World Mission Studies

———

THE CHRISTIAN MINISTRY
IN AFRICA

1. The Rev. Andreas Madide, Zululand

BENGT SUNDKLER

THE CHRISTIAN
MINISTRY IN
AFRICA

SCM PRESS LTD

BLOOMSBURY STREET LONDON

PRINTED WITH THE FINANCIAL
SUPPORT OF HUMANISTISKA
FONDEN

PRINTED IN SWEDEN BY

Almqvist & Wiksells

BOKTRYCKERI AKTIEBOLAG

UPPSALA 1960

CONTENTS

LIST OF ILLUSTRATIONS

Plates are reproduced by permission of the following:

1. Dr. J. F. Holleman, The University of Natal, Durban
2. American Baptist Foreign Mission Society, New York
3. Universities' Mission to Central Africa, London
4, 6 and 8. Society for the Propagation of the Gospel, London
5 a. Methodist Missionary Society, London
5 b. U.M.C.A., London
7. United Church of Canada, Board of Overseas Missions

PREFACE

'Are you in?'—
'We are in, Father. Welcome, welcome.'

Pastor Yonathan Karoma, together with Catechist Yoel Lutasho-bya and the young village teacher, Blasiyo Kazimoto, and three or four men and women from the village congregation, approach on a narrow path through the banana plantations. If they wanted they could see Lake Victoria glittering in a distance in the afternoon sun. But they are not interested in the beauty of the landscape. Hezekiel Mutashaga, an elder in the Kanyigo congregation, is seriously ill. Early one morning, as the pastor arrived on his routine round of the local village churches, he was told of Hezekiel's illness. At once he decided to visit Hezekiel. A few yards from the tall grass hut, he calls out in Luhaya: *'mulimo?'* (Are you in?) After the usual long greeting ceremony of the Bahaya, the visitors sing a hymn, and the pastor and the catechist offer a prayer for their sick friend, for his family, for the local church. The teacher pulls out a New Testament from his brown bark-cloth bag and reads a few verses. His choice of text is perhaps not carefully premeditated. Everybody in the group takes for granted that the reading of the Word as such has a reassuring, perhaps a healing, effect.

Underneath and beyond the praying and reading and singing something happens which belongs to the charm and richness of the life of an African village congregation: in the face of calamity, sickness, and death, sacred ties of friendship and solidarity are knit and strengthened in the name of *Omukama*—King—Jesus Christ.

Whether in the bush or in the city, it is in the local church that the message of Christ becomes real and relevant, or fails to prove itself as the message of salvation. It is well to keep in mind these little groups of pastors and local helpers, going from hut to hut in the banana groves in Tanganyika, or from house to house in Pimville, Johannesburg. Their errand is the most important in Africa.

The International Missionary Council have asked me to write a general volume on the Christian ministry in Africa in which the

problems of ministerial training might be discussed in the wider
context of present social, political and ecclesiastical developments
in Africa.

This purpose has dictated the plan of the book. It begins where
the pastor himself begins: with his calling to the ministry and a
brief discussion of recruitment problems in the African setting.
Next we show that the ordained ministry is a recent innovation in
Protestant Africa and try to explain why this has been the case. We
study the role and function of the pastor in his relationship to
other local leaders, traditional and modern; and with his co-
workers, African and Western. The last and main part is devoted
to problems of ministerial training in Africa. The book concludes
with an attempt to assess problems of Christian theology in African
terms.

The book is intended as a contribution to the ecumenical
debate on theological education, carried on after 1945 in the
United States, Europe, India, South East Asia and elsewhere. It is
our hope that a direction of the study towards specifically African
topics will prove to be of some value for wider discussion; for
the ecumenical debate must of necessity feed on experience at
both local and national levels.

Our study deals with conditions in Africa, and this is a wide
area. A conscious effort has been made to achieve a balance between the various regions of Africa, and we have been helped
here by our personal interviews in every African country South of
the Sahara, except Sierra Leone and Nyasaland. It is inevitable,
perhaps, that the searchlight is turned more on some countries
than on others: my experience as a missionary in Zululand and
Tanganyika (1937–1945) has probably led me to emphasize conditions in East and South Africa at the expense of the Church in
the Congo and West Africa. It will be realized that one of the
main problems of presentation in a study of this kind is found on
this level of geography. In order to achieve comprehensiveness
and accuracy, a conducted tour from country to country and from
Church to Church throughout Africa would be valuable, as each
new aspect of our problem is tackled. But this desire for com-
pleteness defeats itself. We have had to choose another method.
We have had to select representative examples and generalize from
these. Otherwise we should be embarrassed by the sheer volume
of material. We are aware of the fact that some of the generaliza-

tions may be controversial, but hope that the controversial chapters and statements will help to start a debate on theology and theological education in Africa.

The geographical attribute in the title—The Christian Ministry *in Africa*—is important. An attempt has been made to put the problems of ministerial training and theological encounter against an African background. From one point of view, of course, the problems of Africa are those of the whole world at the present time, and there is nothing peculiar or particular about Africans as distinct from other people. Yet, just as the ministry in the United States or in Japan or in Sweden meets with questions that are essentially American or Japanese or Swedish, by the same token there are levels and dimensions of the Church's life and conditions in Africa which are at present peculiar to the countries and cultures on that continent. And we believe it to be realistic if in Africa theological problems are seen against an African background. There are risks involved in this approach: There are obviously many different interpretations and standpoints as to what is 'African', and as a European I shall be told by many that my viewpoints and valuations are very far from being 'African'. These risks must be taken, and with a certain buoyancy. For we also know that the other attitude, that of forgetting or ignoring the national and local context is, even if supposed to be orthodox and safe, no less risky.

As to the method of soliciting fresh material I can limit myself to one observation. In my visits to Africa I found that interviews with individuals or small groups of three to five were much more rewarding than discussions in big conferences. The African pastor or evangelist is like most of us also on that point: he is much more ready to talk freely when in his own home or office than if the interview is to take place in the form of an officious statement in a big conference. Being more interested in overtones and unsolicited reactions than in polished reports, I found that such reactions were more likely to appear in the intimate group in the pastor's own home. To arrange this kind of ideal meeting was, however, more difficult than is sometimes realized. Even when I prepared my own travel routes myself, I was up against what I describe as a 'wall of whiteness': In all parts of the continent, not only in the South, there is at work a machinery of social control that gears the visitor into the right, white channels—if I may say so without appearing too ungrateful to my many Western friends in Africa who went out of their way to make my studies profitable. In order to overcome this wall of Westernness I held before my eyes throughout the years an unwritten rule: 'A day without a visit to an African pastor—in his home or in his office—is a lost day.' There were many such lost days, but perhaps not as many as the case might have been without this golden rule. I was enriched personally by these meetings and am grateful for having been given an excuse for enjoying what I regard as the most rewarding and refreshing of occupations, the making of personal contacts with African churchmen.

In the Appendix (p. 321) we have listed our field studies for this book, and the material is discussed. I have there specified the various groups of African writers who have contributed diaries, notes on the 'Pastor's Week', autobiographies, and letters for this book. I am vividly aware of my debt of gratitude to all these many friends; without their generous co-operation the book could of course not have been written.

So many Africans and Westerners have helped me in various ways that I cannot name them all individually.

I mention particularly my three colleagues on the International Missionary Council Commission to 'Latin' Africa, Dr. C. G. Baëta, of the University of Ghana, Professor M. Searle Bates, of the Union Theological Seminary, New York and Professor Frank Michaeli, Paris. A number of friends gave vigorous criticism of a first draft of the book, and I benefited greatly from the views of these readers, among whom I mention Professor M. S. Bates, Dr. Peter Beyerhaus, Blauberg, Transvaal, Dr. Lyndon Harries, The School of Oriental and African Studies, London, M. Etienne Krüger, Paris, Rev. Fritz Raaflaub, Basel and Mr. Johannes Aagaard, The University, Aarhus. I am deeply indebted to Bishop S. C. Neill, Geneva, Mr. L. B. Greaves, London, Dr. Audrey I. Richards, Cambridge, and Fr. Hugh, S.S.F., Oxford, for having read the proofs and made suggestions of considerable changes in the text. Fr. Hugh also supplied the index. I thank Mr. Eric Sharpe, Uppsala, who revised my English.

I had the privilege of discussing some of the sociological aspects of the study in the seminars of Professors E. E. Evans-Pritchard, Oxford, Max Gluckman, Manchester and T. T. Segerstedt, Uppsala. I am indebted to Professors G. Balandier, Paris and M. J. Herskovits, Chicago, Dr. J. F. Holleman, Durban, Dr. Roland Oliver, London, and Dr. G. Parrinder, Ibadan and London, for helpful discussions and to an ecumenical Africa seminar at Dunford House, Sussex, under the chairmanship of Dr. J. H. Oldham.

For help with my chapter on the Roman Catholic Church I thank Professor Johannes Beckmann, Schöneck-Beckenried; the Rector of the senior seminary at Yaounde, the Cameroons and the Rector of the junior seminary at Kisubi, Uganda and Mr. Roland Hindmarsh, Kisubi.

I thank the Humanistiska Fonden, Stockholm, for a generous grant towards the publication of this work.

I am indebted to the Swedish Institute of Missionary Research, Uppsala, for clerical help without which it would not have been possible from Uppsala to keep in touch with what is going on in the Churches in Africa. Miss Ulla Lundberg, of the Institute, has typed and retyped the manuscript many times, and I am much obliged to her for patience and perseverance.

I thank my wife whose sensitive understanding of African affairs has been, throughout the years, a great challenge to me.

Uppsala, August 1959   *Bengt Sundkler*

University of Uppsala

FOUND AND CALLED

'Nda funyanwa, Nkosi yam,
Nda funyanwa!'

(I have been found, my Lord,
I have been found!)

The Call Came Early

A young South African Methodist pastor sums up his personal experience in that short line from the refrain of a Xhosa hymn. As I read his autobiography it struck me that those few words, sung to a characteristic revivalist tune, express the reason why this particular young man, and thousands like him throughout the continent of Africa, have become pastors. They were 'found', and they had to respond.

The call to the ministry comes much earlier in the lives of African pastors than is generally realized. In fact, not a few could testify that they have had 'the call of Samuel', that they had been set aside for the work of the ministry before they were born. Such is the story of a Zulu pastor, S. M. His father was himself a pastor, studying at the Lutheran Theological College at Oskarsberg in 1912, as one of the first batch of theological students to be received there. 'By then father had had seven daughters and no son. To us Zulus this is very unpleasant. My parents and relatives joined in prayer. In 1914 father made a vow and said: "Should I get a son, I will do all in my power to dedicate him to God and his work." On June 14th 1915 I was born, exactly a year after the vow. When father received the news he knelt in the mud where he was and prayed. He gave me his own and grandfather's name: Simon Andreas. As soon as I was self-conscious, the fact that I am an answer to prayer was drilled into my mind. I had it in my mind and heart right through my school career. It served as a deterrent from all young people's faults. Strangely, from the primary school up to the teachers' training college mischievous boys and girls contemptuously called me *"umfundisi"* (pastor).'

He was trained as a teacher, and gained excellent results. A well-to-do relative offered to see him through his B.A. 'or further'. He reported this to his father. The father said: 'If you now proceed to B.A. or M.A., you will never become a pastor in our church, because salaries are so low. The B. A. will give you honour from the people and also a lot of money perhaps. This is not what you were born for.' Then he hung down his head and said: 'My son, exercise yourself rather unto godliness. For bodily exercise profiteth little; but godliness profiteth unto all things, having promise of the life that now is, and of that which is to come.' The young man decided to refuse the attractive offer, and became a minister instead.

A student at Trinity College, Kumasi, Ghana, relates that from his earliest years he had been interested in becoming a pastor. One day in school, when reading Luke 2: 23 he found that he, as first-born, was predestined by God for the ministry. He promptly wrote to inform his parents that he had to become a minister. The Bishop of S.W. Tanganyika (Anglican) was visited by a man who came to say that he presented the bishop with his son, then a schoolboy, to be trained as a priest. When the bishop expressed doubt about coming to a decision about the child, he was exhorted 'to receive him as Eli received Samuel from Hannah'.[1]

A leading layman in Ghana who is sociologically informed told me that in at least one Church in his country parents would bring a son to the church authorities, during the time of Synod, saying, 'We have sacrificed this son to God'. Similarly it is known that sometimes in the Mar Thoma Church in South India parents offer their sons for the ministry of the Church. We have reason to believe that until recently this has been an important factor in many parts of Africa. The custom is not unknown either in the Roman Catholic Church, and it has a traditional background in Africa, since in former times a child could be given to the chief. About the turn of the century and even later it was not unknown in Uganda that a man would 'give' his child to the European missionary, saying, 'He is yours; you take him to Britain and have him educated'.

The Rev. Dr. C. G. Baëta, lecturer in the Theological Faculty of the University of Ghana, and son of one of the great leaders of the Ewe Presbyterian Church, received his call in the same way.

---

[1] *Central Africa* (U.M.C.A., 1955), p. 173.

'It would be true to say that up to quite recently it was considered the duty of all good church members to encourage youths to enter church service, and naturally ministers tried to lead the way in this respect. In my own case, although I also definitely chose the ministry upon parental suggestion, the reason was slightly different. The boy born to my parents before me took ill on the third day and died after a week. When I was born I similarly took ill and the illness developed in the same way as before. My parents made a vow that if I survived I would be dedicated to the work of the Lord. Ever since I can remember anything at all I was constantly told of this vow. I grew up assuming that I would become a minister and never seriously considered any other profession.'

One Ghana theological student can trace the first stirrings of his call back to a very tender age: 'The initial stages of certain courses of action are indefinable. So it has been with my call to the ministry. I have learnt from my parents that I used to call myself *"Osofo"* (pastor) when I was about two years old in 1928.' If this is rather precocious, others begin to play at pastors very early. This is, in fact, a popular child's pastime throughout Christian Africa. Rev. C. S. from N. Transvaal recalls from his childhood: 'I suggested that we built a church of stones. When it was built, I was the *moruthi* (pastor) and took turns with J. M. The Bible was a flat stone. I also tried to sing the liturgy. When we had finished, I went out first, as the *moruthi* has to do. The bell was a milk tin, and I would shout: *"kwete-nkwete-kwete-nkwete"'* (the equivalent of 'Ding! Dong!').

Throughout Africa, little boys look for a piece of sacking or some other material to serve as ecclesiastical vestments for their service in the bush. The possibility of becoming a priest has crossed the child's mind. Rev. S. Mbatha, Zululand, overheard his two sons, eleven and six years old, talking very seriously one day. The older lectured the young one, whose name was Dumisani, 'Remember, Dumisani, you must never smoke *dagga* (a kind of hasheesh). If you do, the police will come for you and throw you into prison!' Dumisani retorted, very decidedly, 'Have you ever seen a pastor smoke dagga?'—'Whoever said anything about pastors?' replied the elder brother. 'I shall be a pastor when I grow up!' claimed Dumisani. His elder brother replied, 'You a pastor! Well, I shall be a doctor. And if I fail with my patients, I can send them for treatment to Rev. Dumisani Mbatha!'

Incidents from the life of the child can take on a new significance later in life. One Transvaal pastor (b. 1894) remembers how,
during the Boer War, he fell in with some English soldiers. One of
the soldiers took a minister's cap and put it on the child's head.
Half a century later the receiver of the cap writes: 'To-day I realize
that the soldier was fore-telling that I would be a minister.' There
are a number of cases of children overhearing their parents, in
another corner of the hut or house, discussing the possible future
of the children; on such occasions the ministry was suggested to
an impressionable mind as a life's calling. G. S's experience (Methodist; Orange Free State) is one shared by a large number who in
the last generation have grown up in a Christian congregation. 'I
cannot tell how early I started to attend Sunday School and Junior
Class and the Band of Hope. I was so enthusiastic at these children's organizations that very early I was nicknamed *"umfundisi"*,
and I can still remember feelings of childish pride welling up in
me whenever I was so addressed.—But this religious zeal was to
cool off when I entered my teens. This period of barrenness of the
soul, as it were, started when I entered High School.'

The very first years in school have often contributed impressions
which can later be interpreted as important factors in the discern-
ment of a call to the ministry. One of the Congregationalist
students (b. 1929) in Natal recalls that from childhood days he
had felt the attraction of the ministry. In 1939, when he was in
his fourth school year, the teacher—herself a daughter of a minister
—asked the children about their plans for the future. This boy
was the only one who mentioned the ministry. 'After I had spoken,
Mrs. Hlubi shut her eyes as though she was praying but did not
utter a single word. After she opened her eyes, she said I had a
good aim in view. Her shutting the eyes and remaining silent for
some time, and her remarking upon my ambition, remained indel-
ible in my meditations.'[2]

A Ghana theological student expresses himself in more general
terms, and is fairly representative of many who later became
pastors. 'The idea of becoming a minister began working in me
from my early school days, but the notion was not very clear then.

---

[2] Friendship between two or more young boys, on the pattern of *obu-
nywanyi* (blood-brother bond) or of *ndoyi* (association of two or more bearing
the same baptismal name, cf. Balandier, *Sociologie des Brazzaville noirs,* 1955,
p. 163) can also be important as a channel of vocation in tender years.

This impression dawned on me as a result of my personal contact with a minister and as the effects of the stories about Jesus I learned in the Sunday School.' Later, he recalls, the idea was repressed whenever it appeared again, but there came a time when it could be silenced no longer.

A whole generation of pastors, now active leaders in the Protestant Churches in Africa, are sons of pastors or catechists, and the loyalty to the father is in many cases one of the deepest springs of their vocation. Every denomination has traditions of pastoral service within certain families. We mention a few outstanding examples: The Ewe Presbyterian Church in Togo and the Baëtas; Ghana Methodists and the Acquaahs; the Anglican Church in Nigeria has connections with the Howells and Martinsons, the Akinyeles and Oyebodes each numbering two generations of bishops; in the Rhodesias the traditions of the Ramushu family began with a Methodist evangelist originally from South Africa who had three sons in the Methodist ministry; the Lutheran Abraham Serote in Transvaal also had three sons in the ministry. Another Lutheran in Transvaal, Rev. Moses Rakoma II, writes: 'My father was Evangelist Rakoma I'.

The relationship to the father is something deeper than merely 'following in daddy's footsteps'. A young Zulu Anglican priest who had a very promising career as a teacher writes: 'I could not be free and happy, for it was at this time that I began to think of my desire while still young, that of following my father's steps: beginning as a teacher and finally becoming a priest.' Of a prominent Ghana Methodist leader—son of a Methodist preacher—it has been said: 'He felt he was always standing in his father's shoes.' In Sierra Leone Bishop T. S. Johnson, after a long career as headmaster and assistant bishop, decided on his retirement in 1947 to return to the little village where his father had once been an evangelist, in order to rebuild church life there.

To those of a younger generation, who after school have strayed for some time from the fold of the Church, the crisis of vocation is often a return both to the father and to the Church, in the latter case expressing itself in a readiness to become evangelist or pastor.

Yakobo, who was born in 1931 in a Tanganyika mountain district, had had a Standard VI education and worked for a few years as a hospital dresser. Later he became a policeman in Zanzibar. He told me what had happened to him there: 'As a policeman I only followed the ways of this world and I squandered all I had in riotous living. One day, as I went to visit one of my many girl friends, I fell off my bicycle. My left hand was badly hurt. I felt then that God was warning me. I read about the Prodigal Son, and began to repent my sins. I longed to go home, home to the mountains, to my country and to my father. So I went home to my father and as I saw him, I chose to do evangelistic work which could save my soul. In August 1953, I decided to join the M. Bible School.'

It is significant that a decisive vocation to the ministry has in many cases been felt at the time of the father's death. N. M.'s father was an evangelist in Northern Transvaal, and N. M. was a teacher in the same congregation. On his death-bed the father asked for his son and called out: '*Moet my boeke nie weggooi nie*' ('Don't throw away my books', i.e. church books). Twenty years later, his father's words remain indelibly impressed on the young pastor's mind. D. M., a Lovedale student, had a similar experience: 'The reasons why I became an evangelist are two: firstly, when my father passed away he commanded me that I must become an evangelist or minister. He gave me a Bible which he used when he held his services.' (The other reason was more general: 'I decided myself to serve God and show people that God is a living God.')

The father's death and his influence on the life-decision of the son must in certain connexions be understood on a still deeper level. This at least was suggested to us as we discussed with the theological students at Cuttington College, Liberia. It was natural in this particular national context to approach the problem of vocation and its relationship to dream-life. As opposed to the attitude of the African staff of the college, the students held a firm belief in the authoritative character of revelation through dreams, 'particularly those dreams in which the father appears'. In quoting this, we shall resist the temptation to draw too far-reaching inferences from this idea, and shall emphasize that it was brought to our notice only in the special atmosphere of Liberia.

The father's role is often played by an uncle. In cases where the father has died, or is a non-Christian, a future pastor may have spent many formative years in the house of his uncle, perhaps an evangelist or a pastor. 'Somehow I cherished a very great interest in the vocation of my uncle', a Ghana theological student writes.

In many cases it is the influence of a Christian mother that has contributed to a conviction of vocation to the ministry. A Zulu Lutheran was reading in the Bible which had been given to him on the occasion of his confirmation. The passage about a 'royal priesthood' in 1 Pet. 2: 9 puzzled him. He had to ask his mother whether the passage referred to himself 'or to my father because he is an evangelist'. 'My mother said that it referred to me. I asked how it could refer to me, since I was not a priest, and she then replied: "These words prophesy your future." I kept on pondering what she said. Eventually I was convinced that I had to become a priest.' A Ghana theological student was a son of the manse. The father was always away on missionary journeys—'we always felt that something was lacking in our home because of this'—and he grew up 'under the iron hand of my mother'. Those hands were not always of iron. They could be put together in prayer. The decisive impression of home life was his mother's prayer 'for a Joseph in the family'. 'My mother's words for a Joseph in the family came to me more than once. I was now (in Secondary School) beginning to understand what she really meant, and I kept telling myself that perhaps her prayers would not be in vain.'

In certain remarkable cases which have come to my notice, the appearance of the deceased mother in a dream has been a decisive influence. In October 1953, I had the privilege of interviewing Bishop Akinyele († 1958) of Ibadan, Nigeria, and he told me of the decisive event in his early life. In 1888, he moved from the home of his parents to that of a missionary, where he was to receive his first education. The day before he left home, the young boy and his mother prayed together. Kneeling, she made him promise to give his life to God. In school, he soon stood out as a young man of rich promise. In 1891, his mother died. In 1893, he received an invitation to become private secretary to the Governor, Sir George Goldie, in Lagos. This was an honour and, of course, he had to accept. The day before he was to leave, he had a dream. His dead mother appeared and reminded him of the promise he had given. 'I so much would have liked to go to the Governor—but for that dream.' So he chose rather to follow the promptings of his dream than to accept Government service. 'That's the most wonderful event in my life', the venerable Anglican bishop told me, sixty years later.

Where the decision to become a pastor was taken later in life,

the determining event was occasionally the appearance of the dead
wife in a dream; such cases are reported from the Methodist
Church in Wembo Nyama (Belgian Congo) and from the Lutheran
Church in South Africa.

Among first-generation Christians, with their personal contact
between missionary and African local leaders, it is true to say that
a ministerial calling often resulted from the example and influence
of a missionary. In a Lutheran church near Lake Victoria, Matia,
himself of a noble family, had received a teacher's training and in
about 1935 began to show interest in the work of the Church. The
missionary suggested that Matia should be ordained, but he was
not enthusiastic, since he agreed with those of his friends who
thought that a pastor's calling is 'like a rope which binds a man
so that he cannot do what he wants'. In order to escape the influence of the missionary, he left the school and took up business
in Kampala. On a return visit to his village, he was persuaded by
the missionary to return to church work and to keep in touch with
the missionary himself. The poor wages he received as a catechist
—seven shillings a month at that time!—were not enough to meet
his needs. As a catechist, he could no longer dress well, and the
desire for good clothes had originally been one of the principal at-
tractions of the teaching profession. One Sunday he was asked to
preach. (The text was 1 Tim. 6: 3–10.) As he was addressing the
congregation, he heard a voice say to him: 'You, Matia, give up
this struggle with the servant of God.' He returned to the missionary, and to God, and eventually received deacon's orders.

From South Africa an African pastor relates that a deceased missionary 'came in a vision in a heavenly robe. He gave me hymn
no. 173 in Afrikaans and also Psalms 60 and 70.' This was decisive
for his vocation to the ministry.

Pastor Stefano M. on the Rand was for many years a teacher.
His German missionary friends suggested that he should be ordained, but he refused. In 1926 the missionary superintendent fell
seriously ill and calling him to his bedside said, 'Stefano, I must
go. My Bagkhatla will be orphans. They are your flock now. My
son, be a good shepherd to them.'—'Overcome with grief I did not
understand the weight of his words, but later I did. It was the call
to the ministry and I fathomed the meaning of those words.' In

spite of this he hesitated. Finally a missionary called him: 'Think of your deceased minister's last words!' 'There and then I saw the face of my father [= the missionary] and heard him say to me: "They are your flock!"—It was then that my spirit believed in the call to be a minister.'

The Call in the Crises of Life

The African minister carries out his many duties in village and city, among the poor and among the relatively well-to-do. Far away, in the mission boards, or close by, in the modern clubs of the educated élite, people are asking questions about him: What are his educational standards? What are his chances of retaining, under modern conditions, the status and prestige which he once enjoyed? Through all this our African pastor seems quite unperturbed. He is often conscious of his failure to live up to the demands of the present time, but he carries on, confident in the knowledge that his life is a thank-offering. One such pastor sums up his experience in his own words:

'On the 14th of April, 1942, I fell from a bicycle and nearly broke my left leg. My brother took me to the G. Mission (S. Rhodesia) and the missionary brought me the twenty-five miles to the M. hospital. I was a heathen at the time and I was in the hospital for five weeks. I stayed in great fear because I was not used to see people dying. However, the Word of God worked on me, and so I promised God that if my leg was not cut off I would become a preacher. Back home again I told the missionary. In 1950–51 I was at the G. Secondary School. This period was the darkest in my life. I started to doubt my call, and also I had a bad dream in 1951. I did not have peace with God and wanted to withdraw my application as a student of theology... During the ten years from 1944, when I was baptized, to 1954 I experienced great changes in connexion with my call to the ministry. Sometimes I felt the call burning, and at other times it was cold, and I came to the conclusion that God keeps on repeating the call to the individual whom He wants to use in His service.'

In the eye department of another hospital—this time in South Africa—J. N., a teacher, was a patient. Because of eye trouble he had had to leave the teacher training school. 'In hospital I promised that if I recovered my sight, I should become a minister.'

Ephraim A. was a member of the East African forces in the Burma campaign of 1943. His section was under fire from Japanese snipers, and he had dug a deep hole. The British sergeant, who used to show his contempt for the Chagga 'Bible-puncher', as he called him, crept along and asked to be given a foothold in the pit. As the European took shelter, he came as far as saying, 'Let us put our trust in the Lord'. And Ephraim, who knew the reality of these things, gave a promise: 'If I come through this war alive, I shall serve the Lord.' After the war, he made good his sacred promise.

In Ghana, a village teacher hammered the elements of arithmetic into his young pupils. Through it all he remembered how he as a child had been miraculously saved three times. Once, at the age of seven, he had helped his elder sister with the washing in the river. He had naturally played in the water, had slipped, and had been rescued from drowning by his sister in the nick of time. On the second occasion, he had almost drowned in the sea. The third accident resulted in serious burns when trying to lift a pot of palm oil from the fire. He had to stay in bed for six weeks, and as he lay there the thought came to him again and again: 'You have been miraculously delivered, so you have to do God's work.' So when the request came that young men were wanted to do God's work, 'I offered myself for catechist's training'.

He worked for three years as a catechist. 'Then something happened which may be regarded as "the last straw" in my life: My village was burned down, and I was rightly considered to be the cause of it. When I came home after the fire had been put out, the challenge came ringing in my ears, "You must offer yourself entirely to God's work"—In 1952, I was accepted into Trinity College, Kumasi.'

The crises of life have a meaning. They reveal man's dependence on God and call forth man's response through the offer of life-long service. We have not attempted any statistics as to the percentage of theological students and pastors who have felt the irresistible power of God's call in connexion with crises of this kind. Autobiographies of pastors from all parts of Africa give, however, an overwhelming impression of the close relationship between crisis and call.

In special cases, living contacts with the Church in the West may result in vocations to the ministry. I was impressed by meeting in London a Ghana medical student, the son of a Presbyterian minister. In the Western Metropolis he had met with a great spiritual experience—the preaching of Dr. Martin Lloyd-Jones, himself a medical doctor who had become an evangelist. The prospective Ghana doctor knew that he would do the same one day: 'There is hunger in me. I must become a minister. The whole thing is serious in my country and in this country. In 1953, I was called to the ministry, and I have written it down. When I have served a certain number of years as a doctor, I shall go out as a pastor of souls. I shall preach the Word of God, in the Holy Spirit.' We shall not forget the urgency in his voice.

Dreams as Channels of God's Call

'I am glad if and when any of our candidates mention anything else but dreams when applying for ordination', was the remark of a distinguished East African bishop speaking about vocation to the priesthood in his diocese. 'They have all first seen themselves appearing in liturgical vestments in a dream.' This was possibly an exaggerated account of conditions in that particular diocese and is therefore not necessarily of universal validity, although the African principal of a leading East African theological seminary insisted that most of his candidates had been called through dreams, and the late Bishop Akinyele of Ibadan, Nigeria, told us that the majority of the men who offered themselves for the ministry 'had seen themselves in a white surplice and therefore wished to be ordained'. One misses an important aspect of what is understood as constituting a vocation to the ministry in Africa if the dream is overlooked as a channel of God's call.

This is a stage of development. Some have reached a level of intellectual sophistication or of Christian experience in which dream-experience is rejected as a source of guidance. The *Balokole* revival movement in East Africa is a case in point.[3] Here dreams are frowned upon not only by the leaders but also by ordinary village elders, and this, as far as I can see, is an important indication of the Western influence in this revival. A group of Anglican

[3] See p. 71.

Bible teachers in the Embu country (Kenya) was representative of this tendency. 'The time of dreams has passed,' one of them told me. As an ordinary, formal Christian *(mkristo ovyo)* he had had dreams, but not now when he was 'saved'. 'Dreams are of Satan; we always pray God that he will remove them from our minds,' was the comment of another in the group. A Muganda ordinand had felt a longing to enter the priesthood since he was ten years of age. When he became a teacher he had a dream, seeing himself in a surplice. 'For many years I was sure that this dream was God's way of calling me. But when I was saved in the *Balokole* revival I understood that this call was not the true one.' Being 'saved' was the true call. This had financial consequences. As a school teacher he had a salary of Sh. 230 per month. The dream made him take a catechist's position, at Sh. 35 per month. As a deacon of the Church he would eventually get Sh. 120 per month.

Generally speaking, this critical attitude to dreams is not typical of conditions in the Churches in Africa. We have already referred to a theological school in Liberia where students were convinced of the authority of dreams. We felt in discussion with them on this particular issue that they considered Westerners (including Westernized African pastors) unable to understand the workings of the African mind.

The close relationship of dream and vocation was succinctly expressed in the autobiography of a friend of mine, O. N., an evangelist in the Lake Victoria area. *Mambo hutokea,* he said, *na mambo yatokeayo, kwanza yaotwa katika ndoto; baadaye hutokea.* Here, in his Swahili, he has carefully formulated a psychological law, a law of dreams: 'Things happen, and things that happen have first been dreamed in a dream; then they happen.' He referred to the dreams that had preceded his own joining the ranks of catechists.

A Congo pastor made a useful distinction. There are two kinds of dreams: first, dreams about things and conditions of which the dreamer has prior knowledge; secondly, exceptional dreams, about things and conditions of which he has no such knowledge. The latter are inspired by God. If vocation is channelled through a dream of the second kind, it should be taken very seriously in the Synod, he felt.

In other Churches people are anxious to point out that the importance of dreams must not be over-emphasized. A leading

Methodist pastor in Ghana (ordained 1920) told me that if the call to the ministry had been mediated only through dreams it would not recommend itself to the Synod of the Church. The dream had to be corroborated through other indications.

Not only future pastors receive assurance about their calling in dreams. A highly intelligent and well-balanced Chagga (Tanganyika) writes in his autobiography: 'One night I saw in a dream that I must do the work of a Telephone Exchange Operator. I heard a voice from heaven by way of telephone telling me these things.' And a Telephone Exchange Operator he became—in a distant scene, in the capacity of Sergeant-Major in the King's African Rifles, doing signalling work in India and Burma during World War II. It was his experiences in that campaign that made him decide to become a pastor.

There are certain stereotypes in the manifest contents of these vocational dreams. Some describe their dream apparitions as 'Visions of light',—specified by one theological student in Ubangui-Chari in the words 'as light as *Aida*' (Aida being the name of a popular pressure lamp); others have seen someone dressed in white approaching and saying: 'Feed my sheep'; the Lord in a long white robe, or an angel in white beckoning and telling the dreamer: 'This place is too small; my church must grow; you are called.' Or the dreamer has seen himself in a white surplice standing in a church; or again, the dreamer has seen a deceased person, such as a missionary or the dreamer's father, in a shining heavenly robe. This motif is modified by various details.

Another stereotype is based on the experience of climbing—climbing a mountain, or struggling out of a pit. On the top of the mountain there appears a theological college, a scene of ordination or a service of baptism in which the dreamer takes a leading part, the logic of the dream being quite evident.

F. K., a 22-year-old catechist from the Lake Victoria district, expresses himself in very general terms: 'In my sleep or when I walk along I see a picture in my head and I hear a voice in my heart telling me to become a pastor. One day I had this dream: I was baptizing people together with Pastor Matia.' A catechist in the same church had this dream: 'A solid-looking European missionary placed me among a mass of people at Bukiza. Presently he raised his finger, and then the right arm and the left arm and said: "Lo, this man is to rule over you, from Kantale to Buyango." At dawn I asked myself, I don't know this man who placed me in command of other people. I only heard him and know that he will come. After a year Dr. Ernst Johanssen (a well-known German missionary) came. As we went along to greet him, I talked to him and told him that I had in fact seen him before. I asked him: "Sir, where have I seen you before?" He replied: "You have not seen me before. I was here once before but that was before you were born. Perhaps you have been dreaming." *As he was saying this* [my italics], I remembered my dream. I was astounded, for I thought nothing would come of it, and yet, here he was. When I was ready to be placed as a leader of Christians in Bwanjai, I told my people openly about this dream. And when later on Pastor Caesar sent me to God's work in Buyango, I had to remind myself of my dream. I said to myself, "Yes, this is Dr. Johanssen's second hand which he raised at Bwanjai and Buyango in that dream several years ago".'

The 'climbing' stereotype is varied in this way by a theological student from Lango, N. Uganda: 'So many hate theological studies, and priesthood, but the Holy Ghost teaches you to come. When I was at the Teacher Training School at G., I had a dream. I dreamed I was climbing a very high mountain. On the top there was a wide circle with the most beautiful flowers. It was early morning, and the sun had just begun to shine on those flowers. I thought, God wants me to do something. As I thought of this dream, I knew: He wanted me to go to Mukono Theological School. Because as you know Mukono is situated on a high mountain. Again, I had a very long way to travel from my home in Lango country to Mukono, no less than 432 miles. That is why the dream spoke of a long climb. When I explained my dream to my African pastor, he said, "God is calling you".'

The 'pit' stereotype, sometimes connected with a ladder image, is often dramatic. Jafes dreamed of a pit, dug by Satan. Jafes himself was deep down in the pit. A crowd was standing above shouting: 'Do not say Jesus! Do not say Jesus!' Jafes looked up and shouted, 'Jesus has power to save'. Then Jafes discovered that he had been lifted out of the pit, and the shouting people thrown down into the pit. 'I felt I was called. I told the pastor about it. He confirmed this, saying: "God has called you".'

A characteristic combination of the two main stereotypes appears in the following vivid dream, related to me in 1956 by an elderly, leading Ghana Methodist pastor.[4] His dream dated from 1907—half a century earlier. For years, he said, he had not wanted to tell anybody about it; only in his old age was he prepared to reveal a dream experience which obviously had been of fundamental importance for his calling, and for his personal assurance in later life of following the will and way of God:

I was a class leader and organist in a local church in the Volta area. I prayed, 'Father, I want to see you. I really want to see you.' One night I had a dream. I saw an angel sitting on the sea shore, beckoning me to come. I followed him and we came to a group of angels, some of whom were rejoicing, whilst the others covered their faces with their wings. 'Why do some cover their faces like that?' I asked. 'When men sin, the angels cover their faces; when people on earth live according to the will of God, the angels rejoice,' was the answer.

We went higher up and found a group in white. 'Who are these?' I asked. 'Those who have overcome,' was the answer. We went still higher. I saw big men sitting down. 'Who are these?' I asked. 'These are men near the throne,' was the angel's reply. Then he beckoned me to continue. We came to a very beautiful gate. I cannot fully describe *how* beautiful it was. The angel tarried there, but told me to go in through the gate. As I came in, I saw a Majestic Man standing in a garden. 'Oh, Lord Jesus!' I shouted—'but where is God?' Then a voice replied. 'Hast thou seen Jesus and then askest of God? Do you not know?' The angel beckoned me to come out of the garden. I came out through the Gate and came down to those who were attired in white, the ones who had overcome. Further down, I came to the group of angels, and at last I was brought to the shore where first I had seen the angel. Then I awoke from my dream.

Many dreams seem to symbolize a struggle between dark powers and the power of the White Christ. One of the most intense African preachers whom I ever met—a strong, highly assertive personality—relates a dream which, though individually modified, is amazingly representative of many such dramatic dreams: 'I saw a mass of people divided into two groups, and they struggled about me. The one group consisted of the old ones from long ago in my clan (the spirits of the departed), and the others were strangers, clad in very shining white clothes and they had crosses in their hands. One group took one of my hands, and the other group the other and they pulled as at tug-of-war. But the strangers won and brought me with them, and they sang a joyful victory song.'

---

[4] Rev. Charles Graham, who died in July 1958.

Characteristic of some of these dreams is their supposed recur-
rence, a regular number of times, such as three or seven. In cases
where an individual shows greater resistance to the call, the dreams
may be experienced over a long period of time. A Presbyterian
catechist from Ghana did not wish to be ordained, as the itinerant
life of the pastor did not appeal to him. In June 1950, he dreamed
that the Lord was standing before him face to face, urging him to
work in His vineyard. 'I was surprised because I was then already
a catechist, and I thought that was sufficient.' The vision was repeated on seven nights, and at last he had to yield. At the time of
writing about his experience, he was a theological student at
Trinity College, Kumasi. From this and similar experiences one
is possibly entitled to infer that the calling of God channelled
through a vivid dream tends to transform a somewhat reluctantly
executed congregational task into an exciting reality.

In a study of Separatist Churches in South Africa we attempted
to show the importance of dreams in modern Bantu syncretistic
groups, where in fact *the guided dream* becomes a vital factor in
the life of the Church.[5] But in the 'orthodox' churches, the call to
the ministry would seem to be a response to more solid realities
than those of which dreams are made. And this is so; God is
building His Church in Africa, and it is He who calls His servants
to the task. But it would be misleading to ignore the dimension
of dreams as one of the channels used by God as He calls His men
and women to serve the Church in Africa. We have seen how, in
certain sections and at certain levels of the churches, the authority
of dreams is rejected. The actual material found for our present
study has convinced us that under the conventionally Westernized
surface there lie deeper levels to our problem, and visions and
dreams offer a key to these hidden depths.

Yet, the kind of material we have related here does not allow
anything but a superficial presentation of manifest dream content.
The latent content in the hidden recesses of the mind, of which
this manifest content is a symbol, remains unknown to us, as we
do not sufficiently know the personalities whose moral struggles
have expressed themselves in these dreams.

Only the utter rationalist would, however, fail to appreciate the
importance of this dimension. For, after all, we are here dealing,

---

[5] B. Sundkler, *Bantu Prophets in South Africa*, 1948, p. 273.

not primarily with mere organization, even less with material things; we are dealing with religion, and are trying to understand the workings of the inner being of African man as he responds to the call of the God of all men.

We shall, however hesitatingly, venture to make three suggestions related to vocation-dreams.

1. The two main stereotypes we have noticed—the luminous white figure and the climbing from below upwards towards the light—are, we suggest, symbols of the struggle for sanctification and purity—for *ubumhlope* (whiteness), as the Zulus say. The demands of kin and clan, and the conventions and strictures of African environment are ever-present as a counterpoint to the Christian's attempt to live a Christian life. The symbolism of the dream is expressed within the context of the Church, as the awakening mind responds to the vision of the White Christ. The moral struggle is resolved in willing consent to become a servant of that Christ.

2. Dreams and visions are like dew on gossamer shining in the early morning in a clearing in the African bush. They are made of the most fine and delicate stuff, and they reveal the hidden hunger for beauty and holiness and a sacred rhythm of life. The drab and formal Western-style worship in the rough and ready chapel is not always an ideal home for the soul that has caught a glimpse of this wonderful world of vision. Those who attempt to help build the Church in Africa should not be afraid of making it, as far as possible, and in the terms of the Scripture, a 'court of heaven'.

3. The third remark is *per viam negationis*. With a background of vivid vision and dazzling dream one would expect, perhaps, the resultant ministry to emphasize a mystical relationship between leader and led. Generally speaking, this has never been the case, which perhaps demonstrates the great controlling influence of Western missionary organization on the first formative generations in the life of the African Church. For the future one might possibly infer that the more missionary control is replaced by African leadership, the more scope will be found for a ministry which will tend to put its particular emphasis on the relationship between the shepherd and his flock.

Individual Initiative or Collective Control?

Most obstacles to the individual's call and his recruitment to the Church are created by the demands of family and clan. The African pastor is a family man, and a member of his clan. This fact has far-reaching consequences.

In most straightforward terms the problem is the one experienced by a Lango student, about 25 years of age, at an Anglican theological college in Uganda.

'My clan warned me that as a pastor I could not have two or three wives or become a rich man. In 1950, as I succeeded in my entrance exam. to the teacher training school, my brothers persuaded me not to go, because if I did, I would not be able to marry more than one wife. I always regretted that I followed their advice. Therefore, when in 1952, my brothers tried to hinder me once again from coming this time to the theological school with the same argument, I replied: "No, now it is enough. This time, I am going."' His hesitation was finally overcome by a 'climbing dream', p. 28.

The economic obligations to the clan or the family are particularly important. A young man will be told that the clan contributed financially to his education as a teacher; he must not take on a job which will make him unable to show reciprocal favours. In the detribalized South African city or town, the reality of the clan may have become somewhat faded, but the same problem will here have to be fought out within the narrower context of the family. A highly gifted Methodist leader—later B.A., and with post-graduate theological studies in the United States and Switzerland—felt the problem: 'I had brothers whom I had to see through their education and a widowed mother to support; the Church was not paying enough for me to do both these things. But deep down in me somewhere I felt that all this was not thoroughly true.' In 1945 he spent a fortnight in hospital for some eye trouble, 'a fortnight of thought'. On his return home he told his mother that he had decided to enter the ministry. She accepted this news 'with that understanding which is characteristic of mothers'. But his sister, instead of sharing this joy, retorted: 'What are we going to do with this profession of dogs?' 'But I was not easily put off. I had for too long felt like a Jonah running away from where the finger of God pointed me to go.'

Another aspect of the influence of family and tribe on recruitment should be noticed here. As missionary control is withdrawn
in the interest of African leadership, there is a marked tendency
in certain churches both in West and East Africa to stress the
tribal character of the Church, and men who do not belong to the
right tribe are not always acceptable as candidates for the ministry.
We have come across many examples of otherwise deserving men
who have said: 'I was never asked, I was never called—because I
belong to such-and-such a tribe, and am therefore not popular
among the leading African pastors.'

A generation ago recruitment to the ministry did not present
the same dramatic problems as to-day. Missions had, in fact, something of a privileged position in African society. The mission was
the only channel by which a gifted young man could make a career,
and this often meant either teaching or the ministry or both.
To-day, not only does the mission school channel lead to a number
of other opportunities but there are *other channels,* by-passing the
mission—possibly also the Church—altogether. A generation ago,
Rev. E. M. R. of Johannesburg told me, it was taken for granted
that a pastor's or a teacher's son had to become a pastor. R. himself
had a Standard VI education at a well-known Lutheran centre in
Transvaal. In his confirmation class of 30, four were sons of church
elders, and it was regarded as a matter of course that all four were
to go on to the theological seminary. 'This was no choice of my
own. The groove was made for me in advance.' Even secluded
Botshabelo Seminary was not immune to the attraction of other
possible careers. 'Those who had been confirmed before us had
already come home from Johannesburg at intervals wearing beauti-
fully tailored suits and were being admired by the opposite sex.
Adventure, money and luxury appealed to me as to any young
boy—but my father had told me: "After confirmation you will go
to the Seminary. Prepare yourself for becoming a *moruthi*." This
statement was to me like a command and had to be obeyed. As a
matter of fact, my father's words sounded as if they came from
somewhere beyond him—from God.'

The time when the Church found its African leaders in this way
has definitely gone. To-day, the individual's self-determination has
become more marked in detribalized communities. On the other
hand, the pressures of collectivistic trends may, of course, be just
as keenly felt now as they always have been. How is this interplay

of collective control and the individual's choice to be understood in the matter of ministerial vocation at the present time?

In the Church in Africa, the individual himself does not as a general rule apply for the position of catechist or pastor. The Church, through the Bishop, the Synod or through a missionary, extends the call. This, it is explained, is a result of the communal structure of African society. The individual is supposed to count for much less than in Western societies. The group, the collective, is the basic factor.

This explanation is relevant and helpful—as far as it goes. But it does not take us the whole way.

Let us first consider the implications of the 'collective' view. This is obviously connected with the pattern of African society. In modern Bakongo society to-day, it is the family as a totality that decides whether a son should become a mechanic or teacher—or a catechist. In Luluabourg, Belgian Congo, we were told that it is the clan as such which sends a young boy to school—with all the sociological machinery of reciprocal help and obligations that this implies. In the leading Protestant Church in Mozambique there was only one pastor who had offered for the ministry independently. In the case of all the others it was the Synod that had invited the individuals concerned. Among the Kikuyu—a tribe in which traditionally the 'elders' have wielded the greatest authority—the initiative is generally taken by the church elders. From S.W. Tanganyika it is reported that in one Anglican parish the church-wardens' meeting presented the Bishop with the names of two people whom they had chosen for ordination although the men themselves had not been consulted. The Bishop adds: 'It was a fine African gesture in the traditional manner, where the individual is supposed to submit his will to that of the tribe, but unfortunately in this case, the men were too old.'[6] In the same mission a generation ago one was sure to get results when Bishop Frank Weston († 1922) used to tell men of calibre and promise whom he met: 'I think you should consider God calling you to holy orders'. In the same way, missionaries and African pastors have earlier called and still to-day do call Africans to the ministry, doing this in the name of the Church.

In many regions of Africa the individual, as a rule, simply can-

---

[6] *Central Africa* (U.M.C.A., 1955), p. 173.

not allow himself to put forward his own name. The reaction to any attempt in this direction is the one expressed by some Congo Congregationalists: 'If I fail in my ministry after having applied on my own, people will say: There you are. You pushed yourself into this. How you manage is your own look-out!' Africans in the Reformed Church in Mozambique make a distinction between the call to a catechist's work and the call to the ministry. They are keen to offer as catechists, but very chary of presenting themselves as candidates for the ministry. 'We fear the sacredness of the ministry and we do not believe that an African can be a pastor. I am not worthy.'[7] The same was reported from Congregationalist pastors in the Lower Congo area: 'Some men have a call, but do not dare to say so on their own initiative. It is after all a work in the presence of God; that is why men must fear. Jesus Himself had fear for this task.' A French missionary leader with wide experience in different countries in Africa, Jean Keller, has pointed out that the call must be understood in terms of environment and the degree of cultural development. There are areas in Gabon where the strength of clan loyalty can be measured by the fact that if a pastor or catechist for some moral reason has defaulted from service, the clan frequently feels that it ought to offer a substitute from amongst its own group.

The call to the ministry is sometimes a vehicle for tribal ambition, a factor which to-day is at least as frequent as a generation ago. A common motive for joining the ministry has been the idea that it is a matter of honour for a tribe or a town to produce its own pastor. The virile and proud tribal groups in the Cameroons provide striking examples of this.[8] In the Presbyterian Church in the Cameroons we were told that if the young man after completing his studies is posted elsewhere than in his home town, the local congregation which has sent him to the theological school may well attempt to put a spoke in the ecclesiastical wheel. 'He is our man, we must have him back!' is the claim of the group. Here, of

---

[7] For comparison's sake it can be noticed here that at the time of our visit to Mozambique, 1953, there was only one African Roman Catholic priest in the country.

[8] So do church groups among the Temne in Sierra Leone, the Ga in Ghana, or in Nigeria, or in the hitherto somewhat neglected Mishenye area in the Bukoba district, Tanganyika—to choose but a few random instances of an important trend.

course, tribal and family ambitions, and to an increasing degree political interests enter into the affairs of the Church.

The obverse of the collectivistic tendency is the fact that in some cases the religious group does not act and does not extend the call, for reasons which may arise purely from tribal self-interest or from certain traditional social conventions. The conventional dogma about African thought-forms seems thus to apply also in this case. Vocation to the ministry is a matter solely for the group or the community, in this case the Church; the individual does not count.

And yet, it is the burden of our whole argument in this chapter that the problem cannot be resolved by setting the collective call in opposition to individual initiative, and the objective in opposition to the subjective. The fact that the call appears much earlier in the individual's life than has been generally realized; the role of dreams and visions, and of decisions at the time of personal crises, go far toward proving beyond doubt that the collectivistic approach is insufficient, because it is too mechanical. What in fact happens is that *the call of the group actualizes the individual call.* When the call from the Church reaches the individual, he suddenly brings to mind—'remembers', as the Africans say—the call which he had received perhaps many years earlier, perhaps in a mysterious way, through a dream and a vision and a voice. It is against this background that we begin to achieve a sense of perspective, and the great, and growing, recruitment problem in the Protestant Churches in Africa takes on a new dimension of depth: the time of the teens and the twenties, the intermediate period between the early call in the formative and responsive childhood at the one end and the years of manhood and decision at the other is seen as being vital. It is to this period in life—notoriously the most neglected, in Africa, as elsewhere—that the Church must turn its attention if she wants men for the ministry. A representative example will show where the problem lies.

One of the most gifted pastors I have met—in Africa, or elsewhere—a South African, born in 1924 (cf. p. 18), was one of the many Africans who as young boys were determined to become pastors.

> This religious zeal was to cool off when I entered my teens. This period of the barrenness of the soul, as it were, started when I entered High School and discovered the 'treasures of learning'. There was Shakespeare and English literature; history lived and science inspired

me with the infiniteness of human knowledge. It may be there was in all this an element of hero-worship for my college teachers who held as University degrees M.A. or B.A. At the same time somewhere in me there grew a contempt for the ministry, although earlier I had been proud of being counted worthy of this profession of the unlearned and non-intellectuals. My school results drove home into me this idea that going into the ministry would be a waste of my intellectual capabilities.

Few are able to analyse the workings of their own minds as was this pastor. His experience is characteristic of a trend that obviously is going to be more marked in the near future, as the opportunities for secondary and university education spread throughout Africa. It is not a case of attempting to kindle a call to the ministry at that period. For the Church it is rather the task of nurturing and strengthening an interest that very probably had awakened much earlier in a youthful longing for the ministry. One of the International Missionary Council reports on Theological Education in Africa attempts to tackle what is presented as an 'almost desperate recruitment situation', by suggesting that it is of primary importance to establish contact with African youth 'in the top forms of secondary schools and in the colleges'.[9] We welcome this insistence on the duty of the Church towards the students in the top forms of secondary schools. The educational system in Africa is at present being taken out of the hands of the missions, and Protestants have unfortunately not been very nimble in adapting themselves to this situation. Here is a frontier-line, and the struggle is important. When, however, the Church extends her call to the individual young student, there is in many cases a deeper process at work. It is not a question of kindling a vocation through a general call to students in the top forms of secondary schools. Something more important is happening, in the lives of many. As the call is extended, the student is reminded of that vocation which he had already felt as a child, seven or ten years earlier. The call makes him *remember* that which he had half forgotten. If a Church takes its own ministry seriously, it will thus, in extending the call, have to take into account that the official call often functions as a reminder of that early call.

---

[9] *I.M.C. Theol. Report,* III, p. 35.

Three Ladders

A somewhat alarming aspect of what we have termed 'the inter-mediate period between early call and manhood's decision' is the fact that this period now tends to become longer than hitherto. This change is being brought about by the rapid spread of formal school education. Children enter school earlier than before, and, above all, the average school leaving age for the elementary school has rapidly been lowered during the last decade. The secondary schools have not yet to any appreciable extent become educational channels for African pastors. On this point the Roman Catholic Junior Seminary system scores very heavily. There, students who have responded to the early call are not left alone in the hurly-burly of life, but nurtured and guided throughout those most decisive years, as we shall see later.

From various countries there have appeared statements to the effect that this intermediate age is the time when many promising men are lost to the ministry. A Baptist leader in Belgian Congo, E. H. Morrish, pointed out that at present the Protestant Churches do not take care of their young men after they leave elementary school and that these men are therefore channelled into other oc-cupations before the time when students are usually accepted into a theological school. Secondary school education for Protestant youth in the Belgian Congo is comparatively rare. Morrish emphasized the *écoles d'apprentissage pédagogiques* of the Belgian Congo as one possible avenue for Protestant youth in the next few years. From Mozambique it was reported that while the call to the ministry may be experienced quite early in life—between the ages of fourteen and eighteen, or even earlier—the educational situation in that country did not to any appreciable extent allow Protestant youth to be brought straight into the theological school, and most young men took various jobs on the Rand where contacts with the Church were often loose and irregular.

In many Protestant Churches throughout Africa it is still the tra-dition that a man should not be ordained to the ministry until he has reached a more mature age. The autobiographies of theo-logical students and pastors from certain countries in West and Southern Africa provide much food for thought here. In not a few cases young men have applied for admission to a theological school, but have been told that they are too young. With the variegated denominational map of Africa, enterprising young men manage in spite of this however. They apply for admission to other Protestant Churches. As a rule it is particularly Churches of the Reformed-Presbyterian tradition who have lost ground to other groups through this process.

Bishop Stephen Neill has drawn a useful distinction between two 'ladders' of recruitment, the teachers' ladder and the church ladder (or the catechists' ladder, as we would prefer to say).[1] We have, unfortunately, no accurate statistical information as to the relative strength of these two ladders at various intervals during this century. The task of gathering such statistical material is obviously complicated by the fact that at certain levels of the Churches' development, catechist and teacher are one and the same person.

Clearly the catechists' ladder has assured the Protestant Churches a regular supply of pastors, and if a Church wishes to continue this tradition it will probably for some time continue to be able to recruit its ministers from the ranks of catechists. In one Church in a French territory we were told that from one point of view there was no shortage of pastoral candidates. There were 800 such aspirants, for the catechists were 800 in number, and they were all keen to reach the lofty heights of the ordained ministry.

On the other hand, the policy of progressive Churches has increasingly been that of exchanging the large army of catechists for a smaller and well-educated group of pastors aided by voluntary lay helpers. In principle, therefore, the catechists' ladder to the ministry will in the future be insignificant as compared with its role in the first half of the century. The exception to this rule is 'Latin' Africa where many denominations seem determined to retain the older tradition.

The 'teachers' ladder' as an avenue to church service—which was of the greatest importance for the whole of the period 1925–1955— is now rapidly losing its role. The great difference in salary scale between teacher and pastor makes it on the whole difficult for teachers with perhaps considerable family obligations to enter the full-time work of the ministry. There are exceptions to this rule, caused by specific social and political conditions. In South Africa, after the enforcement of the Bantu Education Act, 1953, a great number of African teachers applied to become ministers of the

---

[1] *I.M.C. Theol. Report*, I, p. 17.

Methodist Church. In 1957, eighty such teachers applied from all over the Union. Young pastors of that generation are sometimes referred to as 'Bantu Education ministers'—ex-teachers who have decided, 'this Bantu Education is not for me'. The Methodist Church had, however, to ask also for other, positive signs of a call to the Christian ministry and not all these applicants by far were accepted. Parallel with this development, the Methodist Church in South Africa sees another tendency at present in the number of applications for the ministry from members of the police force and from mining clerks, of whom some have no more than a Std. VI education.

More and more young teachers, secondary school students and graduates refuse to consider the possibility of entering the ministry, since it is generally accepted that theological studies are only for those who have failed to achieve some other academic ambition, in secondary or teachers' education. 'Brilliant students do not become pastors. Theology is for those who have failed to get an entrance into the secondary school', declared a leading African layman from Sierra Leone.

The system which at the beginning of this decade was instituted in the Union pastors' school at Kimpese, Lower Congo, has crystallized this problem. Teachers and pastors studied together for their first two years, and then divided into two streams:—teachers' training and theology. The tendency was for the better student to become a teacher and for the slower to choose theology. We emphasize that this impression, held by increasing numbers, is possibly the most dangerous threat to sound recruitment to the ministry.

In West Africa particularly, secondary education is rapidly becoming the key to the educational and cultural advance of the people. Here also great efforts will need to be made in order to guide interested students towards the ministry of the Church. Characteristically, it is the theological reports on British East and West Africa and on South Africa that have stressed the role of secondary schools in ministerial recruitment. As early as 1950 Bishop Neill wrote: 'I am convinced that one of the crucial points of actual weakness and potential strength is to be found in the two top forms of secondary schools. The development of effective Christian unions at that level is an urgent need. It must be remembered that, though so far Christian schools have outnumbered all others, an increasing number of Christian boys will be getting their education in non-Christian schools. These must not be left out, in the attempt to ensure better Christian training for the younger generation. That this is not impossible is shown by the fact that one of the most encouraging youth groups I met during my travels is to be found in the Prince of Wales College, the government secondary school in Freetown.' And Goodall and Nielsen say about the situation in Southern Africa: 'Renewed efforts should be made to get into touch with African youth in the top forms of secondary schools, and in the colleges. Some good personal work is being done here and there, but much more is needed. The situation would repay the setting apart of men and women to concentrate their time and thought on this problem. The challenge presented to the churches by African youth at this stage of their education and spiritual development can hardly be over-stated.'[2]

The same concern—a solid secondary school education as the foundation for further studies—is voiced by the Commission to 'Latin' Africa, although here there was perhaps more reason than elsewhere to take into account the considerable variety of educational backgrounds, quite apart from the wide divergence of denominational traditions. It was particularly the Frenchman on that commission, Professor Michaeli, who maintained that the secondary school problem is the key to the whole advance of theological education. With his knowledge of French colonial and educational policy, he stressed with assurance the future role of secondary schools in French-speaking Africa also. 'In ten or twelve years' time we shall perhaps have theological faculties in Africa, on a level with the faculties in the West.'[3]

Recent progress in the African work of the World's Student Christian Federation and the Y.M.C.A. may prove to be one of the means by which the Church can in the near future approach its new urgent problem, the task in the secondary schools. This new ladder of recruitment to the ministry needs to be strengthened.

Both the Y.M.C.A. and the World's Student Christian Federation are at present on the threshold of great things in Africa. They should both have great scope for the new youth programmes

---

[2] *I.M.C. Theol. Report*, I, p. 18 and III, p. 35.

[3] *Bulletin Trimestrial de la Fac. Libre de Théol. Protestante de Paris*, Déc. 1953, p. 113. Cf. *I.M.C. Theol. Report*, II, p. 58.

which they are evolving for different levels in Africa, particularly if they establish contact in this field with the Theological Schools.

Similar efforts should be applied to the training of teaching candidates. One prominent Church in West Africa, with an extensive educational programme, has worked out a plan for its teaching candidates. After the teachers' training (four years), the students will be invited to stay on for another year's theological study. Then they will take up teaching for a certain number of years, after which they return to the college for another two years of theological education, followed by ordination. It is too early yet to judge how this will work out in practice, or even to say whether the invitation to stay on for the additional year of theological study will be popular.

The recruitment situation must not be reduced to an interplay of social and economic forces. The other aspects of the pastoral vocation to which we have so forcibly referred above point in another direction. There are splendid examples of men who, under the impulse of the divine call, have given up comparatively lucrative positions in order to become pastors, as we have already pointed out, p. 26. A Lutheran Bena teacher in Tanganyika with a salary of Sh. 300 per month joined a theological school with the prospect of falling to Sh. 150 per month as a pastor; a Methodist Kimbundu Angola carpenter, who earned an income easily three times higher than that of a pastor, gave up his business in order to join the ministry. These men represent a very important section of the ministry in Africa to-day; they and their many colleagues throughout Africa have, in spite of very great hardship, found an assurance which a Zulu pastor expressed thus: 'The little money which pastors earn is *blessed* money. This enables us to live fairly satisfactorily. Many teachers do not believe us when we quote our low salaries.'

The winning of educated youth is an important 'frontier line' in the Church's advance in Africa. On that frontier of the spirit, the need for sensitiveness and real spiritual expectancy is great. I write this remembering a secret revival that took place in a teachers' training school in the Lake Victoria region a decade ago. Thirty young and keen African students suddenly decided, in 1946, to become pastors, the point being that this interest was not only unexpected by the missionaries but has remained largely unknown for a decade, and that it took place in a period during which the missionaries were convinced that the Church concerned was moribund.

One young student teacher, Theophilo, was 'convicted of sin and convinced of salvation'—as he himself expressed his initial experience. He joined forces with four other students and they began to study the Bible and its teaching on the ministry. Very soon another twenty-five—in a teachers' training school of one hundred students—followed their example. They confided their burden to an African seminary teacher of great spiritual experience. He brought them almost daily into the village church, and there, before the altar, they received from him scriptural teaching on the nature of the ministry. In 1947, as the church was invited to send students to a theological school in another part of the territory, the leading pastors were in a position to choose five of the thirty to be prepared as ministers in the Church of Christ.

The present writer formerly had personal contact with that teachers' training school, but he only heard of this amazing student revival nine years after the event, and he is not sure whether any of the missionaries in the district at the time knew what was going on.

It is probably very healthy that church leaders—Africans and Westerners—realize that in this matter of vocation great things do happen without their knowledge, and without their being in a position to guide or direct. The Spirit bloweth where it listeth. And as there exists a Church in Africa to-day, it exists because there was a call, and because men and women have responded to the call. There is a contagious joy in that Xhosa hymn-response:

Nda funyanwa, Nkosi yam,
   nda funyanwa![4]

---

[4] Translation, see p. 15.

· 2 ·

THE AFRICAN PASTOR — "IS HE REALLY
NECESSARY?"

Missions and African Leadership

A century ago Henry Venn, the secretary of the Church Missionary Society, decided to put into practice his theory of a *self*-governing, *self*-supporting and *self*-extending Church. He turned to the Church in Africa. He overcame resistance from the local missionaries and hesitation on the part of Samuel Adjai Crowther, an African minister, and in 1864 arranged for the consecration of Crowther as bishop 'in Western Africa'.[1] This daring and imaginative action had very far-reaching consequences. It showed that Henry Venn's three-'self'-formula was meant to be applied in the life of the African Church. It showed at this early date that African leadership was taken seriously. Missionaries were regarded as temporary agents, serving in the *interim,* until an African Church with an African ministry under African bishops could be fully established.

It was a great experiment—and almost fatal. A serious crisis developed in Crowther's extensive diocese, which made his last years—he died in 1892—difficult and bitter. The name of the African bishop became a symbol not only of African leadership but also of the supposed failure of African leadership. For half a century and more, Africans were considered to be insufficiently 'mature' for leadership in the Church. It was only in 1927 that another Anglican, Roland Allen, showed that Crowther had, in fact, been the victim of an impossible situation. 'There was no African Church in any real sense of the word. Crowther was really an agent of the Church Missionary Society in Episcopal Orders.' And Allen concludes: 'No objection to an apostolic practice can

---

[1] Crowther received his theological education in England and was ordained in 1843. Cf. P. Beyerhaus, *Die Selbständigkeit der jungen Kirchen* (1956), p. 124.

be founded on an instance which did not even remotely resemble the Apostolic example.'[2]

The three-'self'-formula, modified by the American Congregationalist, Rufus Anderson, and a host of other mission leaders, became the corner-stone of Protestant policy in Africa. It was of great service—up to a point. It presented a blue-print of the relationship between Western mission and African Church. As the old ancestral order was dissolved by modern Western influences, the Christian Church grew to represent a new rallying-point, a new order, with a new law, a new life and a new leadership. It was often in and through the Church—the tribe of Christ—and its Book, that scattered tribal and linguistic units were brought together into a greater whole.[3]

Western missions brought to Africa organization, an effective administrative machine, and a new cohesion. In every Church throughout the continent, missionaries and Africans together were engaged in drawing up constitutions for independent, self-governing African churches. In fact, most of the work on village, district, national and regional levels in Protestant Africa was related in some way to this one basic problem: the transfer of authority from mission to Church, the 'devolution of power' from missionary to African leader.

The organization of the Church on the foundation of a democratic constitution was meant to guarantee the fullest possible independence under African leadership. In this context, the training of pastors and catechists becomes a burning issue in the building of the Church.

The transition from mission to Church affected the pastor more than anybody else. He was expected to take over the authority delegated by the missionary and to bear the brunt of the struggle that inevitably had to be fought out—however amicably—when the terms of the transfer were to be decided upon.

---

[2] Roland Allen, *The Spontaneous Expansion of the Church*, 1949[2], p. 193.

[3] An important example is the Ewe Presbyterian Church, in Togo. Cf. D. Westermann in *Neue Allgemeine Missions-Zeitschrift* 1936, p. 217–323. A. W. Schreiber writes: 'The gods of the Ewe died. Thus the Ewe suffered internal and external decline. It is the mission which gave them a common language, the prerequisite for becoming one people; further a common written language and a literature founded on the Bible.' A. W. Schreiber, *Ein Wort zur Kritik Missionar D.Dr.jur. Gutmanns und der Kirchenordnung des Evang. Ewe-Kirche in Togo*. Bremen 1937, p. 10.

From this point of view of the date of transfer, the policy of non-Roman missions in Africa, as elsewhere, proceeded on three different lines.

1. Gradual devolution of authority from Western mission to African Church was the most common rule, this gradualness being more marked in some cases than in others. The development of, and the transfer to African leadership was much slower than Henry Venn himself once had anticipated. Generally speaking, 'self-government' was made dependent on 'self-support'.

2. In some cases, traditional Western mission patterns came to a sudden end because of eruptive political developments. This occurred in two world wars with all the German missions North of the Limpopo. These Churches had to pass through exacting experiences which tested their spiritual strength and suddenly placed a very heavy burden of responsibility on African pastors in particular.

3. In discussing the volume on the Marangu All-Africa Lutheran conference, Bishop S. C. Neill has pointed to a third line. 'The disastrous dichotomy of mission and church ... ought never to be allowed to rise', he claimed, 'If we start with the missions we make almost impossible from the start the natural development of the Church. We must begin with the Church. ... The moment an African is converted there must be a church into which he can be incorporated as a member, and not a mission of which he becomes a dependent. No lesson in mission history seems to me clearer than this. Down with missions!'[4]

It must be admitted, however, that mission history in Africa teaches one other lesson, at least as clear as that to which Bishop Neill refers, namely that this ideal approach has, unfortunately, never been more than a hypothesis. It is the slow devolution process which has been the general rule in Africa.

When the missionary defined the aim of his work as the establishment of an autonomous, independent Church, the main question on the African side throughout the continent and through the entire period under review was, 'When will this happen?' The whole argument between mission and African Church can be reduced to an attempt to decide the time and define the terms of devolution from mission domination to church autonomy. The

---

[4] S. C. Neill, *The Lutheran World*, June, 1956, p. 66–67.

question of the ministries of the Church and their jurisdiction entered as a fundamental issue into these deliberations.

Already in 1916, Dr. H. Junod, the famous Swiss sociologist and missionary in Mozambique, on a visit to a conference at Fort Hare sensed this dilemma. 'When Africans seem to say: "The moment has come. We can manage on our own now. You can go," and when on the other side the missionaries reply: "The moment is far off. Keep quiet and be obedient," *then* the situation has become dangerous. Real insight is needed and above all friendly and intimate personal relations between Black and White, in order to exorcise the danger.'[5]

The terms of the problem varied according to the different and changing denominational and social contexts in which it appeared.

On the South African scene it had a character all its own. Here the official mission policy with its avowed goal of an autonomous Church caused some consternation among the missionaries prior to and around the turn of the century. When John Kilner, London secretary of the Wesleyan Methodist Missionary Society, went on a 'deputational hurricane' to South Africa, he was surprised by what he called the 'amazing modesty' of the missionaries. He emphasized the need of an African ministry. No less than fifty or sixty names were registered of men who might be ordained as 'Native Ministers on Trial'. And Kilner met with opposition from some of the missionaries, who 'felt that the action was too hasty, and there were serious misgivings on the part of some'.[6]

Somewhat the same problem was felt by Presbyterian leaders. Dr. Stewart of Lovedale was not altogether willing to follow the lead from Edinburgh which urged the ordination of an increased number of African ministers. He even seems to have claimed that the main cause of Separatism or Ethiopianism was to be found in the interference of European mission boards in the matter of ordination of Africans.[7]

These examples show that some of the early missionaries in the field—representing some of the most influential missionary societies working in South Africa at the time—felt the danger of a too hasty application of Henry Venn's and Rufus Anderson's principles.

---

[5] *Bulletin de la Mission Romande,* Nov. 1916.

[6] Findlay and Holdsworth, *The Wesl. Methodist Missionary Society,* IV, p. 322, (Wesleyan) *Missionary Notices* 1885, p. 178.

[7] Leenhardt, *Le Mouvement Ethiopien,* 1902, p. 117.

On this question the standpoint of the Dutch Reformed Church in South Africa is of particular interest. At the general missionary conference in Johannesburg in 1925 various missionaries spoke about different aspects of the evangelization of Africa. It is significant that the only Westerners who stressed the role of African leaders in a self-governing African Church were the three spokesmen of the Dutch Reformed Church. J. W. L. Hofmeyer pointed to the experience of his Church in Nyasaland and quoted with enthusiasm the radical ideas of Sidney Clark and Roland Allen on the Indigenous Church. 'The missionary is the transitory factor, the Church the permanent factor.' J. Reyneke, the well-known leader of the work of this mission in Bechuanaland, emphasized that Africa must be evangelized through Africans. He did this in a telling sentence, pleading for African forms of religious expression: 'One reason why Christianity has not swept over South Africa may be because we have not left it sufficiently to the Spirit to give Africa an indigenous African Christianity.' A. C. Murray, of the same Church, wanted all the missions of South Africa to start together 'an undenominational Bible Institute' for the training of African leaders of the Church.

A direct line leads from these 1925 statements to the standpoint of the Dutch Reformed Church as formulated at the famous policy-shaping Bloemfontein conference of 1950. The political climate had now changed considerably as compared with 1925. The self-governing church under African church leaders was still the goal. It was now felt that the policy of building self-governing Bantu Churches harmonized with the *apartheid* policy of the political party in power. *Apartheid* 'facilitates healthy missionary work', it was thought, and was consonant with 'general missionary thinking', i.e. the establishment of independent indigenous Churches.

This official statement was modified, and brought to an energetic encounter with realities in the 'Mission Methods Report' by the Federal Mission Council of the Dutch Reformed Church, possibly the most remarkable, and certainly the most penetrating, of missionary studies in South Africa in the 1950's.[8]

Building on leading missiological studies such as the writings of Roland Allen, Bavinck, Merle Davis and Bishop Azariah, the

---

[8] *Federale Sendingraad, Rapport van die Kommissie van Ondersoek in verband met Binnelandse Sendingsmetodes,* Pretoria, 1954.

Report tries to determine the process of transfer to the 'Daughter-church'.[9] 'The missionary must learn to surrender more and more of the responsibility to African church leaders. In that way he will not hinder the Bantu predikant, for he will appear as his best friend.' This must also be the case in the administration of the Synod. 'This is the direction in which our church must move, and with determination, and we should not be content to say that this [transfer] must be postponed to a distant future.' In this way the mission is aiming at *saambou,* not *opbou* of the Bantu Church, ('building together', not merely 'building up').

We should add here that as a consequence of this general policy, the Dutch Reformed College for Bantu pastors, Stofberggedenk-skool, at present has higher demands for the standard of entrance (matriculation) than any Bantu Seminary in the Union, and gives to its future African pastors a theological education at least as thorough as that offered anywhere else in the country. It is significant however that as a result of the *apartheid* policy of the Government (the Group Areas Act) and the present general up-heaval of many Bantu theological centres in the Union, Stofberg-gedenkskool also will have to be moved from its present place to some recognized 'Native' area.

In the Belgian Congo, missionaries were faced with the ques-tion of African leadership in the Church, but the answer came only slowly and hesitatingly.

In 1918, as the World War was about to end, the American leader A. F. Hensey in a Congo missionary conference made 'the irresistible plea for advance'. In that group, he must have ap-peared as a radical dreamer when he put the problem in these words:

'I wonder if the native Church does not need to be taken more completely into our confidence? Is the time never to come when a conference of representatives of our native brethren shall sit at the same time as this conference? Shall we never have even a Lower House in our deliberations?' There are two things to notice about this exclamation. First, how radical it was in the circumstances can be understood by the fact that only in 1957 did African pastors as officially appointed representatives of their Church take part in

---

[9] Bishop Azariah's important study on *Self-Support* forms the basis of the chapter on 'Stewardship' in the Dutch Reformed Church report.

the meeting of the Congo Protestant Council. Secondly, Hensey, in 1918, was not able to envisage a conference in which Africans and Westerners could deliberate together. The most he could wish for was a Lower House of Africans, although he did not add whether the conventional division of power between Upper and Lower House in the British parliamentary sense was to be followed or not.

The break-through of the Kimbangu prophet movement in 1921 affected the attitude of missionary authorities to a large extent. It seemed that here was regrettable but convincing proof that the African local leaders could not be trusted with that confidence which the official self-government policy of the missions wished to see placed in the Africans. A missionary from the American South in the General Conference of 1921 put the question: 'What is the Congo native worth to the Church?' The speaker had found —and all this could be said as late as in 1921—that intellectually the African 'lacked those traits of mind which have caused his white brother to forge ahead, namely, initiative, a sense of responsibility, the organising faculty, self-control, and the power of will'. And yet, he felt that 'the time will and must come when we missionaries should relinquish the field [to the native]'.[1]

In the twenties the threat from the prophet movement haunted deliberations about African leadership in the Church and hindered an advance towards the training of an ordained African ministry. J. W. Allen, of the Southern Presbyterian Church, USA, speaking to the 1924 General Missionary Conference on 'Leadership' defined this word in a way that could not be misunderstood: 'Leadership: I interpret this as missionary rather than native leadership.'[2] In this connexion another missionary was daring enough to raise the question of ordination of native leaders. He laid down two conditions for ordination: '(a) when men have been serving faithfully for many years they might be ordained; (b) very few men can serve faithfully during their entire life'. This latter observation, sombre as it is, is of course only too true if applied to mankind generally. It is when the judgement is restricted to the 'Congo native' that it strikes a modern reader as remarkable. The hesitation expressed by this missionary was met by one of his colleagues

---

[1] *Congo General Conference Report* 1921, pp. 5 ff.
[2] *Congo Missionary Conference* 1924, p. 67.

from the same missionary society who went so far as to favour the ordination of Africans 'in spite of dangers'.

These quotations from representative debates in the twenties by missionaries in the Belgian Congo, one of the main areas of the Protestant evangelization in Africa, is indicative of an attitude that was general enough at the time, and which was bound to influence the shaping of policy for the following years. That action was so influenced can be seen by the fact that, in 1925, there were only five African ordained men in the Protestant Churches of the colony, two in the Presbyterian Church and three in the organisation called 'Regions Beyond'.

One of the most far-sighted of the missionaries of that time, Dr. W. M. Morrison, however, stressed the necessity of solid theological training as a means to an autonomous African Church. It was largely on his own initiative that the well-known theological seminary at Kakinda was established. As a result of his planning and that of his colleagues, a firm policy of transfer from American mission to African Church was introduced in the Kasai area. It was explained to the Tambaram Conference of 1938 by Charles L. Crane.

Crane regarded the Congolese Church organisation as a training-school for African leaders, looking toward the time when they could finally assume full responsibility. Such full responsibility could not be accorded them 'at the present time'. There were two reasons for this, he told the Tambaram Conference, and his reasons were obviously generally accepted by other missions in the Belgian Congo at the time: deference on one side to Government policy, and on the other to mission policy. Full responsibility for African church leaders—on the eve of World War II!—was dangerous from the Government's point of view, he thought. To hand over full responsibility

> would very probably jeopardize the good relations that now exist between our mission and the Belgian Government, who are exceedingly wary about any tendency towards what is called the *libre examen,* or the too free interpretation of the Scriptures on the part of the African peoples, with the danger of wresting them to perverse ends. Africa—and especially in parts of Central Africa—has seen too many separatist churches grow out of this tendency.

Simon Kimbangu, the Congo Messiah, was, of course, safely imprisoned at the time and his followers relegated from Lower Congo to another part of the Belgian colony, but nevertheless this spectre was still haunting the Protestant missions some two decades after the first outburst of separatist activities, and inhibited them from taking such steps as were otherwise desirable.

The second reason for withholding full responsibility was the fact that the African Church was not yet self-supporting. Only a 'full measure of self-support would entitle (the Church) to full autonomy'. In these words Crane, one of the ablest and most remarkable Congo missionaries of the period, expressed succinctly, and rather dogmatically, the generally accepted mission policy of the time.

By a cautious advance, the mission was trying, he said, 'to steer a middle course between the policy of those who do not place any responsibility on their Native leaders and the policy of those who may have placed so much responsibility on them that evil has resulted'.[3] Crane indicated that the mission had found a method of avoiding the risks. The first pastors ordained in the mission were not ordained as pastors over a particular church, but as 'pastors-at-large', supplementing missionary itineration and serving as assistants to the White missionaries. Their main task was to receive into the membership of the Church the hundreds of catechumens in widely scattered villages.

A considered statement on the ministry was formulated by a group of missionaries in a conference at Bokada, Belgian Congo, in 1951. Theologians among our readers will be interested in the definition of the word pastor, a definition on which this conference in the bush found a common mind:

> It was agreed that the term *Pasteur* be reserved exclusively for those who by training and life are worthy of it. Training would normally include three or four years of theological study after the completion of other education, and worthy life would include the assumption of the responsibilities of Christian marriage and the manifestation of the fruits of the spirit through at least ten years of unbroken Church fellowship and Christian service, so that the Church would not hesitate to ordain the man concerned and grant him the right to Baptize and give Communion. It was agreed that these should be minimum requirements and that all the tendency of the Missions concerned would be to raise these standards in the future rather than to lower them.

---

[3] Tambaram Report (1938), II, pp. 16 ff.

The statement is an interesting indication of an attitude which still obtains in certain groups in Belgian Congo and elsewhere.

Perhaps the most notable consequence of this attitude is the lack of differentiation between pastor, catechist and ordinary layman. The spokesman of an important British missionary group in Lower Congo expressed this at a conference in 1955: 'Our deepest trouble is that we know no difference between pastor and evangelist.' He also pointed out that 'many African Protestant leaders are known as "pastors" without having received the training for this work.' African leaders in this area pointed out as characteristic of the situation that in the African languages there was no difference between 'catechist' and 'pastor' (*nlongi* in Kikongo dialects). This is a typical situation in many districts, particularly of 'Latin' Africa. Some of these groups feel that the African field is a great experimenting ground as far as church offices are concerned. 'We are not tied to any particular system of ministry—we are experimenting and fluid. So for instance we experiment with different systems on different stations and we shall see what the outcome eventually will be.'

Another example is a group in Ruanda-Urundi which had three 'ordained' men and five 'shepherds' to direct their 200 catechists. In Mozambique, that same group stated that after the evangelists' school the students are 'ordained as pastors', while another reported that each outstation was under the leadership of an '*unordained pastor*'.

This view of the ministry has the important practical consequence that it affects recruitment to the ministry, particularly in some Churches. In passing we hint at this recruitment problem in its present dynamic and admittedly controversial context.

This problem is more acute in some Churches than in others. In Anglican, Lutheran, Presbyterian, Reformed and Methodist Churches there has been a tradition of definite teaching on the ministry, and a clear distinction between different orders in the Church. In groups of more radical Protestant allegiance, such as Baptist and Holiness groups, there exists great latitude in nomenclature and interpretation with regard to the ministry. This has apparently led to considerable confusion as to what is meant by a 'pastor' or by other offices in the church groups. For that very reason it is not easy for an educated young man to offer himself for the service of the Church.

We opened this chapter with Henry Venn's vision for the Church and the ministry in Africa. Nowhere was this vision applied with more conscious determination—and indeed with more success—than in Uganda, through the great Bishop Arthur Tucker. We need not go into detail here as we can now refer to J. V. Taylor's admirable book *The Growth of the Church in Buganda*.

The self-governing Uganda Church was Bishop Tucker's goal. The constitution which was adopted in 1909 did not fully correspond to his ideals, and the relationship between British mission and Ganda Church had to be worked out in the course of subsequent history. Here African pastors were to take a leading part.

Bishop Tucker knew that

> in training native Christians in the art of self-government it is a tremendous mistake to hold aloof from their organization, and this for the simple reason that if the work of the European Missionaries is carried on outside the limits of the native Church, there must be an outside organization. In that case the native Christian will not be slow to realize that the outside organization is the one which really settles whatever questions may be under discussion in the Church and that their own organization is more or less a sham ... To my mind, the true attitude and spirit of the missionary towards those to whom he goes is included in the words: 'Forget also thine own people and thy father's house.' Let him therefore throw in his lot absolutely with the natives, identifying himself as far as possible with their life, work and organization.

Taylor has shown the workings of the compromise arranged between mission and Church:

> By means of this compromise the mission was able to be of the Uganda Church, but never under it; to be included in its constitution, but always in an extraordinary position; to be built into its fabric, but always as the keystone. At the Jerusalem Conference of the International Missionary Council in 1928, when several representatives of the younger churches had been voicing their frustration under too much missionary dominance, Mr S. Kulubya, the Uganda delegate, rose to say that this was not so in his country, where the Church had full responsibility. Even today older Ganda politicians say they want to see the Legislative Council fully elected, 'as the Diocesan Council is'.

The role of the African ministry in the structure planned by Bishop Tucker has been analysed by Taylor:

Bishop Tucker took it for granted that the responsible leadership of the Church must be largely identical with its clerical ministry, and that in setting aside men to be catechists, lay-readers and pastors in the Church, he was building up the real hierarchy of authority by which the Church was to be led and governed.[4]

German missions were a special case. The changes and chances of two world wars had a far-reaching effect on their leadership problems and no doubt hastened development towards African autonomy. In Tanganyika—until 1919 called German East Africa —conditions differed somewhat from mission to mission. In 1920, the German missionaries were told to leave the country within three months. In the Usambara field, the Bethel missionaries approached the Universities' Mission (Anglican) with a view to handing over the superintendence to them, but the Shambala lay leaders in the Lutheran Church protested, since they did not wish to become Anglo-Catholics. The German missionaries then called seven trusted laymen together—mission-trained carpenters and teachers—gave them two weeks' training and ordained them as 'shepherds'. Three of these men were hardly able to read a Bible text, and one of them had to be dismissed later because of money troubles, but the others stubbornly carried on, greatly assisted by self-reliant voluntary elders. To a large extent, the local congregations of this Church have been under the leadership of lay elders ever since, a fact which has determined the character of the Church as a whole. Another Bethel field in the same territory—Bukoba— followed another course. Here the African leaders had close contacts with the Church in Uganda, and the Bishop of Uganda, at the request of the orphaned Church, sent an English missionary together with Baganda priests and deacons to lead the young congregation which had been founded only a decade earlier.

The Leipzig mission in the Kilimanjaro area adopted a different method. Faced with immediate internment after the war, the German missionaries did not ordain *in casu necessitatis* as their Bethel colleagues had done. The reasons for the Leipzig attitude were first, a general hesitation on the part of German Lutherans about ordaining without solid theological education and, secondly, the influence of Dr. Bruno Gutmann's ideas. Gutmann stressed the 'primordial social ties' of the African tribe and kin. Building on

---

[4] J. V. Taylor, *The Growth of the Church in Buganda*, 1958, pp. 72, 86, 88.

this sociological foundation he hoped to achieve what he called
'*Selbstbewegung der Gemeinde*'—the initiative of the congregation as a whole. A specially trained group of pastors, or a group
of college-trained teachers tended, according to Gutmann, to form
a possibly dangerous isolationist body, to the detriment of the
group. Gutmann preferred the voluntary church elder who by the
rights of birth and kinship was a leader within his natural social
group and represented the *Volkskraft* of the African group and of
the community as a whole.[5] When a few years later Africans were
ordained in this Church, Gutmann tried to protect what he called
the 'African point of view' by insisting that no man should be
ordained under the age of 40.

Gutmann's views were by no means decisive for his colleagues.
But most of them were at that time, like many missionaries in
other denominations in other parts of Africa, chary of what was
described as 'rash' ordination of Africans. It is characteristic that
when a change on this point did take place, it was brought about
in the Leipzig mission on the initiative of the Home Board. It is
characteristic, we say; for in many Western missionary societies,
from the time of Henry Venn onwards, the Home Boards had to
override the hesitation of the local missionaries in allowing scope
to African leadership.

In 1927, Professor Carl Ihmels, Director of the Leipzig Mission,
made a 'visitation' of the Lutheran field in Northern Tanganyika.
To a certain extent he shared Gutmann's concern. He represented
a point of view that was held not only by German Lutheran, but
by many other missions at that time, particularly such missions
as were under the spell of the Phelps-Stokes reports and the ideas
of Jesse Jones. Dr. Ihmels stressed that the training of African
leaders must not isolate these from the community and from their
own people. Higher education of any kind in Africa had to establish 'organic connexion with the mass of the people'. But here,
Ihmels felt even Jesse Jones and the Phelps-Stokes Commission to
be at fault; they did not offer an adequate account of man as a
member of the whole African society. The highest criterion for

---

[5] See B. Gutmann: *Freies Menschentum aus ewigen Bindungen*, 1928,
particularly Ch. III,
    idem, Die Führerfrage in Africa, in *Lutherisches Weltmissionsjahrbuch*,
1927, and
    idem, *Sage es der Gemeinde!*, 1950.

leadership was not an educational standard but the relationship between the leader and the community as a whole. 'We must therefore be very careful; the training of the leader must always be carried on in the closest touch with his people.'[6] Given this important modification, Ihmels insisted on theological education for, and ordination of, Africans.

The mass movement into the Church in Northern Tanganyika, he claimed, necessitated decentralization of the young Church and the handing over of responsibility to African pastors. There they must not be hesitant or niggardly. 'Do not quench the Spirit. Do not suppress any charismatic gifts.' With regard to the 'form of the ministry' they should not copy conditions in Germany. For the theological training of trusted, experienced teachers a six-months' course would do for a start, he thought. Dr. Rother and other leading Leipzig missionaries in Tanganyika accepted this view, and the missionaries' conference in 1927 decided to launch out on the hitherto untrodden path of theological education and ordination for Africans. Seven years later, in 1934, the first ordination took place in this important East African Church, forty years after the beginning of the Leipzig mission work.[7]

The particular emphasis which Bruno Gutmann gave to the discussion—the religious leader in Africa as representative of the natural group—must not conceal the fact that the fundamental concern of German Lutheran missionaries at that time was one which they shared with the great majority of Protestant missions. Their interest was to create a ministry which was the expression of the Christian community as such, and which was not alien to the religious group it represented. As the ideas of Roland Allen have stimulated the development of the Church in Africa, particularly in 'Latin' Africa, we shall refer briefly to his writings in this context. The Anglican missionary to China who ended his days in Kenya, not far from Kilimanjaro, was as different from Dr. Gutmann of Kilimanjaro as one could imagine. Theologically, their approach was different, for while Gutmann's point of departure was the 'primordial social ties', given through Creation, Allen's was the Third Article and the life of the Spirit. But in spite of this, Allen's belief in what he, and his World Dominion group,

---

[6] Letter from Dr. C. Ihmels 5.11.1930 to Dr. J. H. Oldham, I.M.C.
[7] Beratungsprotokoll, Leipzig Mission, Tanganyika, 11.11.1927.

called 'indigenous Church principles' had certain affinities with Gutmann.

Allen was convinced from the very beginning that 'Church order is not the enemy of the natural and instinctive' and he shared Gutmann's fear of institutions, classing the theological school as a mission 'institution'. According to Allen, 'the education of the leaders of the Church was divorced from the Church through the mission institutions. They were trained not because they were leaders in the Church, and the Church wanted them trained; they were trained because foreigners wanted to train them in their own way. In relation to the native Church they were often as foreign as the foreign missionaries.' The causes of stagnation of the Church lay, he thought 'in the fact that we have despised and set at naught the natural training of experience and have put in its place an artificial and intellectual training before the great body of the people was ready for it, and the inevitable result is that those who receive it are separated as by a gulf from their people'.[8] Gutmann himself could hardly have said this with more emphasis. Despite all the liberating effect that Allen's message had in other spheres of the Church's work, in this field of training of church workers his writings have probably retarded the development of the Church. For with his sharp and witty criticism of solid intellectual training he strengthened the hand of those who only too willingly postponed, or neglected, theological education for the Church in Africa. In the long run too, this retarded—as far as we can see—the aim of instituting autonomous Churches which Allen himself was advocating.

Gutmann's 'self-expression, or initiative, of the congregation' as a unit; Ihmels' (and Knak's) 'organic connexion with the mass of the people'; and even Roland Allen's 'spontaneous expansion' could without much difficulty be reconciled to the community emphasis of Jesse Jones and the Phelps-Stokes Commission reports at the beginning of the 1920's. It is recognized, the Reports say, that 'the training for the religious leadership of the African people is the most vital of all educational responsibilities'. With the practical attitude of the Quaker, Dr. Jones claims that 'every form of leadership is in some respects a religious leadership'. The special-

---

[8] Roland Allen, *The Spontaneous Expansion of the Church,* 2nd ed. 1949. pp. 173, 192.

ized religious training should prepare Africans 'to give the main emphasis of their lives to directing the people to a faith in the Divine order of the Universe'. With his particular interest in education based on the agricultural community, Dr. Jesse Jones suggests that African preachers could also be 'teachers and farmers'. Nevertheless the American recognizes that the training of the religious worker should 'as far as possible presuppose the essentials of secondary education'. This theme is developed in a few characteristic recommendations:

1. The Native minister must have an appreciation of the Bible, of the Christian Church, and of Christian civilization. This means, of course, that there must be careful study of the Bible, some knowledge of church history, and some acquaintance with the social and religious history of European and American nations.

2. Customs and traditions of the Native people must be studied and interpreted in the light of comparative religion and social science. The helpful elements must be distinguished from those that have been harmful and destructive.

3. The application of religion to the life of the individual and the community must be studied, and illustrations from actual life should be brought to the attention of the student. Educational adaptations for the training of the individual and for the improvement of the rural and urban community should all have a part in the preparation of the Native minister.[9]

Other missionary leaders felt that these approaches were not in the best interests of a well-educated ministry and that the identification of leader and group blurred the vision of real leadership. The most interesting spokesman on this side was, characteristically, French. He represented the Latin idea of leadership according to which it was the function of the *élite* to form the mass, as distinct from German and Anglo-Saxon ideas of slow evolution of leadership material latent in the mass of the people. Maurice Leenhardt, the famous sociologist, had begun as a Protestant missionary in New Hebrides and had later become founder and editor of *Le Monde non-Chrétien*. He had made an extensive tour of the Paris Mission fields in Africa (Madagascar, Basutoland, Northern Rhodesia and Gabon) in the twenties, and as a result launched an eloquent and courageous criticism of the policy of his own mission in

⁹ T. J. Jones, *Education in Africa*, N. Y., 1921, p. 75.

Northern Rhodesia. The question which forced itself upon Leen-hardt was the following: Why are African pastors a power in some Churches, but not in others? He refuted the argument that it was a variation in the quality of human material from tribe to tribe. The crux, according to Leenhardt, was to be found elsewhere: in the mind and the heart of the missionary himself. There were three different missionary attitudes to African leadership in the Church, he claimed.

1. Some missionaries felt that the nationals were not mature enough. But by pointing out the religious or intellectual deficiency of the African Christian they obscured their own view so that they did not have an eye for 'innate values'. Such missionaries would soon become incapable of winning the confidence of the African.

2. Others attempted a compromise: 'They invent half-pastors, or substitute pastors, composite pastors,—*Ersatz.*'

3. Finally, there was a group of missionaries 'who run the risk of showing confidence, and they create the ministry'.[1]

The particular background for Leenhardt's argument was the Church situation in Barotseland, the Paris mission field in North-ern Rhodesia. It was founded in 1885 by the famous François Coil-lard, together with a few faithful Sotho evangelists whom Coillard had brought with him from his earlier sphere of work in Basuto-land. Coillard did not find the Barotse responsive. Also his de-mands on African candidates for baptism, and even more in the case of candidates for church office, were considerable. Coillard's heritage of severe pietism played an important role here. There were catechumens who were kept waiting twenty years for their baptism. After 40 years of mission work, the number of communi-cants was 195. The first pastor was ordained in 1950, after 65 years, and only after a considerable change in the theological climate among the missionaries had taken place. To be accepted for bap-tism in this Church was a very great achievement. To be accepted as a catechist was an honour on a par with the Croix de la Légion d'Honneur.

Leenhardt's point was that the mission had not shown enough confidence in the leadership qualities of the Africans, and that

---

[1] *Propos missionnaires,* Febr. 1940 (a missionary review published by Leen-hardt in Paris 1927–1940).

this confidence could be gained only through the re-consideration of the theology of the Church and the apostolate. As both a sociologist and missionary, he was not impressed by an attitude which made religious leadership merely a function of the group— this attitude Leenhardt called Rousseauism. He wished rather to form an élite of men who knew that they were part of *un sacerdoce universel naissant,* men set apart for the order and ministry of the Church, who did not have to dissipate their energies in school or hospital. (In this connexion Leenhardt makes a very strong plea for the Divinity School as the most important place in the mission, a *terra sacra.* His aim is to distinguish sharply between Church and school, and give the Church and its ministry its rightful place.) The Christian pastor, concludes Leenhardt with a definition that deserves to be better known, has spiritual maturity and is, in his environment, the only person who in all things can *porter un jugement de valeur.*

To a certain extent, Leenhardt's attitude was shared by some Anglo-Catholics. The whole trend of Protestant Africa in the period under review was, however, in another direction. That is possibly the reason why theological education became such an embarrassing problem as the years went by. It is at least possible that Leenhardt saw farther than most people. While the view he opposed was a characteristic expression of the twenties, the period of Indirect Rule, Leenhardt's alternative belonged to a period to come. It is possible, we say, that Maurice Leenhardt saw farther than the other mission leaders whom we have just quoted. One thing at least cannot be questioned. He had the great leader's confidence in the African. And this in itself was helpful in creating that new climate in which responsible African church leadership could grow.

We met recently a well-known French-speaking missionary who had given forty years to Africa, rich and fruitful years marked by generous and inspiring contacts with his African co-workers. He had known Leenhardt well and had learned much from him. Now he had retired, and I asked him about his view of African pastors. He replied, 'The one great weakness in my missionary life has been that I did not show *sufficient* confidence in the African.' This insight corresponds exactly to the view of Maurice Leenhardt, to that of Henry Venn and of Bishop Tucker and to that of many gallant missionaries throughout the continent of Africa.

The Ordained Ministry in Africa: a Recent Innovation

'Look at the story of Christianity in the southern two-thirds of Africa, and see . . . how short it is.' Dr. Roland Oliver's wide view of Christian history in Africa has reminded us that it was only in the nineteenth century, and then very slowly, that the serious missionary approach to Africa was made, either by Catholics or Protestants.[2] Only a hundred years have passed since Livingstone opened 'a path to commerce and Christianity'. In many parts of Central Africa, it is only fifty years or less since the first missionary, together with his first catechists, founded a Christian congregation.

From that date to the ordination day of the first African pastor was often a very long step. A glance at African church statistics will demonstrate how very recent an innovation this is.

Africa south of the Sahara but including Ethiopia and Eritrea

	Ordained missionaries	Ordained Africans	Unordained	Christian community
1900	1,200	408	6,000	560,000
1910	1,300	750	18,700	1,700,000
1925	2,000	1,181	38,126	2,200,000
1938	2,463	4,000	76,000	4,900,000
1949	2,810	3,491	79,600	9,250,000
1957	4,208	5,760	82,433	10,950,000

The Protestant and Anglican communities in Africa increased from half-a-million in 1900 to over two millions in 1925, five millions in 1938 and some eleven millions by 1957. The impression of the growth of the Christian community is one of an accelerating mass movement, particularly until about the middle of the century.

Certain countries show a very rapid rise. Nigeria and the Belgian Congo belong to that category. Some countries with a comparatively long Church history showed a more even and steady development. Ghana, Southern Rhodesia and Uganda belong to that category. Then again there is a tendency towards numerical stagnation at least in Sierra Leone, not only for the Christian community but

---

[2] R. Oliver, *How Christian is Africa?* (1956), p. 7.

also as far as the figures for ordained and unordained workers are concerned.[3]

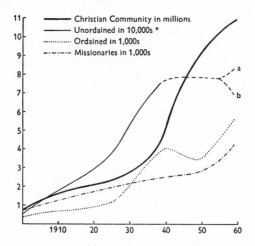

* The term "unordained" includes for the most part (a) teachers and (b) catechists, as we have shown on pages 64 and 95. The teachers' position in relation to the Church altered substantially during and after the Second World War. The dotted line referring to the period post-1940 indicates the problematic nature of the situation with regard to unordained workers. The distinction between teacher and catechist begins to make its presence felt during this period.

―――――――

[3] Ghana 146, 262, 337, 433; Southern Rhodesia 21, 110, 167, 258; and Uganda 145, 329, 490, 444. Sierra Leone 37, 41, 48, 54.

We cannot go into detail here as far as development on denominational lines is concerned. Not all, by far, of the churches included in the general survey are amenable to co-operative contacts with other churches, and the total effort and effect appear to be weakened accordingly. So, for instance, out of a Christian community of some 11 millions in 1957 nearly 1 million comprised Seventh Day Adventists and Pentecostal groups (470,000 and 500,000 respectively), or 9% of the total. Even more significant, perhaps, is the fact that of the 5,760 ordained, no less than 1,141 (660 and 481 respectively), or *20% of the total number of ordained Africans* belonged to these two groups.

The statistics refer to the following sources:

1900: R. Grundemann, *Kleine Missions-Geographie und -Statistik*, Stuttgart 1901.

1910: Dennis-Beach-Fahs, *World Atlas of Christian Missions*, N.Y. 1911.

1925: Beach-Fahs, *World Missionary Atlas*, London 1925.

1938: Joseph I. Parker, *Interpretative Statistical Survey of the World Mission of the Christian Church*, N.Y. 1938.

The position of the ordained African ministry in this period must be compared with that of *the unordained evangelistic staff,* the local catechists and village teachers. Their numbers rose from 6,000 to over 18,000 in the first decade and to over 38,000 by 1925. This total was doubled again, to 76,000, in 1938. From then onwards the figures for 'unordained staff' must be handled carefully and critically. The 1938 survey, however, shows that about 55 per cent of the total of unordained workers were 'evangelistic' staff, i.e. catechists and others, and about 44 per cent 'educational', i.e. teachers. In 1938 it was, however, of small importance whether the local lay-leaders were counted as teachers or catechists, since both categories were church workers and co-operated as a matter of course in building up the local congregations on the frontier of evangelistic expansion. In the statistical returns for 1949 and 1957 these categories are not differentiated. In 1949, and still more at the end of the fifties, a new factor had appeared; the schools were being taken over by the Government, and teachers were no longer, as they had once been, servants of the Church. This meant that even if the total of lay workers was slightly higher in 1957 than twenty years earlier, the Church's position had in fact weakened, as the pastor could no longer muster or control those whom he had earlier been accustomed to call 'his' teachers for the evangelistic and catechetical work of the local church.

These facts must be remembered when the very rapid rise of the numbers for unordained staff in the second quarter of the century is considered. All the same, the achievements of this vast army of lay helpers have been great. Between 1925 and 1957, the numbers of unordained workers grew, in Angola from 760 to 3,580, in the Belgian Congo from 4,300 to 19,350, in Nigeria from 2,650 to 16,740, and in Tanganyika from 890 to 3,616. In Uganda on the other hand, where this rapid development of the system of catechists had set in earlier than in many other parts of Africa, there was a marked tendency to exchange paid catechists for a new system. In 1925 there were some 4,000 unordained workers in Uganda, but thirty years later that figure had fallen slightly, to 3,700.

1949: Bingle-Grubb, *World Christian Handbook,* 1st ed.

1957: Bingle-Grubb, *World Christian Handbook,* 3rd ed.

For the statistical returns and the adjustments which we have had to make, cf. Appendix III, p. 330.

2. Baptism at Vanga, Belgian Congo.

In Africa as a whole, the future of the catechist became a problem, and Protestant mission policy attempted to dispense with catechists in favour of a combination of ordained men and voluntary lay workers. For the building up of the local churches in the first decades of the century the catechists and village teachers had been of fundamental importance. The system of lay helpers was most rapidly developed by Methodists and Anglicans; *in 1900,* nearly two-thirds of all lay workers in Africa belonged to Churches in South Africa (nearly 3,900), of which more than half were Methodists. In West Africa similar conditions prevailed. Almost half of the lay workers in this region (604 out of a total of 1,321) were Methodists and Anglicans (C.M.S.)—381 and 223 respectively. *Ten years later,* Methodists and Anglicans again dominate the scene as far as the unordained forces go. In South Africa, of some 8,300 lay workers, one-fifth were Methodists. In West Africa, more than a quarter of the unordained staff (660 out of 2,300) belonged to this same mission. This fact has wider implications. The Methodist Church brought its 'class' system to Africa, whereby the local congregation was organized in groups, or classes of, ideally, twelve members, each group with its own 'class leader'. This gave to its organisation a vital and dynamic cellular structure (see p. 298), in which lay leadership found its logical and necessary place, a conception the importance of which was not confined to Methodism. It influenced church structure in a number of other Protestant groups, for instance Lutheran mission work in Natal and Zululand. Whether recognized as a model or not, the Methodist class system has been of great importance in adapting the Church to the village and to urban conditions in Africa. From this, and from other points of view, the Methodists appear as the characteristically Protestant Church in Africa in the first half of the twentieth century. Other missions which built up extended systems of unordained staff at this time were the United Free Church of Scotland in South Africa and Nyasaland, the Dutch Reformed Church in Nyasaland, the Berlin Mission in South Africa, the Basel and Bremen missions in West Africa, and the Baptists—British and American—in the Congo.

Against this background, the slow and hesitating way in which Africans were prepared and accepted for ordination stands out in sharp relief. In 1900 the total was 400, and one-fourth of these belonged to the special case presented by the churches of Liberia. The relevant figure should therefore be quoted as 300.[4] In 1925, their numbers had risen fourfold to some 1,200 for the whole of the continent. If we now break down these totals into regions, we find that *in 1900,* in the whole of West Africa *three* missions alone accounted for 137 ordained, out of a total of 160: the Church Missionary Society and the Wesleyan Missionary Society in Sierra Leone and Nigeria, and the Basel Mission in the Gold Coast. Also in South Africa the great majority of ordained Africans were Methodists and Anglicans—90 out of 125. The situation in the rest of Africa in 1900 is easily summarized. The Christian communities from Congo to Angola had *one* African pastor, of the American Baptist mission in Banza Manteke. East Africa, including Nyasaland, had 30, of whom again 24 were C.M.S. priests in Uganda, and five highly-trained priests (educated in England) belonging to the Universities' Mission, in the Diocese of Zanzibar.

Ten years later, *in 1910,* the situation in West Africa had changed only slightly. Here again C.M.S and Methodists provided three-quarters of the total number of pastors. Two continental missions had meanwhile made considerable efforts in the field of theological education. We refer to the Basel Mission in the Gold Coast, and the Bremen Mission in Togo. These pastors had in most cases had a thorough education in Europe in the German language. In South Africa, the dominant Methodist influence is seen by the fact that no less than 245 out of a total of 400 African pastors belonged to Methodist groups, representing some 360,000 Christians. But a new, and portentous, factor had appeared: half of these Methodists called themselves 'A.M.E.'—African Methodist Episcopal Church. The Ethiopian movement had begun. Most of the A.M.E. pastors had broken away from the fast-growing company of Methodist local leaders. Anglicans had 60 priests, various Lutheran bodies some 20 pastors and Scottish Presbyterians about the same number. Also in the Rhodesias and Nyasaland, Methodists, Anglicans and Scottish Presbyterians formed the spearhead as far as ordination of Africans is concerned. But the

---

[4] Of the 250 West African pastors in 1900, 95 were to be found in Liberia, and that number remained stagnant in the period 1900–1950 and largely confined to the capital Monrovia. For our purpose of a general survey of Africa, we should have to disregard Liberia, the ecclesiastical problems of which are peculiar.

competition, if such it was, was not serious. The total of ordained Africans in this part of Africa was only 16. (U.M.C.A. in Nyasaland with six, the Wesleyan Methodists five.) The strong Presbyterian missions in this region were much more reluctant about ordination (Scottish Presbyterians in Nyasaland and the Paris Mission in Barotseland).

The whole region which included the Cameroons, Congo, Angola down to German South-West Africa had only 16 pastors in 1910.[5]

The missionary map for East Africa had by 1910 become slightly more stabilized. The Anglican Church in Uganda with a Christian community of nearly 70,000 had 33 priests and well over 2,000 catechists. The U.M.C.A. in Tanganyika had 17 African priests.

As late as *1925*, the ordained African pastor was still largely an unknown quantity in whole regions of Africa, though West and South Africa and Uganda by now had considerable numbers of ordained men. Sierra Leone, Liberia and the Gold Coast had 100 each and Nigeria 150; in South Africa, Methodists and Anglicans were far ahead of the others in this respect with some 150–170 each, though a number of other Churches, such as the Lutheran, Dutch Reformed and Congregational bodies had now begun to train and ordain Africans. In comparison with this advance, the hesitation shown in other parts of Africa is the more marked. The Belgian Congo, with sixteen Protestant missionary societies and a Christian community of over 100,000, had only five pastors (two for the 'Southern' Presbyterian group and three for the 'Regions Beyond' mission.) Of the eight missionary societies represented in Angola at the time only one, the Methodist Episcopal Church, had begun to ordain Africans—no less than twenty-one men. South-West Africa had none; while Northern Rhodesia—with 11 societies and a Christian community of over 20,000—had four pastors, three of whom were Methodists.

It is at present not advisable to draw too hard-and-fast conclusions from the available statistical material. We should note, however, that in Angola, between *1925* and *1957*, the numbers of

---

[5] Whereas the Christian community in the region comprised slightly more than 100,000, one single mission—the Disciples in Congo—with a total Christian community of only 1,800 reported 52 ordained Africans. Fifteen years later this mission did not claim to have any ordained men at all and it is safe to assume that the generous statement in 1910 was caused by a somewhat peculiar definition of the term 'ordination'.

pastors rose from 4 to 144; in Belgian Congo from 5 to 568; in French West Africa from 19 to some 220 ordained[6]; in Kenya from 16 to 426 ordained; in Nigeria from 151 to 467 ordained; Tanganyika, one of the countries which on account of two world wars had to go through particular difficulties in the field of Protestant missions, shows an increase from 22 ordained in 1925 to 272 in 1957.

In order to interpret this development, and the possible correlation between the rise of the Christian community and that of the ministry—ordained and unordained—one would have to consider the problems of local leadership in much greater detail than is here possible.

But one thing stands out, sharply and unmistakeably: the 1950's have witnessed a fundamental change in the local leadership situation: the unordained staff—teachers and catechists—were, for different reasons, retreating from their previous central position with regard to evangelistic outreach and congregational life. In this situation, the emphasis on the work of the ordained minister became stronger than hitherto, the burden on his shoulders heavier than ever before, the call for better ministerial training more insistent than ever. There was no longer any question as to whether the African pastor was really necessary for the Church.

Mass Movements, Revivals, and the Ministry

The period 1920—50 in the Protestant churches in Africa is characterized by a series of *mass movements*.[7] Ivory Coast, Nigeria,

---

[6] The official figure is 462, but this includes 242 ordained Seventh-day Adventists, in an organization which has not returned any figures for unordained, who presumably are included in the 242.

[7] We have used the term 'mass movement' for the influx of great numbers into the churches in recent decades. We use this term advisedly. As such it is distinct from a 'group movement' in e.g. South India where a sociological group as a totality—a village or a particular caste sector of a village—moves into the Church. The term 'mass movement' should also be clearly distinguished from 'revival'. This latter term should be reserved for a new-life movement, or revitalization of an existing church which in the course of time may have acquired a certain formalized tendency. Unfortunately, the term 'revival' is often used indiscriminately as referring to an influx of large or moderate numbers of non-Christians into a church, which in fact is a mass movement, a transition to a new religious organization, in this case to the Christian Church.

Cameroon, Uganda, Northern Tanganyika, certain parts of the Belgian Congo—such as the district of Kwango—all contribute dramatic examples of mass transition to the Anglican, Methodist, Lutheran, Presbyterian, or Baptist Churches.

The typical character of the mass movement can be seen most clearly in West Africa. For example, the Anglican Church in Nigeria had, in 1925, a Christian community of nearly 150,000. 25,000 of these were communicants, while baptized non-communicants in this Church comprised nearly three times this figure, or 70,000. To shepherd the masses of new Christians there were 100 ordained (among whom there were now numbered two African assistant bishops) and 1,500 unordained workers. The latter were also responsible for the 47,000 or so children in the rapidly expanding mission schools. The Bishop of Lagos writes in 1924 on the situation:

'To baptize the hundreds who are flocking into the Church, unless we are prepared to continue their training and teaching, spells disaster in the future. In a district in which there were over 1,000 adult baptisms last year, there are over 200 congregations, and it takes at least five days to get from one end to the other. There is only one superintending missionary and four African clergy on the staff. The visits of a clergyman must be few and far between. If the present opportunity is lost it will not recur. I do not fear that the growing African Church will be swept away; I am fearful as to the outstanding character it may assume in the future. What will be the general tone and level of the future Church?'

A keen Anglican layman, D. A. Stevens, who between 1921 and 1924 trekked all over Nigeria, contributed an even more alarming report: 'Three years in Nigeria tends to shake a man's trust in Christianity as a world religion.' The reason for his pessimism was the scarcity of clergy, the result of which was congregations practically deprived of the use of the Sacraments. 'The Altar resembles the Jewish Sanctum Sanctorum—it is approached once a year, if then.' Stevens had a solution:

'Laymen must be authorized to celebrate rather than that the Sacraments be rendered inapplicable and impotent. We must be prepared that a calabash for a cup, a camp fire for an altar, and a very imperfect conception of the meaning of the Sacrament may be in God's eyes a much more acceptable service than many that are offered with all the pomp and circumstance of a European Cathedral.'

Stevens had his article published in the official Anglican mission review, *The East and the West,* (1924) and the editor had to put in a caveat, although he admitted that 'the Church is bound to take some action if it is not to suffer irreparable loss'. In the situation the rejoinder from the then Bishop on the Niger was perhaps not altogether satisfactory: 'The desirability of too frequent communions for a primitive people is one which is open to grave question.' The Bishop seemed to weaken his own argument against Stevens when he also conceded, 'The greatest problem which the Church has to face is the rapid growth of its numbers.'[8]

The possible conflict between rapid growth and the 'quality' of the Church's life in these circumstances becomes a central problem. This is a problem which Roman Catholic theologians have characterized as the 'law of strangulation' (*vide infra* p. 81), but it is not limited to the Roman Catholic Church. It seems in fact to be at work in many Protestant Churches as well. There seems to be a certain definite periodicity in the development; a 'first generation' of Christians is characterized by intense conviction and interest, which eventually culminates in one or many consecutive mass movements. This is followed by a 'second generation', where the lack of trained leadership in certain cases results in a loss of interest, and a third generation in which a general deterioration becomes visible.

As the small intimate fellowship expands to a mass movement, there is obviously a greater degree of impersonality; this is a serious loss, for we are dealing with religion, the essence of which is personal relationship. But the problem is deeper even than that, and is more far-reaching than such commonplace sociological observations can convey. How far in all this is the minister—Westerner and African—a pastor of his flock, a priest of souls? How far does the structure of the Church ensure that first things come first?

If the pastor is supposed to administer rather than minister, he may possibly tell himself that he can succed just as well in large-scale administration, with the apparently unlimited resources of a Government or a mining company rather than the creaking ma-

---

[8] Articles by the Bishops of Lagos and on the Niger; and D. A. Stevens, in *The East and the West* (1924).

chinery of the Church. Considerations of this kind pierce deep into the very nature of the Church and its ministry. As long as those questions are answered tentatively and uncertainly, some of the best young people will not consider the ministry as a life calling.

The scene changes, however, when a mass movement is followed by a revival. In certain cases the two are closely intertwined and condition one another. Protestant Africa experienced a remarkable number of local revivals in the 1930's. Looking at the whole canvas of Africa at that time we have been struck by something which almost resembles a synchronization of great revivals in the years 1935–38. Even the most detached historian can scarcely fail to appreciate the spiritual power of these simultaneous signs of awakening in the Church.

The *Balokole* revival in East Africa began in about 1935–36 in Ruanda. A young African minister, Blasio Kigozi, himself a product of a mass movement, grew impatient with the besetting formalism of his church. Convicted of sin, he challenged himself and his colleagues in a Uganda synod, praying 'Lord, revive thy Church—and begin with me!' This East African revival had already begun before this incident, but at that time there was 'a fresh upsurge of life in the Church' (Warren), coinciding with the diamond jubilee of the mission, 1935–36. Dr. Warren has pointed out that these years 'were "a time of ferment" in East Africa—in Ruanda a famine, in Uganda a devastating scourge of locusts, in Kenya growing unrest as new ideas surged in to overthrow the ordered round of an older world.'[9]

About the same time as this revival in British East Africa, there was a remarkable mass movement in Ethiopia, and in 1937 a combined mass movement and revival called *oban* in the French Cameroons. About the latter the American Presbyterian mission writes: 'The evangelistic work in this particular part of the world which has been called a "pentecostal field" continues to be the most encouraging phase of the mission's work. This particular part of Africa has paid higher dividends than almost any other area in the world and still continues to be an amazingly fruitful field.'[1]

---

[9] M. A. C. Warren, *Revival, An Enquiry*, 1956, p. 42.
[1] 107th Annual Rpt, Board of Foreign Missions, Presbyt. Church, U.S.A. 1944.

The results here are ascribed to the work of village evangelists and teachers, the relationship between growth and leadership being clearly seen.

The complex relationship between mass movement and revival can to a certain extent be interpreted in sociological terms. Mass movements in Africa tended to make the Church into a big organization with little person-to-person contact, during such time as there was an insufficient number of local leaders. The greater the success of the Church in statistical terms, the less intense tended to become church life on the local level. The revival—particularly by its emphasis on open confession—went far toward solving the problems of fellowship, by creating small, effective sub-groups in which intense corporate participation was made possible. Here a new form of leadership emerged. Sometimes, in fact surprisingly often, it was identical with that of the official Church, but there were also charismatic leaders, and 'brotherhood' groups with particularly strong ties between leader and followers. It is characteristic of the fellowship experience that the East African revivalists refer to each other as 'brother of the same kin'—*aboluganda*. It should also be pointed out that often Westerners and Africans shared fully this brotherhood fellowship. The revival with its open confession has served as nothing else has done to break down inter-racial barriers, but for those who found themselves left out, these barriers may be more unyielding than ever.

Here the revival changed the whole orientation of the Church, and brought its activity on to another level, revealing a new dimension which mission and Church had hitherto neglected. With the conventional combination of evangelism and education, missions mainly approached the masses on the intellectual and catechetical level. The revivals showed that the masses, and the individuals also, had to be approached on another level. An American sociologist, Priscilla Reining, has pointed out, with reference to one of the peoples near Lake Victoria, also reached by the East African revival, that there existed a general *guilt complex* in the population. They regarded their womenfolk as infertile and prostitutes, and hence felt an overwhelming need of confession. The *abolokole* revival meets this need to a degree which most Westerners fail to appreciate. Obviously, the demands on an African pastor will be different in a revivalist group of this nature from that of a more formalized, conventional bourgeois Western type. In engaging himself in a revival movement of this kind, the pastor becomes a means of intensifying the integration of the group.

On the level of church organization there appears a further factor which also tends to hasten the growth of the Church. As this factor has great consequences for the African ministry we shall study it in some detail. Dr. D. A. McGavran, in his book *The Bridges of God*, (1955) has called attention to the dangers latent in the earlier emphasis on the role of the mission-station and the need for bold decentralization of the local evangelistic work. This is a theme of direct relevance to the African scene and to our study of the ministry, for there are many fine examples of a release of new life and strength, consequent upon the transfer of control from the missionary on his central station to the local centres with their responsible African ordained leaders. There is perhaps no more telling instance of the effect of change of policy on these lines than that of the Baptist work at Vanga in the Southern Belgian Congo.

The success of the Baptist mission at Vanga in the Southern Province of the Belgian Congo was due both to sound planning at the start and courageous decentralization at a psychological moment in the development of the district. Dr. William Leslie, of the American Baptist Mission, had begun his missionary career in the older Baptist districts near Leopoldville. When he had to open up a new area in the Kwango district, he drew upon his previous experience, and insisted that the new work be self-supporting from the start and must not depend upon mission support as had been the tendency elsewhere. The district comprised a population of about 250,000 in some 420 villages, over an area of about 8,500 square miles—the same size as Palestine. After a decade, only about a hundred had been baptized, but there was gradual growth. New villages were added as the evangelistic efforts spread from the central station. About the same time as the mission started, big business reached the district with the commencement of the palm oil industry in the Kwango. Under the influence of the preaching at the central station a 'revival' was reported in 1924, though church statistics show that only fairly small numbers were added at that time; however the foundation then laid was doubtless sound and solid.

A new American missionary, by the name of Lewis Brown,

decided about 1931–32 to break with the central station idea and to decentralize the whole work. Prior to this, *all* the members and catechumens had made monthly trips from their local villages in to the central station for worship and instruction. Now five new district centres were established *under African pastors*. New interest was created, and the work made rapid strides. In 1933 the number of baptisms passed one thousand for the first time in any one year. It should be added in this connexion that motor roads —such as they were—began to be laid about that same time, in order to facilitate the transport of palm nuts and palm oil. Transport thus became easier for the missions also.

The decentralization programme of the Church has been carried through with great determination. The Vanga mission now has 30 church centres and 420 catechetical centres in the villages. Each church centre is under an African pastor, who has had two or three years of study at the Theological College at Kimpese, following upon five or six years of training in the mission station school. The pastor's salary averages 1,000 Belgian Congo francs per month, and there is an attempt to keep Kimpese-trained pastors and teachers on about the same level of pay.[2] Church membership is 26,000, with an additional 3,000 under discipline, and with about 8,000 catechumens under instruction. Parallel with this development, a great many schools have been opened in the district. Apart from the 11,000 pupils receiving elementary instruction from the catechists in the 420 villages, there has been rapid growth of enrolment to the primary schools in the 30 church centres. In these there were less than 1,500 pupils in 1945 but over 6,200 ten years later. Throughout the period the churches have assumed financial responsibility for the schools. The result of the stewardship programme of the Church has been very gratifying—we saw that self-support was the very principle of the work established in 1912. In the ten years between 1945 and 1954 Church contributions in the area increased from 156,000 francs to over 3,300,000 francs. This covers the salaries of all the pastors, catechists, and regional school teachers, as well as the buying of all books and supplies for the churches and schools.

Among factors which have facilitated growth at Vanga the fol-

---

[2] Catechists receive on an average 210 francs per month, with extremes of 110 and 415. To this is added free housing. They also receive 'probably just about all their food' from the Christians.

lowing should be noticed. As a result of the presence of the palm-oil industry in the area, there has not been as serious a dispersion of the male population as elsewhere, since the majority has been able to remain in the area. Men comprise some 40 per cent of the active membership of the Vanga Church. Between 1912 and 1955 about 34,000 were baptized here, and 26,000 are still resident members in good standing, loss by death and removal to other areas over a period of forty years naturally accounting for a considerable part of the fall. The 3,000 under church discipline mentioned above are not included in the 26,000 members.

To a large degree the success of the work is ascribed to the ability of the Vanga Church to retain its graduates. Since 1945 not a single teacher trained at the Mission School at Kimpese has left the church work, in spite of the attraction of work in the palm-oil industry.

The decentralization of the work carried through at the beginning of the 1930's has been of decisive importance, for the missionary staff has been very limited; in fact, during the whole period evangelistic missionaries have never been more than one couple at any one time. For many years, all finance has been in the hands of the African Church itself. Devolution to African leadership has been the watchword.[3] The Roman Catholic Church in Urundi has achieved startling results by a new decentralization policy (p. 80). It is an interesting coincidence that the Baptist work at Vanga and the Catholic work in Urundi had a change of policy at the very same time—around 1930—and with similar effects.

Lack of church leaders in sufficient numbers is the cause of many missed opportunities. In the 1920's, an intense local revival in Gabon was not gathered into the Church but allowed to burn itself out. Fervent catechists waited for missionaries or African pastors to lead the movement. As they had to wait in vain, the catechist became a village headman instead, and the local Christian movement petered out ...

The last generation in the history of the Protestant Churches in Africa has been one of unprecedented growth, characterized by

---

[3] Chester & Margaret Jump, *Congo Diary,* 1952.
Ch. Jump, Typed 'Notes on the Development of the Vanga Work' (1954);
Ch. Jump, letter 11.5.1953 to M. D. Farnum, Gen. Sec., A.B.F.M.S.
Letters from Ch. Jump to the present writer, 1954–1955.

rapid mass movements in certain parts of Africa, but by signs of stagnation in other areas. How did this affect the main agents of Church advance at this time? This was a period when the ordained missionary was increasingly engaged in school work, when the African teacher was drawn into a Government-controlled system of education and when the position of the catechists became more and more precarious. This trend is of immediate concern in our study of the position of the African minister, for on the ordained minister was laid the main burden of the Church's work in Africa.

The Roman Catholic Church

> I repeat that in the same way as the sun illuminates the five continents of the world one after the other, so often does the good God, and I, the Pope, declare unto you that now is Africa's turn.
>
> Pius XI in an audience given to the Archbishop of Carthage.

'You could have knocked me down with a feather, I was so surprised.' He had been a Protestant missionary and theological expert in Africa for some four or five years, and was very sure of his opinion. He was sure he was right when he told us there was not one single African Roman Catholic priest in the particular country which he served. There could not be, because of the celibacy clause, he thought. He was genuinely stunned, however, when we told him that there were at least 200 African priests in that country, and some additional 120 in the adjacent Mandate belonging to the same colonial power.

The story of the development of the Roman Catholic Church and ministry in Africa in this century is astounding, one of the most amazing in the dramatic history of world missions.

From 1900 to 1957, the Roman Catholic community in Africa South of the Sahara has risen from half a million to twenty millions. This rapid growth has been more marked in some parts of Africa than in others. With less than two millions in West Africa, the Roman Catholic Church represents only about three per cent of the total population; the number of African priests is small and African episcopal leadership here is, as yet, slight. 'South Africa the quarry must become the vineyard of the Lord'—that bold slogan is only slowly becoming a reality. The rise in the number of African clergy has been steady but cautious, though generally speaking, African leadership is as yet on the weak side. In East Africa ten per cent of the population—or some three millions—claim to belong to the Roman Catholic community. Here Uganda is strongest with 24 per cent of the population Roman Catholic, but Tanganyika with over a million is not far behind. African leadership is 'moderately strong'.

But all these achievements are surpassed by developments in Central Africa, particularly in the Belgian Congo and Ruanda-Urundi. One-quarter of the population in the Belgian Congo is Roman Catholic and well over thirty per cent in Ruanda-Urundi. The number of African priests in the whole of the Belgian Congo, including Ruanda-Urundi, was less than 80 in 1939. In 1957 it had risen to 461. In the same time the number of Congolese Sisters—called 'the miracle of Africa'—had risen from 175 to 1,075.

This remarkable development is a quite recent fact in the history of the Roman Catholic Church in Africa. The emphasis on indigenous clergy is a new idea in the history of the Roman Catholic missions. Neither the missionary expansion in the sixteenth and seventeenth centuries, nor in the nineteenth century, emphasize the role of a national clergy to the same degree. The leading idea is 'There is *one* clergy in the *one* church'. That means that there are the same standards, in principle, and the same opportunities for all priests, irrespective of race and colour.

The strategy of the twentieth century was directed from the centre, from Rome. It was formed by the great missionary popes of this century, albeit under the influence of missionary leaders in the orders, particularly Cardinal Charles Lavigerie (1825–1892), the founder and general of the White Fathers. This overall strategy is laid down in the missionary encyclicals, *Maximum illud* by Benedict XV, 1919, and particularly *Rerum Ecclesiae* by Pius XI, 1926, where the Pope declared the rapid and energetic formation of an African clergy to be 'Our will and order!' The emphasis is slightly modified in *Donum Fidei,* by Pius XII, 1957, but the main concern is the same. These fundamental directives were underlined by statements of or interventions by Cardinal Prefects

such as van Rossum in 1923 or Papal delegates such as Arch-
bishops Hinsley and David Mathew.

The expansion was directed according to an overall strategy.
Strategy and planning, not improvisation, is the overhelming impression of this development. The Protestant observer notes in
passing that there seems to be at least some disadvantage in all
this, which was pointed out in the Fordham Catholic leadership
conference in 1954 with regard to education in general in Africa.
Dr. Alba Zizzamia, herself a Roman Catholic, who visited Africa
for the United Nations, saw both Catholic and Protestant mission
schools. 'I do say, quite regretfully, that in Protestant mission
schools, whether for boys or for girls, the students seem to express
themselves with greater freedom, poise and assurance; they did
seem to have been given more responsibility and to have developed, perhaps, a greater sense of initiative than the pupils in
Catholic schools. I discussed this with a number of missionaries,
who attributed it to what is perhaps an over-protectiveness in the
Catholic schools generally.'[4] This observation does indicate what
is, perhaps, a weakness on the Catholic side. On the Protestant
side, we have cause to ponder the fact that improvisation, while a
good thing in itself, can be overdone!

The first beginnings of the preparation of African clergy in
modern times in the Catholic Church were a struggle against very
heavy odds, but the directives were there, laid down by mission
leaders such as F. M. Libermann and Cardinal Lavigerie. The
latter stated that 'The most important task [in the mission] is
undisputably the training of an African clergy.' This rule was a
help against the pessimism of some missionaries. Pessimism seemed
well-founded when one looked at the results of ten years theological seminary work in East Africa. During the years 1893–1903, in
the Great Seminary, 300 candidates were educated. How many of
these struggled through to the end and became priests? Answer:
Three!

In Lavigerie's spirit, Bishop J. J. Hirth († 1931) of Uganda put
all the emphasis in missionary strategy on the training of priests.
It is because of his vision and energy that the countries round the
Central African lakes have a large number of theological seminaries, lower and higher. He had no illusions, but he knew what

---

[4] [J. F. Ewing *ed.*] *Local Leadership in Mission Lands* (1954), p. 114.

ought to be done. He writes to the first leaders of one of the seminaries: 'You will perhaps see no result of your labours. God does not demand results from you, but work. And even if the majority of your students never attain to priesthood, they will give the mission great service as catechists who through their strong faith can become a model for others.'[5]

Bishop Hirth's influence was decisive in two of the most important countries in Central Africa, Uganda and Ruanda-Urundi. In the latter country his ideas were carried out under the leadership of the well-known Bishop Classe. Bishop Hirth defined his methods in his *Directoire pour le catéchumenat à l'usage des missionnaires,* 1909. His aim was that of an indirect apostolate; the Africans were to be won by Africans, with the mission station as the centre of the circle of activity. The European missionary, and later the African priest, was forbidden to extend the radius of a station more than four hours' walking distance in all directions. The groups of catechumens and baptismal candidates had to be on the move to and from the mission station four or five days per week for two years. That it was at all possible to make this rule, and enforce it, shows the tremendous authority which the Church exercised over the total social life of the country. The last two months before baptism had to be spent at the station itself.

The teaching task was almost exclusively the concern of the missionary, and eventually of the African priest. Hirth had no use for the catechist as intermediary between priest and the mass of people. He never founded any central catechists' school and did not want to train groups of paid catechists; instead he used an army of young men as assistant catechists who could return to their families every day and who lived as ordinary farmers. As the radius of the station was restricted, those voluntary helpers could to some extent be supervised and given some teaching.

It was a great and courageous scheme, and it worked admirably, up to a point. Above all it hastened the training of African priests. But on the other hand the system carried its own unsolved problems. About 1910–1914 it was felt that the missionary situation in Ruanda was critical. Stagnation threatened. In 1921 Hirth

[5] Johs. Beckmann, *Die Katholische Kirche im neuen Africa* (1947), p. 309 and Fridolin Rauscher, *Die Mitarbeit der einheimischen Laien am Apostolat in den Missionen der Weissen Väter,* 1953.

gave up his vicariate over Ruanda-Urundi. In 1922, Bishop Classe took over Ruanda, while Mgr. J. Gorju, missionary in Uganda since 1895, became bishop in Urundi.

Bishop Gorju waited six years, trying to find a new approach. Then he changed the whole structure and system radically. The Synodal Statutes of 1928/29 laid down the rules for a new missionary method, with the most far-reaching consequences for missionaries, African priests and catechists, and for every catechumen on the hillside.

The results can be seen in black and white:

Roman Catholic Church statistics in Urundi

	Stations	Baptized Christians	Catechumens	European Priests	African Priests
1922	5	14,500	30,000	15	—
1927	10	28,500	44,000	25	2
1935	19	140,000	192,000	49	10
1937	22	253,000	227,000	54	12
1949	34	610,000	240,000	118	29
1957	71	1,200,000	353,000	244	117

Decentralization was the secret. 'Away from the station!' was the slogan. Instead of bringing the catechumens for 4–5 days a week to the station and to the missionary, Gorju reversed the whole process. The Church founded a net of local centres; trained catechists were sent out to be responsible for the work there. The gravitation centre of the whole work was switched from shepherding the Christians to the conversion of the pagans. At the root, there was a difference in theology. Hirth wanted only 'good Christians', who could serve as models of faith and knowledge to the pagans. Gorju was out to win the pagan masses, and he knew that the missionaries could not forestall the weaknesses of the Christians by refusing the catechumens baptism. The six months' final intensive training on the station came to an end. The catechumens were taught in their own village, and the task of the missionary and the priest was to control the work of the catechist. Here Gorju was adamant. The control had to be rigorous. 'Even if all the Protestants in the world were after us, I would not concede this point.' Gorju had the idea that the result of the work of the catechists corresponded exactly to the attention which the missionary and priest could give them.

It must be added that, in Urundi, the evangelization was only to a comparatively small extent dependent on the conversion of the chiefs, but their particular influence was nevertheless important. By about 1948, 32 of the 36 *saza* chiefs and 441 of the 563 local chiefs were Roman Catholics. In Ruanda this element has recently played a much more dramatic role. This incidentally conforms to the vision of Lavigerie, himself once a professor of Ecclesiastical history at the Sorbonne and a keen student of the missionary methods of medieval Europe, who stated that just as, at that time, the masses had been won through the conversion of kings and chiefs, so in Central Africa a Christian kingdom would be built up in that way. In 1943, King Mutara was baptized and three years later he summoned his people to dedicate themselves to Christ and to the Catholic Church.

The amazing mass movement in Urundi, in Uganda, and in certain parts of the Belgian Congo created its own problems of particular importance to our special theme, the training of the clergy. A German Roman Catholic theologian, Augustin Tellkamp, called attention to the problem in his book, *Die Gefahr der Erstickung für die katholische Weltmission*, 1950, (The Danger of Strangulation in Catholic Missions). There is at work in the process analysed in connexion with Urundi a law which Tellkamp, following Fr. F. Plattner, S.J., calls the 'law of strangulation'. This means that the great numerical results in the work of conversion of the masses has a tendency to stifle real growth, as we saw on p. 70. Tellkamp's book is a challenge of great weight. He shows that the number of priests in relation to the numbers of Christians and to the numbers of catechumens is much too low: in Urundi one priest for 4,381 baptized and 1,024 catechumens; in Ruwenzori 1 for 2,763; Karoma, Tanganyika 1 for 2,177; Yaounde, French Cameroun 1 for 2,812; Lomé, Togo 1 for 2,777 and Angola 1 for 4,188. He quotes warning voices who have said accusingly: 'False activism, in order to obtain impressive statistics!' His main solution to this serious problem is one that would have pleased Bishop Hirth: to increase the number of national priests, and to follow a world-wide strategy for placing priests from one country in some other country where they are more urgently needed. Seven years later, the papal encyclical *Donum Fidei* stressed these ideas in an authoritative and imperative way.

The training of a Roman Catholic priest takes some 21 years: 5–6 years in primary school, 6–7 years in the junior seminary (petit séminaire), 8 years in the senior seminary, divided into 3 years in the philosophy department and, after one year of practical church work, 5 years of theology. This latter period may be extended to include practical church work under experienced missionaries.

The Belgian Congo, for example, has 24 junior seminaries with some 2,500 students and 5 senior seminaries with about 475 students; to these should be added another 90 theological students trained by the various religious orders (mainly Jesuits, Dominicans and Scheutfeld). Uganda has 6 junior and 3 senior seminaries. At present, the number of students in senior seminaries is on an average slightly higher than the number of ordained priests in each country in Africa.

The junior seminary gives a secondary education—although different from ordinary secondary schools in that Latin is given a prominent place. There is no Greek, and the course in mathematics is reported to be modest. At the end of the junior seminary course, the students in British areas sit for the General Certificate of Education. Great emphasis is laid on character-training, and the religious community life of the junior and senior seminaries is of fundamental importance. The head of the Kisubi Junior Seminary (Uganda) told me in 1955 that the cycle of the Church Year gives rhythm to the character-training, with for example particular rules of abstention during Lent. 'The African mind likes something clear-cut, and our students want to have definite rules so that they know where they are.'

The emphasis on character-training and on the spiritual life does not cease with the final examination from the senior seminary. Father Anthony Coolen of the White Fathers, who has had unique experience as Professor of Moral Philosophy at the important senior seminary at Kipalapala, Tanganyika, has stressed the need for 'a spiritual year' in the life of every African priest in order to equip him for the task of spiritual leader. In this year— placed presumably fairly early in his career as a priest—spiritual training should be given. Father Coolen suggests that the time would be particularly helpful if they could get 'a well-trained and qualified African as guide, one who knows the theory of spiritual life perfectly and is more aware than the European missionary of the African needs and mentality'.[6]

The most promising of the younger clergy are being sent to Rome. In Uganda, I was told that from that country as a rule about four priests are sent each year to Rome where they study some three to five years. The most prominent of those who have in this way studied in Rome is, of course, Bishop Kiwanuka who took a doctorate of Canon law in Rome, and in 1939 was consecrated as the first Bantu Roman Catholic bishop in this century.

Three factors seem to be of particular importance in the Roman Catholic Church in Africa at present: the 'translation' of Catholic theology; greater scope for an African hierarchy; and scope for the laity. All these factors have a bearing on the place and function of the clergy.

1. Solid theological training for some fifty years is rapidly paying dividends in a spate of books and articles by African priests dealing with the key problem of adapting Catholic doctrine to African thought-forms. The tradition of *theologia naturalis* is re-adapted with enthusiasm by African priests. The book by P. Tempels, *La Philosophie Bantoue,* 1949, has meant a real liberation to a whole generation of these young leaders. An African Church Father of long ago, Clement of Alexandria, presents them with the key idea of *logos spermatikos*. One of the most vocal of these African theologians, Vincent Mulago, launches Clement against what he calls 'Luther's fundamental error' which, according to Abbé Mulago, consisted in the German Reformer's idea of 'the intrinsic and irreparable corruption of human nature'. Mulago exemplifies his natural theology in a very interesting comparison of the Bantu blood pact, *ubunywanyi* (Ruanda-Urundi), and the Eucharist. In the same manner others see the task of African theologians as being the recovery of the sense of community in the Church which has largely been lost in the West. From this standpoint, others again take up a positive attitude with regard to

[6] *Local Leadership in Missionlands,* ed. Ewing, Fordham Univ. Press, 1954, p. 62. Cf. p. 75, discussion.

African culture. This is important in a much wider context than that of the Church itself. In a recent phase of African nationalist development, the *négritude* is accorded a new value by African and West Indian writers. On this point, the writings and attitudes of some of the most vocal African Roman Catholic priests seem to coincide with the aspirations of their compatriots in the cultural field.[7]

2. The development at this intellectual crossroads should be noted, for here the priest comes into contact with leading African laymen. This meeting is promoted chiefly by the recent movement for a lay apostolate in Africa. There is an interesting reaction, both among missionaries and the laity, against clericalism, and an immense effort is being made to give scope for activity and a means of expression to the educated laity. Writers, journalists and doctors are given a place of honour in the affairs of the Church. A most important recent happening here was the First Leaders' Meeting for the Apostolate of the Laity in Africa, held at Kisubi, Uganda, in 1955. Bringing together 250 leading laymen from 43 dioceses, vicariates and prefectures apostolic of 15 countries in Africa and representatives of 14 Catholic international organisations, this conference gave a new impetus to the lay movement in the Church.[8] It should be realized that a great many of these lay leaders were trained with the priests in junior seminaries in different parts of Africa. Many of them had intended to become priests, but now for various reasons serve the Church in other capacities. When it is sometimes said in criticism of Catholic training that only a certain percentage of those who begin in the junior seminaries actually become priests, this latter aspect should be borne in mind.

3. With all this, how far has the fullest scope for leadership been accorded to Africans? It is difficult to judge. But it is much more than symbolic that at present an impressive number of African bishops have been consecrated. We have already mentioned Bishop Kiwanuka of Masaka, Uganda, who was consecrated in 1939 together with Ramarosandratana of Madagascar († 1958). This step towards an indigenous hierarchy remained unique for

---

[7] See V. Mulago, Gérard Bissainthe, Meinrad Nebga, Alexis Kagame, P. Ondia and E. Verdieut in *Des prêtres noirs s'interrogent,* 1956.

[8] *Acts of the First Leaders' Meeting for the Apostolate of the Laity in Africa,* Kampala 1954 (cyclostyled).

12 years. The 1950's have been the first great decade of African bishops in the Roman Catholic Church.[9] Tanganyika received two, in 1951 and 1956, Kenya and Nyasaland one each in 1956, Ruanda in 1952, Nigeria in 1953, Basutoland and Zululand received one each in 1953-54. The 'Latin' Africa countries were somewhat hesitant until in the French dependencies four African bishops were consecrated in 1955-56, and one in the Belgian Congo in 1956. Bishop Dud of Sudan, consecrated in 1955, is also an African.

And while thus the number of African bishops increased in a dramatic way, the late Pope Pius XII directed his bishops in all the world to put at the disposal of the Church in Africa a sufficient number of younger priests to serve in Africa for a certain time. This is the main challenge of the papal encyclical *Donum Fidei*, 1957.

Vocation. A valuable study of seminarians' vocations has been made recently by no less a scholar than Fr. J. Masson, S.J.[1], who in 1956 visited five of the six senior seminaries in the Belgian Congo and Ruanda-Urundi. The enquiry comprises replies from nearly 400 students. The situation in Uganda was referred to in an interview with the head of the Kisubi Junior Seminary.

As in Belgium, the majority of priests come from *large* families. The Congo family is supposed to have on an average 3 children; the families from which these young men come have almost twice as many (av. 5.4). The great discovery on which Masson insists is the importance of *early vocations*. He speaks of a first and a second vocation among 354 students who gave definite answers. The former took place before primary school (11 per cent) or, more commonly, in the first 4 years of the primary school (62 per cent).

In this African community, 179 of the students were baptized at the age of 6 or later, and many of these regarded the day of baptism as kindling their hope to become priests. While most of the students, 278 out of 391, first became convinced of their desire to become priests little by little, 113 speak of a sudden impression which made them want to take this step. It might have been an

---

[9] Cf. Informations catholiques internationales, 15.5.1957.
[1] La Vocation Sacerdotale au Congo et au Ruanda-Urundi in *Bulletin de l'Union missionnaire du Clergé*, 1957, pp. 53-75, 162-171; as separate volume, Bruxelles 1957.

occasional meeting with a man of the Church: with a missionary (66 cases), an African priest (69 cases), or African seminarians (75 cases). It might be the influence of a teacher. 'When I was still a little heathen, the teacher taught us to say this prayer in front of the crucifix: "My God, I adore Thee, I love Thee, I shall give myself totally to Thee."' In Masson's enquiry, the role of teachers and of the school does not otherwise appear to be predominant. We found the situation in Kisubi, Uganda, different. We were told here that, in the primary schools, the boys are once a year, beginning in Primary II, asked the question whether they wish to become priests. This is repeated up to Primary V. In Primary VI they may make their formal application to enter a junior seminary. The method was not without results. In 1955, we were told, there were 45 applications for 25 places in the first class of junior seminary.

Masson has brought out examples of the young African seminarian's first decisive impression of priests. One says: 'Photos of black priests saying the Mass'. Another writes: 'I was so impressed by the gesture of benediction which the priest did towards the people. Sometimes I went on top of a termite hill to make that gesture of benediction. I loved to serve at Mass and to see the priest singing with his arms extended. When I returned home, I would go out in the bush where I looked after the cattle, and I imitated him. A tree stump was my altar.' African seminarians returning home in their habit to the village for the vacation have particularly appealed to the imaginations of boys of eight to ten years of age, who later themselves became seminarians and priests. Some have received their vocation in a dream.

Père Masson draws an important conclusion from his study: watchfulness and kindness towards the children who are at this often quite decisive age. 'This first vocation seems to have made African seminarians perhaps more sensitive (*affective*) than their Western colleagues, and left in their mind a clearer and more luminous remembrance than is usually the case among Westerners.'

As these young men reflect on their first vocation and their more mature decision (second vocation) at the age of about 16, it emerges that their motives have been varied. 'To play a great role in life' among 13 per cent of the students; 'to become a scholar' 20 per cent; 'the dignity of the priest' 10 per cent; 'struggle for personal saintliness' 30 per cent; 'love of Christ'

20 per cent; 'love of the Church' 12 per cent, 'desire to help one's own people' 40 per cent. A more general motive, 'Love of the souls of people, particularly the poor and the sinners' 42 per cent.

Masson also analyses hindrances on the road of priestly vocation. 85 per cent of the students have had to struggle against opposition of various kinds. In 124 cases—30 per cent—it is opposition from the family: 'as a priest, he will not bring up a family and thus he will break the lineage'; or, 'his duty is to support the family, and as priest he will be unable to do this'. It is altogether amazing to find that in no less than 70 per cent of the cases the families have *not* caused any objection. This shows how deep are the Church's roots in the life of the people. The situation in Kisubi, Uganda, was similar. Out of 45 applications for the junior seminary, there was only one case of opposition, from a father where the applicant was the only son. In Uganda, it is still quite customary for the sons of chiefs' families to apply for entry to the seminary.[2]

---

[2] We have not been able to take into consideration the valuable book by Fr. Adelrich Morant, OSB, *Die Philosophisch-Theologische Bildung in den Priesterseminarien Schwarz-Afrikas; aktuelle Fragen des Priesterbildung mit besonderer Berücksichtigung Kameruns,* 1959.

THE PASTOR IN A NEW AFRICA

Africa — Old and New

Just a generation ago Protestant mission leaders met in Belgium to reconsider the policy of their work. This meeting, at Le Zoute in 1926, had a vast representative character. It showed the trend of development at the time and outlined the main emphases in the international missionary world with regard to Africa.

The emphases at Le Zoute were two—and not more than two: first, the need to understand the African's past; and, secondly, the necessity through Western education to prepare the African's future. In this programme there was a hidden tension between the preservation of African culture and the 'remaking of man in Africa'. In the end one of the factors, education, became the dominant interest during the period under review. It is surprising, perhaps, that in a missionary conference of this importance there was little reference to the Church as such. To such an extent was interest concentrated on Africanization that when W. C. Willoughby, the great Congregationalist missionary leader in South Africa, lectured on 'Building the African Church', he mainly dealt with the relation of Christianity to social customs (puberty rites, bride-price with 'other evils of bride-price' and polygamy). It fell to an Anglican missionary, E. F. Spanton, to point to self-support, the administration of Church discipline through Africans and, above all, the training of African leaders as constituent factors for building the Church in Africa.

The African heritage and the Church. After the first world war, missionaries discovered that their own activities did, perhaps, threaten the survival of African cultural values. In the twenties there was a definite change of heart, expressed in some of the most representative missionary studies of the decade, Bruno Gutmann's *Gemeindeaufbau aus dem Evangelium,* 1925 and E. W. Smith's *The Golden Stool,* 1927. On the Roman Catholic side, Père Aupiais of Dahomey began his *Reconnaissance Africaine* in 1925. Dietrich Westermann, the German scholar and former missionary to Togo who became the first director of the new International African Institute in London, likewise emphasized 'the value of the African's past' (1926): 'The Africans have been treated by us as having no religion, no language, no traditions, no institutions, no racial character of their own, as empty vessels to be filled with European or American foods.'[1] Missionary literature in those years was concerned with what seemed to be the great threat to Africa: the break-up of traditional African society. The acids of Western individualism appeared to be eating into the very foundations of African community life. The most thoughtful and the best-informed among the missionaries were determined to make a last-minute attempt to turn the tide.

Dr. E. W. Smith is typical of this attempt. His name is linked with that of the Le Zoute meeting, since he, of course, wrote the conference volume, called *The Christian Mission in Africa*. His book *The Golden Stool* was a challenge to the missionary forces: 'The disintegration of African social life' was his great concern, and his problem as a missionary strategist was formulated in the question, 'Can the Africans become Christians and remain Africans?' or to put this in slightly different terms; 'how to naturalize Christianity in Africa?'

To the problem which he thus put with unrivalled authority, he had a theological solution which was characteristic of his time, the first third of the twentieth century. The religion that had been brought to Africa was, he thought, something 'other than essential Christianity'. It was 'an amalgam of elements drawn from many sources', and it was important not only to distinguish between civilization and Christianity but also 'between vital, essential Christianity and the organized historical institution that embodies it'. It was this 'essential Christianity' of the New Testament—and also, incidentally, of twentieth-century liberal theology—that was now to be planted in Africa. One example of how the ideal could be reached was, according to the Methodist E. W. Smith, already given by the Anglican Church in Uganda. For here the overwhelming majority of clergy were Africans, 'trained locally, living in native style, dressed in native garments, supported financially

---

[1] D. Westermann, 'The Value of the African's Past', *International Review of Missions* (1926) p. 426.

by their own people'. The Uganda Church had approached what ought to be the principle for all, that Africa must be 'evangelized by Africans and that the Church must be built up by its own sons'.[2]

This was a parallel in the ecclesiastical sphere to developments in the administrative field. The 1920's were the hey-day of 'Indirect Rule' in British Africa, particularly in Nigeria, Tanganyika and Uganda. Characteristically, it was Lord Lugard, the protagonist of Indirect Rule, who wrote the foreword to E. W. Smith's important book.

It was a generation of great men who in the 1920's and later tried to turn the tide with regard to the Church's attitude to the African cultural heritage. E. W. Smith, Henri Junod and Henri Philippe Junod, Dietrich Westermann, Bruno Gutmann and Gustav Asmus, Cullen Young and W. C. Willoughby, Bishop Lucas of Masasi, Father Denis Shropshire, C. R.: Methodists and Lutherans, Reformed and Congregationalists, Baptists and Anglicans—among all of them there were leaders who understood that the task of the mission was greater, and more difficult, than some had thought.

'The African has a home, the only one he has . . .' The words are Bruno Gutmann's, and it struck a chord in the hearts of many of the best missionaries in the latest generation. The term 'African heritage' was, of course, utterly vague and included language, certain religious and group expressions, song and music and rhythm, and many other things besides; with the addition of romantic Western ideas of African rural life. It was perhaps just as well that the term was kept vague and all-inclusive, for it was, in the last resort, a concern, an attitude: how to make the Christian Church the home of African Christians.

It is not unjust, however, to say that this interest in the African cultural heritage remained the concern of comparatively few missionaries during the period. And the African colleagues of the missionaries were often even more chary of admitting African forms of expression than were the Westerners. This is a sweeping generalization, but less unfounded than most Africans would now care to admit. The reason for the hesitation on the part of African leaders in the 1920's and 1930's is easy to detect. They were themselves products of first and second generation churches. They had

---

[2] E. W. Smith, *The Golden Stool*, p. 269.

the convert's sharp aversion to anything that had to do with a past which they, the progressive leaders of *that* period, had just left behind, in order to create a Christian future for Africa. Their general cultural background and their theological education was not seldom narrow in the sense that there was a tendency to accept uncritically the word of a particular missionary and the type-written text-books that he had left behind. This did not always foster originality and self-reliance.

The facts of 'the African heritage' were close enough to the African pastor. They were ever-present as stark realities in the recurrent crises in the life of the individual and of clan and community. When, in 1950, a British missionary in Kenya said of African culture that 'it hardly operates in Kikuyu life to-day', this was meant to be self-evident to everybody. But the very real operations that did take place, on rather a big scale, in Kikuyu society only two or three years later, proved that the problem could not be solved simply by denying its existence.

It was in West Africa that the question presented itself in the most urgent form in the 1940's and 1950's. The *Asase Yaa* issue in Ashanti at the beginning of the forties caused a controversy between the paramount chiefs of the great clans, on the one side, and the opinion of African ministers, including Roman Catholic priests, on the other. Thursday, as the Birthday of Mother-Earth *(Asase Yaa)*, was officially proclaimed a non-farming day. The Christian ministers felt that *Asase Yaa* was 'fetish' and that they therefore could not comply with the order. In Nigeria the 'fraternities' issue caused a deep cleavage in the ranks of the clergy itself. The Reformed *Ogboni* Society, a secret society often interpreted as a harmless West African equivalent of Freemasonry, and in any case functioning as a closely knit in-group of influential men in Yoruba society, was bitterly criticised by one section of the clergy under the leadership of S. C. Phillips, the Anglican Bishop in Oshogbo, while on the other hand it exercised a distinct attraction for other sections of clergy and lay leaders in the churches.[3]

With increasing education and self-reliance, there was a growing irritation among a younger generation of African pastors and leading laymen with the Westernness of the Church in Africa, balanced by constant vigilance against syncretistic tendencies, as

---

[3] See S. C. Phillips, *The Heathen Cult called Reformed Ogboni Society,* Ibadan 1956.

proved by the determined stand taken in 1950 by the Gold Coast Christian Council against the Tigare cult.[4] Professor K. A. Busia, sociologist, leading politician, and churchman in Ghana, stated: 'For all their influence, the Christian Churches are still alien institutions.' The urgency of that observation was brought out with great force and directness in a recent remark to us by an African pastor from the Cameroons, studying in the West: 'Christianity', he said, 'is a matter of the Whites. As they leave Africa, Christianity will also disappear.' If there are other pastors as despondent as this one over the Westernness of the religion of Christ in Africa, there is reason to consider what can be done to make African ministers capable of interpreting the Christian message in terms which are recognized as African.

Two Presbyterian ministers in Ghana have tackled the issue in important statements. Rev. E. A. Asamoa, Presbyterian educationist and church leader, challenged missionary scepticism as to the very existence of the supernatural powers of African religion. 'The Church has become in this respect the handmaid of science; and when church leaders speak in denial of witchcraft or *abosom* (lesser gods), they do so as men of culture rather than as Christians.' To Asamoa it was clear that the Church should acknowledge that 'the spiritual world in which the African believes is a reality'.[5]

Christian Baëta, of the University of Ghana, clarified the debate when he pointed out that 'the Church has to do with Africans and not with African culture'. There is not such a thing as a static entity called African culture, but rather the way in which Africans respond to demands made upon them by life itself. He pointed to the great task of re-interpretation that needs to be undertaken by the Church with regard to fundamental aspects of African culture.[6]

In statements like these, one can sense a new African emphasis on the concern which had been that of E. W. Smith, Bruno Gutmann and Dietrich Westermann in 1925. That concern had been repressed in and by African pastors for more than a generation; now it was being voiced by leading African churchmen and theologians. They were no longer going to be content with repetitions of the lessons from the West. The men who best knew their Wes-

---

[4] Cf. Christian Council, Accra: *Tigare or Christ?*, Accra, no year.

[5] E. A. Asamoa, *International Review of Missions*, April 1956.

[6] *Christianity and African Culture*, ed. by Christian Council of the Gold Coast, 1955, p. 60.

tern theology claimed that theology had to be related to the African soil.

Western Education and the Church. 'The horizon recedes. New lands come into view. The world is seen to be larger than we thought.' At Le Zoute, Dr. J. H. Oldham thus opened the vista to new possibilities. 'We are led into a new era: our need is of something radically new.' Dr. Oldham knew that the life of African people was being reshaped by powerful new forces and he urged the missionaries 'not to rest content with being in Africa and preaching on African soil, but to get as near as we can to the throbbing heart and centre of the movement of African life'.

The passport to that new land was education. Oldham had been instrumental in shaping big things for Africa through his contribution to British educational policy laid down, in 1925, in the *Memorandum on Educational Policy in British Tropical Africa*. The Memorandum of 1925 gave to Governments the control of educational policy but guaranteed close co-operation with the missions, through the system of grants-in-aid. In conformity with the British policy of Indirect Rule, the Memorandum aimed at raising the education not of certain élite classes, but of total communities. 'The education of the whole community should advance *pari passu*.' The underlying philosophy of this policy is related to the Phelps-Stokes reports on education in Africa.

In the 1920's, it was Oldham more than anybody else who inspired the missions to engage themselves wholeheartedly in education. Here was a momentous choice and missions should 'seize the opportunity with both hands'. To him, 'education and evangelism were seeking, each in its own way, the same end'.[7] This was a declaration of faith, and only subsequent developments were to prove whether he was right. He was aware of the risk that through too close a connexion with the educational system of the State too many missionaries would become absorbed in institutional work and no longer available for the pastoral care of the Church. But what was a risk implied at the same time a great service to Africa.

---

[7] J. H. Oldham, *The Remaking of Man in Africa*, pp. 20 and 24. For a valuable recent discussion of the mission school in Africa, see F. Raaflaub, *Gebt uns Lehrer!* 1948. J. McLeod Campbell, *African History in the Making* 1956.

If the Protestants, with Oldham, saw and seized the opportunity, the Roman Catholics threw themselves even more determinedly into educational work. In August 1928 the Apostolic Visitor gave his order at Dar-es-Salaam: 'Collaborate [with the State] with all your power; and where it is impossible for you to carry on both the immediate task of evangelism and your educational work, neglect your churches in order to perfect your schools.' Père Dubois, in 1932, wrote in his handbook for Catholic missionaries: 'Who owns the schools, will own Africa.'[8] No doubt, the competition with Rome in Africa added to the Protestant educational impetus—and *vice versa*.

The tension between the two concerns of Le Zoute—preserving the African's past and preparing for the African's future—was, at least for a time, evaded by Dr. Jesse Jones' sociological definition of education as preparation for life in the community. A rural basis of African education, emphasis on the role of African languages and a certain reluctance to accept European languages as media of instruction all helped, for the time being, to reconcile the two interests. When E. W. Smith in *The Golden Stool* developed this theme on the basis of his own experience in Southern Africa, he warned against such education as would uproot the African from his past. 'Surely the first thing necessary is to understand the African and his past, and the second is to plan our educational scheme so that he shall develop according to the laws of his own nature'.[9]

This was greeted with satisfaction in German missionary circles. L. Weichert found that British and American missions had at last, through the influence of the Phelps-Stokes recommendations, accepted those ideas which for a long time had been fundamental to German missionary work in Africa.[1] But whatever educational philosophy was involved here, aiming either at rapid change of African man and society or preferring slow deliberate adaptation, the course was set. In the period 1925–1950/55, the schools dominated the missionary scene in Africa. To choose but one representative example of the explosively dramatic developments: in Nigeria, the number of pupils in primary schools was 95,000 in 1925, but by 1951 it was just over a million. This affected the Churches.

---

[8] Quoted after Roland Oliver, *The Missionary Factor in East Africa*, p. 275.
[9] E. W. Smith, *The Golden Stool*, p. 296.
[1] L. Weichert, *Mayibuye i Afrika!* 1928, p. 269.

Education, as the great instrument of social change, demanded an all-out effort, in men and money, on the part of the missions. Teachers who from 1925 until 1939 were regarded as, and regarded themselves as, mission teachers, after World War II were employed increasingly by the Government and regarded as Government servants. The Development Plan in the Gold Coast, ten-year plans in other territories, the Bantu Education Act of 1953 in South Africa—all were from the point of view of missions and of the African Church indications of the rapid secularization of the schools.

In fact, those great opportunities to which Le Zoute had pointed in 1926, had twenty-five years later become a problem and some-times a disturbing liability to the Church. The whole church pro-gramme had been geared to the educational planning of the Gov-ernments to such an extent that some of the essential functions of the Church were jeopardized. In a famous address, L. B. Greaves, one of those who for two decades most effectively had served Mis-sion education both in West and East Africa, summed up the situa-tion at the middle of the century:

'Use the School to build up the Church' is essentially a pioneering slogan, appropriate, if ever, only to that phase. Experience shows clearly that the time comes everywhere when there is a very strong tendency to reverse the order, and to use the Church to build up the school. We are forewarned of that; we ought to be forearmed against it and check in its beginnings the usurpation by the school of the place that properly belongs to the Church. Here are some of the things that lie ahead: —
A Church impoverished in money and in spirit by the magnitude of the effort diverted to its schools, so that boys and girls leaving the schools are in danger of finding no vital Church ready to receive them. A ministry in bondage to its schools, and, what is worse, hugging its chains: so used to thinking in terms of schools that one of the most over-burdened can plead to be allowed to add to them with the words, 'Without my schools I cannot be a Methodist Minister'.
A teaching body so large that its general Christian level sinks rela-tively low...
Denominational rivalries...
A community increasingly aware and critical of these shortcomings, but unprepared to offer an acceptable alternative... That is the kind of bog to which this road, paved with the best of intentions, sooner or later leads us.[2]

[2] L. B. Greaves, *The Churches' Educational Task*, Address to the Methodist Church, Accra, 1949.

Four years earlier, T. A. Beetham, another Methodist, said at Kumasi: 'In striving for universal Christian education, we must beware lest we wake up in 30 years' time to the fact there is no longer a Christian Church to provide it.'[3]

In view of this situation, Dr. Max Warren called the churches radically to rethink the whole strategy of missionary education in tropical Africa, withal knowing that the Church has 'an inescapable responsibility to educate for life her own members'.[4] In one country in tropical Africa with a very influential non-Roman Church, we found in 1953 that of the total number of missionaries, only six men, including the Bishop and the archdeacon, were engaged in church work proper, while all the others were on the pay-roll of the Education Department. In one very large West African city we were told by an eminently capable observer that 'the Church was only concerned with education, not with evangelism', that the missionaries were mainly directors of schools and that the African pastors wished to reach the same position of honour and influence. The leading African minister of a dominant Protestant church in that city was mainly a big educational administrator. The Church took collections three times on a Sunday for their schools, but there was nothing over for the repair of the dilapidated church building.

From West Africa we turn to the Belgian Congo, where Protestant opportunities in the sphere of education were limited until 1948. Prior to that year only 'national missions'—in fact synonymous with Roman Catholic missions—had received Government subsidies. In 1948, the strong Protestant movement in the Belgian Congo was in principle put on a par with Catholics as far as education was concerned—almost a quarter of a century after the publication of the Memorandum for British Tropical Africa. Here opened a new chapter for Protestant missions in the Belgian Congo. The *Kulturkampf* about the middle of the 1950's, between the Catholic Church and the Socialist Government, in Belgium and in the Belgian Congo, tended to emphasize the principle laid down in 1948 with regard to Protestants. Not all were sure that the opportunities should be seized. Representatives of a leading American

---

[3] T. A. Beetham, Comments on the Methodist Memorandum, 1945.
[4] M. A. C. Warren, *The Truth of Vision* 1948, p. 105; *C.M.S. News-Letter,* June 1953.

mission told us in 1953: 'We are engaged in a battle for the younger generation. If we do not hold our own in education, the younger generation will be lost to the Roman Catholics. Our mission has always been extremely reluctant to co-operate with a state education system. But then the State tells us: "Do you not agree that education ought to be Christian? If you do, join the race for the education of Africa."'

In the Belgian Congo, as in British Africa and elsewhere, the African pastor became involved in this change in the sphere of education. The ordained missionary became more and more inextricably engaged in education, and the African pastor tended to follow the example and find his *raison d'être* in educational activity. Some pastors with secondary and university education were by the same process led from actual church work to the task of being masters or principals in secondary schools, and this was not always calculated to solve the disturbing problem of the Churches: the lack of a sufficiently well-educated ministry. In the latter part of the 1940's, the salary scales for teachers were raised very rapidly, and it is only human that this factor influenced recruitment to the ministry—as we shall see in some detail later.

In all this, the Churches increasingly felt the need for an African ministry prepared to tackle the exacting challenge of a new day: a. A ministry which could give Christian service and leadership, related to the vocal educated groups and classes, formed by that Western education which the missions so effectively had helped to transmit. b. A ministry with a sufficiently solid and well-founded education—from a Biblical and theological point of view —to be able to pilot the Church clear of two extremes: In Africa's new day these extremes represented modern variations of the themes discussed at Le Zoute, and now they both attempt to make the Church their handmaid. Their names are tribalism—or its modern guise of tribal party politics—and secularism. It was rather late in the day when the Churches awoke to the need for such a ministry.

New Africa. 'There is a New Africa.' A generation ago E. W. Smith's book on the Le Zoute Conference of 1926 opened with that statement. Colonial administration; new rail transport; the discovery of precious minerals; 'the discovery of comparatively healthy areas attracted virile colonists; towns and farms began to appear in the haunts of lions and the elephant. And so the New Africa has come into being.'

Thirty years later, and Africa is still expanding. To prove his case, in 1926 E. W. Smith had prophesied that in twenty-five years' time the mileage of railways in Africa would be doubled. It was not foreseen in 1926 that very soon another means of travel would change the face and fate of Africa. The glittering gossamer of airlines was spread far and wide and put Africa into immediate contact with the West and with Asia. This shift from railway to airway is symbolic; it represents the immensely quickened tempo of the Newer Africa.

Mines and industrial plants became the attractive magnetic centres of the continent, though it is still true, of course, that the great majority of the 125 million people in Africa South of the Sahara mainly rely on subsistence agriculture in the many small rural communities. From that point of view Emory Ross is right when he maintains that the Churches have above all to deal with 'the millions of rural men and women in Africa'. He supports his 'Mother Earth' concept for Africa by claiming that 'the more thoroughly urbanized 5 million are only about 3.3 % of the population in Africa South of the Sahara'.[5] At the same time, one must not overlook the established cityward tendency throughout the continent. Georges Balandier has shown for French Equatorial Africa that twenty per cent of the population are urban, and that, in the Southern part of that territory, every uprooted villager is a potential townsman.[6] Already in the 1940's, between 14 and 19 per cent of the populations of Senegal, Ghana, and the Belgian Congo were living in towns, and in the province of Katanga 28 per cent of the population were in towns.[7] Conditions vary, of course, in different parts of Africa, but the cityward trend is there, and it continues with marked determination. During the last decade the size of some African towns has doubled, while others have risen to four times their previous size in the last ten years (Léopoldville, Kolwelzi). This is the social reality in the new Africa of which the Church must be aware.

In the nineteenth century, the missions—whether Roman Ca-

---

[5] Emory Ross, *African Heritage* (1952), p. 21–22.

[6] G. Balandier, *Sociologie des Brazzaville noirs,* (1955) p. 39.

[7] G. Balandier, in UNESCO (ed. D. Forde), *Social Implications* etc. 1956, p. 495.

tholic or Protestant—could afford to create their own sociological groupings in rural Africa. The 'Christian villages' became well-knit communities, African variations of a theocratic ideal, where Christians who had broken away from their tribal environment could form a new tribe of Christ under the missionary or the African catechist as chief. Some of these villages still exist to-day in the bush, or on the mountain slopes, but the general development has moved in other directions.

To-day, industrialism reaches far outside its immediate factory surroundings; it affects also rural Africa. Hon. John Karefa-Smart, of Sierra Leone, has rightly said: 'The peculiar problems facing the West African village to-day are the problems which have arisen out of the increasing contact with, and influence of, the outside world of Western civilization.'[8] This is of course even more true of the new communities in rural areas, the plantations in Tanganyika or Liberia, or the 'new villages' in Kikuyu-land, Kenya, examples of drastically revolutionized social conditions in 'rural' Africa.

New towns create, not new men, but 'new types of social personalities' and new sociological groupings.[9] Old tribal loyalties are not thrown off in the process; on the contrary, there is often an extraordinary emphasis on the old values in a new context. Traditional institutions and culture patterns are 'transferred' to the towns to an extent which appears surprising, but shows a development with which church leaders in towns often have to contend.

The new conditions tend to produce a pervasive malaise, 'a spiritual confusion of the educated African', connected with the social and personal insecurity and frustration of Africans living under westernized conditions.[1] Social isolation is overcome by new patterns of groupings, associations, and mutual-aid societies which proliferate in the cities. These modern associations are not solely an urban phenomenon. In Bukoba, Tanganyika, and elsewhere we observed how the forming of clubs, and various other functional associations (ebyama), were early, flexible acculturation attempts, also in a rural environment, in the 1930's and during the second

[8] J. Karefa-Smart, 'The West African Village and its Problems', in Report, First West African Area Conference, Y.M.C.A. 1954, mimeographed, p. 23.

[9] K. A. Busia, 'The Impact of Industrialization on West Africa', in West African Institute of Social and Economic Research Annual Conference, Ibadan March 1953, mimeographed, p. 33.

[1] Cf. G. Malengreau, in Unesco, op. cit., p. 632.

world war. In most cases these were under Catholic or Protestant lay leadership. At the same time, urbanization obviously has a long-term disintegrating effect on traditional social structures. Above all, the extended family system breaks up under the impact of modern economic conditions. A new family system, oriented to a social structure based on emerging occupational class distinctions, arises within the urban society. The role of women changes rapidly, particularly as a result of new educational opportunities. Twenty years ago, in some urban centres of the Belgian Congo and in the Union of South Africa, wives of educated Africans were rarely literate. In South and West Africa to-day, and increasingly in East Africa (Buganda), such wives are educated and often take the initiative in the westernization of home and social life.[2]

The trend in response to the pull of the new forces lies in this direction, and a Church that wants to be relevant to new Africa must be oriented to these conditions. How far local leadership of the non-Roman Churches has this orientation is a matter for some concern. In order to understand the role of the Church and its leadership in relation to the forces that shape the African society of today, we shall measure here the contacts and conflicts between the pastor on the one hand and on the other hand the accepted leaders of traditional and of new Africa.

Pastor and Chief

The status of the pastor can to some extent be measured in relation to that of the African chief. The status and prestige of the chief himself is no longer, however, what it used to be, and has changed very considerably in the last generation.[3] And yet the chief has his particular power sanctioned by tradition or guaranteed by Western administration. The pastor has to take this into account wherever he moves in traditional rural African society, although for our particular purpose in this study we perhaps do not need to draw too sharp a distinction—however important in itself at present—between the position in (a) a hereditary chieftainship; (b) chieftainship by appointment, or rather by king's favour and (c) chieftainship as a new introduction.

We content ourselves with the general observation that pastors,

---

[2] Cf. D. Forde, in UNESCO, *op. cit.*, p. 44.

[3] L. P. Mair, 'African Chiefs Today', *Africa* (1958), p. 195–206.

teachers and all employees in Western concerns and organizations have a higher status if they live in a society in which the chief is not indigenous. 'No intelligent man could think of becoming a chief to-day', was the comment of an influential pastor in Ghana, himself born into one of the royal houses in Fante country. He could, in fact, have been a Fante chief if he had so desired, but was aware of the loss in real power and influence which chiefs had suffered in West Africa as Indirect Rule was followed by a modern democratic party system. For East Africa, a similar development has been analysed by Dr. Fallers. In a study of the Basoga of S.E. Uganda, Fallers shows how the traditional head of the tribe has become a 'civil servant chief' in a modern administrative system in which old traditions and new loyalties exercise conflicting demands upon him.[4] For French Equatorial Africa, Balandier has underlined the fragile nature of the authority of chiefs among the Fang.[5] These examples must suffice in order to stress the fact that the authority of the chief is contested nowadays as it never was thirty years ago.

East Africa. The relationship between the Christian minister and the chief has developed in a more interesting fashion in Uganda than possibly in any other part of Africa. We take our starting point here. This relationship is closely linked with the history of Church and state in Uganda.[6] It began in 1889 when in the turmoil of political events a Moslem party took the upper hand in Buganda. A large group of the Christians then found a home for a time in the kingdom of Ankole. These 'Ankole exiles' formed a religious party which in 1890 returned to their homeland, ousted the Moslems and gained power. The leaders among these Ankole exiles became the future notables of Uganda. Some of them became *saza* chiefs, others deacons and priests, others again were both chiefs and priests. I found in the priests' register in Kampala that out of the eleven—all 'Ankole exiles'—who were ordained deacons between 1893 and 1896, three in a short while became chiefs.

---

[4] L. A. Fallers, *Bantu Bureaucracy*, 1956, p. 180 ff.

[5] G. Balandier, *Sociologie actuelle de l'Afrique noire*, 1955.

[6] On missions and politics in Uganda at this time, cf. Anthony Low, 'British Public Opinion and the Uganda Question...', *The Uganda Journal*, 1954. pp. 83–100;
Kenneth Ingham. *The Making of Uganda*, 1958.

The 1900 Agreement between Buganda and the British Government was influenced and signed by the Anglican Bishop Tucker. Chiefs and sub-chiefs were given freehold plots—generally four sq. miles, some even ten sq. miles. Priests with high status were given estates, and thereby were assured a good living. They had of course the additional prestige of belonging to the original group of 'Ankole exiles' who had saved the country of Buganda politically. Under Bishop Tucker (resigned 1911) they formed a priestly aristocracy who were unquestionably on a par with the leading chiefs of the country.

That first generation of rich and powerful ministers gave their particular stamp to the work and influence of the Church. Some of these men lived for a long time. Yokana Muyira, who was ordained deacon in 1893, died in 1932; Yonasani Kadzi, who was made deacon with Muyira, retired in 1929; Nasanaeri Mudeka, who was made deacon in 1896 and appointed canon in 1917, died in 1932. This was the first, great generation of Buganda priests. Their prestige was immense in a Church which in their lifetime grew from being a persecuted group of witnesses and of martyrs, to the status of a national Church.

The *mailo* or estates were, however, extended to them as individual family property and not made over to the Church as such. Their sons became rich land owners and sometimes respected laymen in local congregations but never thought of taking holy orders. I was told by a member of one of the most influential families in the kingdom that after 1900—05 only two Baganda of the status of *saza* chiefs have become priests. When one of them made known his decision about 1930 to become a priest, he was told by his people: 'This is not your place, you were intended for something more important than being a priest.' This incident is a significant indication of the fact that an important change in the status of the Protestant minister had taken place in the country of classical missionary effort in Africa.

The traditional political structure in Buganda and adjacent kingdoms consisted in a well-defined hierarchic system of office, from *kabaka* (i.e. king) to village headman. Bishop Tucker adapted the administration of the Church closely to this traditional structure. It is generally recognized in Buganda that the political and ecclesiastical systems of office used to correspond very closely:

Kabaka	Bishop
Saza chief	Rural Dean
Gombolola chief	Priest
Muroka chief	Deacon
Mutongole chief	First letter catechist

The African rural dean usually lives near the *Saza* residence and there are many points of contact.

But there are also big differences between the two. In a culture where money plays a great role as a basis for status, it has not gone unobserved by the general public that the priest nowadays has an altogether much lower financial position than the first generation of church leaders. While these owned rich land, a priest nowadays 'is lucky if he on his small salary can put aside a sufficient sum of money to buy two or three acres to which he can retire when his time of service is over', as a leading Buganda priest put it to me.

The tradition of close church-state relationship is of course still there. At some receptions by the Kabaka, *saza* chiefs and priests sit together and 'thus have the same rank', as one priest put it, unaware perhaps of the view of the *saza* chief as to this particular problem. Dr. Fallers, referring to Busoga country, says that 'the rural dean is the religious *saza* chief'. He also notices that an ordinary priest addresses his rural dean as *mukama wange*, (my king, or my chief) i.e. in the same manner as a *saza* chief is greeted.[7]

With the lower income and, most often, the lower educational standard of the priest, as compared with that of the present-day civil servant chief, the influence of the priest with the chief depends to a large extent on his personal qualities. 'A socially-minded priest who can make friends with people always calls on the *saza* chief to discuss matters with him', I was told by one informant, who himself held a leading position in the field of theological education. 'When the District Commissioner is to come, the *saza* chief informs a priest who has such qualities. He calls him to the meeting with the Commissioner and perhaps asks his advice in advance.'

But there are other cases where chiefs have long recognised that the power of the Church is a matter of the past; in such instances the priest is hardly more than a poor relation. A sociologist who

---

[7] Cf. L. A. Fallers, *op. cit.*, p. 198.

herself knows East Africa well spent a couple of days with the wife of a *saza* chief, at the chief's residence. One day at tea-time, the chief himself turned up. His wife poured the tea, but the chief was not pleased when he discovered that she was using an ordinary cheap enamel tea-pot. 'Why do you treat our distinguished guest like this, serving her tea out of a clergyman's tea-pot?'

Sometimes there is danger that the priest may become financially dependent on rich chiefs who are not exactly paragons of Christian virtue. One pastor complained that certain chiefs, although nominally Christians, had polygamous households and would not come to church. 'So when I come to visit him, the chief asks himself, "Why has that priest come here; does he want to warn me against my sins?" Before I know where I am, he has called one of his wives and asked her to prepare tea and nice food for me. Then you can see on his face how he is plotting to hinder me from referring to his polygamous family life. "Do you intend to build a new church?", he will ask. "Do you not need money for a new Church at X? Perhaps you need a hundred shillings?" If I don't pray hard to God, I really cannot preach the Gospel in such a place. You just take the money, and off you go.' This degradation is a far cry from the glory of the Ankole exiles in the early days of the Church, and certainly should not in any way be taken as typical. It is quoted here as an indication of a loss in personal authority which is much more important than any such decline in status as can be measured in terms of salary scales or educational standards.

There is not much that remains of the church-state system established by Bishop Tucker around 1900, with its well-defined reciprocal relationships on various levels between the two hierarchies of Church and State. The system of rank as such still exists, of course. Wherever two people meet, in the whole region around Lake Victoria, immediately the problem of status comes in. *Baingana bituuro,* the Banyoro say: people are equal in the grave (and nowhere else!).[8] The position of the Christian priest has in popular opinion been steadily redefined by a complicated process operating with the three variables: blood, wealth, and personality. In Buganda he is now probably placed between sub-county and 'parish'

---

[8] Cf. J. H. M. Beattie, 'Nyoro Kinship', *Africa,* 1957, p. 317, and 'Nyoro Marriage and Affinity', *ibid.,* 1958, p. 1.

chief.[9] That also is true for the Bukoba district in Tanganyika (Reining).

Priests of noble families in East Africa. An outstanding socio-logical fact about the Bantu living near Lake Victoria is the dif-ferentiation between the cattle-owning nobility class and the peas-ant class who depend upon agriculture for a livelihood. The for-mer are of Hamitic origin, and are referred to as Hima (Huma). The peasant class comprise the great majority, and are referred to as *abailu,* the serfs, in Ankole and Bukoba.

In Ankole, the social differences among the people were, until very recently, markedly reflected also in the Church. From the beginning of the Church's history the priests as a rule were of Hima origin. It was regarded as a matter of course that the two rural deans in the district belonged to this class. After 1945, how-ever, most new priests came from the peasant class. Generally speaking, the relationship between ministers belonging to the two different sections was strained and unhappy. A student from An-kole told me as an incident of great significance that in 1955 he had seen a Hima rural dean and a peasant-class priest eating together. 'They ate goat's meat, and they ate together. This *never* happened before.' The objective truth of this statement is less im-portant than his subjective impression of its exceptional character.

Towards the middle of the 1950's the process of democratization on the part of the Uganda Central Government resulted in a social revolution which gave Ankole a peasant-class Prime Minister. At about that time, a priest of this same humble origin was appointed as new Protestant rural dean. This rapid change-over makes it in fact very difficult at present to appoint a dean or an African bishop belonging to the nobility.

In the adjacent Bukoba area (in Tanganyika) a similar social revolution, although less drastic than in Ankole, is taking place. Three of the fifteen Protestant pastors (one of these is now the rural dean) come from noble families. From the point of view of these three men, good contacts with the chief were useful for the Church and gave the pastor added prestige. One of them told me: 'The pastor ought to be a friend of the chief. That has helped me. Everybody sees that I visit him and that we talk happily.' But

---

[9] According to Dr. J. Goldthorpe, *Outlines of East African Society* 1958, ch. VIII.

church leaders of both sections insist that if they visit the chief's residence they must not stay too long. *Omukikale biliho ebintu* (in the palace certain things happen), I was told. If the pastor makes his visit too long, people might think that he drinks with the chief, and the custom of eating and drinking together has a deep meaning. In Bukoba, however, a chief and a pastor cannot eat the traditional food of plantains together. But the pastor can, in spite of this, enjoy a degree of table fellowship with the chief. On such occasions as church festivals they can have tea and bread together, since the eating of modern European food is not accompanied by traditional associations and sanctions.

Priests belonging to the nobility section in these kingdoms are in the middle of a rapid democratic revolution, conscious of the fact that their heritage gives them a particular advantage over their colleagues of a more humble origin. 'We know the secret of leadership. Those from humbler families do not understand this secret as well. *Obuzana bwasikwa mugolewe,* runs the Haya proverb: "when a housemaid takes over the responsibility of her master", [then, of course, everything goes wrong]. Men from noble families, however, do not seek honour. They do not need it.' This statement made to me by a well-known leader in one of the churches near Lake Victoria is significant of the extent to which the problem of status is the object of reflection. The priests and pastors of noble blood feel that their number is rapidly diminishing but are the more convinced that their conciliating influence is greatly needed in the social revolution of which they are a part. When an Assistant Bishop, coming from the peasant class, dared to challenge the moral standards of the head of his state, priests belonging to the nobility were strongly critical of the bishop's prophetic outburst.

In one very important kingdom where for different reasons even the kingship has recently undergone a drastic crisis, impartial foreign observers feel that there is a need for a greater contribution from noble class pastors. 'The present group of clergy are afraid of X-[referring to the head of the particular kingdom], as they have never been before. They now no longer have the support of a European Government.' An injection of a group of pastors with stronger social background might strengthen the Church at this juncture, it is thought, and help to balance the suddenly unlimited power of the head of the state.

Moving further east we notice that in Tanganyika the U.M.C.A. priests in the Shambala-speaking area belong to the leading Kilindi clan, and there is thus a connexion between priest and chief's clan which is typical of the development of the the first generation in African Churches. In Northern Tanganyika, there are Lutheran chiefs among the Arusha, Meru, Chagga and Pare peoples. Some of these chiefs were teachers or hospital dressers before being elected as chiefs. They are in certain cases related by marriage to leading Lutheran pastors, and the pastors seem to have relatively easy access to the chief. One Lutheran pastor told me how the chief used to ask his advice in secret about the affairs of the tribal council, such as the appointment of councillors. Here efficient co-operation was established, and this greatly enhanced the prestige both of the pastor and of his Church.

In rank-conscious *Southern Africa,* Bantu priests and pastors often come from chiefs' families, at least in the first two generations. St. John Evans, writing on Southern Rhodesia, has pointed out that one of the four first African deacons raised to the priesthood in 1926 was a nephew of Chief Khama.[1] In the matrilineal Thonga society of Mozambique and Nyasaland, another problem presents itself. At least among the first-generation Christians, there was a tendency to elect sons of headmen as catechists. Because of the social structure of their tribe these sons of headmen could not themselves become headmen, and they found a chance for leadership opportunities in the modern power group, the Church. A study from this point of view of church leadership in matrilineal societies throughout Africa would be of great value. There is at present strong tension in these societies between the father's right and that of the mother's brother. Modern influences—from both State and Church—work against the matrilineal tradition which is however attempting to assert itself. How these tensions work out in the life of the Churches and the local congregations is largely unknown.

Sometimes such close personal contacts have been established between chief and local church leader that the pagan chief feels quite possessive over 'his' catechists or pastor. Hlongwane was a teacher at the headquarters of the chief of the Amangwane tribe

---

[1] H. St. John T. Evans, *The Church in Southern Rhodesia,* 1945, p. 41. For South Africa, the pastor-chief relationship has been analysed by G. Brennecke, *Brüder im Schatten* (1954).

in Natal. The Lutheran missionary came to inform the chief that Hlongwane was to be ordained. The chief retorted in a characteristic soldierly combination of husky harshness and personal devotion: 'I am really against you, *bafundisi,* for taking this brother Mfinfi (Hlongwane's tribal name) to be a minister. Really I would like to stop you from doing so. What I dislike is this. When I allow you to have him ordained (!), you will then simply transfer him any time and to any place, I don't know where to. My desire is this. In case I die, he must bury me, and if he dies, I must bury him here in the midst of the Amangwane tribe.' This request was granted. On the day of Hlongwane's ordination the chief gave a fine fat sheep to the theological school.

A Lutheran colleague of Hlongwane's, Rev. A. Lathane, served the famous Rain Queen of the Lovedu, Modjadji (d. 1959). He knew that she was not far from the Kingdom of God, and regularly read to her from the Book, in a Sotho translation. He was a respected member of the leading group around the Queen, and is now a member of the School Board. He had easy access to the Queen every time he wished to discuss church matters with her. When she was ill, he would be there praying for her. With all this the pastor is a fearless preacher of the word of God. He writes: 'A pastor who drinks beer at parties and who relies on witch-doctors and who has no true words is despised by Christians and pagans alike. A pastor must abide with the Word of God, and must be ruled by it, honouring the Queen (Modjadji) and the people of the royal kraal and should be ready to assist and help everybody. Thus he will himself be esteemed.'

An able, well-educated pastor working in Central Zululand analyses his relationship with the chief: 'In Zululand proper a chief eats with nobody. In civil matters a priest can go to the chief for advice, but there is always suspicion. A chief never calls a priest for advice in civil matters. Very few chiefs ask priests for help in educational matters and when judging cases in which two Christians are involved.' In his part of Africa, very few chiefs have aligned themselves with the progressive forces, and the pastor must orientate himself towards other sections of the community.

Central and West Africa. In Angola the problem does not exist in the form in which it presents itself in non-Portuguese territories, for the simple reason that the old chiefs have been dethroned.

As most pastors have royal blood in their veins, they can, if they have strength of character, assume the role of judge and arbiter in the community, at least up to the limit set by the colonial power in question. In the Coquilhatville district, Belgian Congo, we were told that at present the pastor wields a much greater influence than the chief. So, for instance, almost 90 % of all minor legal cases, 'palavers' in the Church, are settled not by the chief but by the pastor.

In Ubangui-Chari, all ten theological students in a Bible school belonged to chiefs' or blacksmiths' families, and 'therefore were respected'. For in the traditional creation-myth in their part of Africa, the blacksmith plays the leading role, and his modern descendants in the nascent Christian Church have now to hammer out a new role of religious leadership. In the French Cameroons, the catechist is treated as a kind of village chief and is recognized as such by the French Administration. In other cases, in this same country, the catechist served as the secretary of the village chief, since he was, until very recently, the only literate person in the community. The small tribes in the Douala district each want their own pastor, and it is a matter of great prestige that they should find and educate a future pastor. When he is ordained, the tribe considers itself to have an unalienable right to claim the new pastor for itself. The new pastor has prestige because he belongs to the right tribe, their own.

Many leading churchmen with whom I came into contact along the coast of West Africa belonged to chiefs' families. In a number of cases, in Nigeria, Dahomey, Togo, and Ghana, it was explained to me that So-and-So belonged to the chief's clan, and could have been a chief himself but for the fact that he had chosen the Church. The way of honouring a chief is sometimes also shown to a pastor in Ghana. You take off your sandals and slip down the cloth so that the shoulder is free. 'Many do this to us because we are *osofo*,' an old Methodist minister said, 'we do not ask for it and most times we do not even allow them to do it, but they insist on showing us their esteem and respect in the way they are used to with regard to chiefs.' Bishop Akinyele of Ibadan was the brother of a chief, and was himself, he told me, as an aged bishop made an honorary chief. It was the case of an old chieftainship which had lapsed but had been revived in order to honour the great ecclesiastic of the Yorubas. The old bishop valued his contacts with chiefs very highly, and was pleased that he had been able to introduce a special united service for them in the cathedral. Thirty-three chiefs of Christian profession graced the occasion with their presence, Not all church leaders are as impressed by chiefs. They are aware of the fact that in modern Africa the time of the chiefs is past. In Eastern Nigeria the situation is different. There people remember the time, not too distant, when African priests used to rank above chiefs who were mostly petty chiefs. My informant commented that with the rise of education this relationship had rapidly changed, and that the Church had fallen behind. In Sierra Leone where—in the Protectorate—things have not as yet developed as fast as in some other parts of West Africa, chief and pastor do not eat together. Some chiefs in Sierra Leone with modern education tend to regard the pastor as a non-progressive.

In West Africa, more than elsewhere, the relationship between pastor and chief is affected by modern democratic movements which with breath-taking speed are overtaking both of them. In traditionally rural areas in which the old glory of chieftainship is still upheld, the minister may be given additional prestige through his friendly contacts with the chief, or lose status, as the case may be. To an even greater extent than in other parts of Africa the personality of the minister is of importance in the establishment of influence in a rapidly changing situation.

The Chief as Pastor. This analysis of chief-pastor relationship lacks one very important aspect, seen in those cases in which a modern educated Protestant chief in fact becomes a pastor of souls, unordained, probably without an official standing in the Church and yet, through example and precept, bearing a far-reaching moral and spiritual influence. We think of men such as Chief Njock Bot in the Cameroons. After three decades of service as teacher and influential lay-leader in the (American) Presbyterian Church he was in 1952 elected and appointed chief over a district of some 14,000 people in 38 villages. An energetic and fearless reformer, introducing drastic measures against alcoholism, polygamy and bride-price, he has built up something of a modern theocracy within the framework of his district administration. Chief Daudi of Bugufi, Western Tanganyika, has exerted an influence as a revivalist Christian leader in word and deed at least as effectively as any pastor in the region. Or that anonymous village headman in Bechuanaland, a Congregational layman, who attends to all matters—secular and spiritual—in his village and whose service hereby has become relevant to the whole of life in that village. In this community, where one does not (and should not) differentiate between a secular and a spiritual realm, the chief or this Christian village headman, just because he has secular authority, has to perform pastoral tasks. There are highly modern parallels to this situation in the West, where the same rule applies to some leading managers in industry.

The Church and Tribal Values in the Cities. In order to understand the particular Church problems of modern Africa it is necessary to stress the role of tribal outlook also in town congregations. In fact, it is here that the pastor often meets one of his most persistent difficulties. The town is the meeting-place of a great variety of African tribes, representing varying linguistic and cultural backgrounds. Traditional institutions and cultural patterns are 'transferred' to the new conditions of the city, and this 'transfer' in many cases has a tendency to result in 'super-tribalization', to use a term coined by M. Jean Rouch in connexion with his study of the immigration of people from French territories to certain towns in Ghana.[2] This exceptionally strong emphasis on tribal values is, however, not confined to certain groups in Kumasi or Accra; it is a phenomenon which at the present level of development appears as one of the strongest factors for small-scale integration and large-scale disintegration in the urbanized areas of Africa.

The emphasis on political and economic *Africanism,* or pan-Africanism, sharply expressed at the end of the 1950's by Dr. Nkrumah at Accra is thus, we claim, offset by a competing tendency toward *tribalism.* The problem presents itself in a clear-cut way in the strained relationship between the Ewe and the Minha in Lomé, the capital of Togo. Linguistically the difference between the two peoples is slight. The Minha are, relatively speaking, newcomers in Lomé. The change from German to French administration, as from 1919, gave the Minha their social and economic opportunity, as the Minha came from the adjacent French-speaking Dahomey. The fact that the Ewe usually are Reformed

---

[2] UNESCO, *Social Implications of Industrialization and Urbanization in Africa* etc. (ed. D. Forde), 1956, p. 38.

(Bremen and Paris missions) and the Minha are Methodists was used as the denominational reason for the separation of the two Protestant groups. For a pastor working in a church situation of this kind, the problem of intensified tribal consciousness will be ever-present, and he must be careful not to allow himself to be used as the leader of tribal group differences instead of acting as a servant of the Church of Christ.

On the other side of the continent, in a coastal town in Tanganyika, Protestant missionary work was begun in about 1890 by a German mission. The local tribe was the Digo. Around the turn of the century, evangelization showed promising results. The Islamization of the coastal belt however proceeded at rather an alarming speed in the first half of this century, and the Christian congregations of the Digo tribe were reduced to little family groups without much more to show than the supposedly glorious traditions inherited from the first days of Lutheran missions. The rapid expansion of the sisal industry has meanwhile brought Christian groups from a great number of East African tribes to the coast. The Digo remnant feels its traditional superiority over the newcomers, and tribal tensions are brought into most aspects of the life of this town congregation. These same inter-tribal tensions are felt between Zulu and Sotho and Shangaan in Johannesburg, between Kongo and Luba in Leopoldville.

Tribal differences loom large on the horizon of the African, and also of the Christian African. A reminder of this was given to the European lady in Kenya who, on a Christian day of prayer, asked an elderly Kikuyu priest to pray for the three races of Kenya. He did so gladly, offering his prayers on behalf of the Kikuyu, Embu and Kamba!

An interesting light on the strength of the tribal loyalty within the Church is shed by the example of an East African driver coming originally from a tribe near the coast with a relatively old Christian community. He had lived for 30 years up-country on the western side of Lake Victoria, and had become a recognized lay-leader in his adopted Church. But as his children grew up and approached the time of confirmation he saw to it that each one of them was sent to his own tribe and confirmed in the Church of his youth.

The loyalty to the tribe thus survives in the new conditions of the town, and most townspeople aim at retiring to their 'home'

3. Building Together

in the Reserve, or some other rural area. There is in fact a constant interchange between town and country. Rev. J. J. R. Jolobe has expressed this in the following manner for South Africa: 'A sharp line between the country and the town cannot be drawn these days. The country is in the towns, and the town is in the country. We find bits of each in either and a minister, in order to be of service to his community, must have such a broad training and outlook that he may be able to adjust himself easily to whatever locality or situation he is called to serve.'[3]

Town and city conditions may thus lead to an extraordinary emphasis on the values which are connected with one's own particular tribe. A good leader can try to utilize this tendency in the interest of the Church and allow legitimate competition between tribal groups to become a stimulating factor in church work. But sometimes tribal tendencies lead to isolation and stagnation.

The whole trend of development in Africa is away from the countryside, to the mining and industrial centres, the towns and the cities. Are the Protestant Churches prepared for this fateful overall tendency in Africa?

'A million and a half people in the Congo now live in cities and in industrial areas, receiving less than their share of church and missionary attention. Luanda and Lobito, Douala, Abidjan, are not staffed as their portion of population requires.' Thus the International Missionary Council theological report on 'Latin' Africa (p. 40). The measured terms do not sufficiently bring out the critical urgency of the situation. And if—as usual—it takes a comparison with Roman Catholic achievements to make us sit up and take notice, then it is perhaps sufficient to point out that the traditionally Protestant Douala in the Cameroons has now two Protestant missionaries, as compared with forty Catholic priests and a great number of Catholic sisters. In Yaounde, the administrative capital of the Cameroons, the Presbyterians before 1939 had 96 local church centres, a number which has since been reduced to 32, because of the lack of evangelistic workers.

An example from South Africa was illuminating not only for a particular situation but for the more general question as to whether or not Protestants are prepared to adapt themselves to the fact of the rapid and inevitable urbanization of Africa. We

---

[3] *Ciskeian Missions Council Rpt.*, 1949.

met a dynamic French missionary in Johannesburg struggling with the overwhelming task of caring for the tens of thousands of Protestant Sotho on the Rand, most of whom had once come from Basutoland. In Basutoland the Protestant mission in the nineteenth century had built an admirable system of eleven mission stations and many educational institutions which in more senses than one changed the face of Basutoland. But mission stations and institutions, once they are there, must be looked after, and that, of course, is what missionaries are for. So the missionaries stayed in Basutoland, devoting themselves to the great tasks there. In the meantime, however, it happened that gold was found on the Reef, later called the Witwatersrand, or Johannesburg. Half the male population of Basutoland moved to the Rand, many of them taking their families with them. The mission could spare only one missionary couple from the eleven mission stations in Basutoland to go to the Rand.

In the cities and towns the churches met with problems of new dimensions, and of a nature very different from those which they understood in the traditional tribal context. From the point of view of long-range church history, one would have expected that Protestants would find their place without much difficulty in urban conditions. As the Protestant ministry emerged in Europe in Reformation times, it was largely an urban phenomenon; it was the Protestant élite of the cities—Wittenberg, Strasbourg, Basel, Geneva and Copenhagen—who changed the countries at that time, by adapting themselves to the new sociological forms and technological expressions of a new culture. In Africa to-day, the task is fundamentally the same. If the Protestant Churches feel that their distinctive contribution is really wanted in Africa, they must reach out—through their African leaders and Western advisers—to the masses and to the opinion-forming élite in the urban centres. Here again theological education in Africa has a very necessary part to play.

The combination of denominational isolationism and tribal nationalism is one which at present is, and possibly will increasingly become, a cause of stagnation in the Church. West, East and South Africa at present offer examples of this isolationism causing an obvious lack of missionary *élan* and evangelistic urge. The Church concerned spends its remaining energy on a misunderstood 'churchiness', and in that process tends to become a modern religious rationalization of tribal cohesion, and not much more than that. If this is stagnation—from a Christian point of view—there is a reason why it was brought about.

In the present situation it is more necessary than ever that the intellectual and personal preparation of the pastors of the Church should be geared to the situation we have indicated. The problem of language medium in the theological school, for instance, is affected by this. A theological training which is to be relevant to the modern situation for the Church of Christ in Africa should not be exclusively hemmed in by the narrow limits of the vocabulary and idiom of a small tribal language. The Protestant Church respects tribal and national differences. It tries to realize the wisdom of what Margery Perham has said, that tribalism should be 'sublimated rather than superseded'.[4] And yet, sublimation requires wide and free vision, in this case, the vision of a universal Church, within which the differences which God created may play their appointed part.

The universal, the catholic dimension, is of the *esse* of the Christian religion. Below and above all the paraphernalia of organization, administration and constitutions, the Church of Christ consists in a living and constant flow of nourishment from the Root of the Vine. The Church is universal and must transcend the frontiers of tribe and nation, denomination and generation.

Pastor and Teacher

For a church in Tanganyika, things had really come to a pass when one Sunday morning old Rev. Father Y. Mn. got up in his pulpit and shouted at his congregation: 'Don't come to us priests for a cup of tea! We have no money to buy tea any longer! We are as poor as church mice!'

He remembered wistfully the not so far distant past. Until 1939–45 in his particular area the priest as a matter of course had the highest salary in the community. It was taken for granted that as a representative of the Church he was a leading personality, and he should be paid accordingly. Sh. 50 per month was considered a good salary. The African supervisor of schools only drew Sh. 40 at the time. For a teacher to become a priest was a promotion also from a financial point of view. The post-war period brought a

---

[4] Quoted after J. V. Taylor, *Christianity and Politics in Africa*, 1957, p. 102.

total change in these conditions; in a few years' time, the same supervisor of schools had a salary of Sh. 600 per month, Grade II teachers (nine school years' experience) who used to get Sh. 35, could start at Sh. 180. The priest after many representations and discussions had his salary raised to Sh. 140, but his own daughter could start straight from teacher training school with a salary of Sh. 200.

In this as in other territories, British or non-British, there had been 'headlong change and development' in education after 1950 —to quote the Cambridge Conference Report on *African Education*.[5] Government planning in education got under way towards the end of the 1940's, and those who saw the situation in perspective knew that there was no way back. Dr. L. P. Aujoulat, the French politician and colonial expert, put this in memorable words, representative of the development in Africa after 1950. The Africans, he said, had criticized the colonial powers for having been too slow in offering educational opportunities. These powers had tried to defend themselves by pointing out that educational advance had to move hand in hand with the economic development of the country. But, Dr. Aujoulat goes on to say, by being too cautious, the colonial powers missed their goal. 'Young peoples are readily totalitarian in their demands. When once you have started on the road of a development which is considered normal elsewhere, you must have the courage to carry it through to the end.'[6] Conscious of the need for rapid development, British, Belgian and French governments have raised the whole educational system in a few years, at every level, from primary school to university. A key problem in this development was a teacher training programme supported by a dramatic rise in teachers' salaries.

The new economic status thus conferred upon the school teachers had wide consequences. The teaching profession has been the solid ladder to influence and power in 20th-century African society. If the teachers did not stay on in their schools, their profession served as a ladder, *until 1950*, to positions as ministers of the Church; and *after 1950*, at least potentially, positions as

---

[5] *African Education, A Study of Educational Policy and Practice in British Tropical Africa*, 1953, p. 5.

[6] *Enseignement Outre-Mer, Bulletin de l'Inspection*, Dec. 1952, p. 13 cf. L. P. Aujoulat, *Aujourd'hui L'Afrique*, 1958.

ministers of State. Admittedly, this is a somewhat sweeping statement, but the tendency is there, for everybody to see.[7] The whole
generation of those who became pastors in Africa in the period
1926–1956 had started as teachers. Not that this was unique for
Africa. When, during the Lambeth Conference of 1948, Bishop
Akinyele of Ibadan, Nigeria, told his life-story to the Archbishop
of Canterbury, Dr. Fisher beamed, 'I had exactly the same career
myself: first headmaster, then bishop!'

The Church in Africa in the last generation depended on the
schoolmaster for the conscientious teaching of Scripture in the
school and for a great amount of voluntary church work. The
teacher in many parts of Africa was paid by the Government, but
through the mission, on the premises of the mission or the Church.
He was a 'mission teacher'. The African pastor had a tendency to
feel possessive over the school and would refer to 'my teachers'.
He could get away with this as long as the teacher did not have a
higher education than himself, but with the rapid rise of teachers'
training, secondary and university education, the tables were permanently turned.

A generation ago, Dr. Hensley Henson, late Bishop of Durham,
wrote about the teachers in Britain:

> The whole question of 'religious teaching' in schools has to be con-
> sidered with reference to a new and waxing factor—the professional
> *amour-propre* of the teachers. They will no longer, or only for a little
> longer, tolerate any arrangement which seems to place them 'under the
> clergy'. They are often better educated: and better paid: they are
> always better organized. They know themselves to be, both politically
> and socially, a more considerable force.[8]

Thirty years later, that statement, word for word, could be
applied to all of Africa.

From almost all countries in Africa there is the same story.
With rapidly increased salaries, the teaching profession has acquired a new status as compared with the clergy, both in society
generally and in the school itself. In a rural district in East Africa—
it was here that Rev. Fr. Y. Mn. made his startling announcement
to the congregation not to visit their impoverished priests (p. 115)—

---

[7] In rich Katanga, Belgian Congo, the great majority of teachers were attracted to well-paid jobs in the mining companies.

[8] E. F. Braley (ed.), *Letters of Herbert Hensley Henson* (1950), p. 30.

the following income hierarchy could be established about the middle of the nineteen-fifties:

1. University-trained teachers
2. Ordinary school teachers
3. Artisans, hospital dressers, drivers
4. Clergy
5. Ordinary peasants.

In the same district some priests consider it their right to walk into any school at any time in order to give a Scripture lesson. They are not a little upset when the teacher tells them to stop it, and when they really discover that he is now under another authority, that of the mighty Government.

With reference to West Africa, an example of the same change could be quoted from Sierra Leone. A leading Creole layman writes: 'In former years Africans in the civil service received a salary of about £150 per annum, some receiving £100 per annum. The clergy were then in a higher income group. To-day the clergy is in the lowest income group of the civil service.' Ghana, Nigeria and Katanga (the copper belt of the Belgian Congo) provide striking examples of the same tendency.

The change in salary scale and educational attainments has brought about a change in attitude. This is true already of the relationship between the younger generation of teachers, with secondary education, and their somewhat older colleagues who have not had the same opportunities. One example must suffice. I met a well-known Buganda headmaster who had been one of the first students at Makerere College. But, he said, he did not want to refer to himself as a Makerere man any longer. There had appeared on the scene a new generation of highly educated Makerere masters, and he felt old and out-of-date when compared with these. This was in 1943. Towards the end of the 1940's and at the beginning of the 1950's the new universities were established in West, East and Central Africa. My old friend who felt out-of-date in 1943 must feel even more so today.

The pastor, with his more humble educational background, is even more subject to this feeling of inferiority. In a situation where the roots of modern culture are short and sparse, money and educational standards tend to become the exclusive criteria of prestige and status. The pastor may be tempted to assert the authority he once had—the natural reaction then being: 'Just imagine a pastor with a Standard VI education trying to enforce his archaic ideas on a School Certificate chap! It is most absurd.' That is the final judgment of a Makerere student on the pastor-teacher relationship in Northern Tanganyika.

Teachers with ordinary training college education soon adopt the same attitude. At Mukono, Uganda, in 1955, I met a group of some thirty primary school teachers who were called in for a refresher course. Here are a couple of their remarks on the pastors: 'They try to enforce their authority. They do not want to look small.' 'But I am the father of these young teachers, our pastor says. He thinks we are conceited because we receive a higher salary than he does.' In Bunyoro, Uganda, young men say they do not wish to become teachers because of being subject to the oversight of pastors. It is characteristic, however, that these indications of tension came from the more sophisticated parts of Uganda. The districts with more recently established contacts with the Church and Western civilization appears to accept church leadership with better grace.

A very important consequence of the rise in the Church's educational commitments is the fact that some of the pastors who are best equipped intellectually tend to be absorbed by educational institutions, and cannot give more than a fraction of their time to the work of the Church. So for instance several of the few ordained African graduates in the Church have gone into such institutions. They have of course very legitimate reasons for doing so. A Zulu friend of mine has this to say about his case: 'When I went to the theological seminary in 1938, I had passed Junior Certificate and had begun preparing for matric. by correspondence. When I finished the theological course in 1941, I asked the Synod to allow me to study for matriculation, and I was allowed study leave. My wife went to work as a teacher, and I got a Government bursary which I supplemented by loans from the Mission. At the end of three years I had borrowed about £200. A pastor's salary was £5/10/- per month in our Synod then. From that salary it would have been impossible to pay the mission a loan of £200. I went to teach at our teacher training college for seven years. From there I came to O. to teach, but owing to the shortage of pastors I soon had to take charge of the church work in the district as well. I am drawing a teacher's salary only, however. There is need for me to do whole-time church work, but hitherto the Church has not been able to make the special arrangements that are needed in my case, so I continue teaching.' The inverse of this is that some of the best potential leaders in the Church will not be in a position to give their time to church work in a more exclusive sense. This sketch would be altogether one-sided if we did not add that quite a few well-equipped and well-paid teachers have gladly given up a higher salary in order to join the ministry.

The Pastor and the Educated Élite

The teaching profession is the spearhead of the new educated class in Africa, the *évolués*.[9] The status of the pastor should be measured not only in comparison with teachers but also with the class of educated laymen in the towns and cities. We shall ignore for the moment that there have been in the past different policies —British Africa *versus* 'Latin' Africa—as to the wisdom of encouraging the development of a class of *évolués*. The point is that this class exists to-day, in the new towns and in the rapidly growing cities. This class fashions public opinion to an ever-increasing degree, even in the Church. It comprises the lawyers, doctors and politicians in British and French West Africa; mine company clerks and journalists and many others in Belgian Congo; Government clerks and teachers in East Africa; men with secondary and university education who, like the headmaster of a big school in Lagos, read their daily airmail copy of the *Manchester Guardian*, or who, like that headmaster in Uganda, refer to themselves and their friends as 'Old Budonians'—'we Old Budonians are trained to think fast and freely'.[1] We think, too, of the headmaster *cum* postmaster in a town in Angola, who comes to church on Sunday morning carrying a hymnbook and a Portuguese edition of Dale Carnegie's *How to win friends and influence people*; or the young African politician in Ndola, Nairobi or Abidjan—these and thousands like them are the *évolués*.

---

[9] We are aware of the fact that the latter term, until recently fashionable in the Belgian Congo, is no longer altogether acceptable to leading groups among African progressives. Cf. (J. F. Ewing, ed.), *Local Leadership in Mission Lands* (1954), p. 21, statement by Dr. V. van Bulck, S.J.

[1] The King's School, Budo, near Kampala, is the Eton, or Harrow, of Uganda.

There are different categories of élite. G. E. J. B. Brausch has drawn the distinction in the Belgian Congo between a traditional élite—chiefs, leaders of age-groups—and an intellectual élite. In 1954, the latter totalled 11,572 members for the entire Belgian Congo while in Portuguese Africa there were, in Angola, 15,747 *assimilated* men and 14,342 women, and in Mozambique 2,561 men and 1,788 women.[2] This intellectual élite, according to Brausch, includes 'medical and agricultural assistants, clerks, ministers and priests, together with university graduates from Belgium or the two new Congo universities (Kimwenza and Usumbura)'.

S. B. Ngcobo, writing on the African élite in South Africa, mentions the following groups as belonging to the educated élite: 'ministers of religion, teachers, supervisors and sub-inspectors of schools, clerks, agricultural demonstrators, journalists, editors, nurses, sisters, social welfare workers, sports organizers, musicians, medical doctors, lawyers, university graduates, including lecturers and professors, mainly at the University College of Fort Hare'. He adds the important groups comprising 'the occupational élite': boss boys in mines; skilled workers in secondary industries (of the 135,000 African workers in secondary industries 5.4 per cent were skilled; he mentions that factory employment has become a preferred occupation among Africans); bus drivers and conductors in public transport services, and others making up a class of African *entrepreneurs*.

Dr. K. A. Busia, writing on Ghana, mentions both a traditional élite and new literate élite. He suggests the following criteria for defining an élite, which seem to be valid also for most other countries in Africa: (1) persons of eminence, (2) some degree of corporateness, (3) some consciousness of position occupied in society, (4) enjoyment of high status, (5) imitability.[3] We shall see later that there are interesting differentations in the élite among women, particularly in West Africa, p. 172. Pastors are here included in the category of the intellectual élite. In fact, some priests

---

[2] *Assimilado* is the equivalent in Portuguese Africa of *evolués,* but in Portuguese areas assimilation involves a juridical process bringing exemption as Portuguese citizens from the disabilities of the mass of the people.

[3] Cf. papers by Busia, Brausch, Ngcobo and others in the No. 3, 1956, issue of *International Social Science Bulletin*. The whole number deals with African élite groups.

and pastors have excellent and frequent contacts with members of these classes: in cultural clubs and associations in Durban, Johannesburg, Douala and Cotonou; or as pastors of souls to groups of teachers, nurses, university students, or to African middle-class homes in the new cities.

And yet, generally speaking, the pastor, once himself the leader in the forward movement of education, often shuns real contacts with the intellectual élite. He feels outdistanced by them, and fears their comments. A 'good' pastor, a man who had done excellent work in a rural district, was sent to the town adjoining one of the biggest airfields in East Africa. In the town he was a dismal failure; after a couple of years it was found out that during all that time he had never preached in the township and only visited the country parishes. The town and the educated class overawed him. 'The priests retire into their little corner and are afraid of us,' was the comment of a leading headmaster and politician in that particular country.

On the Copper Belt (Northern Rhodesia) where one would expect the need for effective church life to be very acute, one African minister, bewildered and overwhelmed by the pressing problems of city life, is quoted as saying: 'The young teachers and workers are not interested in Christianity and you cannot build a church here. Let us go where we can build a church.'[4]

In Luluabourg, Belgian Congo, the young educated generation in the age-group 25–35 is in danger of being lost to the Church, and only a sufficient number of African ministers, especially trained to work in urban conditions and among the modern educated classes emerging there, could avert this danger. The pastor cannot help comparing his modest lot with that of the younger educated groups. In Leopoldville a Congo pastor told us: 'There is always a voice in my heart reminding me: "I am elected to be the servant of God." And it is the voice of God Himself. And yet—look at my position. I know old students of mine who to-day earn 3,000 francs per month, while I myself get only 600 francs. Of course, I am happy that I am a pastor—and yet, *on est humain, quoi!*' In Douala, Lomé, Abidjan, the *évolués* in the churches are known to be not a little fastidious. They find out beforehand who is going to preach and do not come if the pastor

---

[4] *I.M.C. Theol. Report,* III, p. 32.

does not speak good French. In Douala and Lomé this has until recently been a special problem. Some of the most outstanding among the pastors had received their theological training in German—once upon a time. 'But at 40, such a man was a generation older than everybody else'—as a French missionary remarked. Some pastors try to hoist themselves up to the supposed cultural level of évolués and attempt to win them this way. In a very fine old church in one of the largest cities in West Africa, we took part in Evensong, at which a highly refined priest preached a sermon in impeccable English to his upper-class African congregation. He was elegant, eloquent, well-versed in 19th century English poetry—and dead as a door-nail.

South Africa is characteristically different. Rev. S.M., a fearless Lutheran leader in rural Zululand, has a small group of University graduates and other educated people in his large congregation. In his sermons he sometimes tells the congregation, 'Now you can rest for a while. I am going to speak in tongues now! I shall now turn to our educated friends and speak on their level.' And so he does, with great fluency and effectiveness—with the result that the university graduates say afterwards: 'We got something out of the service to-day.' Rev. E.M.R., a man with long experience of school and church work, has this to say about the pastor and the educated class: 'The status of the minister is the same as before—with a little difference. If he is not highly educated, he does not get respect from the educated class (court interpreters, C.I.D. officers, teachers). They still say, "Good morning, mfundisi", when they meet him in the street. But they lose interest in his sermons. "The sermon was not worth the trouble of going to church", they say. On the other hand, where a minister is well-educated and can preach on to-day's level, he attracts the educated class. They form a choir, teach in the Sunday School, help in the youth movement.'

This statement to a certain extent holds also for the situation in urban areas in other parts of Africa. But there are—it seems to me—certain overtones in the South African situation which distinguish it from church conditions north of the Limpopo. The colour issue, being the key-signature of the South African cacophony, enters deeply into the matter of the status and prestige of the minister of religion and welds him to all elements of the dominated caste. There is, of course, a wide latitude between dif-

ferent economic and educational levels among the Bantu themselves, differences which begin to constitute a system of class differentiation in the Bantu population. But the pressure from the
one overwhelming social problem—race and colour—is so heavy
that class differentiation is more easily forgotten and overcome
than in Central or West Africa. In this situation, even an indif-
ferently educated Christian *mfundisi* is forced to play a role which
is not altogether restricted to his church office. Deep down in their
hearts, people may feel that their *mfundisi*, in a crisis, may emerge
as a potential Moses, liberating his people from the heavy bondage
of the present.

This expectation from the group, combined with the personal
aspirations of the pastor, not only influences the concept of the
ministry in the African Church (see p. 304) but also modifies the
course to be taken by the Church over against Western political,
social, and missionary domination and African nationalism. Here
educated laymen join with simple mine-labourers in helping to
build up the Moses-role of the pastor and in singing their part in
their own variation of the African's song of liberation.

> Go down, Moses,
>   Way down in Egypt land,
> Tell ole Pharaoh—
>   Let my people go!

The Pastor and Politics

The over-emphasis on tribal values is one of the problems in the
modern cities and towns, which can cause the pastor great difficulties and may often isolate him, at least for some time, from
large sections of his congregation. Modern party politics is another
dilemma, puzzling, sometimes dangerous. In fact, the two issues
sometimes coincide, the local party political struggle being a rationalization of tribal tensions. What should be the attitude of the
pastor to the political problems of his country?[5]

The close connexion between tribal loyalty and political loyalty
can be seen in Sierra Leone, where we are told that a chief may be

---

[5] Obviously this is not the place for a detailed study of this problem, and
we limit ourselves to a few observations. We refer the reader to J. V. Taylor's
Penguin book (African Series), *Christianity and Politics in Africa*, 1957.

offended if the pastor makes a statement against the interests of the party to which the chief belongs. 'Some pastors have been persecuted for that.' In at least one other West African country the dominant Protestant Church was closely linked with the politically strong anti-colonial aspirations of the tribe—a tribe which in fact is divided under two or three different colonial administrations. The leading pastors in this particular case are personal friends of, and even close relatives of the foremost African politicians, and no doubt effective co-operation between the political party and the Church is being established here. At the same time this has obviously implied an extremely delicate relationship with the administration—not an easy performance for the pastor.

There are at least two or three views on the part played by Protestant pastors in the political struggles in Ghana and Nigeria. One well-informed observer summed up the situation, which is becoming increasingly representative for the whole continent with its present-day nationalism:

Some of our pastors have been strongly engaged in the national liberation struggle. Three considerations, however, made a more intense investment in party politics difficult. 1. There was not in the Church that sense of frustration that was felt in political circles. Our Church was not in any sense controlled by the mission. The policy of self-government for the Church in our case began in the 1890's. To-day all the thirty Church circuits, except three, are under African superintendents. Also the important educational institutions are under African leadership. 2. The low level of the political debate was not attractive to us pastors. The dominant X.Y.Z.-party has practised heavy mud-slinging in which no pastor could take part. 3. By joining one party the pastor cut himself off from other groups in the community. As pastors we have therefore preferred to make our influence felt in the background rather than coming forward as fully-fledged party members or as members of the Assembly. The reaction from the X.Y.Z.-party has been sharp. They have been largely anti-church, saying that the Church, and particularly the pastor, was under the thumb of the white man and subscribed to the 'spiritual imperialism of Western missions', etc. We have been for political self-government but critical of some of the political methods used.

In a few cases, pastors have allowed themselves to stand as candidates for the Assembly. In Western Nigeria, some Anglican priests have become members of the House. The late Bishop Akinyele told me his view on these things: 'When politics are on the side of the Church, we should be on the side of politics.' The Anglican priests have later stood down, because of the ruling of their synod. In the Methodist Church, a minister is considered to lay down his office during the time of his service in the House of Assembly—a situation which has arisen both in Nigeria and in Ghana. In local councils in Ghana, the minister may sometimes be selected as an impartial chairman. This was the case with the well-known Methodist, the late Charles Graham of Accra; he had to chair a council with strong C.P.P. (Nkrumah's party) dominance, at which it was taken for granted that the pastor-chairman should open the meeting with a prayer. Graham had a high opinion of the work of his local council: 'We only seek the common good.'

Leading laymen in West African churches generally recommend that the pastor take a balanced stand in politics. 'He should be interested in politics, but in a temperate manner in order to reconcile the two opposing views.' Not that that standpoint is particularly easy! In a French-speaking country in Western Africa the political issue is still largely undecided. One leading African pastor has had particular difficulties from his own church because of his failure to come out enthusiastically for immediate political independence. A budding young politician was a member of his church. When this man propagated his radical views, the pastor told him: 'If you are a Socialist or an M.R.P., that is all right, but if you are a Communist—as I suspect—then you are an enemy of the Church and you can no longer be a member of my congregation.' The man left in anger, and the pastor had stored up tremendous difficulties for himself. The church choir changed its attitude, as its members favoured immediate political independence for their country. Just as the pastor was about to begin his sermon, the choir used their secret weapon, a song on the Resurrection of Christ, based on Matt. 28: 5–6. They kept on singing this song for more than an hour, thus effectively hindering the politically unpopular pastor from preaching. He had to leave the chapel, still listening to the song on the Resurrection.

In Belgian and Portuguese Africa, mobility and initiative on this political level is fairly restricted, particularly for a Protestant pastor, and the problem does not arise in the same way as in French and British Africa.

British Central and East Africa present a different political scene. For Northern Rhodesia, Dr. A. L. Epstein has in a most instructive way analysed the emergence of political leadership, showing how the 'tribal elders' in the mining districts have been succeeded by leaders of so-called 'welfare societies' and eventually by officers of the African National Congress.[6] On the Copperbelt, all kinds of leadership tend to be adaptable to other situations, so that the same men may be in some sense both political and church leaders. Many of the leaders of the welfare societies had at one time been church leaders or evangelists and lay preachers. The important, alarming recent development is that many of these men had taken an attitude to the Church which is at best passive, at worst hostile. Pastors have to be careful not to be classed as 'agitators'. On the other hand, they no longer can, or wish to, turn to the Administration for support, the political pressure from their own group being too strong. Here again, the situation just at present seems to be somewhat less inflamed in East Africa. The churches in some tribes have long experience to draw on. Chagga church leaders in Northern Tanganyika recall that in the struggles over the K.N.C.U.—local coffee co-operatives—some pastors took sides with the one or the other of the two contending parties, and thus became enemies of the opposed group. The general comment was that this must not happen again and that a pastor should not be engaged in party politics. In other parts of East Africa, the present course of events makes it very difficult for local church leaders to stand aside from the national struggle.[7]

South Africa is different; but even there it is possible for African church leaders to take two opposite views.

A Lutheran Zulu minister, born in 1915, is representative of one extreme. 'A minister who mingles in politics is really a criminal', he claims. He went along to a meeting of the African National Congress, but the position taken by this organisation did not win his approval, and he told them so. He did this in terms which correspond to Rom. 13 and Luther's Small Catechism but hardly to the African nationalistic temper of to-day: 'Political bondage is nothing. It only lasts a life-time. But a life-time is

---

[6] A. L. Epstein, *Politics in an Urban African Community* (1958) and *idem*, 'African Leadership on the Copperbelt', *Listener*, Oct. 1956.

[7] With courage, competence, and balance, E. M. K. Mulira of Uganda has discussed the principles involved on the Christian frontier in politics, 'Some Thoughts on the Christian Frontier in East African Politics', *Christian News-Letter*, October 1955.

short. Then comes eternity. Spiritual bondage is the thing we should fear.'

The pressure from radical political organizations is felt by the church leaders, particularly in the many recent crises. The civil disobedience campaign in South Africa during 1952 was a serious challenge to African ministers. Some joined the movement, and had to pay the price. One internationally well-known Methodist minister describes the agony of twenty-four hours he had to go through until he decided not to take part in the campaign. This was the same man who, when in 1950 the African National Congress attempted to found an African National Church, decidedly refused to co-operate in that move. Others again take a much more decisive standpoint. A highly-educated Nguni priest writes in this modified, yet determined way: 'I was not happy during the resistance movement. Many resisters had not reached maturity in the "spirit" of pacifism. But I am a member of the African National Congress. My pacifism loathes the hatred of the white man which one meets frequently among the general African public. But one is not surprised. It is their reaction to policies which set out directly to make the African accept the position of permanent inferiority. It is good to see that my people will never accept this. Therefore they have a future. But we need much Christian influence.'

Some African pastors in this situation have decided to throw in their lot with the social and political aspirations of their own group and have joined a particular political party or organization. In South Africa a well-known Anglican priest is on the executive of the African National Congress. There are, no doubt, dynamic factors in the present situation in South Africa which, with an inner necessity, will force the African minister to take a more decisive stand politically. One of the very best, a highly-educated and deeply responsible pastor, told me recently: 'You cannot have a place of responsibility as an African in this country without getting into politics. And we cannot keep quiet any longer without feeling that we are selling our people into bondage.' This particular pastor, a man of fine theological understanding, finds the ultimate solution in the Bible: 'I study the Old Testament and I find that we Africans, like Israel of old, are a nation in God's school. It is a hard school, but it is God's. Our glory is not in attaining freedom, but in achieving an understanding of God's work in history. The great Biblical characters show me the balance between resignation and struggle, between peace and strife, which we need.' In his case this theological interpretation does not for a moment make him relent in the political struggle. With this prophetic view, he has arrived at the level where the Church can make its most significant political contribution to the new men of Africa.

The Younger Generation

'To me and my parents our pastor is the mid-man between God and ourselves.' These words by a Methodist schoolboy in Lagos, Nigeria, are surprisingly characteristic of the attitude of the younger generation. 'God's representative in the local community and in the church' is the definition offered by a Methodist schoolboy in Kumasi. 'The majority of the community look upon him as the man who represents God, as they cannot see God themselves' (same school). At my request, some three hundred secondary school students all over Africa have written essays on 'The Pastor in our Local Church'. Some of those who stress the role of the pastor as 'mid-man between God and ourselves', are at the same time aware of the fact that this attitude is not very 'Protestant', yet they cannot free themselves from a valuation for which as Africans they have, perhaps, a special propensity. 'We attach great respect to the work and position of a minister. As some Roman Catholics say, the minister is representing God to us on earth' (same school).

The 300 essays are exciting reading. For one thing, these African students know their pastor. If young students in the highest form of a secondary school in my country, Sweden, were told to write an essay on 'The Pastor in our Local Church', I fear that many of them would simply admit that they have no idea of the man or what he is doing. To African students the pastor apparently is much closer, a well-known figure and friend. A good percentage of students in African secondary schools were once *discovered* by the pastor. On his tours of the schools in his district he had open eyes for promising young lads and girls. In many cases these future African politicians, doctors, journalists and Government school teachers spent some of their first school years in the pastor's house, treated as his own children. In a Uganda teachers' conference in 1955, with twenty-seven attending, I asked how many had been 'discovered' and helped on the way by African pastors. Six felt that this influence had been decisive in their lives; another four in this group were sons of ministers.

In this and other ways the pastor is well known to the younger generation. We shall let a Ghana Methodist schoolboy describe what he has seen of the pastor's work:

> As the Circuit to which I belong is too big we should have had two ministers but only one is there. He has a big task, for he travels more than thirty miles to some stations and has about thirty churches to visit each month. He holds morning prayers with his household, he helps the class meetings, he goes round after class meetings or ordinary meetings to visit those who absented themselves, asks them the reasons why they failed to attend; if they are not well, gives them encouragement and advice. He checks the class and ticket money, district extension funds and all collections made by the church. He represents the church during Synod session. He sees that the schools in his district are all in good order. If I were to tabulate all these it would occupy many pages.

> It is not only the church duties that he shows keen interest in but he also respects the townsmen. He sometimes pays visits to the chief's house, invites him to the church and comforts the weak. He invites not only the chief but the prominent people in the town to be chairmen during harvest time. All the people in the town respect him because of his good behaviour in the town.

Generally speaking, the school-age generation appear to appreciate the work of the pastor—although we shall probably do well to discard some of the most enthusiastic expressions of praise. They have discovered the fundamental role which the pastor plays as a social and religious leader in the local community. The historical perspective in which a Ghana Presbyterian schoolboy sees the arrival of the pastor is conceived in terms which we regard as memorable: 'It was one Sunday morning when the church room was crowded with people. Our catechist introduced the Pastor who had been commissioned to take charge of the Church in my area. *That was the first time in history*.' He was right, of course. The arrival of that pastor did mean, perhaps to an even greater extent than the schoolboy had perceived, a new chapter in the local history of that church.

Critical voices are not lacking. Many of these youngsters feel that the pastor has a tendency to forget the downtrodden and favour the leading people in the community. In certain West African countries they criticize the pastor on account of his supposed membership in secret societies and there are sometimes veiled hints about his moral life. Above all, he is criticized by these youngsters because of his lack of general education, and particularly because they consider that he does not know English or French as well as he should. In this connexion some of the pastors are criticized in their capacity as preachers; they cannot capture the interest of the younger generation because of their lack of culture.[8] Progressive Nigerians are apt to feel that their pastors as yet do not measure up to their national aspirations. A Yoruba schoolboy writes: 'Things have improved considerably in the past few years, with regard to Athletics, Politics, etc. for we can see Olowu making headway in athletics, Awolowo in Politics, Maurice Fievet in Arts, and Fela Sowande in Music—*but what of Religion?*'

But even the critics do not doubt that the pastor is in some way a 'mid-man' between God and the congregation, the one who prays to God on behalf of his flock, and who can bury their dead and thus in some way assure them safe keeping and life eternal. In secularized Lagos a Methodist schoolboy opens his essay with the following statement: 'I feel that the pastor is somebody that should be respected as it is through him that God speaks.'

The essays from South Africa are different in one respect. They alone introduce one particular issue: colour. They want to be assured that the pastor is an African, not a European: 'Our minister,' writes a schoolboy belonging to a Reformed church, 'should be an African in order to prove that to be a minister is

---

[8] An Anglican girl in the C.M.S. Secondary school for girls in Freetown. Sierra Leone—age about 15—begins her essay with fully-fledged journalistic verve:

The parson of my Church. 'And now unto God the Father. ... Goodness! The sermon is at an end at long last. I was actually day-dreaming during the talk, and I did not realize that the preacher had come to an end. He seemed to have been talking for ages, and I cannot even remember what the text was. ... The other day I overheard a girl asking her companion if she was going to church the following Sunday. She said 'No' definitely and when asked for her reason replied that Rev. Boring was going to preach, and the sermon was sure to be irksome. If it had been Rev. Interesting she would have gone, as his talk would be worth hearing. I immediately agreed with the girl because it was during the sermon of Rev. Boring that I had been day-dreaming the previous day.'

not meant for Europeans only.' Others again write, 'We need
Bantu ministers, because they are the ones we can follow properly.'
'By white ministers you get the opinion that God is from the
Whites and for the Whites; the African minister alone knows our
way of thinking etc.' European ministers 'are not closely sociable
with their Christian members'. These young writers will however
claim in the same breath that their Bantu ministers should receive
their theological training overseas, and some will even admit that
Western missionaries are necessary for the well-being of the
Church: 'A foreigner is needed for the widening of Christianity,'
is a statement by a young student from colour-obsessed Transvaal.
His view shows that there are those who wish to transcend the
tribal and racial barriers of the Church and stress the universal
dimension of the Church, its 'width', as he calls it.

Some of the youngsters are critical of the pastor but even when
they criticize there is in their voices a longing for leadership and
guidance from the man who is a 'mid-man', a representative of
God on earth.

The idea of the minister as the representative of God is of
course even stronger in essays written by secondary schoolboys in
Roman Catholic schools. The students of one such school in East
Africa also wrote essays for our present study. There hangs a real
threat over those who do not fully appreciate what the priest is
doing: 'If there is any Catholic who does not see the part played
by the priest in the life of the Christians it would be better for
him to perish than to live, and lose his everlasting happiness, for
there is a possibility of his departure from the Catholic Church.'
What is this part and position of the priest? He is 'the civil servant
of God and has an enormous responsibility toward Him. All the
work which should have been done by God Himself, if He were
bodily present in the same form as we are, is accomplished by the
priest.'

No wonder then that the Roman Catholic youngsters have
admiration for the priest! 'They are highly respected by everybody
not only because they are highly educated psychologists but because they were empowered by Jesus Christ to call God daily in
mass and try to incorporate us in Him by communion.' It is all the
more necessary, according to the young essay-writers, that there
should be a great number of priests. They all stress the need for

building new seminaries and for young Africans to respond to the highest call, that of a priest. 'Thus the number of Catholics will multiply very enormously.' This is a concern that they all have and one which their Protestant contemporaries do not seem to express in their essays.

Pastor of the Past or for the New Day?

'Look at my earlobe, Bwana. The right one has a hole in it; my father arranged that it was pierced according to the custom of our tribe. The left is not pierced. You see, the right earlobe is the olden times, and the left is the modern time. But the head is one and the same! That is what I am always telling my people, caught as we are in the whirlpool of rapid change in Africa to-day. We have to move with the time, but not too fast, because if we do we shall be torn to pieces.'

The eternal snow of Kibo, Kilimanjaro, shone above him, and the endless plains of the Masai stretched out below him as he explained to me, early one morning, the position of the African pastor on the threshold between the old order and the new.

Does the pastor to-day represent the past or the new day? The very fact that the question is asked at all shows that conditions have changed radically in the last fifty years. As the Church was slowly being established in tribe after tribe, it was conscious of shaping the future. A Zulu pastor in Johannesburg, now about 55 years old, writes in his autobiography that he was born 'in an atmosphere of conversion'. People were converted and changed, and expected the community to change with them. The school as the handmaiden of the Church was the great instrument in achieving this change. The Church was on the side of education and progress, and the Gospel taught that new wineskins were needed to hold the new powerful ferment of ideas.

What about the attitude to-day? The reply is, there is no one attitude. The problem cannot be solved in one simple formula; it varies from situation to situation, and largely also from individual to individual.

The question includes another problem. What, from the point of view of the Church, is 'the future' or 'progress'? These terms are not necessarily the same to the Church as they appear to a colonial administration or to an independent African state. From the characteristic point of view of the modern political organisation or the welfare state, the African pastor does not to-day represent the 'future'. This is, of course, the one complaint of the *evolués,* the teachers, the political leaders throughout Africa. His standard of culture and his education do not correspond to the exigencies of modern urban community life. His ideas in politics are too old-fashioned, too closely bound up with the old colonial system; 'he does not understand modern science; the pastor is *très dépassé'*.

But this is a judgement from outside. What do the pastors themselves feel about their situation? Some of them do not seem to pay much attention to the problem. There are among them, as elsewhere in the world, people who are by nature conservative and who only too easily confuse religion and tradition. The traditions introduced by the first missionaries—the Victorian hymn tunes, certain chance details in the arrangement of the congregation in the Church service, and also, and this is more important, an inveterate way of thinking in terms of Africa as only rural, forgetting the cities and towns to which in fact the 'progressive' part of the Church has already moved—become sacred and must not be changed.

A young student from Ghana had listened to sermons preached by such a pastor. His best sermon, he says, was that on 'Contentment': 'He made it clear that everybody must be contented with what he has in hand. He drew the attention of the congregation to the Tenth Commandment and summarized its contents. He referred to Cain and Abel. Cain was not content with his gift and had to slay his brother Abel. He gave us an example of a dog with a piece of meat, that passed a bridge and saw its reflexion in the water. Because the dog was not contented with what he had in hand *(sic)*, he jumped into the brook to seize the other piece of meat. We should be content with what we have!'

The deliberate emancipation from dependence on the missionary may accentuate the choice between traditionalism and progressivism in a rather interesting way. Here is a 1957 example from a Lutheran Church in Central Africa. A nursing student, an eighteen-year old girl, was to be confirmed in the church at the hospital centre of N. The African pastor insisted that according to the tradition of the tribe her head must be clean-shaven for the *rite de passage* in question. The girl refused, for she was just about ready to take her nursing exam., and would then be entitled to wear a new nurse's cap: but this cap would only fit a person with hair on her head. The European missionary defended her viewpoint and pleaded that she be confirmed without having to go through the hair-ceremony. The pastor stood his ground however: 'Here I decide. I follow our tribal custom. The White man must not put his nose into this.' From the point of view of Western civilisation, the pastor in this case appeared stubbornly to uphold the traditions of the past. In the eyes of African nationalistic leaders in the district he very likely was hailed as a progressive, as certain African traditions tend to be regarded as symbols of modern nationalism.

But it is invidious to make such references, if we do not at the same time point out that there are pastors in some of the cities and townships to-day—names in Johannesburg and Durban, Accra and Lagos, Yaounde and Fort Portal (Uganda), come to mind— who are as representative of modern life and progress as anybody else in the community. To them, and through them, the Church has a relevant answer to the agonizing problems of modern life. They make a conscious effort to stand on the frontier of the future, and to mould the local Christian community into a flexible instrument of social progress, in order that it may be a real help towards the integration of personality, group and nation.

There are other pastors who sense this problem, whether they represent the 'Past' or the 'New Day', as an intensely personal concern which sometimes creates in them a wistful desire to participate in some other task more in consonance with the future. Rev. X. Y. in Johannesburg, a man with an excellent mind, author of a few books in his own vernacular, has a son who was educated in the United States and in Europe and a daughter who is principal of an important girls' school. Why did he become a pastor? The answer is simple. He grew up on a mission station and is a third-generation Christian. His father was a catechist. 'The groove was made for me in advance.' There are moments now when he feels that he serves a lost cause, that the Church is too timid, too quiescent, too little in contact with realities. If he could begin again, he would not just follow the groove. He calls these thoughts his 'moments of doubt', and it is only Easter, in his church on the Rand, which helps him to dispel that doubt each year. He may serve an institution linked primarily with the past; but Easter does hold out a hope for the future, not least in that chapel on the Rand.

In the Congo, a group of old and young pastors have come together. One of the older generation speaks on behalf of himself and the others: 'I was a teacher at 15, catechist at 19, and after another 16 years of service, they decided to call me "pastor". I grew up with the Mission, and it is my home. It is more difficult for the younger colleagues. Some of them feel imprisoned in the Church. They cannot do what they want. They have chosen this work and feel they have to carry on in the service of the mission until death. But some of them would like to go to town where they can do what they want.' Here the work of the Church is not satisfying and frustration knocks at the door. In a large French-speaking Central African city, a group of pastors expressed themselves in the same vein: 'Things change nowadays as fast as an aeroplane flies. Our fathers had sufficient education [these pastors were second-generation Christians], but that is of no avail to us now. We belong to a past time. I just had six years in school and then three years in the Pastors' School. With that kind of background I ask myself if I really am a pastor—or what I am.'

'The African pastor is a lonely man', Mabel Shaw told me after a tour of Africa visiting a great many churches in many countries. The pastor—*un grand isolé*—was the comment of two Swiss missionaries of the older generation who have served in Mozambique. That loneliness and isolation is a fairly recent phenomenon. A generation ago, being on the side of what was then 'progress' gave assurance and relevance to the daily tasks of the pastor, the interpreter of white religion, civilization, and law, in his corner of Africa; now the new political nationalism often isolates the pastor from the modern progressive groups and powers. A Methodist minister in Central Africa writes: 'In these days of tension and national aspiration the pastor is confronted with many problems, especially among the young people, who suspect that he is being used by the White missionary as informer on what is going on in the political field.' He would not wish, or even dare, to turn to the administration for support. The mission and the missionaries appear to be on the way out, achieving their famous *euthanasia* (withdrawal of the mission in the interest of the national Church), and the rapid turn-over of missionaries at present confirms in the mind of the African pastor that this declared policy is being carried through.

How far the connexions with the chief and the teacher, the African representatives of Administration and Education, offer a substitute for these other fast-disappearing contacts, is a matter of daily concern to the pastor—as we have tried to indicate.

In order to understand the present position of the pastor we have studied his relative status as compared with the spokesmen of the traditional values and of modern aspirations in Africa. At the same time he would probably himself ask, and rightly ask, whether in fact the category of status is one in which the contribution of the Christian ministry ultimately should be measured. In the last resort, it may well be that status, prestige and position is not the measuring rod with which to gauge the influence of a ministry the nature of which, by definition, is service: 'I am among you as one who serves ... let this mind be in you, which was also in Christ Jesus ... who took upon Him the form of a servant.'

Yet, this ministry of service (if the tautology be allowed) is incarnated in men similar to most of us. Africans are at least as susceptible as others to the constant psychological weighing process implied in the creating of a fruitful relationship with one's fellow-men. Above all, the African minister would like to be convinced that his contribution is relevant to those whom he is to serve.

In the very limited library of one of the pastors in Angola we found a few copies of books in English, among them Elton Trueblood's *Alternative to Futility*. I was not sure how far the message of that book had influenced its owner, but there was something in the title which seemed revealing.

If the African pastor is left with the impression that he no longer measures up to the demands of the new day, he may soon come to regard much of his work as futile. The more necessary it is that he be given tools, scope and opportunity for a service which is felt to be satisfying and relevant.

· 4 ·

THE PASTOR AND HIS CO-WORKERS

Meet Pastor Ulwendo!

'Ulwendo' is a Konde (Southern Tanganyika) word for *safari* or journey. It is chosen here as a fictitious name for a few Bantu pastors whose acquaintance we shall make. All over Africa, the pastors are 'in journeyings oft'. Before attempting to define in general terms the nature of the African minister's work, we shall let a few of them open their diaries and tell us of their daily activities.

I. *Rev. B. K.* is an evangelical priest at St. Paul's Cathedral, Kampala, (Anglican) and one of the leaders of the Revival movement in Uganda. First a headmaster at the school in Entebbe, he joined the *Balokole* Revival movement in 1935—on the same day as his wife. 'My wife and I confessed our sins to one another. Since then we have walked together all the way. There is no darkness between us.' As a theological student he was one of the 1941 rebels, who left the Theological College because of disagreement with the Principal over the Revival question. Later he returned and was ordained.

My daily routine

Every day early in the morning about 6–6.30 a.m., my wife and I read the Word of God, usually from the Scripture Union daily portions. Having meditated in silence on what we have read we have prayers together before I go to church.

7.15–7.30 a. m.	Morning prayers in church according to the Prayer Book; usually not a big congregation at that time.
8.	Breakfast.
8.45–9.	I take prayers in one of the schools on the Namirembe hill in turns.

9–12.	Office hours, during which I have baptism and confirmation classes. Sometimes members come for a baptism certificate which they may have lost, also for problems concerning marriage difficulties. Again during this time I supervise the work of keeping the church tidy.
1–2 p. m.	Lunch.
2–2.30.	Rest (when I am not needed).
2.30–3.	Quiet time, usually in the church. This time I have private prayers, reading of my Bible etc.
3–7.	Visiting Christian homes, Bible classes and/or the hospital.
8.	Family prayers—we parents and our children having prayers together: A hymn, then a portion from the Bible and a short talk about what we have read. Our grown-up children are free to lead us in prayers, otherwise we—my wife and I—take it in turns, whoever feels free to take it.
9–10.	Reading books, letter writing.
10.	Supper.
	(Our children under 9 years of age have their supper early. These children have prayers themselves before they are put to bed.)
11.	To bed.

My diary, August 1957

1 August. I attended a clergy meeting eleven miles away. We met to discuss the matter concerning the Uganda Diocesan Mission. I enjoyed the meeting.

2 August. Every Thursday in the week, I take preparation for marriage. These are the people who are to be married one week later. 9–9.45. We start with Holy Communion. 9.45–10.15. Writing various forms. 10.15–12. Talked to those couples about Christian marriage through the Word of God. They are free to ask questions. They were six couples. 3.15–4. Two marriage registrations were done. 4–6. I visited Christian and non-Christian homes helping them where necessary and praying with them. 6–7. I visited hospital as usual.

3 August. 9–12. Office hours. A class of fifty candidates who are being prepared for confirmation attended. This time I revised what they had learned before they were sent to me. They came

from various schools and villages round here. This was the first time they had attended class. 3–4.30. Attended a reception given to the graduate students by the headmaster and staff of one of the C.M.S. schools here. 5–6. *Fellowship meeting,* held every Friday.[1] We read the Word of God and pray together.

4 August. 7.15. Morning prayers. 10 attended. 9–11. To town to do some shopping. 11 a.m.–2 p.m. I washed clothes and helped in the home work. 3–6. We had a meeting of fathers and mothers. We discussed the Christian home. The subject was 'Who is responsible for Bible reading and prayers in the homes?' Every one was free to talk and the talks from either side were of great value and helpful. It was understood in the end that mothers (wives) have greater responsibility than men, because the mothers are always indoors and they are very much concerned with bringing up the children.

5 August (Sunday). 9.5 a.m. Went to preach at the Kampala Technical Institute. About 60 students and the staff attended. 2–4. Rest and preparation for Evensong. 4–5. Preached the afternoon service. It was a broadcast service which was a big opportunity to pass on the Lord's message to the people in the whole of East Africa. 5.30. I went away about 75 miles to pay a visit to my relatives.

6 August. Bank Holiday. I came back to Kampala, arriving very late in the evening.

7 August. 9–12. Office work and confirmation class teaching— 53 attended. 2–3 p.m. Bible class with the hospital nurses. This time I took Sin and Repentance as subjects. 3–4. Visited prison and prayed with the inmates. 6–7. Visited Christian homes. Going round these homes, I come across some people who have problems specially in small things which are caused by misunderstanding between man and wife.

8 August. 7.15. Morning prayers. Nine attended. 8.45–9. I took prayers in one of the girls' schools on the hill. 9–10. Confirmation class teaching. 10–12. Went to town to do shopping; buying things for church use.

9 August. 7.15. Morning prayers. Twelve attended. 9–12. Preparation for marriage as last week.

---

[1] Fellowship meeting, referring to the weekly *Balokole* 'revival meeting' usually held on Friday afternoons through East Africa.

10 August. 7.15 a.m. Morning prayers. Fourteen attended. 9–12. Office work and confirmation class teaching. 54 attended. Again Christians came for their baptism certificates. 5–6 p.m. Fellowship meeting, during which we heard news from different parts of the country that God saves people from sin. We praised and prayed for those who were being saved.

11 August. 7.15. Morning prayers. Nine attended. 8 a.m.–1 p.m. I helped in the home, washing clothes etc. 2.30 p.m. Attended the Re-United Budonians' Golden Jubilee Celebration. This took place at Budo [10 miles from Kampala].[2] About a hundred Old Boys attended. 3–4. We were taken round to see the College buildings and the work done by the students. 4–5. Tea served by the students. 5–6. Games. Tennis and football match between old and present students. The old students lost! 6. I took the evening service in the College Chapel. 7.30. Supper and a talk given by the headmaster. 9–11. Concert by the old students. Singing etc.

12 August (Sunday). 7.30. At Budo (Golden Jubilee) breakfast. 9.15. Morning service. Many of the old students attended. I conducted the service and the headmaster preached. 3–4 p.m. I attended a fellowship meeting at Kawolo, 30 miles away from Kampala. Many brethren of different nations and languages attended it. God spoke mightily to our hearts and we went home praising Him.

13 August. Usually I am off duty on Mondays. I spent this day helping in the home. At 5 p.m. Deanery Council. I took the Chair. Discussed various church affairs.

14 August. 8.45–9. I took prayers in one of the girls' schools. These are grown-up girls from 15 years and upwards. I allowed them to ask questions concerning their spiritual life. Such questions are: 'How can a man know that he is saved? Is public confession necessary? If we confess to God only is that not enough?' To answer those questions, I had to give them my testimony how God saved me. This helped them to understand what it means to be saved. I read with them the Word of God. 9–10. Confirmation class. Only 15 came this time! 10–12. I attended the group mission leader's meeting, during which we had to read the Word of God and to pray for the Mission to Uganda.

15 August. 8.45. Took prayers in the School. 9–10. Confirmation

---

[2] See p. 120, note 1.

class. 25 attended. 11–12. Office work—letter-writing etc. 3 p.m. I took Bible study with the hospital nurses. The subject was 'Eternal Life'. 5–6. I attended Sanyu Babies Home's committee. We thought of the ways in which these babies (motherless babies) can be helped financially.

16 August. 7.15. Morning prayers. Eight attended. 9–12. Preparation for marriage, as last week. We start with Holy Communion and then I start to talk to them.

17 August. 7.15. Morning prayers. Ten attended. 9–11. I had a baptism class of 20 pupils. These come from schools and some adults from villages around. 11–12. Went to town for shopping. 2.30–4. Quiet time. Afterwards I did some accounts. 5–6. The weekly Fellowship meeting.

18 August. 7.15. Morning prayers. Nine attended. 8 a.m.–2.30 p.m. I stayed at home, washing and helping. 3–6. Conducted marriage service. I had eight couples.

19 August (Sunday). 7.30. Holy Communion service. 250 people attended. 9.30–11. Morning service including Holy Communion. I took the service and preached. 4–5. p.m. Evensong. I read the service. 5–6. Visited the hospital, talking to the patients individually.

20 August. It was free Monday, so I stayed at home and helped my wife with the work.

21 August. 7.15. Morning prayers. 13 attended. 8.45–9. I took prayers in one of the schools. 9–10. Confirmation class, 43 attended. 10–12. Office work: church accounts. 2 p.m.–5. I went with some friends of mine some twelve miles away, to attend a funeral service. I took part in the service.

22 August. 7.15. Took Holy Communion service. One Christian family had their 34th anniversary, therefore they came to give thanks to God; 13 attended. 8.45. I took prayers in one of the schools here. 9–10. Confirmation class teaching. 48 attended. 10–12. In the office doing the accounts. 3–4. Bible class with the hospital nurses. 5–6. Visiting the patients in the hospital.

23 August. 7.15. Morning prayers. 13 attended. 9–12. Preparation for marriage, 16 attended. As usual, we started with Holy Communion service.

24 August. 7.15. I went to see one Christian three miles away who was ill. I had prayer with those who had also come to see him. Then afterwards I prayed with the sick person, reading for

him some verses from John 11. 8–12. At home getting ready for the Diocesan Conference at Mwiri [some sixty miles away]. 5.30 p.m. Mr. X and I started the journey and we arrived at the conference at 7.15 p.m. 8.30. We started our quiet time with an introductory talk by the Bishop, who was to lead the conference.

25–26 August (Sunday). The Diocesan Conference.

27 August. I rested at home, reading books etc.

28 August. 7.15. I took morning prayers. Eight people attended. 9–10. Confirmation class. 10–12. Office work: correspondence.

29 August. 7.15. Morning prayers. 12 attended. 8.45–9. I took prayers in one of the girls' schools. 9–12. Mr. X and I went to town to buy things required for visitors. These visitors were the Ordinands from the Upper Nile Diocese. 2–3 p.m. We prepare the place and get ready to welcome the visitors. 3–4. Bible class to hospital nurses. 5–6. Visited Christian homes.

30 August. 7.15. I took morning prayers and eleven people attended. 9. Went to town to see the public water supply officer on account of my complaints about the running short of water in our home; the matter was dealt with fairly well. 11–12. Baptism class. 1.45 p.m. Two Christians came to see me about their marriage registration. 3–5. My brother and I went to see our aunt who was very ill and we brought her into hospital.

31 August. 7.15. Morning prayers. Eleven people attended. 8.30–12. I took round the visitors (Ordinands) to see some important places in my parish, starting with the Diocesan Offices, then to the C.M.S. Hospital. They visited the Nurses' Training School, Maternity building, Clinic, Wards and Operating Theatre. After leaving the hospital, we went to the Sanyu Babies Home for motherless children. It was a very interesting time. 2.30–3. Dr. X asked me to go and talk to one patient in hospital about her spiritual needs. 4–4.45. Baptism service in the Cathedral. 5–5.30. I attended the Fellowship meeting; only thirty minutes. 5.30–6.30. Attended the choir practice for the Sunday service.

II. *Father X.Y., Anglican priest in the U.M.C.A. of S. Tanganyika, visits his flock in the mountains.*

August 6th. Started a big 'ulwendo' to the stations on the Manda-Milo road. I left the head station for Mfufu, a walk of 2 ¼ hours to the north: in the afternoon eighteen Christians came to confession, following Evensong and Preparation for Communion. In the morning, according to his custom, a priest says his prayers and after these he begins Mass. But there are some difficulties in this parish; some Christians stay in their houses when the priest arrives and then come early next morning wanting to make their confessions and to communicate. To cure this bad custom we must refuse their appeal and teach them that it is the work of a priest in the morning to prepare himself before he begins Mass; the time for his other works, except when there is really good reason, is in the afternoon soon after his arrival in the village.

August 7th. On the second day, after Mass, I heard cases needing church discipline, counted and wrote up the collection, and then set off for the next village. I walked for just over two hours to Ndilima; it was a cloudy day, more like May than August, and it even rained a little. After resting there, I began hearing confessions at 3 p.m. and at 4 we had Evensong and Preparation for Communion; in all there were sixteen communicants next day.

August 8th. A walk of 1½ hours next morning brought me to Lupila. The monitor was not there; he and his wife had just gone home without waiting to ask his priest-in-charge's permission, leaving the station without anyone to look after it. So it was for the padre himself to do all the works of the station, his carriers blowing a ram's horn to call people. After a long time of waiting, only three out of the total of eleven Christians of the village turned up; some had gone to find food as it was the hunger-season.

August 9th. After Mass, when the three Christians communicated, I walked to Kilumbo, a distance of four miles. There I called the four young unconfirmed Christians and the one catechumen to see what they knew of the Faith. They only looked at me without saying anything; they have no teachers to take their classes, and they cannot be expected to learn much when a priest can only come once a month to their village. After this, five communicants came to their confessions; Evensong followed.

Rain and cold was heavy every day after we left Kilumbo. I was very glad to climb a high hill, up, up, up and up until we reached the top.

August 12th. It was so cold at night that I could not sleep. After Mass, when four communicated, we journeyed for an hour to Ngalawale. There were eighteen confessions here, and after Mass

4. "In journeyings oft. . ."

on the 12th we left for Mene, the last Manda mission station on the road to Milo. Sixteen Christians came to confession and Communion here, and there was an Infant Baptism after Mass.

We went on down the hill, down, down, down, until we reached Nindi. Fifteen Christians came to confession and Communion. Then I remembered that for two years running I had been on a journey for the Feast of the Assumption and so was unable to sing the Festival High Mass; but it is all the same, 'the offering of the Lord's Sacrifice', whether High Mass, Sung Mass or Low Mass.

At our next village, Mhangaji, the monitor had had to be dismissed from his work for receiving a dowry for a bad marriage of one of his relations. There were only four communicants; the offertory was 30 cents (= 3 ½ d.). Our flour was now finished and there was no more tea.

August 16th. I left Mhangaji for Mukwe through similar country, hills and gorges one after another for 10 miles. Now I can be proud of my race; certainly I am 'an African of the Africans', and it is for me to work for the Africans. I live as they live, and if they are short of food, and have only water, I also have the same experience, and work for them gladly. Assuredly I am proud to be an African priest and to work as an African for the Africans.

Mukwe is not a good place; except for the monitor and his family, all the Christians are under church discipline for marriage irregularities; I heard some of these cases after Mass next morning.

It was a 2½ hours' walk to our next village through Makata where there is no longer a monitor, and the Christians are living idle, refusing to build a church; I talked to the men about the meaning of being a Christian and urged them to cease being lazy.

Hurrah! when I reached Idusi the monitor gave me a letter from my wife; she had also sent me some flour, having heard of our hunger on the journey. I was getting tired by this time and had caught a cold. Our next stop was Mpela, the last station of our journey. My cold had developed into a fever, but I have finished the work in all the villages I intended to visit during August. When I got back to my station at Kipangala, Paul, my youngest child, did not recognize me; he had not seen my face for 17 days.

The work at Manda is not large, but it is hard; it is discouraging; its greatness is of walking. Many of the Christians in the parish are under church discipline, and they know very little about Christianity. I am very disappointed here at Kipangala; although there are 70 communicants, the average on Sundays is only 20; they are more fond of drinking than of coming to the Holy Sacrament. I am trying to teach them about the Sacraments on Sundays when I am here; I do this after Mass in order that they may have time to ask questions. It looks as if many of the Christians in this part of the country were baptized, confirmed and began to communicate too soon; they know not what the Sacraments of the Catholic Church are, nor how we can receive them, nor in which ways they can use them.

III. *Rev. D. M. R., Central African Federation*; pastor of a Methodist Church in mining area. In 1892, D. M. R.'s father, a Sotho catechist, was sent from Transvaal to assist the missionaries in Rhodesia. D. M. R. has two brothers in the Methodist ministry. Mrs. R. is employed by the B.H. Mine Welfare centre as senior African Woman Assistant Officer, and works among the women living in the Mine Compound. The family has one boy and four girls still at school: one is doing senior secondary education, two are doing their junior secondary, one is doing nursing and the youngest is still in elementary school.

Daily routine: 5.30 a.m. quiet time for prayers. 6–7 (or 8) a.m., odd jobs at home, breakfast. These routine notes are omitted here.

August 1956

11th. At 5.30 a.m. got up for quiet time of prayer. At 5.45 a.m. odd jobs at home. These include vegetable garden, flower garden and cleaning the surroundings before breakfast. My wife (Mary) shares this work with me before we go to our actual work.

8.15 a.m.: Saturday morning is usually set aside for interviewing teachers as well as the Circuit and District Evangelist. At 11.30 a.m. they all left, and I went to town to collect mail and to do a bit of shopping. At 12.30 p.m. returned to my office to carry on with my work. 2.45 p.m. to 5.45 p.m., Leaders' Meeting. We get reports from leaders in different sections of the town. Some are very encouraging reports; others very disheartening. After the meeting had a talk to a few individual leaders about their personal problems. At 7.30 p.m. went home for dinner. At 8.30 p.m. returned to my office for Sunday preparation.

12th. At 6.30 a.m. went to Hospital to pray for very sick patients. At 7.30 a.m. returned home for breakfast and after that went to the church to arrange pews before people come. The minister has a duty to train them so that in the future as they gradually learn they should be able to do these things for themselves. At 9.30 a.m. went to my vestry till 10.15 a.m. At 10.30 a.m., a united service lasting until 11.30 a.m. At 11.45 a.m. Holy Communion (N.B. In the Urban Area, Holy Communion is administered every first Sunday of the month; in the Rural Area once a Quarter only.) At 2.30 p.m. went to Central Prison for service. At 3.30 p.m. left for Adult Preparation Class in Baptism which is held at the main Church. At 5 p.m. to hospital for evening service with off-duty hospital orderlies and patients who are permitted to leave their beds. At 7 p.m., returned home; after dinner, Scripture reading, and at 10 p.m. retired to bed.

13th. At 6 a.m. went to Five Acre Plots to supervise building repairs being done on one of the class-rooms. At 8.30 a.m. returned home. Paid the Contractor some cash in advance. At 9 a.m. called on the Education Department Officers to make enquiries. From there I proceeded to Bw. five miles out of the town for pastoral visit. Here I met one of the women who was once a member of the Watch-Tower Movement. She now wants to join us, so I advised her what to do. At one o'clock returned home. At 2.15 p.m. went to Mine Western farms. There are three elderly men who no longer come regularly to church. On arrival I found that two had fallen into bad habits of heavy drinking, whilst the third was hindered by ill-health from coming to church. I prayed with these men individually in their homes. At 5 p.m. returned to the church for the Catechumens' Class. (N.B. this class is under a trained Leader who very much appreciates my presence.)

Whilst in this Class a woman arrived to tell me about the trouble between her and her husband. I decided to go with her at once. On arrival, the husband did not want to listen to me. He was furious, and wanted to get rid of her at once. He thinks that by going to church his wife meets with other men, so he must send her away and find some one who has no interest in religion. I invited him to come with her to church so that he can see these things for himself and not be misled by other people, but he could not decide just then. I asked him to join in prayer with us in his own house and he agreed, saying she could stay while he thinks what next step to take. I felt he was convinced by the power of the Spirit of God. At 12.45 a.m. returned home.

14th. 8.45 a.m.–11.30 a.m. worked in the office on Government and District correspondence. 11.35 a.m. went to see how the couple whom I had counselled yesterday were getting on. I was gratified to see that he had now decided not to send his wife away. He only said, 'You pierced my heart by what you said to me last night'. At 2.30 p.m. went out for the School inspection at Five Acre Plots, four miles away. I returned home at 7 p.m. and found two teachers from the Government school waiting for me. One of them had come to ask me if I could conduct his wedding. At 11.30 p.m. retired to bed after some reading.

15th. 8.45 a.m.–11 a.m. Office work: typing Government & District correspondence. At 11.5 a.m., a message from hospital to say that one of our members from the Rural Area is seriously ill, and has just arrived by ambulance. On arrival I noticed that at this stage doctors cannot do anything to save his life. I knelt and prayed for him and his wife and young brother who stood by. At 1 p.m. returned home. Just before I could sit down to have my lunch a message came again from the hospital to say, 'Come quickly, that man is about to die'. I left immediately. At 3.30 p.m. returned home. Went into my Church vestry, began to prepare my talk for the Wednesday evening devotions. After devotions, returned to hospital to see J. K. and still found his condition the same. After praying for him, returned home at 8 p.m.

16th. 6 a.m.–8.10 a.m. Hospital, found J. K.'s condition still the same. 8.15 a.m.–10.30 a.m. visited the rest of the Hospital wards praying for those in need. Returned home. Started preparation for my Rural Tour. At 12 went to collect mail. 2.15–4.10 p.m. worked in my office. 4.15 p.m. left for hospital. Found J. K. about to die. At 4.55 p.m. J. K. passed away peacefully. Prayed for the family and then returned home. After dinner continued with my preparations for my journey tomorrow.

17th. At 8.10 a.m. went to hospital to find out about the exact time for the funeral from the relatives of the deceased. I was told

2 p.m. But with the African, '2 p.m.' may mean anything up to 4 p.m. At 2 p.m. I returned, and waited patiently at the mortuary until 3.30 p.m., when some one came to say that the funeral had to be postponed until tomorrow morning. Then I pointed out to the people that I must leave tomorrow for a place sixty miles away to take service and Holy Communion on Sunday and the people are expecting me to arrive on Saturday afternoon. After some discussion with them we finally agreed that the funeral service should take place at 9 a.m. on Saturday. I returned home. I have wasted much time to-day. Nothing good was achieved.

18th. 8.45 a. m. went to the mortuary and still found that nothing had been done. Some of the relatives of the deceased arrived by train this morning from the Copperbelt. His sister especially wanted him to be taken home fifty-two miles away to be buried there. This meant looking for transport. A lorry was found for this purpose but the owner charged 2/6 per mile. This they could not afford and finally decided to have him buried here in town. It was 12 noon. What shall we do? Funeral 2 p.m. Did we start at 2 p.m.? No! It was not until 4 p.m. that we left the mortuary for the cemetery, six miles away. We got there at 5.10 p.m. and I conducted the funeral service. At 6 p.m. left them and rushed home in order to start for my long journey of sixty miles, for I must get there for the morning service and Holy Communion service on time. I tied my bedding onto my bicycle, and after dinner cycled until I got to my destination at 3.30 a.m. On arrival I went straight into a class-room and slept until 6.30 a.m. I was tired and appeared still half-asleep.

19th (Sunday). At about 7 a.m. the nearest village to the school heard of my arrival. Elderly people came to greet me. Messages were sent to other villages to let them know that I had come. At 10 a.m. we all gathered at the small chapel built by the villagers themselves, and had our service with Holy Communion. After break the Leaders and Local Preachers went back with me into the chapel for the Leaders' Meeting. The evangelist who was stationed at this place resigned because he wanted to take up farming. So the people were left without a shepherd. Two of our Local Preachers promised to look after the spiritual side of the Church without pay. Reports from Class-Leaders received. Two headmen who were once disciplined applied for restoration. Their cases were referred to the Circuit Quarterly Meeting. At 3 p.m. I went as usual to give Holy Communion to two invalided members. I returned at 5.30 p.m. After dinner I went back into the village for a Camp-fire prayer meeting.

20th. 6 a.m.–7 a.m. Got myself ready for the inspection of the school. Visited the new site where I am building a new two-classroom block and a teachers' house with burnt bricks. Work was very slow, through lack of proper supervision from the contractor. At 8.30 a.m. returned to the school to see the children and their teachers at work. At 4.30 p.m. left Sh. School for Kw. Church ten miles away. I got there just before dark. After dinner had a talk with the elderly Christians.

21st. At 10 a.m. United service with Holy Communion. After a short break, the Leaders' Meeting took place. Several matters were discussed, including two cases of discipline; the two men concerned had divorced their wives and got married to younger ones. Both were referred to the forthcoming Quarterly Meeting. At 2.45 p.m., I left for Ka. School where I arrived in the evening (twenty miles distance). After dinner I called for a Camp-fire meeting. It was well attended. This School was opened last year in July. Apart from the teacher there are no Christians, as yet.

22nd–23rd. School inspection.

24th. Spent most of the morning in my office. At 11.45 a.m. went to the bank to draw money for teachers' salaries. 12.30 p.m. returned home. Soon after lunch a woman arrived, Mrs L. M. N., complaining about her husband. She is one of our oldest members in S. The husband, once a Jehovah's Witness, is now a member 'on trial' in our Church. I advised her to return to her home since I could see nothing serious in what she had said. But I told her that I would call on them on Saturday afternoon. So she left peacefully. At 3.30 p.m. went to the M.W. Farms to visit my elderly men and one invalided woman member. At 4.30 p.m. returned for Bible study-group. Special lessons are prepared for this group, and in my absence they continue to meet on their own. 6.10 p.m. to the hospital. Had prayer with those in need. 8 p.m. returned home. After a meal, did some reading.

IV. *Rev. L. C., Johannesburg.* His father began about 1890 as a houseboy of the first representative of a Scandinavian Lutheran mission in Natal, and has remained one of the most solid Lutheran laymen in the district. L. C., now about 35, had four years in a teachers' training college, served for some years as a teacher, then four years at the Lutheran Theological Seminary. Being placed in Johannesburg he seems to have been slightly influenced by the bewildering religious atmosphere of the Rand in which African churches of Ethiopian and Zionist types and European-governed ecstatic organisations such as 'Full Gospel' flourish, and exert an influence which colours important sectors of African church life on the Rand. The city curfew between 10 p.m. and 5 a.m. has stimulated churches of this kind to have all-night shouting services in their chapels. As members cannot return home during curfew time they prefer to spend the night singing, preaching, and praying.

Oct. 29th. At 8.30 a.m. I went to my office and prepared the sermon for the coming Sunday, using Lange's Commentary. But I have to hurry and prepare myself for the Executive Committee meeting of the Johannesburg Regional Christian Council, to be held at 10 a.m. Quite a lively spirit was shown throughout the whole discussion in the Committee. But I did not join any of the discussions with the exception of a few direct questions asked by the chairman, which I had to answer. Matters are tackled at a top level and quickly come to decisions. I was the only African member present, so I had to be very careful. The meeting closed at 11.45 and I was asked to lead in prayer.

At 2 p.m. I had a wedding service to take. We had to wait until 2.30, when the bride came to tell us that the bridegroom had gone home to Delmas to fetch a ring. The bride's father left for work at 2.45, being discouraged. We decided to have the wedding service at 9.30 the following day if both bridegroom and ring were available.

After that I was in my office preparing examination questions for my night-school class (adult education): mental arithmetic and arithmetic. I prepared 20 sums for mental arithmetic and 10 sums for arithmetic.

At 6 p.m. I went down to the basement where the classes (Intermediate and the Seniors) are. 6.30, they do mental arithmetic for 15 minutes and 6.45–8, arithmetic. At 8 p.m. Sithole, our principal teacher, closes with a short prayer.

We have our supper at 8.30 p.m., sour milk. My wife, who does not take sour milk because of her bad chest, takes sausages and bread. We have a short prayer and retire for the night.

Sept. 27th. At 8.30 a.m. two women come from Pimville Location, one of them a church member who no longer comes to church but of course regards herself as a Lutheran; the other woman is a friend of hers. She complained that her son, who should have been married some time last year, has not been married even now, because the father and mother-in-law had quarreled about the *lobolo* money. During this long discussion Rev. F. (a European missionary) came and I had to attend to him for about seven minutes, discussing some things required for the new Kwasakaza Church Hall, while they still waited for me in my office.

Sept. 29th. Today I was at home the whole day. I finished my sermon preparation, and helped a little in cleaning the yard and the house. At about 11 a.m. I went to town for shopping. At 1 p.m. I came home again, and found Ambrose Gumede, who is the chairman of the Youth League in Doornfontein, waiting. We prepared a short programme for the Youth meeting to-morrow. Mr. A. Mohono came. He is organiser of the Johannesburg Bantu Sunday School. He uses our church basement every Saturday for the training of Sunday School teachers. We had a little talk with him and he started his work at 2 p.m. At 3 p.m. I took a confirmation class. Only one had come at the beginning. I continued for 45 minutes.

At 8.30 p.m., after we had our supper, Mr. Cornelius Masikane, chairman of the 'Sons of Luther' here in Doornfontein came to tell me that they were ready to open a meeting and that I had to lead the devotions. This was held in our new church hall. This was a revival meeting invited by *amadodana* [the Sons of Luther] of Doornfontein; others from outstations had also come. They had invited others from other churches who also came wearing their uniforms. The women members accompanied each group. So everything was quite interdenominational in form. After a hymn and prayer, I read from Rom. 10: 8–13, which was used by all those who were testifying or preaching for the whole night. After that Mr. Masikane asked others of our church who were to lead the meeting for the whole night, and all the leaders of different groups were also asked by Masikane to take the front seats. After the two leaders had both preached on the text for the night the meeting was declared opened to anybody who felt like saying anything on the text. At 10 p.m. I went to bed and left them by themselves. They feel happier when they are left alone without a minister for the whole night. They continued until 4 a.m. on Sunday morning.

Sept. 30th. Sunday. We got up at the usual time in the morning. After cleaning the house and yard we had prayer together. At 10.30, I put candles and flowers on the altar. The Coloureds, who have the 11 a.m. service in our church, started with their service.

Our Zulu service which followed at 3 p.m. started with the Baptism of a child of Christian parents of the Shezi family. The Shezis are for a while staying with us in our house. After the service we had the meeting of elders. This was a very short meeting for the sole purpose of opening Thank-offering envelopes. It was conducted by the chief elder, Moses Mkhize of the Norwegian Mission in Natal. The collection was altogether £7.12.4, which brings our total to £83.2.9 so far collected.

While the elders were meeting, the young people had their meeting and I was there conducting a lesson on the persecutions of the early Christian Church by pagans. I read the story from the book 'How the Gospel Spread' (in Zulu) by B. A. Johanson of the Swedish Alliance Mission. The meeting started with a devotional prayer led by Timothy Shezi, and my lesson followed, taking some 50 minutes. After that, Lazarus Kumalo said a few words about what they had gained from the lesson. We had to close earlier because the 'Sons of Luther' and most members of the meeting were invited by the Shezi family to a prayer meeting.

The 'Sons of Luther' and some of the elders gathered at our house in the dining-room. Mr. and Mrs. S. had prepared some tea and cakes. After tea Moses Mgabadeli led the prayer service. This was a very great spiritual occasion for the Sons of Luther and for the Shezis, because this child was an answer to their prayers since the Shezis had had no child before. Moses Mgabadeli also mentioned that before he had heard anything about Mrs. Shezi's pregnancy he was told in a dream that he should not be worried because Shezi would get a child by the name of *Uzwelihle esiya kulo* ('The beautiful country to which we are going'). Cornelius Masikane, the chairman, suggested that a collection be made for the boy. In a short time £2.6.0 was on the table. This was given to Mr. Shezi, who said a few words thanking all for what had been done for his son. He also asked me to say a word of thanks on his behalf, which I did with pleasure because I wished to thank the 'Sons of Luther' and the elders who had prayed for my wife last Sunday. She has been better since then. Our prayer meeting was closed very late at 8.45 p.m.

After this many departed, and the committee of the Sons of Luther had to meet because Thimothy Shezi, who is their treasurer, was leaving for Natal the following day. All money had to be handed over to the vice-treasurer, Mr. P. N. This had to be done before the committee. They continued with this in our sitting-room until 10 p.m., when they left. We had our supper at 9.30 and rested with joyful hearts after a long and blessed day.

Pastor and Catechist

'The village catechist, with his slender qualifications and very modest pay, is the real hero of the Christian situation in Africa.'[3] Bishop Neill is right in this generous appraisal, and many missions and Churches agree with him. Representative voices in the Presbyterian Church in the Cameroons bear witness to the tremendous role played by catechists in the rapid advance of that Church since 1937. The revival in the Cameroons from that year onwards brought about the rapid opening of no less than four catechist schools (2-year courses) in that one Church. These have now been closed, but the men trained there still form the backbone of the Presbyterian Church. To a large extent it is the catechist who performs the real pastoral work—except administering the sacraments.

The Presbyterian congregations in Southern Angola (Mission Philafricaine) provide another example of an organization in which catechists still play a great role. Here, we are told, there are two kinds of catechists, those who have had four to six months' training 'but not ordained' and those who receive three years' training and who are 'ordained as evangelists'. All the pastors come from this latter category. The pastors have all been catechists and evangelists and have had one year's additional pastoral training over and above their previous evangelists' school. In parts of East Africa and Nyasaland catechists are still regarded as leaders in the local

---

[3] *I.M.C. Theol. Report* I, p. 9.

communities. 'For twenty-nine days in every month, these communities are looked after by a teacher, who is already fully occupied in running the school, or by a catechist, who may not always have been very well instructed himself. Apart from the small amount of attention that a priest can give on his monthly visits, the entire work of teaching catechumens, confirmation candidates, first communion classes and penitents' classes is done by the teacher or catechist.'[4]

But if there is thus a hero in the African situation, there is indeed very little hero-worship; in fact, the catechist has of late become the object of sharp and persistent criticism in most Protestant churches.

'It is degrading for an educated man to go into a rural district and become a catechist.' 'We must get rid of our group of catechists.' 'Of our 1550 catechists some are well trained, others are a bunch of riff-raff. They are not qualified to take any other work. The name catechist has fallen into disrepute in our country.' These are some of the comments made by African pastors and Western missionaries in French Equatorial Africa and the Cameroons in conversation with us.

The situation has changed greatly in a couple of decades. In the 1920's and 1930's, most of the work on the frontier was still the responsibility of the teacher-catechist in the village. He had an important position in the community. On the great day when the French or Belgian or British administrator inspected the village, it was taken for granted that the catechist would be there with his school class, in his capacity of trusted representative of his African group and of the White mission. In his world he represented the religion and the power of the Whites and had a certain prestige because of this. In parts of the Cameroons and elsewhere he is still the big *massa* of the village. More important was his place in the irresistible advance of the missionary occupation of Africa. As the man on the frontier, he was in immediate face-to-face contact with paganism; he represented the decisive forward thrust of a great religious movement throughout the Continent.

To-day, with the rising level of general education, catechists are becoming more and more isolated. Most of the evidence goes to show that the position of the catechist is not very strong.

---

[4] E. A. Maycock, *The Vocation of an African Priest*, 1956, p. 4.

He is still there, of course, in his little wattle-and-daub chapel, but aware that he has become something of an embarrassment to the mission and to his Church. His position half-way between pastor and voluntary lay helper is felt as an anomaly. Many churches have time-regulated plans with a view to reducing their number of paid catechists and replacing them by ordained pastors *and* voluntary helpers. A strong Protestant Church on the Ivory Coast —the outcome of the great Harris mass movement—with a Christian community of some 50,000 (20,000 full members) had three pastors and 160 catechists in 1949.[5] Three years later the proportion of pastors to catechists was 6 : 126, and the dynamic British missionary in charge—single-handed, but undaunted—was determined to reduce the number of catechists drastically and treble the number of pastors. Instead of salaried catechists, voluntary 'local preachers' were appointed. In this Church, the declared policy has been put into practice with great determination. Must Churches in other countries share the same intent, but sometimes do not translate it into action. With rising general education possible candidates for the catechist's task become fewer in number, and most new catechists nowadays are to be found among those who have failed to get an entry into ordinary centres of higher education, or who have proved unsuccessful in examinations. A leading, highly educated African pastor in the French Cameroons was emphatic on this point: 'For the future, the catechists must disappear. Those we get now only destroy our work.'

The Methodist Church in Ghana has had reason to give special attention to this problem. In principle, missions of Methodist polity rely on a corpus of class leaders and local preachers. Dr. S. G. Williamson, of the University of Ghana, has pointed out that this system has in fact never been developed in Ghana. From the beginning the paid catechist was used to shepherd the local congregation and this fact then removed the necessity for voluntary class leaders and local preachers. At present the corps of trained catechists is dwindling; the catechist's salary is relatively poor, and most who have any ability take up school work or some other more lucrative employment. 'The churches have therefore to fall back on the much poorer, untrained catechist, locally recruited;

---

[5] The Harris Prophet movement in West Africa 1913–1915, Cf. C. P. Groves. *The Planting of Christianity in Africa*, IV, 1958, p. 45.

and he is generally only marking time until he can get into some better sort of employment, or into a training college for teachers. And because through the years we have relied upon the paid agent, there is now no reliable body of class leaders and local preachers to carry the work in the churches. In the towns there are the ministers; it is the villages that suffer.'[6]

In 1957, in a clear-sighted report entitled *Lay Leadership in West African Churches,* the Methodist Missionary Society stressed that in West Africa they should first of all move towards the provision of a greater number of ministers. 'We need more ministers far more urgently than we need catechists.'

The precarious situation in which catechists find themselves has brought about a fairly rapid turn-over in this group of workers. A Uganda pastor had this to say: 'Very few men stay on as catechists for life. In olden times our catechists used to stay. But the financial situation nowadays makes this difficult. Only those with a reasonable prospect of advance wish to carry on to-day. The others get tired and become whole-time farmers.' There are other openings for such men in Uganda. As a lay-reader a man is in theory supposed to get seventy shillings per month, but often finds that in his particular congregation that sum of money has to last three months instead. He then takes on a job in the Public Works Department or as an office 'boy' and has a guaranteed wage of 150 shillings per month.[7]

In Dahomey, the Methodist missionary reported that some 80 per cent of the catechists were absorbed by business soon after the completion of their training. In the British Cameroons the catechists in 1951 had progressed so far as to stage a strike.[8] Whether this method is going to be used in other parts of the continent

---

[6] S. G. Williamson, 'African Theological Survey', dated 9.2.1950. Typewritten.

[7] In the period between the two world wars the Protestant catechists in the Belgian Congo had in most cases to perform heavy state-required labour, particularly road work. New legal conditions were officially laid down as from 1945. Catechists and others employed by the missions, and totally dependent for their living on mission remuneration, were exempted from such duties. Voluntary helpers, on the other hand, who did not work 'full time' for the mission, had to take such tasks along with their fellow tribesmen. G. Sand, head of the A.I.M.O., Belgian Congo, 5.11.1945 to H. W. Coxill.

[8] *Evangelisches Missions-Magazin,* 1951, p. 111.

remains to be seen. The promotion from church catechist to garage mechanic is one which is quite alluring in South Africa and elsewhere. A catechist in Western Tanganyika whom I knew in about 1945 as a dynamic preacher and fisher of men is to-day the local president of the communal hunts of wild pigs. Why had he given up his church post? Well, he had 'simply got tired', and—as the local Revival group suggested—'he loved wordly glory and he hoped to curry favour with the Government'. His case is not unique. There are many who like this man retire from the catechist's work, although of course not all of them will rise to the lofty heights of president of a local hunting association!

But there are also hundreds of wonderful examples, throughout Africa, of Christian men who have withstood the alluring possibilities of better pay and higher status in society, in order to serve their Lord as simple catechists. We knew personally a case in Western Tanganyika, Filipo K. was in 1944 one of the twenty-two students in the final class in a Swahili teachers' training college (the standard at that time was 6 years at an elementary school and 3 years' teacher training). Filipo was the only one who failed in the examination. While his comrades became comparatively well-paid teachers and some of them eventually pastors in the Church, Filipo disappeared for a few years. In November 1953, I was to meet the new catechist in the township of the area. It was Filipo. He had gone through a deep spiritual renewal through his contact with the *Balokole* revival and now served the Church. We asked him about his experiences: 'Well, Bwana, I always thank God that I failed in my exam. that time. Because if I had passed, I might have become the kind of a teacher who does not pray to God. But now God found me in my misery and I live to serve Him.'

Generally speaking, there exists to-day a remarkably high degree of co-operation between the pastor and his catechists. The latter have of course their particular authority in their local congregation. In Angola we were told that only few pastors dare tell an evangelist about some mistake which the latter is supposed to have made, though on the other hand there are many cases in which the pastor tends to be fairly domineering with regard to the group of catechists. In some Churches one hears complaints that the pastor treats a catechist as his 'house-boy'. In the Cameroons, a pastor may, for instance, expect the local catechist to work for him in his garden, although this is becoming more and more resented. Where caste distinctions are upheld between nobility and peasant groups (cf. p. 105), it has until recently been the rule that a priest belonging to the nobility group cannot eat together with cate- chists of the peasant class. Against this background I understood more deeply—and not without being moved—the comment made by two simple Pygmy catechists, now priests in the Anglican Church. They spoke to me about Apolo Kivebulaya—the Ganda preacher who became the apostle of the Pygmies: 'Apolo bap- tized us, and—he took his meals together with us.'

Pastor and Elders

The voluntary elders are the pillars of the local congregation. They represent in fact considerable influence and power. In the Haya Church, Tanganyika, this fact is marked by their position in the church house at Sunday morning services. While the or- dinary church members are seated on the grass, the elders sit on stools or chairs, from whence they survey their flock. This sym- bolizes their position in the whole of the local congregation; they are the eyes and ears of the pastor and are supposed to report to him any development which requires his individual or their com- mon attention.

A sympathetic description of the urban elder's church work is given by pastor S. M. on the Rand. His words also interpret very well the relationship between pastor and elder in a Lutheran Church in Alexandra Township, Johannesburg.

> Every week I have a meeting of elders. In our very thickly populated urban area we have nearly every week some new phase in our work, which has to be dealt with as soon as possible, if not in some cases immediately. Our aim is to get a fair synopsis of our work, co-operate in all we do and have a common understanding of how to meet problems cropping up daily in our work. We unite in prayer and think of the individuals whom we are serving or of the problems laid before us and ask for guidance. We discuss the cases brought to us and always consider what the Word of God can tell us on the subject. Every elder knows that he has been chosen to serve God and his fellow- men. He has to be a leader and he is responsible for the well-being of the congregation, the property of the Church and of every individual soul under his care. He visits the sick, the ones in need; he tracks the

lost or those gone astray; he comforts those in sorrow and those bereaved. Very often if they are free and I have to serve on our out-stations, they help in holding services, and perform emergency baptisms, which of course afterwards have to be confirmed by the minister should the child survive. They bury the dead, when I am unable to attend. I try to let them feel their responsibility. Church-work is an 'every-man's work'. We all must confess our faith and here is the chance to practice it. This applies also to the prayer-women.

The personal contact and co-operation between pastor and church elder represent the unifying cement of the local Church. If these ties are strong, church life will thrive. In some city congregations, tribal tensions may sometimes cause difficulties. A local congregation under an elder representing a tribal tradition other than that of the pastor may come to experience considerable tensions. There are East African coastal towns where the local elders rule dictatorially over the Church and the pastor, who hails from a mountain tribe some hundred miles away, is despised and criticized.

The intellectual standard of village leadership being what it is, a great deal of tact and generosity of spirit is required of the pastor in order to keep the church work going. From Central Zululand the following case was reported to me by the pastor, a very gifted and balanced leader: 'At outpost X., we have an elder Y. He has only had a Standard III education, is a first-generation Christian and has all the rigorous zeal of the convert. He has translated the traditional Zulu manliness-ideal *(ubudoda)* into terms of the Church in such a way that he has a tendency to be too rough; in church discipline he always wants rigorous methods. He antagonizes the pagans rather than tries to win them through kindness. I tell him: "We must be kind and friendly towards the pagans." He then bursts out: *Sus 'abahedeni pakathi kwethu, bahlal' endaweni yabo* (Away with the pagans from our midst. Let them go where they please). The congregation felt that elder Y. went too far. They also feel sorry for me, as he always opposes me. I am in his way and he thinks that his ideas alone are Christian. The local Christian group have in fact approached me with a wish to having Y. replaced by somebody as an elder. But I need opposition, and in the end I shall win this man. So when the local congregation insisted that Y. be replaced, I managed to keep him at least as a substitute.'

5. The Ministry of the Word and the Ministry of the Sacraments

This case reflects rather well the delicate balance between local leader and local group, and the task of the pastor.

An interesting situation arises when a well established voluntary elder holds sway and a young, recently graduated and ordained pastor appears on the scene. One such case which I know personally fairly well springs to mind. Elder Timoseo holds a very solid position in his congregation. Recently he built a magnificent stone church for his local group and by the great influence of his personality managed to collect 30,000 shillings—three-quarters of the total cost. Pastor Teofrasto had been a school teacher for a few years and was ordained after three years of theological education. He was posted to Timoseo's church, but never succeeded in gaining the confidence of the congregation. At district meetings he managed to keep away and it was natural that Timoseo, the elder, represented the group. Another pastor, chary of what he regarded as too strong lay tendencies in this and other local groups, commented: 'Timoseo is the Great Elder in this congregation, and the pastor has no words. But this is all wrong, the pastor ought to be The Great One *(omukulu)* in the congregation.' In the end, the Synod decided to move the pastor and have him replaced by an older man. In this particular case it was not, however, a case of the victory of seniority over youth, for this particular tribe sets great store by youth at the present time. It was rather the weight of the elder's personality that counted.

It would, however, give a one-sided picture of pastor-elder relationships of we did not bring out something of the generous and friendly co-operation and fellowship between these two parties which in many cases form the backbone of local church life in Africa. When one takes into account the reverence for seniority which characterized traditional social relationships in Africa in the past, it is gratifying that generally speaking the young college-trained pastor is readily accepted as a leader or a potential leader. In the pastor's co-operation with the Council of Elders (or equivalent terms), on matters relating to church discipline, or extension work, some of the most solid and enduring congregational work is taken care of.[9] There are examples of a willing give-and-take be-

[9] O. Mannoni, in his important study of the 'psychology of colonization' and the 'vacuum' experienced by politically dominated people, has for Madagascar made the helpful suggestion that the *fokon'olona,* or the village council, be rejuvenated in order to fill out this vacuum. Mannoni, *Prospero and Caliban,* 1956.

tween pastor and elder, an exchange of experience and information and, on the deepest level, real fellowship in prayer to God.

We are now in a period when African pastors write in their
own languages studies of the ministry of the elder in the Church.
One of the most remarkable of such books is written in Kinyanja
by Rev. J. S. Mwale of the Dutch Reformed Mission, Nyasaland.
In the Appendix we reproduce a translation of the table of contents of this little book, Appendix IV, p. 333.

A special case of leadership by the elders is the church choir-
master in some of the cities, particularly in Western Africa. The
fundamental role of song and music as necessary expressions of
religious group life is accentuated in some of the autonomous
and semi-autonomous churches on the West coast. In the first
place, African leadership will tend to stress the role of song and
music in the church services more than the Western missionaries
ever thought possible. At Sunday morning services in some congregations in Douala I discovered that the whole worshipping
group did in fact consist of the sum of five solid choirs who all in
turn made their lively contributions to the service. But these
choirs have not only musical interests. They have become associations for mutual help and assistance, in the case of marriage
and dowry problems, weddings, sickness, death, burials, in fact, of
all that matters in life. (Burials belong to this last category as
Herskovits has pointed out in the case of Dahomey: 'burial is the
most important thing in life'.)

In this situation, the clerk, or secretary, of the church choir,
achieves an importance of the first order. He it is who allows,
or refuses to allow, a choir to be sent to this or that wedding or
burial on a Saturday, or to this or that chapel on Sunday morning. The pastors have to keep on especially good terms with this
church officer; he can make or break great occasions in the life
of the local church. His role also shows the emergence of new
group-integrating offices in the church, and it is characteristic of
Africa that this innovation is in the field of music.

Leader and Followers

With the rapid development of the Church into a complicated
machinery of inter-relations between the leaders and the led, a

pastor's administrative ability will often be tried and tested. Some have shown remarkable administrative powers which increase the more the African pastor is trusted with responsibility. Others perhaps, lack administrative ability but show other leadership gifts.

A well-known church leader in West Africa died at the age of 70, having completed over forty years in the ministry. A Westerner who knew him well has this to say of him as a leader: 'Z. was born into one of the "royal" houses. He could have been a chief of one of the important X. states if he had desired. He was a real expert in and exponent of the X. language. He was a poet in his own language and wrote innumerable lyrics. None did more to make possible the publication of the Bible in the language in question. He had had such secondary education as was available 60 years ago. His personal prestige, his family relationships and his innate shrewdness made him an able counsellor to his people. He was, of course, constantly being called upon to "settle their cases". When he was 65, he was elected Chairman of the District. He brought dignity to the office. He was a tall figure, upright and upstanding. But as an administrator he was not competent. Deskwork, planning ahead, chairmanship of committees were not very well done. He lived in the past. He could tell in great detail what happened 30–50 years ago in the country and in the Church, but he could not do the same for what happened a year or a month earlier. A number of great opportunities for the Church were missed, or only very partially taken, during his period of office.'

In the modern world as it is construed, administrative ability will be valued very highly. In the case of Z. his other personal qualities could not altogether counterbalance his failure as an administrator.

With this example from West Africa we contrast one from South Africa. 'To keep a congregation alive there must be visible action.' Thus writes Rev. Stefano Makhobe, at Alexandra, on the Rand. He describes how he leads his people on to their goal:

'To reach my goal I always conferred with my elders and staff of teachers, especially with my helpers and my two evangelists and last but not least with the leaders of our women's prayer league. We built our church, we started to buy a site for our school, we enlarged our existing school, we built a church on an outstation. The women were responsible for the cleaning of the church and its decoration and even outfit. For all this, money is needed and in conformity with my elders and prayer-women's league—the latter under the leadership of my wife—ideas and plans were worked out and carried through. In all the minister must always be the leader and adviser and have organizing ability to keep things in their right place and have the right spirit.

We have records of all baptisms, confirmations, marriages and members in books supplied. We also have a record of all the contributions as paid by each member per annum in a separate book, and a record of all who partake in the sacrament of Communion on each occasion. As regards the statement of finances we have two accounts: the Synod Fund and the Congregation Fund. Our system is supervised by our missionary, accounted for by our secretary and our elders' deputies. This has awakened a keen interest and even competition amongst congregations. For the congregation account the African minister and his elders are responsible and have to report to the congregation.'

Here the pastor reveals himself as the efficient administrator. A conscientious and ambitious African Church leader has managed to create a well-oiled machinery of church organization. His large congregation gladly responds to this initiative.

It is the Methodists who more than others have laid the foundation for efficient church organization in Africa, and other Churches have learned from them. The Quarterly Preaching Plan idea, first introduced by Methodists in West and South Africa, was taken over by other Churches, undoubtedly to their great benefit. With local congregations growing rapidly and expanding over a widespread industrial, semi-urban or country area, it was necessary to hold the total of village leaders together by some such plan as this. Having one's name and particular number on the Quarterly Preaching Plan gives prestige to a local preacher and makes him feel a sense of belonging to a powerful organization. But all this administrative work on the part of the pastor tends to cover up a multitude of problems. As most Circuit Quarterly Plans indicate, the pastor will, at best, visit a particular local group only two or three times a year, perhaps not more than once a year. In these circumstances, the grander the Plan the more symbolic it becomes of the dilemma of the African pastor as a leader of souls: depersonalization instead of immediate personal contact. Some congregations in populous areas are better placed here. At Dabou, the centre of the Harris-revival Methodist Church on the Ivory

Coast, two hundred and seventy-five catechists congregate every Saturday to hear their pastor preach a sermon which on the following day they repeat and modify in their own individual ways; here the personal link is still maintained, and in interesting fashion. In Douala, pastors, catechists and helpers meet every Saturday for sermon-preparation, study and discussion.

But as soon as the congregation spreads and comprises a large number of local groups, represented by particular figures on the Church's Quarterly Plan, the real problem begins. A number of pastors, of course, do not feel the problem. They have taken over from the European the administrative ideal, the ideal of the efficient executive, and this is satisfying, up to a point. Even in rural areas with but weak contacts with Western patterns, Africans are impressed by the paraphernalia of church organization, with its concomitant constitution-making, and its endless row of committees. I found the following case interesting. A church near Lake Victoria has been strongly influenced by the *Balokole* revival. The radicals among the revivalists threatened to break away to establish a more 'spiritual' church on their own. Their opponents, however, were sure that they would not really leave the Church, because, as they told me: 'They love our committees, the newspaper committee and the finance committee.' Administrative know-how has a fascination of its own in Bolenge and Bukoba just as it has in Boston, Birmingham and Bielefeld. The pastor who has a knack for these things emerges as a leader.

On the local plane, the pastor reaches out to a fairly restricted group near his own headquarters. In most churches, more particularly in the 'Christian villages', the Protestant pastor takes morning worship every morning in person in his church or chapel. In essays written by the younger generation for our present study the writers are careful to point out that their pastor establishes personal contact with all. 'He wakes up early in the morning before the church-bell tolls and calls for worship. After morning worship in chapel he shakes hands with his people one after the other where the congregation is not very large, showing a clear face to each one of them before they go to their different tasks.'

'The gifts are manifold', and the leadership qualities required by the African pastor vary. It seems to me, however, to be characteristic of the interplay between African church leader and his flock that a certain quality of large-hearted generosity and humour must be there, while meanness and smallness make for trouble.

One Zulu pastor failed in spite of energetic efforts to lead his flock. He was a man of good intellect and had a training above average. But he had a way of pushing himself without giving due consideration to his people. *Lomuntu uyabusa* (that man does throw his weight about) was the angry comment of the congregation. The missionary tried to warn him but he would not listen. The pastor was killed in an accident, and many complaints against him then came to light, insignificant little things which the conservative congregation could have taken in their stride if it had been another man with just a little more humour and generosity.

As a general rule, however, the African pastor, possibly to a greater degree than his colleagues in other parts of the world, has an innate capacity for establishing contact and for creating a happy and generous atmosphere of fellowship. Rev. M. L. has announced that he must visit Biirabo where church contributions are lacking and the congregation has shown a tendency to slacken in their interest. On the appointed day, he begins his address with a humorous story and all have a hearty laugh, which spreads like an electric current through the whole of the group. Then suddenly the pastor turns around and applies the story to the local church situation. They gasp as they discover the connexion with their own situation, and the pastor has already won his case. They are prepared to do something now.

Such leadership is in the last resort a question of personality. When personality and a consciousness of being a God-ordained pastor and priest are combined, then the kind of leadership is born which carries weight in even very delicate and difficult situations.

Weddings and funerals offer other important contacts between the pastor and his flock. Cases of church discipline and the care of souls bring the pastor and the individual Christian in close touch with one another. Here again it is reported that the wide areas to be looked after by one pastor do not afford the necessary opportunities of unhurried fellowship. In West Africa church members complain that pastoral care has become the prerogative of uneducated catechists, while the pastor on his routine tours of the congregations is drastically referred to by some as 'a commercial traveller in sacraments', but without that personal contact which by definition should belong to his pastoral work.

Too big congregations and too few ordained pastors is not only a question of statistics. It is a question of life and death to the groups, and to individual Christians. The dilemma which the Roman Catholic author Augustin Tellkamp has described by the alarming term 'the danger of strangulation' is one which is well-known also in Protestant churches in Africa (cf. p. 81). The rapid development in evangelistic work has not been followed by a corresponding rise in the number of ordained clergy. The masses are not seldom left without real spiritual care. But the pastor by the same process misses something which is vital and essential. He may be drawn into a big administrative machine, and he may perhaps like it as he seems to control all the wheels and the many modern gadgets. But the face-to-face contact with a real, living, local group may be jeopardized. And if that goes, that which possibly is the charm and charisma of the African pastor—creating real Christian fellowship and community—is in danger of being lost. That would be a great loss indeed.

The Leadership Sieve

How does leadership emerge on the purely local level? If you ask the pastor, he will reply that it is the local congregation which elects its elder or helper. If you ask the people in the congregation, they say that it is the pastor, or priest, who decides. The truth is that the decision is taken by both parties in combination. The finding and appointment of local leaders is an important area of contact and co-operation between the pastor and his flock. Generally speaking, the Western missionary has no longer any influence over appointments on this local level. We shall see how this works out in the Haya Church in Tanganyika.

Elder A. in village X. has just died. His successor must be found. How is it done? Pastor Edward Nchwande replies: 'Men and women in the village begin to discuss names. Why don't we take B? When he passes through our village on his bicycle, he does not do as C., who just passes proudly by. No, he jumps off his bicycle, and approaches and says: "How did you sleep? How are you? How are things? And the other things?" And then he talks! He is the right sort; humble, friendly, approachable.' In another village, on another occasion, they discuss a similar problem. 'D. is our man',

they will say. 'He is always prepared in his heart to help if somebody is ill, or somebody is dead. We must choose him.' Or in a
third village: 'E. is the man we need. He is particularly eager to
inform our pastor about the sick or the dying or when somebody
is in any danger. And our pastor seems to like him, because he is
helpful.' Perhaps in this village there are more than one who
could be selected, a certain *akiba* (supply of leadership timber).
Then of course the pastor chooses between them.

In this particular tribe and church, all my informants stress that
in choosing their local leader they look for the man with the
friendly and ready smile, an open and joyous face. This is evidence that he has no deceit, in short that he is a man with Christian
humility and love. But not only that. They want a person who can
be expected to help them and 'defend them in front of people in
authority', that is, a representative and courageous man who is
not afraid to plead the cause of his group.

In a very real manner, the pastor can influence the choice of his
own men. Rev. S. K. told me how he goes about this: 'Z. had been
elder for a long time, and there was not much energy and initiative
left in him. I had to get him away. I could not do that directly,
for that would have made him bitter. I called a villagers' meeting
when he was away. There I put a few questions to them: "Why are
there no catechumens coming forward from your village? Why are
the church contributions so low? Why has not the church house
been cleaned?" Then they are bound to reply (and I never need
to mention Z's name): "The one whom you have put in here as
our leader never told us to do these things. We have no leader.
Give us a new leader!" Then I can turn to him directly, in a
private talk. I speak nicely to him and I say: "My brother, just
tell me if you find that this work is too heavy for you." Then he
will reply: "I am old and tired. Let us have a new elder in this
place." Then I call the group of Christians together and I tell
them about this. I also exhort them saying: "See whether you
have got somebody among you who is a man with energy and a
sense of responsibility. Take him." When I arrived in this Church,
there were forty-two elders. I had to dismiss twelve in this round-
about way. Now there are over a hundred elders, and they all co-
operate well both with me and their local groups.' This pastor
was sure that in his particular church both pastors and local
leaders were regarded as emerging from below, from among the

church people themselves rather than imposed on the Church from above.

Finding the right man for village leadership is one of the most responsible of the pastor's many tasks. It is perhaps not always easy for the most capable man to be available as an elder. The educated layman in town is probably only free on Sundays and cannot give much time to the Church's work. The Usambara Lutheran Church (Tanganyika) on the other hand is a typical elders' Church, largely run by the elders who together have much more power over the affairs of the Church than the ordained pastors. These elders are independent and relatively well-to-do farmers and carpenters who can make themselves free for days in order to do a particular job for the Church. That the sociological and economic basis plays a great role is obvious.

As a general rule, local group and elder get used to one another, grow together and sometimes age together. But crises appear from time to time, and that is where the pastor has to be called in. 'Village A. near Lake Victoria has an elder X., a great leader who has helped his flock very considerably. All of a sudden he gets himself into trouble (this was referred to as "saying certain words"). He takes to drink, starts to beat his wife, drives her away and has dealings with other women. Then some of the Christians warn him, but he won't listen. This goes on and it cannot be kept secret any longer. People begin to gossip and say: "As he went to such-and-such a house, he did this or that, and now we hear that he has had dealings with a girl." Then these people call him before their own local group and accuse him. He listens. Then he says: "Let me decide this case" (kata shauri). Then the whole group, all at once, first mutter and then shout: "No, we won't have that. You cannot decide the case. You are no longer in a position to do so." If X. is a very bad man, he will probably go straight to the pastor and try to accuse his accusers. But the pastor calls the church court together, and then the truth will be found out, and X. will have to be replaced by a more worthy elder.'

In Uganda, a Lango catechist told me that he knew that his own character and that of his colleagues was constantly studied by both priests and certain leading laymen. Reports were written about them to higher and more central authorities, and the ones who were regarded as promising would be invited to go further on the ladder of promotion in the Church. At the same time it was stressed that also in the Lango country villages, leaders were chosen by the local Christians themselves. 'We know the life of So-and-So. We look at his work. He does not drink, nor does he go to dances. He leads a really full Christian life. We want him to lead us.' The man's name will thus be sent to the priest, and the priest's council will probably agree to appoint him.

A Methodist leader in Ghana spoke for Methodist Churches in all Africa when he claimed that the 'class' system of his Church provided the selective machinery with regard to local leadership. Somebody will stand out in the local Methodist 'class' as a man of particular promise. 'Every minister must go about with open eyes looking for budding exhorters'. The weekly leaders' meeting, or an occasional camp meeting will bring out the particular gifts displayed by a young prospective local leader, and that may be the beginning of an important career in the Church.

In many tribes the premium put on seniority will determine the choice also of local Church leadership. Miss Greet Sluiter found that among the Kikuyu, the local groups of Christians in selecting their leaders look for people who are first landowners and whose economic position is comparatively good, and secondly those who are old.

In this respect—as in many others—there are parallels between Kenya and South Africa. Among the Christian Africans who work on European farms in South Africa, the church elder will often be a farm foreman. In the Reserves, if possible, a man belonging to a clan of higher rank will be chosen. At least, that seemed to be the case in Zululand, where the solid chief-type of leader would be preferred to others.

Compare this last point with the conditions in the Central African local group already quoted (p. 167), where humility and helpfulness are the character traits looked for. One cannot altogether avoid a tentative conclusion that there is a parallel, a correspondence between the configuration of the attitudes which traditionally were regarded by the tribe as valuable and the character traits which people expect from a church leader.

The authority and influence of the pastor is enhanced by his skill in handling this important aspect of his work. Catechists in Uganda told me that they know they will not advance higher on the ladder of church offices if they refuse to carry out the priest's orders. On the next step of the ladder this system for some time had a tendency to retard development; the rural deans have until 1952 had a decisive say in choosing catechists and lay readers for preferment. It is recognized that they had a tendency to choose their own yes-men, discarding outstanding men with strong opinions, and in certain cases avoiding also the enthusiasts and revivalists. A new centralized system, introduced in the early 1950's, is expected to overcome this difficulty.

In a more general sociological context, this process has been termed 'sifting' (Siebung). Thurnwald calls it 'the sifting out of personalities perhaps not objectively superior, but conforming to pre-existing value-systems'.[1] In local Christian groups throughout Africa, in villages and city communities, this process goes on continually. From the anonymous mass of believers local forms of leadership emerge within the framework of the Protestant Churches. Decades before political democracy was introduced, simple and ingenuous forms of self-government on the most local level had already begun to develop within the Churches.

In all this, the pastor had, in principle, a decisive role to play. And if he did not play that part—in a situation where there were altogether too few pastors—something very vital was missing from the roots of the Church's life in Africa.

The Pastor and the Women of the Church

Islam is a men's religion, in Africa as elsewhere. The Christian Church in Africa is to a very considerable extent a women's organization. This is the case among Presbyterians in the Cameroons. 'Our Church is a feminine Church.' 'It is thought feminine to go to Church.' In the Reserves in Southern Africa, the congregations consist mainly of women. The Zulus often refer to the Church as an *ibandla labesifazana*, (a women's Church), because of the simple fact that the men are away. They are working on the Rand. The men who stay in the Reserves have for the most part not joined the Church, because of the polygamy issue, or, if baptized, will in many cases keep away from the life of the Church for the same reason.

In some African tribes, women traditionally play a subservient

---

[1] Cf. *American Anthropologist*, LVI, 1954, p. 866.

role. There are other tribes, particularly such as are matriarchal, where women wield a very considerable influence. For the Luapula villages in Northern Rhodesia, Ian Cunnison has pointed out that the village headman's wife and her matrilineage are in a very special position, for they can virtually make or break the village. The ritual depends upon her as much as upon the headman.[2] *Mwadi e mwata*—the queen is the king—is a phrase often heard in connexion with Kazembe and his first wife, Kazembe being the Lunda chief who more than 200 years ago reigned over the villages in that part of Africa. The Rain Queen of the Lovedu (Transvaal) is another famous example. The role of the Queen Mother in Swaziland is still another. The most striking indication of the enterprising spirit of African women under new conditions is afforded by the highly successful market-women in Nigeria and in other countries in West Africa. We refer our readers to an analysis by Sylvia Leith-Ross. She distinguishes three groups of leading women in Southern Nigeria to-day: (1) the traditional élite, chosen 'not by age, and not by money and not by power (descent) but by wisdom'; (2) the élite of wealth, i.e. the 'big' women traders, to whom we have just referred; and (3) a new, intellectual élite. She makes an important point which seems relevant to countries other than Southern Nigeria. Even if there is, here as always, a danger that the new élite may draw apart from the mass of the people, this danger is less among women than among men. 'It is as if the bond of womanhood in itself overrode all the jealousies, rivalries and suspicions which cause so much conflict among the men.'[3]

Women leaders in the churches have a very responsible task. The Church Women's organizations often appear as the very backbone of church activity, though this book is not the place for an analysis of their work. Suffice it to say that their organizations deserve a profound study which will show, I venture to suggest, the great liberating role that the Church is playing in the life of African women and, on the other hand, the role that women are playing in the well-being of the Church.

Local leadership by women presents particular problems to the pastor. In the Cameroons pastors feel that prospective catechists might be crowded out if women were given too free a hand in

---

[2] Ian Cunnison, *Africa*, 1956 (XXVI), p. 13.
[3] S. Leith-Ross, 'The Rise of a New Elite amongst the Women of Nigeria', *Internat. Soc. Science Bull.*, No. 3, 1956, p. 467.

the running of the Church's affairs. Both in Ghana and the Cameroons it was reported to me that women tend to be jealous of each other as leaders, and this was put forward by the men as sufficient ground for keeping the women away from office in the local church. But the situation changes. The example given by the state of Ghana, where African nurses are trained as leaders in mass education campaigns, helps Church people to accept women the more readily as catechists. The Presbyterian Churches of the Cameroons rely to a great extent on the work of women. They have been well trained in democratic procedure by American missionaries, and they never hesitate to express their views in Church meetings. 'It is just wonderful', was a pastor's comment on the contribution of women in the councils of the Church.

In many Protestant Churches, local women leaders are invited to preach. An old experienced Ghana Methodist pastor commented: 'It is a treat to hear them preach.' It is characteristic that it is in a Methodist Church that they serve in this way. A well-known sociologist and churchman (himself a Methodist) pointed out that in Nigeria women have greater responsibilities in the Methodist than in the Anglican Church. On the other hand, Bishop Odutola of Ondo-Benin has instructed his Church that in the diocesan elections they must appoint some women as representatives from the parishes to the Synod. The organization of South African Methodist women, known as *manyano,* is very important and it has influenced other Churches, such as the Lutherans. In Katanga, in the Belgian Congo, the *kipendano* organization of Methodist women has a relevance not limited to the church sphere in the narrower sense. For instance, they run a co-operative bank for their sick. Pastors' wives traditionally play a central role in these groups, and the pastor exercises most of his influence in this important sector of the Church through his wife.

At Dondi (Angola) and Bolenge (Belgian Congo) women without much elementary education but with much energy, enthusiasm and good-will have taken on the task of 'deaconesses' in the Church, and are known to do excellent work in this capacity.

How far a leader should go in promoting women's leadership is, however, a matter of concern to many pastors. In a Lutheran Church Council in Natal a young woman teacher had been given the office of councillor. As soon as the missionary left on furlough, she insisted that she could no longer serve in this capacity and that she had been forced into the job by the missionary. Her Zulu pastor strongly supported her plea—he had possibly inspired it in the first place—and she withdrew. The fact that she was rather young probably had something to do here with the attitude of both Church and pastor. The missionary had been eager to have a young representative on the Church Council, while the pastor, being a Zulu, set more store by age.[4]

Conservative pastors who insist on Western patterns in the worship-life of the Church are sometimes put off by the fact that in the women's groups African behaviour-patterns show through with greater liberty than in other sectors of the Church; in the *Nsamba Binga,* the Presbyterian women's organization in the French Cameroons, women dance as they sing their Christian songs. The Methodist women's choir in Kolwezi, Katanga, in the same way dance happily as they sing their hymns and songs. In Sierra Leone, Methodist women have their own particular shouting services at least once a week. The East African revival has played a great role in liberating the women, and has given them a new self-assurance in their Christian witness.

In the comparatively few cases where more imaginative forms of group expression are to be found they are not seldom the result of Western initiative. As the Western missionary left, the African leader sometimes had a tendency to be over-cautious. Here is a point which might well deserve to be taken up in group discussions in theological seminaries.

A survey of the Christian Ministry in Africa which did not treat of *the pastor's wife* would be overlooking one who is often a pillar of strength in the local Church. The Protestant pastor in Africa is *a family man*—in that phrase much of the strength, and weakness, of the whole Protestant movement in Africa is summed up. Weakness, because through the family he is tied, by a thousand strong bonds, with the clans on his side and that of his wife. Traditional religious valuations and inherited reactions, and financial

---

[4] Of great importance is a recent development in the (Anglican) Diocese of Pretoria. On account of the Group Areas Act, European sisters can no longer do the work in the locations. The Bishop has started a scheme for training African women teachers for one year for work in the locations.

commitments all exercise their inevitable influence on the pastor's life and restrict his sphere of influence. On the other hand, and at the same time, these same family ties may be of the greatest importance for the pastor's task in reaching out with the Gospel to the community.

It is a source of strength to the Protestant Church in Africa that the official local representative of the Church is not an individual, but a team of man and wife. Their working together as a team is one of the most important factors in the work of the Church. How far is she at present prepared to take up a task of leadership together with her husband?

First, it must be considered that the educational standards of pastors' wives vary considerably from country to country, and from Church to Church. A leading Anglo-Saxon woman missionary with quite unique experience in the field of girls' education in Central Africa told us after her recent visit to many churches in Africa: 'All senior pastors have married uneducated women.' In 1953, we came across theological schools where only some of the wives of students were able to read and write. In a French-speaking theological school of high level the Principal said of some of the students' wives: 'They have got atrophied intellects.' Others again in the same school were alert and capable. In a well-known East African theological school we met a student who had come up against this problem in a way which, unfortunately, is not al-together unique. He had courted a girl who told him that she had a Standard VI education, whereas she was in fact illiterate. She had a sister in a secondary college for girls but this sister was told by her parents not to return home for some time, for the elder sister had to be married off first. In the circumstances, our student married the girl. In the coastal area of East Africa it is the tradition that girls marry very early, not much later than 14 or 15 years old. This often means that until recently they have been illiterate. A woman missionary active in the Mothers' Union in Tanganyika found that even one or two years' education made a great difference to church work as compared with the work performed by a completely illiterate wife. When the *desiderata* have to be reduced to this level, it is a symptom of one of the fundamental weaknesses of general education in certain countries in Africa at present. In recent years great strides forward have been taken by Governments and Missions in the field of women's education, but we found none who thought that complacency about the situation was warranted.[5]

There are other households, particularly in West and South Africa and in Uganda, where the wife has comparatively high qualifications—teachers' training or secondary education—and takes her place among the progressive élite of the community. Recently we discussed this matter at Orlando, Johannesburg, with the wife of a well-known pastor, who himself has played a leading role in local politics. She is class teacher and headmistress in a primary school, leader of the church *manyano* and organist and choir-leader in the congregation, and had also to look after her growing family. 'When in school I worry about the *manyano,* and when I am with the *manyano* women, I worry about what to buy for the evening soup; it is a full life,' she said with gusto and a confidence that belied her complaint about the worrying. A high percentage of pastors' wives, particularly in the urban area in Southern and West Africa, are, like her, full-time teachers. We made special enquiry into the conditions and the role of women leaders in the Methodist Church in South Africa.[6] In a considerable number of cases, the wife of the pastor is engaged as teacher, social worker etc. and we had the overall impression that local women leaders are playing an increasingly important role in church matters.

In one well-known Protestant Church in West Africa, we were told, quite a few of the ministers' wives had their own business in the market, and in this way contributed very considerably to the family income. 'She keeps him in the ministry,' was the comment of a well-known sociologist. The Methodist Church in Nigeria formerly had rules prohibiting such extra income, but it seems that the rule is no longer strictly upheld. The demands from visitors and local neighbours on the hospitality of the manse are often a heavy burden. In Northern Tanganyika, we were told, 'the manse is regarded as an inn where all and sundry think they have a right to stay', and this experience is shared by pastors' families all over the continent. In these cases the extra earning-power—as a teacher, through market business, gardening, farming, knitting—of the wife becomes a very real issue. Above all, in these

---

[5] Cf. Max Warren, *C.M.S News-Letter,* Feb. 1952.

[6] A questionnaire was sent in May 1958 to 300 Methodist pastors. See Appendix V, p. 336.

6. After Church, Sitholeni, Transkei

circumstances she may not find time for church work, and this sometimes leads to tension between pastor and church.

In other cases, and as a general rule, the pastor's wife plays a very considerable role in the Church. Among the Bakongo, we were told, she leads the morning service in the local chapel and takes the catechumens' class. She settles family quarrels, and the pastor, who regards it as his task to be the ultimate umpire, will sometimes be told: 'You are a man and you don't understand these things. Mary, your wife, understands, and we prefer to listen to her.'

The *Balokole* revival movement in East Africa affords some of the most remarkable examples of team-work in the Church between husband and wife. Rev. B. K. and his wife are among the leaders of the movement in Buganda. Characteristically they were converted after both had had a similar dream the same night. 'My wife and I confessed our sins to one another.' Pastors' homes permeated by this revival exert an unmistakable radiation of spiritual power.

The minister's wife through her personality, and often her comparatively good education, can exert a real influence in the local Church. It requires a great deal of tact. She must not push herself forward, and she must show deference to the pastor, who is after all both the minister and her husband. A Zulu minister on the Rand, in his frank autobiography, has some memorable lines on the role of his wife, which in an inimitable way interpret the relationship in the team of husband and wife in the service of the Church:

'God has blessed me with a wife, who at all times was one with me in everything I was able to do, whether at home or in the congregation. She partook in all, was it joy or grief. She was my mirror. I never regretted to have received this comrade of life through the grace of God. As an example of the way my wife and I live together and try to help each other I may mention an incident.

A serious disciplinary case in my congregation and the attitude of a certain group in the congregation gave rise to fear in my heart, that evil manners and disrespect of church rights and order would create a precedent. This would distort our church community and later undermine the respect our Church enjoyed amongst our Bantu people in the Transvaal. I therefore resolved to reprimand my congregation. After a morning service, I asked them to remain and I explained what had happened and the danger it might lead to. Finally I demanded that they should answer me. Several members rose to speak for and against. It appeared as if a heated debate would follow. My wife fearing trouble arose to speak. She did this, to my surprise, unawares and in spite of the tact she usually had shown. But this time I felt, "in a wrong moment". I stopped her with these words: "A Sotho woman does not speak in a *kgoro* (public court-yard in front of the chief's kraal) unless asked to speak or give witness. St. Paul again says: 'Let your women keep silence in the churches, for it is not permitted unto them to speak in the church. Please sit down!" I saw tears in her eyes because I had reprimanded her in the presence of the congregation and of her family relations. But she obeyed. The congregation understood what the point in question was. They saw that due respect had to be given to the WORD OF GOD even if it hurts. Going home, I felt sore at heart having seen the tears. When I entered my home, who was awaiting me but my dear Andronika, still with tears, yet with a thankful smile. "*Morena waka!* (my master!) Thanks for the warning and that you kept your guarding hand over me. Forgive my eagerness to speak, since you are the voice and not I."—I need not mention how I thanked God again for this true comrade, who had understood me.'

The scope and role of the women must be a central concern of the Church. Too little is being done by pastors to give real instruction to the enthusiastic groups of church women. The pastors have not been trained to attend to this important aspect of the Church's life, and their wives are not always capable of doing this, although some ministers' wives play a very considerable role here.

The Pastor and the Missionary

The relationship between pastor and missionary is affected both by principles and personalities and we shall here consider the effect of both.

1. The policy of Protestant missions in Africa was the formation of autonomous churches. Missions of all denominational shades subscribed to the idea. In the nineteen-fifties great strides forward were made. The creation of Anglican provinces of West Africa and Central Africa (and corresponding plans for Uganda and East Africa); the organization of the Methodist West African Council; the dramatic transfer in 1957 of authority to the Presbyterian Church in the Cameroons by the Board of the Presbyterian Church in the United States of America, were examples of a development that was regarded both by Westerners and Africans as necessary and wholesome.

The development on the level of mission policy presupposed another development that was no less important: transfer of real opportunities for leadership to Africans trained for the task. The consecration of a number of African bishops and assistant bishops in West and East Africa is an important case in point. Through these African leaders in our own day, Henry Venn's great initiative is vindicated in happier circumstances than in the days of Bishop S. A. Crowther (p. 44). But the issue had to be fought out on all levels of the Church. It particularly concerned the transfer of authority from the local missionary to the ordinary African pastor.

In order to understand how this worked out in practice, we shall follow in some detail one such example, that of a Scandinavian Lutheran mission in Zululand, where mission work was begun in 1844. Fifty years later, there were gathered 1000 Christians; in 1900 the total was 3000, in 1925 12,000 and 28,000 in 1958. In about 1910, the training of catechists and pastors was begun. The 'visitations' of the General Secretary—one in 1928 and the other 20 years later—resulted in great strides forward on the thorny path of devolution. Here as in other missions it was often the missionary on the spot who represented caution with regard to African leadership, while the mission leader in the Home Board, with a wider experience from other parts of the world—in this case Madagascar —pushed ahead. In 1928, self-government was made dependent on self-support in a way which was regarded as daring at that time. 'When the Zulu Church contributes two-thirds of its expenses, the African Synod will be allowed to take part in electing a European as Superintendent. When the Zulu Church has been able to place African pastors as ministers-in-charge of all the districts and at the same time is responsible for three-quarters of the expenses, the synod may elect an African or a European as Superintendent of the Church.'

The long-range policy in 1928 was not only to increase the number of pastors but also to place these pastors as ministers in charge of local congregations, on a par with Western missionaries.

In order to achieve a better-balanced budget, more easily to be carried by the Church itself, plans were made to reduce the number of catechists. In 1932, this Church had 90 catechists. Of these, 23 had had regular training for three years in a Lutheran Bible School, 9 had studied at a teacher training school, 4 had studied in a private Bible school, and the others—no less than 60 or two-thirds of the total number—were without any particular cate-chists' training. This state of affairs may be taken as fairly re-presentive of corresponding conditions in Protestant missions at the time. In the 1930's efforts were made according to a definite 20-years' plan to reduce the number of catechists in favour of a corresponding rise in the number of pastors. How do such plans work out in actual practice? In 1936 the Church had 13 pastors and 96 catechists. In 1945 they were 17 and 70, in 1958 18 and 55.

In the Church synod in 1945 the leading Zulu pastor, M. J. M., had tabled a question, as innocuous in appearance as such questions always are in synods among the Bantu: 'How can we encourage the local districts in the church?' As the speaker developed his theme, he reminded his listeners of the hundred years of faithful mission work. 'Now we have to develop our Zulu church, born of our dear mother, the X.M.S.' There follow pages of assurances as to how happy he and his colleagues were about the Mother Church. 'We need the missionaries. Without them we would be like orphaned children, and much good work done in love, blood and tears [there is a faint allusion to Churchill, 1940, here] would come to nothing.'

'But in spite of all this, we would not be very happy if the Mother Church is now going to send out a great number of new missionaries, because'—now one could see why our Zulu pastor had done all the humming and hawing—'because this would hinder Zulu pastors from becoming district superintendents. Another mission which began its work in 1876—thirty years later than our dear fathers and mothers in the faith—has already given such responsibility to one of their Zulu pastors. We know this man. He was instructed with us in the theological school, and we may say that he did not then in any way, in knowledge or anything, surpass us. Fathers, let this be the last great gift out of your goodness. Let not everything remain static as in former times. We do discuss these things among ourselves. We do not want to slander you behind your backs. Therefore, Fathers, we speak openly; we are not your enemies, we are co-builders with you; we do not fight. But we speak to you as the child speaks to his father at home. We do not force you, nor do we wish to leave you. We only lift up our hands to our superiors, so that they can think of these things in their missionary conference and forward our wishes to the Mother on the other side of the sea, so that she can decide what she wants to do for us.'

June 1945. This little speech delivered in a Zulu synod is characteristic of a whole epoch in African church history. The attitude is characteristic of time and place. You can see this Zulu pastor, hat in hand as it were, bowing, smiling, pleading, reproducing the whole play of veneration towards the European authority, that play which makes any African into 'a good African' in this corner of the continent. June 1945! It is only a few years ago. And it could happen in so many synods in other parts of Africa even to-day.

And the upshot? The missionaries found it reassuring that the great majority of Africans in the synod seemed to oppose M. J. M's proposal. So many 'good' Africans were there, after all. Was not spiritual power needed for the task? Had Africans such power? (That Europeans had it was taken for granted.) And what of the dangers of nationalism and communism? 'Our pastors might . . .'

A few years passed. The executive director of the Home Board visited the Church in 1949. He was determined to make things move. The earlier long-range plan of devolution had not worked. Twenty-year plans of slow devolution could not stir the imagination. This time, a four-year programme was introduced. In four years the Church had to become self-supporting. Within one year, six or seven pastors *had* to be placed as district superintendents— 'and I don't take "no" for an answer!' Without delay five pastors were accorded status as 'ministers-in-charge'.

June 1951. M. J. M., himself one of the five new ministers-in-charge, rose again the Synod. 'We must not move too quickly. Let us go slowly so that this whole endeavour won't end in a fiasco.

Only men of experience and proved capability must be appointed. Five are enough. The others may not be able to carry this responsibility; then we shall all lose our prestige.'

He was old now, and cautious. He had forgotten the challenge which he himself had given, circumstantially perhaps but courageously, six years earlier. He had become a 'good' African.

Our short story had a happy ending though. The director of the Home Board went right against the cautious hesitations of the leading African ministers (and of the missionaries). Leadership in the Church is part of the apostolic commission given to the Synod, he claimed, and such a commission cannot be waived.

2. Religion is a matter of relationship between persons. This is not the whole truth about religion, but an important part of the truth. The Christian religion first spread in Africa because of personal contacts of love and loyalty between Western missionary and early converts.

The first congregation was the missionary's household. Dr. Ernst Johanssen has interpreted this in an admirable way with reference to the beginning of Protestant work in Ruanda.[7] His example is relevant for all Africa. Personal friendship between T. B. Freeman and Chief Shodeke in Abeokuta and between Pilkington and Duta in Uganda—this was the stuff of which the beginnings of Protestant Church history in Africa were made. A fairly high percentage of the first generation of pastors had as youngsters served as house-boys in missionaries' homes. They learned English or German or French from the missionaries' children, and picked up European ways. 'The old missionary took me into his home as a son'—that statement in the autobiography of a Zulu pastor, now working in *apartheid*-ridden Johannesburg, is the epitome of the early lives of many pastors and teachers throughout the length and breadth of Africa. We have already noticed that a great many African teachers received their calling to the ministry through the example of the missionary. The Anglican catechist Hugh Semboja on his deathbed thought that he saw Bishop Frank Weston of Zanzibar beckoning him to come to the heavenly joy.

In those early days the personal contact with the White missionary—who in his turn possibly had easy access to the officers of the colonial administration—gave the African a certain status

---

[7] Ernst Johanssen, *Führung und Erfahrung*, vol. I, 1932.

and prestige. As a preacher of the Christian religion, the African knew he had the backing of the missionary and the administrator and of the two mighty systems or powers which these two White men had come to represent.

Things have changed quite considerably since then. The change which has taken place in the Church has an interesting parallel in the State. Dr. Fallers, writing on the Basoga in Uganda, observes that the older generation of *saza* chiefs had grown up in the homes of English missionaries and had received an intimate knowledge of European ways which the modern secondary-school-trained generation of chiefs does not possess to the same degree, although they may be much more fluent in the English language.[8] 'Techno-logical progress has tended to decrease the intimacy of Soga-Euro-pean contacts. Aloofness... has its dangers. The official imper-sonality which in the Western world is accepted as part of the civil service pattern may in Busoga take on overtones of racial discrimination in the minds of Africans.'

This process is not unknown in the realm of the Church. A pastor (b. 1915) in Central Zululand writes in 1954, 'The pastors, evangelists, and members of the congregation have experienced a change in the relationships between them and the Western mis-sionary. Cars have contributed much to this change. Many if not most missionaries do not visit kraals any more. They meet the people on Sundays only. The relationship between the missionary and the lay White men who care very little for Christianity seems to be cordial. The African asks why, and gives detrimental answers to the question.'

There is a tendency to idolize the old missionary at the expense of the modern one. 'They do not come down to us', was the phrase used by an African theology teacher in a country which at the time was supposed to be the paradise of race-relations in East Africa. 'They do not visit our homes. They do not attempt to learn our language, as the old missionaries used to do.' While at the beginning of missionary work, contact with the world of the Whites gave prestige to the African pastor or catechist, to-day this same contact has become a problem, and a threat to his very status. In a hundred different languages the verbal equivalent of 'stooge of the whites' is to-day being thrown at anybody who in

---

[8] L. A. Fallers, *Bantu Bureaucracy*, 1957, p. 213.

an atmosphere of intensified anti-colonial nationalism works for 'White' concerns. Balandier has shown the extent to which *mundélé-ndombe*—stooge-of-the-whites—is an accusation against the white-collar employees class in the French or the Belgian Congo.[9] But this applies also to the Church. In a conflict within a group of pastors or a group of catechists, this invective will often be hurled as the last and final missile. Conversely that old pastor in an East African coast town who was accused of embezzlement of Church money and who for that reason was to appear before the White mission superintendent could resort to a stubborn position of defence: 'I refuse to go through the cash book together with a *mzungu*' (white man). Within certain African churches the remaining traces of White domination are now being felt as heavy chains. This has, of course, its particular overtones in colour-conscious South Africa. The appointment of a young English superintendent to a missionary district in a well-known South African church called forth the following comment from one of the African pastors: 'It is madness to put a small White boy over me!' Here again, the early days of the first missionaries will be idealized, and in African ministers' private meetings the present situation is summed up in a phrase which in South Africa is felt much more bitterly than it appears at first: 'The age of the missionaries is gone. Now we live in the age of the sons of missionaries.'

The independence of the new generation of African pastors over against the missionary is of course from one point of view the outcome of conscious missionary policy—that of establishing a self-governing Church. But in Africa, as in other parts of the world, it was perhaps unfortunate that this necessary independence was not seen as part of a necessary interdependence within a universal Church.

A recent visit to South Africa has convinced me of one thing, that relationships between African and Western leaders in the mission churches are more strained than is generally realised by Westerners. This was patent not least in some very influential Churches known to the outside world as staunch centres of liberalism and brotherhood. It is indeed later than we think.

Let us move to the other extreme of the African continent, West Africa! In one of the oldest autonomous churches, with but

---

[9] Balandier, *Sociologie des Brazzaville noirs,* 1955, p. 159.

very tenuous connexions with one or two 'expatriate' missions, a leading pastor told me he thought that he was regarded as pro-white and that therefore, in his dealings with missionaries, he felt that he had to give the impression of being anti-white.

Racial attitudes and nationalism being what they are, both missionary and African pastor feel the tensions. African pastors feel the distance and the aloofness which sometimes has developed between themselves and the missionary. Visiting Protestant Africa in 1953, 1955 and 1957–58, I was disturbed by the lack of natural, matter-of-course relationship between the two parties. I found such contacts in parts of Africa, but in other parts there was surprisingly little of it. As a Protestant, I had reason to be disturbed by the fact that in many countries, not least in the Belgian Congo, African pastors would contrast their own position with the supposedly warm fellowship between Roman Catholic priests of both races. In Tanganyika, I was told by an influential pastor who has seen the world: 'The Roman priests laugh at us, because there is no real fellowship between us and the Western missionary. Among ourselves we often say, we should like to write a book called:

Guide to Missionaries.

Chapter I. How to establish real brotherhood *(undugu)*;
Chapter II. How to get to know African pastors;
Chapter III. How not to be in a hurry.'

Sometimes this attitude takes on a bitter aspect. In one of the 'Latin' Africa territories we were told by a group of pastors: 'Our voice is not heard in the Church. We are called African pastors but we are not allowed to administer the sacraments on our own. In order to baptize or administer Holy Communion we must ask the missionary's permission each time. We were told that this is a Government regulation regarding Protestant missions in this country, but we have been told by others that this is not true.' The most embittered pastor we met in Africa was one serving in a mission of rather radical Protestant type, in Central Africa. The missionary had brought him along to introduce him to a newly arrived European administrator. *Voici notre catéchiste*—may I introduce our catechist—he had said. This was years ago, but the minister who after all *was* a pastor harboured the grudge with unholy pertinacity. (And, come to think of it, as a pastor, the African was just as much pastor as his Western colleague.)

A highly educated African pastor in South Africa brought the problem to a level where the deepest need is felt but where perhaps far too little is being done at present. 'What we need', he said, 'is a *pastor pastorum,* a missionary who is able to act not only as a financial administrator and bank-manager but as our spiritual guide; a man to whom one could turn for confession and absolution.' Perhaps, after all, the very business of the Church is not busy-ness, but the patient care of souls, not least the souls of pastors. It is on this level that ultimately the relationship between Western and African pastor must be judged (and will be judged). This care of souls is of course not a one-way traffic but a matter of mutual help and responsibility.

So much in the Church in Africa at present hangs on the relationship between African pastor and Western missionary. Not all on either side of the fence feel this problem. But the awake, the large-hearted and the open-minded, among missionaries and African pastors, are aware of what is happening under the surface. They are still, as in the day of Aggrey, interpreters in two directions, misunderstood by both sides, and yet perhaps understood and supported by some.

Attempting to interpret the relationship between Western missionary and African pastor, I am more than almost anywhere else in this book conscious of not being penetrating enough. For the situation in this encounter is serious. A parallel to the situation in China prior to 1949 is not out of place. David M. Paton has put forward the thesis that God's judgment to-day, particularly upon missions to China, 'is being executed upon His Church by political movements which are anti-Christian'.[1] If, under the impact of African nationalism, such a judgment were to come upon missions in Africa, the bitterest accusation would very likely be directed against missionary omissions in this fundamentally important field of human relationships between Western and African ministers of the Gospel. On this level of daily contacts, we must redeem the time lest a Moslem 'brotherhood' or a Communist

---

[1] D. Paton, *Christian Missions and the Judgment of God,* 1952, p. 18.

'comradeship' become determinative factors in to-morrow's Africa. Between 'blood-brothers'—redeemed by the same blood—there should be complete and open fellowship. In so far as this happens, the multitudes will understand that the message of the Church and of its ministry has a relevance to Africa.

· 5 ·

THE THEOLOGICAL COLLEGE IN AFRICA

Education for what?

At the international missionary conference at Willingen, Germany in 1952, we took part in a group discussion with the late Dr. J. Nhlapo, of Johannesburg, who was one of the most popular members of that memorable international gathering. He had come as a representative of the Churches in Africa to an international conference in Western Germany, that highly-efficient industrialized country. He introduced his remarks with a phrase that caught the imagination of some of us: 'Africa has been filled with machinery', he said, referring to Westernized administration in African churches. He regarded that efficient 'machinery' with some degree of admiration, but also with uneasiness, as organization and administration which seem to suit the West so well but which has not necessarily become a part of the life of the Church in Africa.

How far is theological education part (perhaps a 'spare part') of that Western 'machinery' to which Dr. Nhlapo referred? Both theological student and minister are bewildered. What should the theological school attempt to do in Africa? The issue is sometimes represented in terms of two supposedly contradictory alternatives, with the emphasis either on intellectual training or on worship and character training.

An Anglican theological teacher at Umuahia, Eastern Nigeria, writes:

> In view of the work for which the ordinands are being prepared, the training may be said to have a threefold purpose. First, a man needs to acquire a power of ordering and organizing his own life and work. African life is still on the whole 'easy-going' about the use of time. The African generally has 'time for people', and this sociable outlook may make him a very good pastor. Unfortunately the traditional attitude to time goes so far in this direction as to be incompatible with modern life. The clergyman, like other busy men, has to

modify it. Though he cannot altogether impose Western patterns of behaviour on himself or his people, he can improve the efficiency of his work by learning orderly ways of setting about the multiplicity of things which he has to do. In the college the day's work is organized with this purpose in mind, to give practice in orderly living.

A second aim of the training is to develop the ordinand's intellectual equipment. His mind needs to be flexible, to keep pace with the rapid changes in his country, and to be well stocked and capable of future study, so as to cope with and help the increasing number of educated people to whom he will minister.

The third purpose of the theological college is to help the ordinand to develop his inner life and move towards spiritual maturity. Growth in the Christian virtues and progress in prayer may have to be made in the teeth of opposition from without and from within. Even the vocation to the ministry seems sometimes, in Nigeria as elsewhere, to be a matter of mixed motives.[1]

Here an attempt is being made to overcome the one-sided emphasis on merely the one alternative or the other, and we wish to align ourselves with this attempt. With Richard Niebuhr we recognize that the theological school should be an 'intellectual center of the Church's life'[2], for intellectual work, bringing reflection to bear on the teaching of Holy Scripture, is not opposed to but in support of the Christian interpretation of Revelation.

But there is another aspect of the Church's life which must find a place in theological teaching in Africa. It is often somewhat neglected. In stressing only the theoretical side of education, the dimension represented by the worship-life of the individual and of the group is sometimes neglected. And with this, there is a neglect of those things which could give movement, colour and richness to the life of the Church, in Africa rather more so than elsewhere: ordered prayer life, the rhythm of the Church's year, music. The life of the Church in Africa is greatly impoverished if that emphasis and dimension are missing. The theological school is the place where experience of the wholeness of life can be recovered, and, we suggest, must be recovered. It should be done now, in constructive co-operation with sympathetic Western teachers.

Dr. Keith Bridston, whose contribution to the discussion of

---

[1] John Goodwin, in [D. Webster ed.], *Truly Called*, 1954, p. 33–35.

[2] R. Niebuhr, *The Purpose of the Church*, p. 107.

theological education has been of particular importance, summarizes the aim of theological training in terms of the Church, the world and the individual student.[3] This is a useful approach which we shall follow here, up to a point.

1. *The Church*. The concern for the Churches in Africa is that the theological schools should produce ministers, 'more and better ministers', for the Church. But in order to understand the aim of theological education, a 'time-and-motion' study of the pastor's job does not take us very far. If, in certain Churches, the pastors seem to be chiefly engaged in chasing around on regular 'communion rounds', a practically-minded theological teacher, in order to prepare men of this order, could of course concentrate on liturgical know-how and a few useful hints about the care of motor-cycles (or a car, as the case may be). In a large number of cases the work of the minister is conceived in terms of office administration and of the orderly keeping of files and accounts. This secret clerk-ideal means much to quite a few of Christ's good men in Africa (and elsewhere, e.g. in Sweden). A curriculum organized to prepare men for this 'machinery', (in Dr. Nhlapo's words) would obviously be useful, but if useful, would perhaps not fully express the real aim of theological education, in Africa or anywhere. This aim must be derived from the nature of the Church of Christ and of its ministry.

One of the aims of theological education, we suggest, is to interpret, with the student, the sacred deposit of the Faith in Scriptures, Creeds and the History of the Church. That is why the 'conventional Western theological subjects' in the curriculum are neither primarily Western nor conventional. They are just as much Eastern and African, for they are part of the heritage of the Catholic Church. Theological teaching in Africa, or elsewhere, if it is to be faithful to the true interests of the Church, dares do nothing less than transmit that heritage. And it is transmitted to the theological student as a future pastor with a view to his passing on this heritage to his team and his flock. In this study, we specifically stress the pastor's relationship with his local co-workers, those laymen and women who together with him form the leadership of the Church, and we emphasize that his task is to inspire, nurture and lead the local leaders, to be a *pastor pastorum*

[3] Keith R. Bridston, *Theological Training in the Modern World*, 1954, (cyclostyled, W. S. C. F. Grey book).

in the district. This is of greater consequence for theological teaching than is perhaps at first realised. It implies that the knowledge is not prescribed solely for the individual consumption of the theological student. *He receives it in order to transmit and translate it to his team and his flock.* Education—for this reason—does not consist of lumps or blocks of unrelated and undigested information, however sacred the contents may be. Education is a flow, a flow of ideas from sources outside and beyond the learner, flowing through him in order to be shared with others. Only in these terms is it alive and can it bring new life.

Knowledge cannot be packed and tied like little parcels. It is a flow of ideas, a give-and-take from *both* sides, both from the teacher and the student, and it is when the theological insight and understanding is transmitted and translated that it is really 'assimilated' by the student-translator. In this process, and with this dynamic aim in view, the subject-matter takes on relevance and urgency. Here is suggested a new aspect of the function of the pastor, and for that reason something of a new aspect of theological education. This task must be understood not as a speciality, but as a necessary *dimension* in the pastor's work—and this affects the very method of teaching in the theological schools.

2. *The Student.* Dr. Bridston's scheme had the following order: Church, World, Student. We shall modify this order somewhat: Church, Student, World. There is a reason for this. In the contact with African theological students, we have been impressed by their particular appreciation of the content of their studies. The student accepts as important and interesting only that which can clearly be related to his particular existence, his experience, environment, aspirations and hopes. Theological knowledge is not objectivized into abstract truths floating about in the thin air of academic reflection but is essentially related to the student's own life and to the life of his church.

A student at Trinity College, Kumasi, Ghana has this to say: 'In the theology course, I find "Life after Death" most interesting. I regard the course in the proof of the existence of God as of less importance. The belief in the existence of God is not alien to any nation or race, and it is only the fool who says in his heart, There is no God. This proving of God's existence does not help me in evangelizing among the heathens because even the fetish priests acknowledge God's existence and His power over their gods.' And he adds: 'Least interesting is the course on "the Holy Spirit", because the subject is too abstract and dry. However it makes a very good and high intellectual exercise.'

I think many theological teachers in Africa would agree that the attitude of this student is representative of that taken by a great majority. It is not only a case of the African's supposed lack of interest in abstract ideas; the important point to note here, and with all students, is their tendency to 'assimilate' only that which is recognized as, or can be shown to be, relevant and important.

Our observation is perhaps very commonplace, and clearly does not only apply to the situation among African students. Dr. Bridston puts the general principle very well: 'In the student the general aims of theological training become specific. Outside of him all other aims [of education] become abstract and irrelevant.' If this is true in the West, it is even more so in Africa. And it is this which makes the educational task in the Theological School so responsible, difficult, and thrilling.

Theological study, on all continents, is closely connected with the student's own personal spiritual life. That is why, in dealing with theological education and the Church, we stress corporate worship and the teaching of Prayer. It is a central aspect of the whole theological school, without which all the rest will be well-nigh worthless.

In this necessary relation to the student, theological education aims at providing 'a principle of judgment' from which the pastor can serve the Church. Not all theological teachers seem to be aware that this is the most important service which the school can render to the student. Not all students—in Africa or elsewhere—arrive at that maturity which is capable of taking a balanced overall view. We know an African pastor, a friend of ours, who had found such a principle of judgment. It satisfied him fully, and I think it satisfied his own followers and others whom he met, and that, when all is said and done, is the main thing. 'All theology is summed up in Luther's Small Catechism. It is all there. Uneducated people and B.A's come to me for advice or come to argue with me. I am not afraid to tackle anybody, for the whole of theological knowledge can be derived from that small seed.' His standpoint is probably far from universally acceptable. But it is a standpoint.

3. *The World*. The ship of the Church in Africa has to steer

between Scylla and Charybdis. The two dangers are those of becoming, on the one hand a frightened ghetto, and on the other a glorified religious expression of the secular aspirations of a tribe or a people. The secularized educated generations are slipping away from the Church, and the pastor's temptation is to be satisfied with a smug little group in a corner. Political nationalism will use both traditional African religion and modern creeds to further its ends. These ideas and forces go to make up the front line where the Church in Africa encounters the world. The ministry is there to minister to, or serve, all God's children, whether they accept it or no. And it is in this evangelistic and intellectual encounter with the old African heritage and new Western doctrines that theology in Africa comes alive and becomes relevant and necessary.

Entering College

There are Protestant groups in Africa which at this late hour lay down 'ability to read in the vernacular' as the standard for entering college. They claim that they are running a Pastors' School and they call their men, trained for some three years (if that), pastors. While being fairly vociferous in claiming that their attitude to preparatory training and theological education is the only possible 'indigenous', 'democratic' and 'Biblical' one (a combination of these adjectives is popular), they soon tend to follow the general trend which definitely points to higher educational standards.

In some Churches, the 'ladder' system of the Uganda type still offers the main approach. Here experienced catechists will, at 35–40 years of age, be promoted to the theological school. With the general policy of substituting voluntary helpers for the old catechist system, the 'catechist-ladder' is now beginning to be too weak and shaky as a line of approach. The other ladder, teachers' education, is at present, generally speaking, the prevalent one both in 'Latin' and British Africa, but there are here characteristic efforts to establish secondary education as the normal avenue.

A unique position is taken by the Stofberg-Gedenkskool of the Dutch Reformed Church, South Africa, 'one of the best-equipped theological schools in the Union'.[4] Here there are two lines, for pastors and for evangelist-catechists. Entrance standard for evangelists is now the Junior Certificate, and the entrance requirement for the ordination course is matriculation. This high standard is maintained against some opposition, but with remarkable results. In an interview with the members of the faculty I was told: 'We find that matric. is necessary as standard for entrance. Theological education must aim at bringing the students *to think for themselves*. This can only be achieved if they have a sufficiently good background of general education. In this way, it will also be possible to integrate the theological course into Bantu universities in the near future.' White leaders of the Dutch Reformed Church are aware of the fact that their Church is the object of much criticism from various quarters. But they are the more determined to keep the standards of theological education high, and progressively rising, in view of the envisaged development of *apartheid* policy according to which Bantu leaders, in Bantu areas, will have responsibility and independence which, it is thought, can never be obtained in areas dominated by the Whites. Thorough theological education for Bantu pastors is thus here accepted as a necessary consequence of the *apartheid* policy.

In order to raise the level of theological education in certain other Churches there have recently been created *preparatory schools* for catechists or others who are interested. The Presbyterian College at Bibia in the French Cameroons has taken a single large class for a four-year preparatory course, with the hope of bringing possible candidates from the ranks of the catechists up to the required standard. The structure of this preparatory school was mainly modelled on similar previous experiments in Brazil; the Roman Catholic idea of a *petit seminaire* also played a role. The course is parallel to the French *brevet* course, but the emphasis is on languages instead of the scientific bias typical of the *brevet* course at, for example, Libamba Secondary School, in the Cameroons. Required of the students are *certificat d'étude*, equivalent of six years primary studies, Christian experience, Church work, and the writing of a brief autobiographical note. French has been the medium of instruction right through the school, with English as a second language, whilst the staff of the school is the same as that of the theological school.

[4] Goodall-Nielsen, *I.M.C. Theological Report*, III, p. 16.

The (Southern) Presbyterian mission in the Luba region in Belgian Congo recommends pre-theological training. 'We cannot suspend theological seminaries in thin air with an educational vacuum underneath. The level and quality of theological institutions will continue to be below the level of our ideals until we develop preparatory schools that will provide an adequate foundation for advanced work.'[5] African pastors in the Cameroons, the Belgian Congo, Angola, and also in Tanganyika and Nigeria have expressed to us strong interest in preparatory schools of this type. The demand for an education of this sort is quite general, although some missionaries express their doubts about such courses. After the prep. school, they think, students may be tempted to abandon the thought of theological training in order to take up better-paid secular jobs. At Bibia this eventuality is guarded against through a rule that no diplomas are awarded.

Lutherans in South Africa have introduced similar preparatory education. The minimum entrance requirement for the Lutheran Theological School (Oskarsberg) is now the Junior Certificate in the same way as for the Anglican Theological School at Rosettenville. For suitable Standard VI students a two-year preparatory course at Untunjambili has been arranged. The main subjects are English, General History, Geography, and General Bible knowledge.

In respect of the raising of pre-theological educational standards, there is a characteristic difference between the I.M.C. theological commissions to 'Latin' and to Southern Africa. The former, studying a situation in which until recently Protestant missions have struggled with great initial obstacles with regard to education (due in part to the Government and, in certain cases, to the general policy of the mission boards concerned), had, in the circumstances, certain specific proposals to make to the missions:

'Complete secondary training is desirable, preferably of the classical or cultural type. The pastors' schools in the Belgian Congo and the Cameroons should move promptly toward that level of entrance, considering conscientiously the reason for co-operation as they do so. Secondary education is spreading and the missions and churches will wish to further their own efforts at that level, if possible transferring some missionaries from the primary and teacher-training schools. Teacher-training courses on the

---

[5] Africa Committee DFM-NCCC, New York, 6.VI.1955. Supplement to A. 765.

higher level, such as the four-year *moniteur* programme in the Congo, are the next best preparation. In the Cameroons and the other areas in the French system, the *brevet élémentaire* indicates the standard to be sought at this moment; and, in the Portuguese territories, the second cycle of the *liceu*.'

'When the requirements in general education are set low, or are laxly applied, the training school is often driven to use a great deal of time on general subjects, making up deficiencies in language, and trying to help students who are really not ready to do advanced study. This preparation should be done *before* they enter the pastors' course, in order that the latter can really do its proper work.'[6]

In regarding secondary education as the key to the whole situation, the commission had support from a number of leading missionaries and Africans. On the other hand, this recommendation will for some time be a counsel of perfection, serving as a challenge rather than a definite rule.

The I.M.C. commission to Southern Africa had to deal with a situation where general education is more advanced than in the Protestant communities in 'Latin' Africa but it did put forward an argument which seems relevant to *all* regions of Africa. The commission makes a fundamental appraisal of what is meant by 'level of education':

> We clearly recognize the need for raising of entrance standards; with the rapid growth of a more educated African population there is pressing need for African ministers whose formal education does not lag behind that of those to whom they will minister. However, the question that poses itself in this connexion is whether such an educational development *eo ipso* 'improves' theological training, and whether indeed it does not only touch *one* particular aspect of the needed improvement. Much of the thinking on this matter seems to us to over-simplify the issue. Theological training is not necessarily improved by raising the college entrance from Standard VI to Matriculation and providing a theological road which promises a B.D. on the horizon. When for instance, as in one case which came to our notice, the raising of the academic entrance standard to Junior Certificate had 'improved' theological training in the sense that the students were now asked to discuss the question of the authorship of the Epistle to the Hebrews, the probability of a proto-Luke, etc., this did not seem to us necessarily to indicate an improvement of theological training.

----

[6] *I.M.C. Theol. Report* II, p. 58.

The improvement most urgently needed is in another dimension; it is the need to improve and make more living the theological training at *any* educational level, even one which begins—as in many instances and for a long time to come it must begin—well below a Matriculation entrance standard.[7]

We are impressed by the common-sense and wisdom of this statement. It is geared to the flexible and varied conditions of the educational systems of the Churches in Africa, in a way which is at the same time liberating and challenging. If it is not used as an excuse for the possible absence—in certain cases—of sustained efforts to improve teaching standards, it could serve as an important lever in the actual situations in the theological schools. Also the commission to Southern Africa has stressed the general need for the raising of entrance standards.

When they do this, they meet a need expressed with increasing emphasis by African church leaders. It is particularly interesting to note that the loudest clamour for higher standards comes from African pastors already long in the service, men who themselves cannot expect to benefit from a reform but who know only too well that in the Church of to-day drastic improvement of standards is necessary. The interest from the African leaders in higher standards is connected with another factor. They know that a higher level of entrance is of importance for the recruitment to the ministry. Theological schools that accept anybody who has had an elementary education do not attract the best-equipped among young African Christians to-day. An educational institution without effective intellectual standards is not regarded by them as worth their while. If they prefer to apply for other posts, their decision is not solely dictated by a concern for financial or other gains; to some degree it may imply a considered judgment upon the level of theological education which *they think* is being offered.

The standard and reputation of the theological school as such either has, or has not, attraction value. One of our finest observers —placed until recently in the most populous country in West Africa—expressed this in the following words: 'The best Africans, those who wish to offer themselves and their lives to something great and worth-while, do not want to commit themselves to anything as uncertain as a theological course, such as they see it

---

[7] *I.M.C. Theol. Report* III, p. 43.

to-day. They feel there is no future in this for a man who wants to do anything real.' The language medium of the theological school is important in this connexion. If the young man has a secondary school education in English, French (or a comparative level in Portuguese), he will fret under a situation which expects him to join a theological course with an African teaching medium, as this language more likely than not is *not* his own!

'Good Company'

Professor Monica Hunter Wilson has shown that the Nyakyusa of Tanganyika regard 'the enjoyment of good company' *(ukwangala)* as of the highest value. 'It is by conversing with our friends that we gain wisdom' *(amahala)*, one of the informants told Dr. Wilson. 'Good company' is not a bad term for the atmosphere of a theological school in Africa.[8] The community spirit is one of its great assets. Without an awareness of that deep fellowship between the students and, in many cases, between students and staff, one does not begin to sense the atmosphere of the theological school.

Some theological schools have a higher degree of this atmosphere of 'good company' than others. A school situated in the bush can, it would seem, make this more of a reality than a school in the city. There are also differences between denominational traditions. The Anglican theological schools, both Anglo-Catholic and Evangelical, have a particular strength in this respect, as far as a non-Anglican is in a position to judge. The most important reason is to be found in the Anglican understanding of theological education. Archdeacon R. G. P. Lamburn—late warden of St. Cyprian's Theological College, Tunduru, in the Masasi Diocese (Anglican), Tanganyika—dismisses the idea of a theological college as 'a place where students are taught certain things' and regards it as 'primarily a place where they grow into the habits of the priestly life'. That this definition is going to have consequences for the whole structure and life of the course is obvious.

[8] For our particular purpose it would be pedantic to add that in traditional Nyakyusa society *'ukwangala'* implies 'to live with contemporaries'. In the sense of discussion and easy give-and-take it is 'made different between men of different generations by the respect required of sons for their fathers'. M. Wilson, *Good Company, A Study of Nyakyusa Age-Villages,* OUP, 1951, p. 66. This modification shows that we are not altogether entitled to use the term for the relationship between staff and students in a school.

In the (Anglican) diocese of Nyasaland the theological school is, as in much earlier centuries, regarded as belonging to the Bishop's 'household'. Here the theological school is primarily a 'community of devotion', to employ the definition used by the Anglican Central Advisory Council of Training for the Ministry (CACTM). It is in accordance with this that the college chapel and the daily Eucharist constitute the heart and centre of the College. An Anglo-Catholic tutor, Rev. J. Poole-Hughes, Tanganyika, reports in 1956: 'The first aim of the course is to develop the prayer life of the students and for this cause ascetic theology plays a large part in the early lectures and individual tutorial assistance in the personal prayer life is given. The Mission rule for clergy to say not only Morning and Evening Prayer but Sext and Compline means that the framework of college routine is in chapel which students also use for most of their private devotions.'

It should be added, perhaps, that this concentration on worship does not need to imply a division of life into the dangerous dichotomy of a sacred and a secular order. The 'good company' in this context is interpreted in terms of wholeness and community. Of Dom Bernard Clements, O.S.B., one of the greatest theological teachers in Africa, (Kumasi 1926–1931) it has been said: 'Hoe and broom were as often in his hands as the breviary'. From these activities of body and spirit he and his students went to the theological class and then on again to deeper experiences.[9]

Mukono, Uganda, is an important Anglican example of community life in the Evangelical tradition. The imaginative leadership given by men such as John V. Taylor, principal of the College 1945–1954, has given the students deep insights into the meaning of worship. Here a main concern has been to relate the prayer life of the community, of the students and their families to the common experiences of the home and garden and market-place. The very structure of the time-table has been conditioned by this concern. The daily corporate worship in the chapel takes place as late as 11 a.m., in order to let the students' wives take part in the service. The ordinands' village at Bishop Tucker College, Mukono, was the most advanced we saw anywhere. In this case there has been an interesting co-operation between Church and State. Miss N. Threadgold, who has made an important contribution to the care of family life in Uganda, describes the Mukono village.

[9] G. Laing, *Dom Bernard Clements in Africa*, 1944.

About ten years ago, it was realized that if the Church of Uganda was to go forward, then the wives of the African clergy should be trained as well as their husbands. Six temporary houses were erected, made of mud and wattle and with thatched roofs. Each ordinand brought his wife and two small children with him, and the little village soon became an integral part of the College life. In time the Government saw the possibilities of such training, and it is because of the vision and foresight of the Church, backed by the generous financial help of the Government, that we have our own permanent 'village' today. Our aim has always been to show our students the 'wholeness of life', so that even the smallest tasks become sacred.

Today, in place of the old thatched houses we have a new 'village' nearer the College. A generous Government grant enabled us to build twelve houses in the form of a horse-shoe, with the 'Wives' College' in the centre, and the Nursery School just below. Each family has its own house, consisting of three rooms, two bedrooms and a sitting-room, with a small store, and outside kitchen and separate bath-house and latrine, and as the families come for two years we have an opportunity of really getting to know them. We give them essential food, but they have to grow all their own vegetables, and each family has its own plot of land for cultivation. The men do whitewashing, cementing, thatching etc. and we have a grand 'Field Day' on Fridays, when both men and women work in the village together.

The students' wives have a varied programme. Most of the theoretical work is done in the mornings, and the practical in the afternons. As well as Bible Study, Mothers' Union work and Pastoralia, the wives learn Hygiene, First Aid, Nursing, Infant Welfare, Housewifery, Simple Accounts, Handwork, Needlework, Mending, Cooking, and above all they learn to live together as a Community and to help each other. As to follow-up work, we are organizing refresher courses for Mothers' Union leaders and pastors' wives in many parts of the country, encouraging them to go back to their villages with new vision and greater enthusiasm to pass on their knowledge to others.[10]

Another important feature of the community life at Mukono is the imaginative use of religious drama to enhance the sense of

---

[10] Some of the ministerial students' families have a considerable number of children. Sometimes statistical problems are involved. In the Masasi area, Southern Tanganyika, one of the students had filled in his application form to the theological college, stating his personal circumstances, number of children etc. Then he had suddenly to add a P.S. in Swahili: 'Ongeza jumla. Tulipata mmoja zaidi usiku huu.' (P.S. 'Please add to number stated above. Another baby arrived last night.')

participation in the Church's year. The students themselves have made creative contributions here.[1]

At the Anglican theological school, in Ibuye, Ruanda, worship is very particularly dominated by the fact of the East African revival. As the theological students participate in the fellowship of the Revival, new levels of Christian experience—in the context of an episcopally-administered Church—are reached.

One could add examples of community life from other denominations. The common concerns of evangelistic field-work play their role in cementing staff and students together and create, on this level, a fellowship which very probably is felt to be satisfying and meaningful. In certain schools, however, inter-tribal tensions can become an important issue in the life of the students. The Theological College at Amanzimtoti, Natal, South Africa (now at Modderpoort, Or. Free State) had until recently received only Zulus of the Congregational Church. One of the Zulu students writes of his experience in adjusting himself to a change of policy in the school, whereby the school was put on an inter-denominational basis and was opened to students of other tribes than Zulus.

In 1954 it was not difficult; but the difficulty came in 1955 when we were more than one race [by 'race' is meant tribe: Zulus, Sotho, Xhosa]. The difficulty lies here: we are mixed races, people of different languages—to have people of different languages created some misunderstanding, because what was a joke to some was not so to others. That was one of the causes of misunderstanding. The other thing was that because we are people of different languages our customs are different; this again created friction for some time. In our custom we Zulus do not greet a person more than once. Once you have seen a person you need not greet again that same day. Our brethren of other races are not used to that. It seems to me that each time you meet him you must greet him. At first we did not understand each other on these matters. Life at first was really difficult for one to adapt oneself. The difficulty was not that either race was insolent, troublesome or boastful but the difficulty was in failing to understand each other. This was a struggle from 1955 up to the first two months of 1956, but after that everything went well.

In considering theological education in Africa the searchlight has been concentrated on the educational standards and the personal qualifications of the students. Less interest, perhaps, has

---

[1] Cf. John V. Taylor, *Afrikanische Passion, The Passion in Africa*, 1957.

been shown in the staff, Western and African. And yet, in a recent important survey of theological education in the United States, the theological faculties were the object of penetrating enquiry, and by the same token we cannot in this African survey altogether overlook the role and the problems of the faculties as such.[2]

In fact, the main problem here is already implied in the somewhat generous use of the academic term 'faculty'. For the typical situation is that of the one-man faculty, where one single missionary, sometimes assisted for Practical Theology by an African pastor, has to carry the whole teaching load, besides caring for the college administration, the personal problems of the students and the supervision of their field-work. And that is not all. There are recent and representative examples of an even tighter squeeze than that; the superintendent of a large Church, with a great number of African pastors, was at the same time President of an inter-Church federation and in his spare time had to run a theological school with over twenty students. When he was away on *safari,* an African pastor had the unenviable task of being a substitute-teacher in any of the subjects taught in the school. In Central Africa, we came across one school run by the superintendent of the mission, whose basic training was agronomy rather than theology and who gave three hours' teaching per week. The real anchor of his school was a valiant African pastor who had received theological education on a higher level than that given in his own school. In this and similar cases, the tutor had to fight against very heavy odds. 'The perpetuation of one-man colleges', say Goodall and Nielsen, 'is obscuring the gravity of [the] failure [to provide for that which is most fundamental to the life and witness of the Church in Africa] and [is] doing far less than justice to teachers and students alike.'[3]

Above all, in a one-man college the students will be intellectually and spiritually dependent on *one* man—and for three or four formative years!—to an extent which may not always be valuable. This seems to be particularly dangerous when some idiosyncrasy tends to influence the teacher. We came across a Western teacher in a school (non-Anglican) of this kind who had formed the interesting

[2] H. R. Niebuhr, D. D. Williams and J. M. Gustafson, *The Advancement of Theological Education,* 1957, pp. 54–77.
[3] Goodall-Nielsen, *I.M.C. Theol. Report.* III, p. 45.

idea that most of the individuals with whom Jesus came into contact in his ministry later turned up as bishops. He knew for instance that the little child blessed by Jesus (Matt. 19: 13–15) eventually became bishop in Antioch and was named Ignatius. This is of course an imaginative method of integrating New Testament and Church History teaching but has insufficient support from any historical document. With one man of this calibre in charge of theological teaching there is not always sufficient width of outlook. Even a one-man college can, of course, achieve remarkable results; but the system can also lead to stunting isolation and narrowness of view. A faculty of three or more teachers will, as such, present a richer variety and a healthier intellectual and spiritual atmosphere than the one-man college.

The role of the teacher in situations of this kind becomes of decisive importance. The I.M.C. commission to 'Latin' Africa has this to say on the point:

> Missionaries on the staffs of the training schools include some of the finest Christian workers to be found, excellently fitted for their present responsibilities. They include others of equally good spirit but less conspicuous in talents and in aptness of training and experience. Among them are also found individuals who are not clearly suited for such work, or who do it as duty without joy or particular interest.

We would add that the really dangerous teacher is the conceited fellow who thinks he knows all the answers, who preaches down to the supposedly low level of his African students and who is allowed to carry on like that for decades, because for reasons of missionary politics, he is supposed to be irreplaceable. Having said that, we quote the I.M.C. commission again:

> These things are not said in a critical mood, but simply to emphazise the enormous importance of the teacher in these rather small and closely knit schools. The best that the mission can possibly provide in personality and competence is not too good.[4]

Some of the most remarkable missionary contributions to Africa have been rendered within the four walls of the theological class. While at the beginning of the period under review there was a tendency for missionaries near or past retiring age to be delegated to the theological school, many Churches nowadays have recognized

---

[4] *I.M.C. Report* II, p. 55.

that theological teaching is an exacting task, requiring contact with recent developments in theological thought, and younger men are consequently engaged as tutors. The furlough, which from one point of view tends to break the continuity of the theological school—periods in most cases being dependent on the furlough conditions of the European tutor(s)—can in other cases be very advantageously used in acquiring new inspiration and orientation. Richard Niebuhr makes an interesting remark, referring to conditions in the United States: 'Men called from the pastorate to the theological faculties are occasionally allowed a period of study in order to prepare themselves for a designated post.'[5] This arrangement, no doubt, is no less necessary in the case of theological staffs in Africa.

Among Westerners who have served as theological tutors, one thinks of names such as Henri Junod at Ricatla and Paul Fatton in Lorenzo Marques, Mozambique, Dom Bernard Clements at Kumasi, Ghana, Bishop Leonard Beecher at Limuru, Kenya and Bishop Newell S. Booth at Mulungwishi, Belgian Congo—to mention only a few, and necessarily omitting names of those at present engaged in this task. The personal and intellectual impact of the teaching on the students has in many cases been considerable. In order to understand the staff-student relationship in the schools we have attempted to gather information not only as to how the teachers regard their students but also—and it is a viewpoint at least as important—how the students regard their teachers. We were impressed by this testimony of a pastor in Mozambique: 'The greatest thing I learned was the teaching about the martyrs of the Church. Mr. Fatton used to explain this to us. I looked into the face of Mr. Fatton, and we all felt that his own heart suffered with the martyrs then and the martyrs to-day. His teaching and example is left indelibly on my heart until this day.' About another theological teacher, Maurice Schaller, in the same country and of the same nationality, a former student writes,

> Schaller's teaching method is to make the student find the solutions himself. The master remains in the background and he helps his student to search and to find. He is 'eaten' by the urge to know the African languages well and the meaning of our terms and cannot allow

---

[5] H. Richard Niebuhr and others, *The Advancement of Theological Education in the United States*, 1957, p. 54.

himself to be beaten in understanding the meaning hidden in our words. So he searches in the Hebrew and Greek and French and English languages and compares with our African languages. Then he discusses various shades of meaning. He doesn't like that in us which is imitation or 'copy', for to him man is not a machine. When we study science or the Bible or any other field of knowledge with him, he is never satisfied with a student who repeats the words of the book. When a student replies in the words of the book, M. Schaller exclaims: 'That is machine work! You must not be a gramophone!' He makes his students think. What strikes me about him is that throughout his life he has had hunger and thirst for knowledge. He has the gift of wonder; he will stop and admire things or happenings. And then he calls out to us: 'You must know to admire and marvel and wonder!' (*Vatatana!*). He himself walks about with open eyes and admires. Whatever he says is full of teaching to us.

Or we turn to an Anglo-Catholic monk, Dom Bernard Clements in Kumasi, as interpreted by Canon G. E. F. Laing, an African ex-student of Dom Bernard.

> Father Rector came to us as our teacher. At lectures we drank deep from his knowledge. He made all subjects interesting and easily understandable. He would make us laugh one minute and not very long afterwards carry us to another world; and when he brought us back into this one you could hear every student sigh. His knowledge of Latin was thorough. He would go either to his hall or to the college library and bring a volume of Moral Theology in Latin, and would read it to us as if reading an English version. His favourite subject was Ascetic Theology. This subject was as easy to him as it was delightful to us, because we saw in the life of the teacher the practical expression of that branch of theology.[6]

The I.M.C. Theological Commission to Southern Africa has in a most convincing manner advocated the need for 'listening'

---

[6] G. E. F. Laing, *Dom Bernard Clements in Africa*, 1944, p. 23. 'Dom Clements once, according to one of his African students, had asked his class to write a sermon to suit Holy Week. A student wrote on the humility of our Lord. In the course of the sermon he wrote: "It would be better for the Kingdom of God if all His ministers were prepared to wash the feet of those to whom He sent them!" After a day or two Father Bernard called the student into his room, showed that part of his sermon to him and said, "You wrote these words, and I thank you for writing them. Would you allow me to wash your feet?" With great reluctance the student agreed. Father Bernard then fetched water and soap and his own white towel, and stooped down and washed the feet of the student—and kissed them.' *Ibid.*, p. 36.

teachers and criticised the tendency to doctrinaire sufficiency and narrow handbook-teaching.[7] The examples quoted show how this quality of imaginative listening and creative teaching is appreciated by African students.

In united theological colleges there is at present a tendency for the various church traditions to be represented each by one *African* tutor. Limuru, Kenya, with two Western tutors, one Anglican and one Presbyterian, has, in principle, two Africans on the staff: one Anglican and one Methodist. In Southern Rhodesia, where British and American Methodists combined in theological and catechist training from 1959, there are in each of the two schools (Epworth and Old Umtali) two Africans representing the different traditions.

In most theological colleges there is at present on an average one African tutor whose education generally speaking is equivalent to that of the school itself, supplemented by some years' experience of practical church work.[8] To take some examples, there are on the one side Mukono (C.M.S., Uganda) with three African tutors, of whom one has been the warden, another chaplain; or Kakinda near Luluabourg, with the same number of African tutors. On the other side there is a number of colleges with no Africans on the staff. 'Tutors should have university degrees and since we have not as yet Africans with degrees we have not appointed any of them to our staff', 'We urgently need Africans on the staff, but they are not yet up to the mark.' In most cases, the teaching duties of the African tutors lie in the field of Practical Theology— Pastoral Theology, sometimes Homiletics and often Singing— supplemented by African Studies, and occasionally the study of Islam.

Among the African tutors whom we met, one taught at a well-known East African college. Son of a minister and grandson of a church teacher, he had himself been a schoolmaster for 14 years and after theological studies at the school where he was serving had been ordained priest in 1952 (deacon 1950). He taught the

---

[7] *I.M.C. Theol. Report* III, p. 47.

[8] A questionnaire on African tutors was sent in August 1957 to the theological colleges in Africa. Answers were returned from 44 colleges (West Africa 8, 'Latin' Africa 13. British Central Africa 9. South Africa 6, and East Africa 8). In these 44 colleges a total of 36 Africans were engaged as tutors.

Gospels, Church History and Pastoralia in the vernacular to a Lay Readers' class. We asked him about his experience as a teacher. He found Church History and Pastoralia easy to teach. In Church History, the Middle Ages was the most important period, he thought, 'For they had many brave men then in the Church. After the first centuries of persecution when the Church was not so developed, the Church, in the Middle Ages, begins to have a firm structure and a real understanding of Christianity.' St. Augustine and St. Basil were among the most outstanding Church leaders, he felt. The former was particularly important because he separated the Church from the world. In Pastoralia, our tutor had no books to rely on but had notes from his own student days, and he could draw on his three years of pastoral experience. Teaching New Testament, he felt, was more exacting than anything else. 'History can be taught without religious experience, but the Gospel which you teach must first be in your life. When I teach about Christ as the Light of the World, I must myself have the light in me.'

His experience of theological training had been brief. In all too many cases, the characteristic weakness of Protestant theological teaching in Africa is shown in the fact that there is a rapid turnover in the African staff. Their appointment is often a case of a temporary stop-gap, and as they are capable men with church experience, their own local congregations exert pressure in order to get them back into 'practical' work.

On the other hand there are splendid examples of African tutors who have been allowed to serve over a longer period of time and who have a reasonable hope of regarding theological teaching as their life calling. The Rev. Joseph Tjéga, of Bibia, Cameroons, should be cited in this connexion. His contribution to the Theological School, and that of quite a few others in similar positions show the very important role which African tutors fill, and which they only can fill to the same extent. They alone can fully understand the African students and the educational and personal problems involved in theological teaching on the particular level of the students. In a very real sense they contribute—or fail to contribute—to the community spirit of the school. And they have a special responsibility—and should have time and opportunity for fulfilling this responsibility—for the production of theological literature in the vernacular which is adapted to the special conditions of the Church. We urge in this book a theological teaching which has as its aim *a process of 'translation'*: of transposing the Bible and the history, doctrine and worship of the Church into African realities and terms of expression. There is none who can do this *trans-latio* as well as an African tutor who has been called, trained and encouraged to this task. (Only people who know something about Africa realize why we say 'encourage'; to show unstinted and unlimited confidence in men of this calibre is important.)

Some of the most remarkable teachers we came across were Africans. The African lecturers at the universities of Ghana and Sierra Leone have a unique position, not only because of their post-graduate studies in the West followed by constant conference and study visits to Western universities, but also because of their contributions to church life in their own countries as well as to the Ecumenical movement. Such scholars include the Rev. Christian Baëta, who is chairman of the Christian Council in Ghana and chairman of the International Missionary Council, and the Rev. Harry Sawyerr, who has represented the Anglican diocese of Sierra Leone at Faith and Order conferences and on other occasions.

An article on China in *The International Review of Missions,* July 1948—one of the very great articles in that review in the post-war period, and written by a Chinese theological scholar, Dr. T. C. Chao—springs to mind. He writes about theological education in his country. Ten years later we quote his prophetic words, applying them to conditions in Africa. They may be even more relevant to the theological school in Africa than at present they can be in China.

> The Church in China has arrived at a stage of development at which she needs not merely an educated ministry but also fully-fledged scholars, writers, churchmen and, most important of all, theologians. Thus far China has not offered to the Church ecumenical any theological thinker and writer. She needs to hurry up and produce such scholars. She needs them for herself and the world Church is impatiently awaiting their appearance. One of the reasons why no Chinese theologians have emerged is that the Church has not made serious attempts to discover and educate them. It is clear that to-day the theological school must make a strenuous effort to call them forth. It must be understood, however, that three years of theological study, following a college education, is utterly inadequate. A theologian cannot be made in ten or twenty years. He must be developed from childhood and then

flower out in the college, in the theological school and in post-graduate studies. He needs all the protection, care, nurture and education that both the Church and the seminary can give. There should be a plan for the emergence of theologians in the scheme of theological education to-day. There must be the allurements, the challenge, the stimulus, the call and the place for such a person before he can appear.

The seminary is a place where the budding theologian finds the kind of climate and new atmosphere in which to grow to full stature.

For the words 'China' and 'Chinese' substitute 'Africa' and 'African'—and you have a cogent and urgent challenge to Church and mission in Africa to-day. It conveys a message which no Church can afford to overlook.

The days of geographical pioneering in Africa ended some fifty or a hundred years ago. A new kind of pioneering is, however, very much needed, not least in the theological school—pioneering in human relationships. In one particular corner of Africa, special laws are now enforced, we are told, in order to ensure territorial and functional *apartheid* between the races. But north of the river Limpopo these conditions do not obtain, and here are great opportunities for making the theological college into a family of Christ. While obviously this is a task for *both* parties, both Africans and Westerners, equally obviously great responsibility lies with the European teachers. In a penetrating study of 'Missionary–Africans Relations', Dr. Robert T. Parsons, Dean of the Kennedy School of Missions, Hartford Seminary, says: 'What kind of partnership do the Africans desire? One answer is found in the reply of an African minister who when asked what kind of a missionary he would like to have in his country said, "We want missionaries who *respect* us, *trust* us, and *love* us, and we want to do the same to them".'[9]

Our study is called 'The Christian Ministry in Africa' but we deal, in fact, only with the African Christian ministry in Africa. This limitation reflects the actual social situation in the countries under review, more particularly in Southern Africa, but we should at least point out that it *is* a limitation, and that there is in principle no reason why in certain cases there should not be common training for African and European students, once the same entrance requirements can be approximately met.

---

[9] *Civilisations*, Vol. III (1953), (Brussels), No. 4, p. 512.

We believe that there should be scope for representative experiments in common training and living in the theological college. Young theological students from the West planning to become missionaries in Africa might consider studying for some time in a theological college in Africa. The results of such experiments could be of great benefit to all parties concerned.

The Search for an Integrated Curriculum

One theological student in West Africa writes: 'The most interesting subject in our college is Pastoralia, because it is well taught. Music I find less important, because conditions do not permit of full teaching of Music as it is done in the School of Technology or other Schools of Music.' Another student writes: 'I am keen on this subject of Bible Study. I know of many ministers who have failed in their work, because they did not really live up to what this beautiful study upholds.'

The reading of a number of similar essays by theological students on their work in the theological school gives much food for thought. These men are interested in a particular field of study for one of two reasons, or for both: because a subject has an existential importance to him personally and to his Church or because a good teacher has made it relevant and exciting.

In personal interviews or written essays on the curriculum in the college, students express themselves very freely. They obviously feel that the problem affects them personally. All will first mention the one great preliminary without which they do not seem to be able to move much further: *Culture générale*—the need for a broad and solid basis of general education in languages, philosophy and world history. The need for this foundation is strongly felt by old pastors and young ordinands, and there is a general disappointment with the achievement of Protestant theological training in this field.

Then they mention some of the subjects which are not included but which for some reason they consider ought to form part of the school programme. The practically-minded Methodists in Mozambique—trained in a tradition of Agricultural Missions—told us, 'We are doing well in Theology and Agriculture, but not in Handwork. ... We also need better knowledge of Veterinary

Science and the planting of trees and soil conservation. We need better training in Hygiene and Sanitation. We should be taught the principles of modern community work. ... There should be a course in typewriting.'

All this is very useful, no doubt. Yet, they are well aware that the fundamental emphasis should be on what, in fact, is treated as the heart of the programme.

The curriculum was established mainly under the influence of traditions from Europe or America. Two of the I.M.C. commissions have noted this. Bishop Neill says: 'The Westernness of all our methods is too plain to need much comment.' Goodall and Nielsen put it this way: 'In general, theological education in Africa has so far been conceived almost wholly in terms of transferring to Africa the kind of pattern which has long been familiar to the West.'[1]

With all our well-founded lamentations about the Westernness of the training, it is perhaps not altogether out of the question to stress that there is to some extent a certain inevitability in this. Christian theology as the organized intellectual expression of the historical religion of Incarnation has to transmit a deposit of knowledge which—if it is to be Christian and theology—must be common to all times and places. It is perhaps not so much the 'Westernness' in the geographical terms of Europe and America with which we have to deal as with the actual historical phenomena of the Revelation and the Church.

This has been pointed out by one of the leaders of the Church in India, Dr. Russell Chandran, head of the United Theological College of Bangalore. In a lecture on 'Trends in Theological Education to-day and their Relevance in South-East Asia' he stresses that any reorganization of theological teaching with a view to obtaining greater 'relevance' for Asia 'must not be done at the expense of the core curriculum, which is rooted in the faith once delivered as well as related to the environment'.[2] What is, and what should be, this 'core' curriculum? The very term suggests that it is organized round some central idea, which gives unity and consistency to all the different subjects. African students are most concerned to discover some common denominator, some

---

[1] *I.M.C. Theol. Reports* I, p. 23, and III, p. 44.

[2] *Record of Proceedings, Conference on Theological Education in S.E. Asia,* Bangkok, Feb.–March 1956, p. 15.

universal rationale by which the diversity of the various subjects can be integrated, a principle by which organic unity can be achieved in the whole body of knowledge with which they are confronted.

But we should not be over-hasty in drawing our conclusions, since the problem is not easy. Its implications and qualifications have recently been brought out with great wisdom and insight in the recent American report on the advancement of theological education.

> The search for this internal consistency of the Christian understanding of life involves many subtle questions. Superficially it is possible to outline a scheme of studies in which each has its place and in which the relationships are formally stated. Such a theological encyclopedia can display a rational order and designate the relationship of all human inquiries to the theological themes. But the real key lies in the nature of the Christian faith itself and hence beneath the surface of any formal scheme. Because the Christian faith has at its center a personal response to the reality of the creative, redeeming, and inspiring God, the unity in our faith must be found through personal discovery of the ultimate reality which shapes the whole of life.[3]

The American report finds two alternatives as solutions to this problem: the way of 'personal synthesis' and the core curriculum. The first is represented by the new plan put forward by the Yale Divinity School and intended for students 'at the B.A. level, responsible enough to be able to have a choice in planning their own course of study'.[4] Here all topics in the curriculum are interconnected and bound up with life-experience in such a way that the student discovers exciting new possibilities through that central reality in his faith which gives meaning to the whole. The 'core curriculum' plan is particularly represented by the Federated Theological Faculty at the University of Chicago and the Perkins School of Theology (Southern Methodists). An attempt is made to discover those basic contents and methods which are the foundation of all theological study. Chicago speaks of seven such 'core courses': Bible, Church History, Theology, Religion and Personality, Ethics and Society, Religion and Art, Christianity and the

---

[3] Rich. Niebuhr—Williams—Gustafson, *The Advancement of Theological Education*, 1957, p. 82–83.

[4] Dr. Liston Pope, at the *Bangkok Theological Conference, Record of Proceedings*, 1956, p. 16.

World Religions. The Perkins School counts four 'core courses': the Bible, the Christian Heritage, Christianity and Culture, the Local Church.[5]

We are conscious of the fact that these courses are mainly for students with a B.A. education, and that our particular concern is on another level of academic attainment, yet our reference to the discussion in America indicates two things: the importance of rethinking the whole of the theological programme and the possibility of combining the two alternatives in relation to the particular needs of the Church in Africa. In Africa, after all and in spite of all, we are not bound to the same extent as in the West by certain denominational traditions, and the need for rethinking the teaching programme should be realized by African church leaders as well as by missionaries. While recognizing the need for a core programme, the school should at the same time be aware of the necessity of relating it to the personal interests of the students and to particular national and local environments. We say this, while keeping in mind that the quest for a possible 'Common Principle' in the theological curriculum in Africa should not be summarily prejudged by a Westerner. It can only be settled by African theologians.

There is another aspect of a more general nature which we emphasize before considering the different fields of study. It concerns the method of teaching, in the sense of the *direction* of this teaching. We have been impressed by certain observations made by a great number of theological students and African pastors: 'I am interested in the New Testament *because* it helps me to teach our catechists and elders when I become a pastor.' 'I regard Theology (Doctrine) as the most important subject *because* it helps me to answer people who do not believe.' 'I find Homiletics more interesting than anything else we are doing here, *because* it helps me to organize my thoughts as I am going out to preach as a minister of God.'

The discovery that some subjects are not simply a sum of facts to be learned by heart but necessary tools for the minister's work and a living inspiration to share with the Church, constitutes a dimension of study which, we think, deserves to be more emphasized than is possibly the case at present, at least in some schools. The African student, no less than theological students in other

---

[5] H. Richard Niebuhr and others, *op. cit.*, p. 84–85.

parts of the world, needs to feel that what he is attempting to learn has a meaning, for himself as an individual and also for the Church which he hopes to serve. It is when facts and phenomena are presented in that context that many students discover a new relevance in their studies.

The Bible. The teaching of the *Old Testament* presents special problems. There are European tutors who are genuinely perturbed by the incessant interest in the Old Testament. One of them—in Sierra Leone—reported in 1939 that his students 'knew a great deal about the early part of the Old Testament but practically nothing about the New. The emphasis had been placed at the wrong end of the Bible.' But fifteen years later this Western hesitation and abstemiousness with respect to the Old Testament had already had striking results in another West African theological school, for now a student informs us that 'the mythical stories in the beginning of the Old Testament fall below Christian standards and they are not historical in the proper sense of the word', and that therefore he is not really interested in the Old Testament as a field of study!

As far as the Old Testament is concerned, we should notice that translations of this part of the Bible are not yet available in many African languages. In other cases, such translations have been published only quite recently even in important and influential languages (e.g. Kikuyu and Fang, Gabon, about 1950). 'The Old Testament is virtually unknown in many churches', was a statement from French Equatorial Africa. When it becomes available—in a translation understood by the people—it invariably evokes great interest.

The parallel and the similarity between certain customs and institutions among the Hebrews and the Africans catch the imagination of ordinary African Christians and of the theological student. It has also been pointed out by certain observers—among others, J. R. B. McDonald of Buwalasi, Bishop Neill and Dr. J. W. Welch—that the African pattern of thought is nearer to Hebrew concepts than to Greek ideas.[6] This to some extent ex-

---

[6] J. R. B. McDonald, 'Classical Theology and African Thought—What are we trying to do?' Mimeograph.

James Welch, *Religious Studies in an African University,* Inaugural Lecture 1950, Ibadan University Press, 1951, p. 18.

S. C. Neill, *I.M.C. Theol. Report* I, p. 23.

plains, or at least indicates, the predilection for the Old Testament, the strength of which sometimes surprises the Western tutor. Here is, perhaps, the greatest and most exciting—and exacting—adventure waiting for the theological teacher in Africa. An advance in this field is particularly propitious at the present moment. Of late, there has taken place a remarkable revolution in Old Testament studies in the West. Building on painstaking research into the thought-world of the Old Testament background, scholars have, once again, established the Messianic line as the *leitmotif* of Old Testament revelation. This is of primary importance for an understanding of the 'wholeness' and 'organic unity' of the Bible, and will immediately be understood in these terms by the African theologian. Furthermore, this approach is fundamental for the establishment of a typological 'harmony' between the preparation in the Old Testament and the fulfilment in the New.[7] Some of the most fertile research at present is being done in the field of typology, a valuable result being the discovery of what has been called the 'Plenary Sense' *(sensus plenior)* of Holy Scripture.[8] Theological teaching in Africa, no less than elsewhere, is a risky business. It is 'one of the dangerous industries', in the words of P. T. Forsyth. So the teaching of the Bible is a challenge. It is not only a question as to how much the African students can 'assimilate'; it is a challenge also to the tutor and his understanding of the Old Testament. The age-old and highly modern, Messianic interpretation of the Scriptures affords a key which we have no right to withhold from African students. And possibly this opens a path upon which African theologians of to-morrow—with their greater propensity for an understanding of the cosmological dimensions of the Biblical faith—will together with their Western colleagues bring us deeper into the mysteries of Revelation.

If the Bible is studied as the story of God's education of the People of God in history, we have again struck a chord which first of all is in accordance with the facts of the Bible, and which at the same time finds a response in the African sense of the corporate. The idea of the People of God serves above all to give

---

[7] Cf. J. Coppens, *Les Harmonies des Deux Testaments,* Tournai—Paris: Casterman, 1949.

[8] Cf. R. E. Brown, 'The *Sensus Plenior* of Sacred Scripture'. St. Mary's University, Baltimore, Md., 1955.

a sense of continuity from Abraham through the Old Testament, through the Church of the New Testament and indeed throughout the history of the Church.

We came across a few cases in Africa of a somewhat anaemic fastidiousness, on the part of Western tutors, with regard to the historical books of the Old Testament, and are not fully convinced that this attitude is altogether helpful in this situation. The parallels between Hebrew and African concepts and institutions which the African student seems to discover have in many cases become important stepping-stones for the integration of the entire corpus of theological interpretation.[9]

Old Testament expectation is fulfilled in the *New Testament,* or rather in the Person of the Messiah. This emphasis on the Person of Jesus Christ seems also to offer a solution to the ever-present problem in African churches, that of legalism. Suggestions as to how this question can be tackled in the teaching of the New Testament are given in a thought-provoking article by Paul D. Fueter.[1] He reminds us of the experience of not a few missionaries 'that the Epistles of St. Paul are hardly understood by African Christians'. One should add, perhaps, that one of the reasons why St. Paul is not understood is due to the quality of the translations of the Pauline Epistles into many African languages.

What about the Biblical languages, Hebrew and Greek? New Testament Greek is optional in a number of Colleges, but the claim for the introduction of Hebrew appears to be crying for the moon. The I.M.C. reports are remarkably silent on this topic. The Commission to 'Latin' Africa has only one phrase on the subject, a phrase not without overtones: 'The major Greek and Hebrew terms, as conveyors of meaning, should be known *at least to the teacher*'.[2] It is perhaps one measure of our achievements

---

[9] An interpretation of the Decalogue such as that of Professor J. J. Stamm (*Der Dekalog im Lichte der neueren Forschung,* Bern 1958) shows this. It demonstrates how sound Old Testament teaching overcomes the tendency towards legalism. In the Pentateuch the preaching of the law is closely related to worship, to the *Heilskultus* with its historical orientation. As Professor Carl Keller has put it: 'God liberates his people and gives it his law in order to preserve its freedom. The Decalogue means joy, freedom, blessing.' Cf. *Evangelisches Missionsmagazin* (Basel), 1959, p. 44.

[1] Paul D. Fueter, 'Theological Education in Africa', *International Review of Missions,* October 1956.

[2] *I.M.C. Theol. Report* II, p. 60 (our italics).

(and of the problems of staffing) and, even more, of our conventional Western attitude to African capacity, that as far as is known Hebrew is not taught, even as an optional extra. In the French Cameroons we were told of one African pastor who before going on a long *safari* into the bush borrowed a Hebrew grammar from the missionary. When he returned after some weeks he had taught himself the elements of the language and had the thrill of having mastered the first eleven chapters of Genesis.

Dr. Frank Michaeli, Professor of Old Testament in Paris, himself a member of the I.M.C. Commission to Latin Africa, has stated, on this problem of two Biblical languages: 'For my part, I have been convinced that the moment is close at hand when the study of the Biblical languages in Africa instead of complicating the problem will make it easier.'[3] He goes on to explain his position: 'Not only is it easier to remain faithful to the Bible text in making one single translation rather than two successive ones (e.g. from Greek directly into Douala rather than from Greek into French, and from French into Douala) but also and above all I have the impression that the Biblical languages—particularly Hebrew—are much closer than ours to the African mentality and even to their languages, which are concrete languages, poetical, metaphorical and realistic.' A Swiss missionary with long experience of Bible school teaching in Mozambique, M. Schaller, gives his opinion on this point in the exclamation, 'When are we going to get Africans who are masters of Hebrew? Then we shall have dazzling Bible translations!'

In the meantime, we would advocate an approach which attempts to make constant translation work into the spearhead of Bible teaching. Students should be made aware of the obvious fact that any translation, and particularly those made by foreigners, are necessarily temporary. There could be a degree of expectation and *élan* in a Bible teaching which aims at enlisting the creative co-operation of the students both during their school years and in their life-work as pastors. The I.M.C. Commission to Southern Africa has valuable suggestions to make on this point.

More time should be given to the thorough study and discussion of the most fundamental Biblical words, tracing their usage through

---

[3] F. Michaeli, 'L'enseignement théologique dans l'œuvre missionnaire en Afrique', *Bulletin de la Faculté de Theol. Protestante de Paris* (XVI) Déc. 1953, p. 117.

the Old and New Testament and noting how the essential beliefs of the Christian hinge upon these basic conceptions. Such word-studies would be studies in that 'Communication' which is more than translation; through conversations and discussions a thorough attempt should be made to get deeply into the thought-forms of the various African languages represented in the student body. This would also help the students to get a much clearer understanding of their own background, of the beliefs of their own people and the distinctive standpoint and content of the Biblical revelation.[4]

We have advocated a dimension of teaching which always aims at *sharing* acquired knowledge with the Church and putting it at the disposal of the Church. Here the teaching of the Bible is of particular importance.

Church History. 'The Bible is a tree-trunk, and all fields of study in theology are only branches growing out from that tree.' Thus mused Rev. Sibane of Mozambique—and he was right. The History of the People of God in and through the Church is a continuation of that history which began in the first book of the Bible. The I.M.C. commissions were told that African students do not easily take to Church history. They lack a sense of history, it was said. In Southern Africa it was reported that 'Africans have no conception of history, no capacity for apprehending notions of time and sequence and the relatedness of events'. In these circumstances, we were told, it is almost impossible to teach Church history with any meaning. In one case the subject had been given up for this reason.[5] We shall let a West African student, from Ghana, speak for the others. His sigh is one which gives an echo in many minds, possibly not only among Africans. 'Church history', he writes, 'is uninteresting, because it is difficult for me to learn dates by heart or commit them to memory, but Church history is full of dates. It is not the fault of the master, for he tries to explain every point as well as possible. I shall welcome any method that will help me to understand this lesson!'

There has been much speculation on Church history teaching in Africa. But very little solid research has been done, and we suggest that there is an important study to be undertaken here in order to understand where the real difficulties lie. Such an under-

---

[4] *I.M.C. Theol. Report,* III, p. 45–46.
[5] *I.M.C. Theol. Report,* III, p. 46.

taking will be helped by recent research into the African's traditional sense of history.[6]

The complaints about a lack of historical perspective among African ordinands cannot very well be taken seriously until we have first provided two things: solid teaching of general history as an epistemological framework—for Church history must take full account of the fact that the Church is a church in the world and for the world—*and* well-conceived text-books on African Church history. By this latter term we mean interpretations in which African leaders are not automatically subordinated to the Western pioneers. The essence, and thrill, of African Church history surely is an account of the response on the part of African groups and individual leaders. This interpretation on the continental, national, and possibly the tribal level must be put into relation to ecumenical history and wide universal trends.

1. There is a tendency to treat Church history as a catalogue of unrelated data, so-called 'historical facts'. This tendency is one reason why the subject is difficult for students to learn. The most important recent development in the West in the field of Church history teaching is a new awareness of Church history as a *theological* discipline, and when the full implications of this insight have been grasped the subject will come to life in a way which no mere catalogue of events ever can. Church history takes us straight into the most burning theological issues of to-day: Scripture and Tradition; the nature of the continuity of the Church and its relation to the particularity of the individual Church; the problem of 'development'. The German scholar Professor Gerhard Ebeling has recently defined Church history as 'the history of interpretation *(Auslegung)* of Holy Scripture', and by this definition has stressed the theological importance of the historical character of the Church. The definition also in a suggestive manner binds Church history as a theological discipline to the study of the Bible. Church history becomes a wide screen on which the rays of Biblical revelation are thrown, and the continuous reflection and response of European, Asian, African and other churches to this

---

[6] J. A. Barnes, 'The Perception of History in a Plural Society'. *Human Relations*, The Tavistock Inst. of Human Relations, Vol. IV, No 3, 1951.

Ian Cunnison, *History of the Luapula*, Rhodes-Livingstone Papers, No 21, 1951.

Biblical radiation constitutes the Church's history.[7] It is in this theological context that the African student will discover the dynamic relevance of history to his own situation. In any case we believe that it is incumbent on the Church history tutor in Africa seriously to accept this challenge of regarding his subject as a task of theological interpretation.

Any Church history teacher worth his salt has an ambition to 'cover the ground'—that is, he persuades himself and his students that his aim is to present the whole of the Church's development. This is *always* a fallacy. We all inevitably select and reject, deliberately or unwittingly, and our selection becomes intelligent in the measure in which it is deliberate. We need a principle of selection, and Church history tutors in Africa need to have not less, but possibly more courage than elsewhere in this process of selection. A suggestion made by an experienced Indian Church history professor, Dr. C. E. Abraham of Serampore, seems to be well worth consideration. *Ceteris partibus* it appears to be applicable to the situation in Africa also.

> The best results are perhaps obtained by a combination of an intensive study of the history of one period or country with a survey course of the ecumenical history that is apposite to that period or country. By intensive study is meant not merely acquaintance with the details of developments in the Church but also observation and study of the Church (understood in the wider sense of the community of God's people) in relation to its environment on the one hand and its objectives on the other; or in other words, the Church, the Gospel and the World in their relations to one another... This intensive study must, however, go hand in hand with a comprehensive survey, a panoramic view of the particular period or area covered so that the field of study may be seen in its proper perspective.[8]

Professor John Foster, whose well-known books on Church history—*Then and Now*; *World Church,* etc.—have been of great service also in theological colleges in Africa, makes his choice on lines which seem to have a general appeal to Protestant teachers. 'If I had to choose two periods, instead of three, I should have

---

[7] G. Ebeling, *Kirchengeschichte als Geschichte der Auslegung der Heiligen Schrift,* Sammlund gemeinverständliche Vortäge, No. 189, 1947, and *idem, Die Geschichtlichkeit der Kirche and ihrer Verkündigung als theologisches Problem, ibid.,* No. 207/208, 1954.

[8] C. E. Abraham, *Indian Journal of Theology,* April–June 1957, p. 45–6.

no hesitation in saying first, the early centuries and secondly, the nineteenth century, which Professor Latourette has called "the Great Century".' To this should, we feel, be added the *caveat* that the choice need not be reduced to two periods, and if that need were to arise, there are many who would not choose the nineteenth century however 'great' it may have been from the point of view of Protestant missionary expansion. Surely the Reformation period has a claim here to our particular attention. Above all it was a period when the great issues of Church history became burning and living as they need to be burning and living issues even to-day. An interesting point was made by Bishop Neill.

> What do we really want our African students to learn from the history of the Church? What parts of it are really relevant to them at their present stage of development? I could not but feel profound symphathy with the African student, who remarked, 'It seems to me that missionaries are much too hard in their judgments on the African churches. Did you never have a period of struggle in your own countries?' Indeed we did. In that moment I suddenly saw that, for the African Churches in their contemporary struggle, the most important period is the one that ordinarily we never teach them in detail, the Dark Ages. Alcuin, the Venerable Bede, St. Boniface, the foundation of Cluny—these are the things that would be really illuminating to them, as they wrestle with precisely the same difficulties, and are called to find anew the way out of the twilight of the co-existence of old and new into a more genuinely Christian life and social order.[9]

The need for a well-balanced Church history text-book written for African students is deeply felt in many theological schools. Combining a universal and African-national approach, it should as far as Africa is concerned bring out the main trends, the great ideas and movements, rather than presenting merely a catalogue of the names and dates of missionary societies and individual missionaries. It is particularly important that the African response to the challenge of the Gospel should be given an essential place in the whole panorama. African church leaders, such as Crowther and Aggrey and Baëta, Jabavu and other Bantu leaders in South Africa, Avirama Ngulu of Angola and Apolo Kivebulaya; the martyrs of Natete, Madagascar and elsewhere;—all these names and many others belong to that great and inspiring company for

---

[9] *I.M.C. Theol. Report,* I, p. 25.

whom there must be an honoured place in the history of the Church.

This again demands work at the grass-roots, in the local situation. There is not much hope of presenting Church history as the thrilling and exciting subject which it in fact is, until the necessary research work about the local churches and its African leaders is being carried out on a wide scale and its results are being published. We need a re-orientation here. The facts about the missionary pioneers from the West are fairly well-known, but with every year that passes now, opportunities are lost for collecting first-hand knowledge of the early converts and of the equally important and interesting second and third generation African leaders. The initiative taken by the Reformed Church in the French Cameroons is of particular interest and consequence here. They have formed a 'Committee of History and Necrology' with a view to preserving biographical and other Church history material relating to the African leaders of the Church.

2. Has the usual approach to the teaching of Church history in Africa been sufficiently relevant? I felt I had to ask that question during the ten weeks in 1941 when in an emergency I had to teach Church history to a class of Zulu theological students. As I suddenly had to adjust myself to this new task, I found that the text-book was quite familiar to me; it was an English translation, published in the United States, of a Swedish Church History, by N. Lövgren, who first drafted his book in 1888. Lövgren was a Swede of the Swedes, and his text-book has a tendency to take in the mighty sweep of Church history from the Swedish point of view. That made the task at least superficially easy for the young Swedish tutor; but I reminded myself that this was not necessarily the most intelligent approach to Zulus, and, after all, my students were Zulus.

This example from my own experience is representative of what is going on, possibly on a big scale, and explains to a greater extent than is generally realized why the teaching of Church history seems to present particular difficulties. The problem is not merely, and not really, that the orientation is 'too Western'. The religion of Incarnation, born in the Holy Land, has for many centuries been particularly influential in the West; no 'indigenization' of Church history-teaching can overlook this stubborn fact of history. With the recent experience of Asia before our eyes we predict that the more political nationalism becomes victorious in Africa, the more the Church will discover the need for the Catholic and universal dimension of its history, and consequently the more Church History teaching must stress the anchoring of the 'facts' and data in the *whole* history of the Church.

The difficulty and the deficiency lie elsewhere, in the lack of teaching of African Church history, and the lack of a creative tension between the national and the universal dimensions. In the same way as Swedish theological students find it natural to base their knowledge on a study of Swedish Church history, so also for African students Church history begins at home. In the same way, African churches everywhere should be made aware, in and through the theological college, of the need *now* for thorough research and study of their own local history.

There are interesting examples of classroom-teaching related to the immediate environment of the African student. Bishop L. Beecher of Nairobi— himself once a teacher of Church history at Limuru—relates his experiment from the 1940's.

> A 'time sense' is not an easy thing to inculcate. So a 'Stephen King Hall approach' was tried. We traced Church history backwards, starting with the diocese of Kenya and other denominations in the country, going back to the arrival of the first Protestant missionary, Ludvig Krapf, in 1844. But Krapf, the German in the service of the Church Missionary Society, had before his arrival in Kenya attempted to reach the Gallas of Ethiopia and spent some time in that country. Krapf thus came not only from Germany, the country of Luther's reformation, but also from the country with the oldest African church. There were then two historical threads to trace back, one to Europe, the other to Ethiopia, and the latter, by way of St. Frumentius, takes the student back to St. Mark in Alexandria and the Apostolic Church. Having thus reviewed Church history in reverse from a highly selective viewpoint, the process was then changed, and the ordinary chronological sequence could be followed—although once again definitely selective.

P. D. Fueter, with experience of teaching in a Bible School and a Theological College in Tanganyika, has made imaginative efforts with regard to teaching through the reading of the Bible text, valuable also for the teaching of Church history.

> These men miss what I would call the fundamental ability of thinking whilst reading. I believe more and more that we fail generally in Africa, because we often try to teach theology before people

have been given the tools of thought. I have now started to teach straight-forward grammar, e.g. the building of a language, which I believe fundamental. It seems that the teaching of history can also be improved considerably. We get further by taking as basis the genealogy of Christ in Matthew. They have to learn the 42 names by heart in the same way as most of them know the names of their own ancestors at least up to the 4th generation (one even knew up to 10 generations). By using names instead of figures for measuring history, we seem to get some-where, and I am sure that if a further course was given making the link between names and figures, they would be up to our conceptions of history.

Doctrine. At Kumasi, Ghana—where the Trinity Theological College is a neighbour of the Government Technical College—one African theological student writes, 'Theology is a subject of great moment, for although it is not religion, it is to religion as geology is to mining; it is the very handmaid of religion.'

A variety of levels in the quality of teaching is characteristic of this subject in various colleges in Africa. We visited some schools where one could sense, on the part of the missionary, a certain hesitation with regard to this whole field of study. 'In our school we study the Bible, a revised form of catechism, Church history and Homiletics. But theology, no, we don't teach that!' It is of course a matter of definition. This missionary wanted to say that he did not teach a prescribed course in History of Doctrine or in 'Dogmatics'. But he was himself not fully aware of the fact that as he opened his Bible and explained the Word of God, he did in fact, on his particular level, teach theology. On this level there is in the seminary rather a catechetical approach, although this kind of theological teacher will declare that he does not recognize the value of catechisms—for his own church 'back home' is against the use of a catechism.

On another level altogether is the teaching of Doctrine pre-sented by churches belonging to Presbyterian, Methodist, Lu-theran, and Anglican traditions. In the Swiss Theological School at Ricatla in Mozambique, there was a conscientious analysis of theological terminology with comparison between terms in French and the African languages concerned. This attempt seems to be of great value. It expressed in tangible terms a most relevant dimen-sion of theological teaching in these parts of the world: a method aiming at the translation into African thought-forms of fundamental Christian concepts. In this connexion it is often stressed by African pastors that a more thorough grounding in philosophical concepts is needed in order to make the study of Doctrine worthwhile.

In making a plea for *translated Dogmatics* we are not primarily concerned with denominational teaching varying from one Church to another, nor with a fully-fledged history of doctrine which, however valuable, cannot easily find its place in the time allotted. The important point is that Doctrine must be seen in its organic connexion with the Bible, 'All fields of theological study are branches on the Tree of the Bible.' This very definitely is the case with Christian doctrine.

In Africa, Biblical revelation has to be affirmed in the encounter with a number of competing forces.

a. *Latent or renascent paganism.* Ancestor-worship and its concomitant ideas on God present the Doctrine class with great opportunities for an approach to the Biblical teaching on the cosmos, creation, revelation, Christ the Mediator and the Fulfiller, on Christian eschatology, on the life after Death, on the understanding of the role of Saints, particularly so in the African context.[1]

The Zionist separatist church movement in South Africa with its Bantu-Christian syncretism is a serious indication of the direction which Christian groups in Africa can take if they are not sustained and nurtured by sound and solid Bible teaching. It should not be taken for granted that such problems as ancestor-worship, magic, and the role of jujus are no longer known to younger generations of African theological students. The faculty would be well advised to discuss these things with the students as being of greater personal relevance to them than is generally realised at present. Against this background the fundamental truths of Christian doctrine stand out in sharp relief.[2]

b. *Islam* presents its particular challenge to the very concepts of theology which the Christian Church preaches. In East Africa we found certain cases in the coastal area, where Moslem fatalism had conditioned the Christian understanding of the nature of God ('*shauri la Mungu*', act of God). This is possibly even more the

---

[1] Vide infra Ch. VI, pp.

[2] Cf. B. Sundkler, 'Response and Resistance to the Gospel in a Zulu Congregation', in *Basileia,* Walter Freytag zum 6o. Geburtstag (Stuttgart 1959), p. 128–145.

case in certain parts of West Africa, and here and elsewhere African pastors need to be well equipped in Christian and Islamic doctrine in order to engage in that 'dialogue with Islam', which Dr. J. S. Trimingham has urged so convincingly.[3]

c. *Modern nationalism* and *Western materialism* both make the teaching of Christian doctrine relevant and necessary and present a challenge and an alternative which serve to sharpen the issue.

As an example of an imaginative and helpful approach to the teaching of Biblical doctrine in an African setting we quote from a letter to us from Rev. P. D. Fueter, then at St. Philip's Theological College, Kongwa, Tanganyika.

> We have been led to start from the Bible and to leave out nearly all reference to the actual history of doctrine. Not of course out of principle, but for lack of time. Our course starts with the question of 'Revelation' which includes a study of God, then the work of Christ, then man, sin and grace, finally, the Trinity, Incarnation and Predestination. We leave the tough bits for the end. We have called this the helicoidal approach to dogmatics, i.e. starting from very far to go to the nucleus, not in a straight line, but in a spiral. I feel that this is the method of approach of Africans generally, who never go straight to the point, 'tournant autour du pot', as the French say.
>
> It is always the conflict between 'tribal thinking' and Christian thinking which is puzzling. The concept for instance of 'luck', *bahati*, has been arresting our attention. Students, themselves keen Christians, said: 'We have always thought that if a man under discipline came back to the church *in extremis,* he had been lucky.' The grace of God seems to be misunderstood. The Divinity of Christ seems to be generally accepted. But we had great difficulty in getting across that Christ was not *kama mwanadamu,* but *mwanadamu* (not 'like man', but 'man'). This seemed to be a blasphemy to many students. I was rather astonished to find unanimity among the students that Islam was a church: *Kanisa la Islam,* with the idea that actually Islam was only another denomination.

Obviously, the teaching of Doctrine presents the *ecumenical* problem in its most acute form. It is felt in theological schools where staff and students represent different traditions, whilst in other schools it is sometimes avoided altogether.

---

[3] J. S. Trimingham, *The Christian Church and Islam in West Africa,* International Missionary Council Research Pamphlets No. 3, pp. 40–53.

Christian Morals are centred in the great principle of respect for every human being as a person in the image of God and for whom Christ died. All teaching in this field should derive from, and continually return to, this major doctrine.

When rules of conduct are determined and applied apart from the basic doctrine, and apart from the second commandment of Christ to which it is allied, moralistic legalism endangers the whole Christian position. No thoughtful Christian teacher in Africa needs to be reminded of the omnipresence of this peril in the current practice of churches and missions.

Since African morals are so strongly identified with the customs and the opinion of the group, and are so easily externalized into collective conformity, sound and thorough teaching of the Christian principle is necessary if any personal sense of sin is to be realized, and if church discipline is to be more than the organizational policing of a social group.[4]

An interesting approach is the one taken by the two Anglican schools in Uganda. Both Mukono and Buwalasi have felt that the 'usual academic Ethics course' was out of the question. Instead they have devised a syllabus called 'The Christian in his relationship' which include in one two-year course teaching on prayer and the growth in grace, sex-teaching and marriage, the Christian's obligations to his Church, to society and to the State.

Fortunately, valuable books are available in English relating to these questions. S. H. Childs' *The Life of Holiness* has grown out of Ethics teaching in an Anglican theological school in Nigeria. Thomas Price on *African Marriage* is an 'International Missionary Research Pamphlet', summarizing the important *Survey of African Marriage and Family Life,* edited by Arthur Phillips. Nationalism and politics is a fundamentally important concern for the African Church, and J. V. Taylor's Penguin Book (WA 9) *Christianity and Politics in Africa,* 1957, treats this subject in an admirable way. It also has a useful bibliography.

It is in this context that the teaching of African culture finds its most relevant place in the curriculum, not as an isolated chapter of African *Religionsgeschichte* but as a living part of the African cultural heritage. The difficulties in teaching this subject are real, and sometimes complex, but the case for training and instruction is strong. Few missionaries or Africans are really qualified to

---

[4] *I.M.C. Theol. Report.* II, p. 63.

conduct such a course. That is, perhaps, a measure of the need to begin to teach it as a necessary part of the curriculum. It is also 'an indication of the considerable distance often maintained between the missionary's message on the one side and the inner problems of the African convert on the other.'[5]

Pastoralia. This subject, in our opinion, is so important that it ought to be one man's whole work. There is room for some original study and thought concerning the nature of the 'sermon' in African worship. This applies to the whole field of pastoral theology; it is here that the encounter of Christianity with the pattern of African life, in its various forms, is immediately reflected. It often seemed to us that pastoral theology and homiletics were being taught within a situation in which the unknown factors were most important. The adequate handling of these subjects waits on the emergence of African teachers; in the meantime, we would venture to say that perhaps one of the most essential responsibilities of the tutor in carge of the subject is to listen.

We recognize that the teaching on *'Worship: Its form and conduct'* and its practice in college chapels must reflect the standpoint and practice of the church with which the college is associated. We nevertheless urge that instruction in the form and conduct of worship should be related not only to denominational practice and the wider history of liturgy but to the possibilities and special insights of the Africans themselves. Once again, the need for 'listening' teachers must be emphasized. Some of the liturgical developments in the African separatist chuches would repay special study. Many of the more orthodox churches seem to be meagre and severe in their liturgical life, continuing the European traditions out of which the particular mission grew. The terms 'devotional' and 'dignity' should not be used solely with the meaning which they naturally convey to Western ears. 'Rhythm' may have a much fuller part to play than is commonly recognized in a form of worship that is both Christian and African.

Many congregations and whole church bodies would do well to develop the use of the Church year and its great festivals, in suitable public worship. The rhythm of the agricultural year should also be heeded in the annual programme of worship.[6]

---

[5] *I.M.C. Theol. Report,* II, pp. 72–73.
[6] *I.M.C. Theol. Reports,* II, p. 65–67, and III, p. 47.

By the term 'rhythm' we emphasize a dimension of theological teaching which some schools at present do not seem to stress sufficiently. Only seldom is 'Music' taught as a subject, and where it is taught the central importance of the training is perhaps not fully grasped. We are therefore not surprised when a young West African student writes, 'Music is the least important field of study, because already before a student enters into college he knows most of the hymns in his hymnbook. The rest of the hymns, which he does not yet know, can be learned by singing them over and over. It is not important to give music a place on the college time-table.'

This opinion is a measure of the unrelatedness of the theological course which we have achieved! One can see how such an attitude has been formed. If 'Music' is reduced to the learning of tunes out of Moody and Sankey, we should not be surprised when African students feel that they ought not to waste valuable time in repeating these hymns. If, on the other hand, rhythm and drama and music are seen as conveying a total expression of corporate Christian experience, then the subject comes alive and can be treated as vitally important. In thirty or forty years' time there may possibly appear some African church leader or theologian who will claim that the approach through African Christian music is the key and the organic principle of teaching of Christian theology as a whole in Africa. Such an attitude could very well appear, by way of reaction to a supposedly sterile Western intellectualism in the approach to theology. This again is a challenge to Western and African teachers alike. This approach should be kept in mind at least in the appointment of African staff — bearing in mind that in many cases the African Christians themselves violently oppose the use of African music in worship.

Research work has recently been undertaken into African music and the means of using form-elements of this music in the Church services. Mr. Henry Weman, the Chief Organist of Uppsala Cathedral, has made an important contribution here. We believe that his book on the subject, which contains constructive proposals for African Church music, will prove to be of particular value in a field which has been tragically neglected and which possibly represents the most important dimension of the Church's life in Africa. Much valuable research has also been made by Rev. A. M.

Jones—formerly of Northern Rhodesia (U.M.C.A.), now at the University of London—into this subject.[7]

Pastoral care. In his attempt to interpret the new conception of the Protestant minister which seems to be emerging at present in America, Richard Niebuhr speaks of the minister as a 'pastoral director', whose primary function is that of building up or 'edifying' the Church, by an activity on behalf of individuals which is expressed as 'pastoral counselling'.[8] Obviously the situation in the Church in Africa is very different from that now emerging in the United States. When we here stress the importance of the teaching of pastoral care, it is also less as a preparation for a form of ministry which already has emerged than as an expression of the need which the Church in Africa feels deeply at the present time. Revival movements such as the *Soatanana* in Madagascar or the East African *Balokole* have stressed public confession. This form has forced its way to a dominant place in the Revival, in spite of resistance showing how deep is the need for the confession of sins. Yet it must be admitted that at present the Church in Africa hardly functions as an 'institute of the care of souls' for its masses of second and third generation Christians. To some extent this could be remedied by creative teaching of pastoral care in theological colleges. This in its turn presupposes an effective pastoral relationship between staff and students, for the only way to learn pastoral care is to be the object of someone's pastoral care, and many theological students complain, we found, that the thing they miss above all in the colleges is intimate skilled pastoral care. Theology is a science *ad praxin,* and this certainly is true of the teaching of pastoral care. Have we perhaps with all our modern rationalism forgotten this function of the ministry at its deeper levels, not to administer an organization, but to minister to sin-sick souls?

The Bible School — School and Power House

The task of the Theological College is to train candidates for the ordained ministry. The Bible School prepares unordained

[7] A. M. Jones, 'Hymns for the African', *Books for Africa,* (27), 1957, Sept.—Oct.

H. Weman, *African Music and the Church in Africa,* Uppsala, 1960.

[8] Richard Niebuhr, *The Purpose of the Church and its Ministry,* pp. 79–94.

workers for the Church: first and foremost the catechists who, more than anybody else, have been the real builders of the thousands of local churches throughout the continent of Africa. But that is only one aspect, and a passing aspect, of the role of the Bible School.[9]

1. The whole concept of the Bible School is changing in Africa at present, and much of the real advance of the Churches—in numbers and depth—is, we think, linked up with a renewal on this decisive front. The training of catechists has been a valuable contribution to the life of the Church in Africa in the last two generations, and still is of very considerable importance. But the scene is changing. The catechist always presented something of a problem, placed half-way between pastor and layman, supposedly as a bridge between those two. The better trained catechists soon wanted to know why they were not given the status and pay of pastors; the less qualified among them, as the time went by and church, education, and society changed, seemed to be more of a burden than a bridge.

The general trend in church policy at present is to form groups of voluntary church workers, laymen and women, willing to carry local responsibility in the Church, and this, not only in order to 'help the pastor', but to demonstrate the local reality of the Church and the fact of the general priesthood of the body of believers.

Our concern is the laity of the Church in Africa, in its original meaning of the *laos*, the whole people of God, and its Christian education 'unto the measure of the stature of the fulness of Christ'. We are aware of the Church's difficulty of getting at 'the real layman', and that more often than not progress beyond the ecclesiastical layman, who by birth, environment or other contacts has been brought to feel his responsibility for the Church, is well-nigh impossible. However that may be, the problem of a deepened and quickening Christian education of the total membership of the Church remains to be solved.

The task of the Bible School has to be seen in a new light, and in a new perspective. We envisage it as a Christian Life Centre, a Power-House of the Church, where men and women could come

---

[9] A thorough and efficient study of the Bible School in Africa is very much needed. In the meantime we would like to believe that our presentation in the following few pages—however superficial—presents a perspective that cannot altogether be left out of the context of ministerial training as a whole.

for inspiration and knowledge and from which a well-equipped team of Bible teachers could go out to conduct short Bible courses in the different districts and parishes. This does not need to imply the ever-present risk of multiplying institutions; it is in fact a case of taking the Bible School seriously and equipping it accordingly—in staff and vision. As general education is being taken over from the Church by the State, the Church can now concentrate in a new way on its evangelistic task, through the Bible School. 'Mobility' is an important part of the plan; the Bible School staff has to be prepared to plan its work in such a way that it can share the courses run at the School and those directed on the parish level. At the Bible School itself there would be short local catechists' courses, and refresher courses and spiritual retreats for youth workers, elders, intellectuals, and women leaders. On the parish level the need is great for mobile local catechists' courses, Sunday school courses, etc. By this interchange between centralized and district teaching and by mobility and determination in planning, the Bible School can achieve a a new relevance to the whole life of the Church.

A plan of this kind implies a shift in the policy of the Church from a preoccupation with elementary education—which is being taken over by the State anyway—to the training of voluntary church workers and the evangelistic outreach of the Church. But we must be aware of a risk inherent in a change of this kind: a narrowing of the cultural and social horizons of the Church. This risk—the more fatal as general education is rapidly rising—should be met by a balanced educational programme in the Church as a whole. This should include a vigorous encounter with the social, political and cultural problems of new Africa. The 'Lay Apostolate' vision of Catholic Action in Africa, enlisting the loyal and enthusiastic co-operation of African writers, journalists, radio-commentators, politicians, educationalists, and businessmen, is one example of this necessary encounter. The radiation from the Bible School, and the Theological School, would above all help towards a renewed encounter with traditional African valuations and reactions and would strengthen the evangelistic outreach of the Church.

This concept, incidentally, also has repercussions on the training of the ministers in the Theological School. It ties up with the particular 'dimension' of theological training which we have attempted to emphasize: a teaching which in all fields of study aims at preparing the future minister for his essential task as a servant and leader of local leaders, as a guide and teacher of local Bible courses and refresher courses.

This new aspect of the Bible School as a 'Christian Life Centre' or a Diocesan (District) 'Retreat House' has been influenced by experience, not least in the United States. The Moody Bible Institute, the Providence Barrington Bible College, and the Lutheran Bible Institute, provide examples of what could be attempted, on an applied scale, for the churches in Africa. In a thought-provoking article in the *International Review of Missions,* October 1956, Rev. Carl J. Johansson, of Tanganyika, has pointed out the new possibilities of the Bible School, thereby building on first-hand experience from his work at Mwika Lutheran Bible School in the Kilimanjaro area. 'The potentialities are enormous. The Bible School seeks to form a stream of evangelism and evangelistic activity within the churches that it serves.'

In the case of the Mwika school, the main programme of work consists in a series of six ten-week periods, spread over two years, attended both by future catechists and by interested laymen. But parallel with this programme, there are weeks of Bible conferences or 'Bible camps', the running of Bible correspondence courses, Sunday school conferences, the writing and distribution of simple Biblical tracts. Special refresher courses for church workers are also held.

Rev. T. A. Beetham, of the (British) Methodist Missionary Society, who has been an inspiring influence in the whole movement towards a new conception of the Bible School and of the training of laymen, particularly in West Africa, sees the School as 'a place of refreshment and re-invigoration for church members, a District "Retreat House".'[1] The Methodist plan on *Lay Leadership in West African Churches* published in 1957, contains valuable suggestions for effective training in a new age, for voluntary service, thereby attempting to maintain the initiative in the field of the training of lay members.

In their valuable report on *Theological Education in South-East Asia* (New York, 1952), Dr. S. R. Anderson and Dr. C. Stanley Smith demonstrate the great appeal which Bible schools make to

---

[1] Cf. T. A. Beetham, *Report of a Secretarial Visit to West Africa,* (1951), p. 17, and *Lay Leadership in West African Churches,* 1957, pp. 12–24.

young people in that region, and their particular appeal to the laity because of a certain evangelistic aggressiveness in their programme. In many places the Bible schools are filling a vacuum. In Africa, these institutions have hitherto played second fiddle to the theological schools and, above all, to the up-and coming teacher-training schools and secondary institutions. There are indications, however, that the role of the Bible School has not ended. It is on the threshold of taking a new, and exciting, part in the evangelistic outreach of the Church.[2]

2. The change of policy with regard to the place and function of the catechist in the Church obviously affects the Bible School as traditionally understood. The whole trend is to replace the large number of salaried catechists by ordained ministers and voluntary helpers. The development within the West African Methodist Conference is important. In the 1920's a number of well-equipped multiple institutions were started here, designed to train three groups of men: ministers, catechists and teachers. To-day, in most cases, these colleges are teacher-training centres, and most of the ministerial training is carried out in newly-organized united theological schools, such as Umuahia in Eastern Nigeria, and Kumasi in Ghana. In the 1920's, it was hoped that the following twenty years would see the end of the employment of untrained catechists. There are to-day about a thousand such untrained catechists in West African Methodism.[3] The policy at present is to eliminate the untrained catechist eventually, and replace this older type by two different groups of effectively trained men, by short courses and longer catechists' courses.[4]

This is not the place for a detailed study of catechists' training in Africa. We restrict ourselves to a few notes on this important subject.

A large number of churches on the radical fringe of Protestantism, and representing missions that are often highly endowed

---

[2] These suggestions and references to recent experience and planning must suffice. As we are preparing this chapter, an excellent book from India reaches us: Wilfred Scopes, *Training Voluntary Workers in the Service of the Christian Church in India*, NCC Nagpur, 1957. It contains a wealth of valuable material presented in a practical way. We hope (a) that the book becomes widely known also in Africa, and (b) that Africa will soon get a comparable study, adapted to the particular needs and conditions of the Churches in Africa.

[3] T. A. Beetham, *Report of a Secretarial Visit to West Africa* 1951, p. 11.

[4] *Lay Leadership in West African Churches*, 1957.

from the West, prefer to develop their training of catechists in and through the Bible Schools. Here the number of applicants for the catechists' courses is regarded as gratifying. The Free Methodists (U.S.) in Mozambique receive twice as many applications as the number of available places in the School, to give one instance of a tendency which still obtains in many similar groups.

In some Churches there is only one central Bible School, which sometimes plays a great role in the spiritual life of the whole Church, while in other Churches the system of catechists' training comprises a certain number of local Bible Schools, preferably under African leadership. An example of the latter type is 'the Bishop Tucker system' in the diocese of Uganda, with three local centres for the training of 'Second Letter Catechists' (one in Buganda, one in Busoga and a third in the Western Province). Here the training is under the inspection of the African rural dean and the staff consists of an African priest and a deacon.

A recent Lovedale (S. Africa) Bible School evangelists' course had some 25 students, of whom three are Coloured. Half of the 22 Bantu students were Xhosa, four were Zulu and the others were Sotho, Pedi or Shangaan. (The average educational background, before entering the course was $4\,^4/_5$ Stds, ranging from Std I to Std X (the latter in the case of one of the Coloured students).) The educational attainment of five standards is in many cases—in this and many other Bible Schools throughout Africa—combined with a strong personality quotient, good intelligence and energy, all of which are heightened by personal Christian experience.

In the French Cameroons, the American Presbyterians have four local Bible Schools. They feel, however, that the quality of men is at present falling until 'near-illiterates' have to be accepted as students. Further North, dynamic Bamiléké pastors (Paris mission) all have their own local catechists' training, either in the form of a regular Bible School, or as at Nkongsamba, a catechists' course during one week in each month.

In certain extreme cases, the narrowness of the individual catechist's educational background has its equivalent in the intellectual outlook of the particular group of missionaries dealing with the situation. The combination is interesting. Western missionaries of the Assemblies of God in Liberia told us that they had organized the curriculum of their Bible School with a view to preventing their catechists from being exposed to the usual secular temptation, which is to leave God's work in order to take up well-paid jobs in the world. 'Therefore, in teaching geography we concentrate on the map of the Holy Land; in history we teach the history of Liberia only, and the maths. course does not take them any further than helping them to count church money.' 'Then you are safe?' we asked, having an incurably inquisitive mind. 'Yes, sure,' was the answer.

Three years is generally regarded as a sufficiently long time for the catechists' training in the Bible School. Courses lasting much shorter time are not uncommon. Africans complain about this. Baptist catechists in Angola—with a nine months' Bible School —said of their opportunity, 'It is like sitting down to eat really good food without time to eat it, for something suddenly happens, and you have to break the meal without warning.'

Professor Busia has warned us that 'for all their influence, the Christian Churches are still alien institutions (in Africa)'. If this fundamental weakness is to be overcome, this must take place on the local level. And here the local leaders—catechists and voluntary helpers—are engaged in an all-important task. In and through the Bible School, African leaders and missionaries make the attempt to overcome this foreignness and to make the Church into a home, a Family of God.

The Bridge of Understanding

What language-medium should be used in the Theological College? Should it be a European language—English, French, Portuguese, Afrikaans—or the mother tongue, the African vernacular, of the students? The subject is controversial. People get quite worked up about it, and well they might, for it is an important issue. Let us first dispose of the current propaganda missiles and if possible dismantle them.

There are two different camps, those of the 'integrationists' and the 'differentialists'[5], in French called 'indigénistes' and 'européanistes'. Those in the first camp insist that to use a European

---

[5] Cf. O. Raum, in *Yearbook of Education,* 1954, p. 218.

language is to 'adhere to the nineteenth-century imperialistic spirit of Europe', to quote an article in *The International Review of Missions*.[6] This supposed adherence to Western imperialism may be quite unconscious, the author of the article admits, but he is apparently convinced that it is nevertheless real. A few lines later, the author has jumped to the conclusion that the protagonists of the use of European languages 'would regard an indigenous African theology so far (for how long?) as being out of the question'.

The other camp hurls the term 'romanticists' against their opponents, and the present writer, unfortunately, cannot enter a plea of 'not guilty' on this count.

It would perhaps not be a bad idea to ignore the propaganda phrases and attempt to face the real situation. This can only be done through a sustained debate, in which African theologians must play their part. This debate must be carried on through continent-wide surveys as well as through local studies.

What are the arguments of the 'integrationists'? The article referred to approaches the problem from the three angles called the practical, the philosophical and the missiological.

In the first place the christianization of African languages had developed quickly, according to von Sicard; the Bantu languages 'abound in preciseness of expression to a much greater extent than do the European languages'.[7] A practical consideration is the size of the language groups. When small European language groups such as the Finns have produced a considerable literature on their own, the smaller African language groups may take courage. Small populations can become bigger. 'We should not overlook the great fecundity of the Africans and the rapid increase of the African population.' Sticking to his argument about the Finns and their neighbours Estonians and Latvians, the author asserts: 'In some of these instances the amount (of theological literature) is not greater than the existing theological literature in Swahili, Suto or Zulu.' This argument is perhaps not as 'practical' as it is supposed to be,

---

[6] H. von Sicard, 'Language and Theological Training in Africa', *International Review of Missions*, April 1955, p. 147.

[7] Here the writer's authority is the German philosopher Cassirer. This is surprising, perhaps, for one would have thought that in this field the author himself is in much better position to judge than the German philosopher, who knew no Bantu languages!

for, apart from the fact that the Finns are four millions in number, most of them have at some time in their lives read some
Christian book, and their Church has of course a long and distinguished theological tradition stretching over many centuries.
It is not very practical to make a comparison here.

Secondly, there is a 'philosophical' aspect. The African peoples
have their particular philosophy of life, expressed in their language, therefore 'African theology should be built on African
foundations'. The author has not discussed here the tantalizing
problem of what is meant by 'African foundations', but one gathers
from the context that he mainly refers to the myths of African
culture, particularly the mythical accounts of the origin of man.

Thirdly, there is a missiological aspect. The use of non-African
languages will retard the churches in Africa. 'They will for a long
time remain "young" [churches].' Therefore missions 'must choose,
and choose now, at this decisive moment', and, of course, choose
the author's main conclusion: 'All theological training in Africa
ought to be given in African languages.' We are also informed by
the author that 'Asian and African Christian leaders have already
made their choice. They will approach Christianity theologically
from a non-western outlook which has found its expression in
their own languages.' There is no modifying clause here, and
some readers may perhaps find the assertion somewhat sweeping.
The trouble is that at least as far as African church leaders are
concerned they are not particularly vocal. And those who are
have made a choice which is much more complicated than this
statement on their behalf seems to imply.

This position is buttressed by other similar arguments which
the I.M.C. theological commissions in Africa met. The African
languages are preferable as medium of teaching for the following
reasons:

(a) The minister must be enabled to preach to his own people
in that language in which they can hear and think. For the overwhelming majority that means, at the present time, an African
language. (b) The mother-tongue is peculiarly the language of the
inner life and of prayer.

An interesting expression of the same attitude has been formulated by a Swiss Reformed theological teacher, until recently at
Ricatla (Mozambique), Maurice Schaller. His experience has been
with catechists' training but he would claim that his argument

applies no less to the teaching in the theological college. Says
M. Schaller:

> It is *impossible* for me to teach the African in any other language
> than his own. It happens that in teaching I fall into Portuguese, but I
> have the feeling that the words rebound like a tennis ball hitting a
> wall. I do not say that I am not sure whether I have been understood,
> but rather that I am sure not to be understood, because of the fact
> that the associations brought out in the African student by these
> words in, say, French or Portuguese, are inevitably poor, and poor to
> a degree which we are incapable of grasping. The deafness which has
> become my fate helps me to understand how painfully poor those
> musical sounds have become which once were so rich. It is exactly like
> that when a European expresses himself in an African language. But
> our task is to find, in the student, that deep region of the soul from
> whence come the words which express his *Weltanschauung* and his
> universe.[8]

We notice that these observations reflect the impression of a
personally-engaged theological teacher and do not claim to represent the reaction of his African students, particularly as the
writer indicates that the European's use of an African language
may also involve problems of its own.

We have quoted two distinguished missionaries from Southern
Africa as protagonists of the African languages as the sole medium
of teaching. It is interesting to find out what theological literature
—apart from Bible, hymn book, small catechism, etc.—exists in the
languages which they represent, Karanga in the Lutheran mission in Southern Rhodesia, and Ronga-Tsonga in the Reformed
mission in Mozambique. Through the combined literary efforts
of the Dutch Reformed and Swedish Lutheran missions there
exist the following books in Karanga: Five books by Rev. S. K.
Jackson, varying in length between 24 and 85 pages on 'The
Christian Home', 'Tribulations', 'The Growth of the Christian',
etc.; two by Dr. W. J. van der Merwe—same sizes—on Palestine,
and a Missions History of Africa; a book of Church history
biographies; and a larger Catechism (Lutheran) of some 100 pages,
adapted to African conditions of life.

In Ronga-Tsonga 'practically nothing is published; neither commentaries, nor Church history; there exist a printed Catechism
by Luther and a Catechism for Youth by a Youth Worker, whilst

---

[8] M. Schaller, *Aide mémoire*, (typed), 1953.

in mimeographed form, there exist an adaption of the Heidelberg Catechism and a Sunday-School lessons course on the Bible.'

A realistic survey and interpretation of the situation with regard to theological literature in African languages does not exist, but would be extremely worth-while. It would do more than anything else to settle this argument about the medium of teaching. Such a survey must not be content with an enumeration of titles of books which at some time were produced in the languages concerned. Apart from the cogent question as to whether any particular book is still in print, literary quality—from an African point of view—level of expression and theological quality ought to be measured. We have ourselves made fairly extensive enquiries into this problem in recent years (1951–1957). As our sampling is possibly not sufficiently representative, we shall not attempt a detailed interim report and shall instead be content with a few broad lines.

There are a few African churches which have a considerable vernacular theological literature, outstanding among which is the Presbyterian Church in Southern Congo. Thanks to the great achievements of two missionaries, C. L. Crane and J. W. Allen, the Luba language now has a valuable set of commentaries supposedly to all the major books of the Bible, though we have not been in a position to analyse the commentaries, not knowing the language. We are informed, however, that 'Crane and Allen followed standard English commentaries, but their work was not literal translation. It was rather a compilation of the best features of several works, with explanations and illustrations especially chosen for the Congolese'.[9] Here is an altogether remarkable achievement.

We shall also admit that in the case of a *lingua franca* such as Swahili the problem presents itself in a different light from that of the smaller languages. So far all non-Roman churches in Tanganyika and Kenya have used and are using Swahili, while Uganda for historical reasons has insisted that Swahili is unacceptable, and therefore has until recently concentrated on Luganda.

As to Swahili, a great church leader and linguist such as Bishop L. Beecher, Nairobi, says: 'After a good deal of thought and study, I am still inclined to suggest the medium of instruction should be Swahili. This does not, of course, mean that English as a subject will not be taught to the students; unquestionably it must, and be taught very well. But if most of their ministry will

⁹ L. A. McMurray, 29.11.1956, to the author.

be spent in preaching the Gospel in a vernacular environment, then it is essential that they should learn to think about the Gospel in a vernacular, and to develop a system of theology in the vernacular. For this, Swahili is particularly well equipped — — — as a hybrid language which combines a fairly considerable Arabic vocabulary with a Bantu African grammar and basic vocabulary.'

The theological literature in Swahili has been produced mainly by the U.M.C.A., the Church Missionary Society and the Lutherans, and a considerable part of this literature dates from the period before 1914. As a foundation an 'Introduction to the Old Testament' and 'Introduction to the New Testament' are often used. A study of these representative and fundamental works is interesting. To take an example: from an Evangelical stand-point surely the teaching about 'sin' and 'grace' is important. In the Swahili 'Introduction to the New Testament', the chapter on St. Paul states that according to the Apostle, 'sin' *(dhambi)* was 'a kind of sickness' *(aina ya ugonjwa)*. Whatever St. Paul taught about sin, he most certainly did not teach this. Particularly in an African setting, this theological definition has its obvious limitations—to put it mildly.

The example is quoted in order to show one little fact which sometimes is forgotten in this debate, that the African text, of itself, does not make the theology good. So far, almost without exception, all theological text books in African languages have been written by non-Africans. With all respect to the great efforts that has gone into adapted or original work of this kind, one must not always take for granted that the text is above reproach from a linguistic or theological point of view.

In any case it should be remembered that Swahili, as a *lingua franca,* on the one hand represents a foreign language and is of course not the 'mother tongue' of most of the students and that, on the other hand, it has some religious and theological literature which hitherto has been of real service to the development of the Churches in Kenya and Tanganyika (and to a certain extent in the Belgian Congo). But the Luba situation and the Swahili *lingua franca* are exceptions, and must not be taken to represent the whole picture. Even as we write, the official status of Swahili in Kenya has been definitely reduced as the Education Department has changed its language policy from an emphasis on Swahili to a preference for English.

The *average inventory* of theological books in the vernaculars probably includes one meagre little commentary (of some 60–100 pages) to one of the Gospels and possibly another to a few chapters in Genesis; a Church history of varying size and quality; perhaps a more developed catechism serving as a foundation for Dogmatics; a few brief biographies of the heroes of the Protestant faith, plus possibly some refutation of Roman Catholic teaching.

In one important area in Belgian Congo, with a language spoken by some 100,000, we found the vernacular theological literature to consist of a few mimeographed *compendia,* written by the missionaries. Being especially interested in Church history we gave some attention to the volume of eleven pages which summarized—that *is* the word—the mighty sweep of the two thousand years of the history of the Church of Christ. Here the period A.D. 1517–A.D. 1950 was neatly packed into three pages. Martin Luther had half a page, while Calvin and Calvinism had to be content with a few lines. The Counter-Reformation had one page, and World Missions, from William Carey to the present day, one page.

In the last generation the problem of vernacular literature for the Protestant Church has been discussed with perhaps greater intensity and vehemence in the French Camroons than in any other country in Africa. In the 1920's and 1930's, the policy of the Paris Mission was to treat two of the leading vernaculars as selected ecclesiastical languages, the Douala language for the southern part and Bamum for the northern part of the country. By this method an attempt was made to find some possible way out of a situation complicated by the fact that there are not just one or two 'mother tongues', but a great variety of languages in the French Cameroons. This mission policy led to endless palavers and to actual skirmishes between different tribal interests. The struggles over this issue had as one result that some of the best African catechists had to be dismissed by the Mission—a serious loss to the life of the Church.

One of the most progressive of the Cameroon peoples at present are the Bamiléké. It is all very well to argue that theological education for the Bamiléké should be solely in the vernacular; but so far, the only literature produced in the language comprises two of the Gospels in translation and a 'Bible History'. The Presbyterian Church in the Southern Cameroons (American) has particularly used the Bhulu language. This language has been the medium of instruction in the theological school, which has meant that students of the Basa people have also had to learn Bhulu, a language which is very far from being their 'mother tongue'. In the Bhulu language the following books of a more 'theological' character are printed: 'Life of Jesus' and 'The People of God'. Of the language in the latter book we were told by a good Bhulu linguist, an African: 'It is English Bhulu'.

But not only the Basa were dissatisfied with the mission policy of putting a premium on the Bhulu language. Another small tribe, the Ngumba, live as a well-knit sociological entity, an enclave, in the centre of the Bhulu area. In 1898, an American missionary, Robert Oscar, generously promised this group that they would get the Bible in their own language. They waited, but in vain, for a few decades. On Christmas Day 1933, the Ngumba Church with chief and pastors and all the faithful decided to walk out and be separated from 'the Mother Church'. They formed a discontented, energetic religious tribal group, proud of upholding the Protestant claims of the mother tongue.

At Lomé, Togoland, we came in contact with the famous Ewe Church, independent since 1919, one of the great show-pieces of church autonomy in Protestant Africa. There is a Bible in Ewe, but we were told by Dr. C. G. Baëta that the present generation have to read the Old Testament in French or English *in order to understand their Ewe Old Testament.* There is a neat little collection of some 20–25 theological books in the Ewe language, a monument to the tremendous energy characteristic of the German missionaries who worked in Togoland prior to A.D. 1914. These books cannot be expected to reflect the theological climate after World War I. Obviously the problem becomes particularly acute in the case of the smaller languages. How the situation works out in connexion with some of the theological schools we reported in the I.M.C. theological report, and we quote:

> The scattering of language groups is illustrated by the seven or eight major and twenty minor languages among the scant two million people in Liberia; and by the twenty-odd languages in the field of the Methodist Missionary Society among the two million people of the Ivory Coast. At Libamba in the Cameroons, the secondary school conducted jointly by the Paris Society and by the American Presbyterian Mission, recently counted representation among the students of twenty-seven tribes, with almost that many separate languages.

Regular Sunday-school classes are conducted there in six languages. At Ndoungué, also in the Cameroons, the ministerial training school of the Paris Society, which has been serving a few students from Togo and from French Equatorial Africa, recently had students from sixteen tribes, who could communicate with each other more or less satisfactorily through four principal languages. Church buildings in Yaoundé, capital of the Cameroons, have on Sunday successive services in five or even six languages. In another territory we have seen a hymn-book in four languages; and in still another we have witnessed the announcement of hymns with numbers for three different books, each in a separate language. In the Belgian Congo and Ruanda-Urundi the minor languages are many, even two hundred, say certain educational documents.[1]

In many African languages the books were produced in, and are a reflex of, a by-gone age. It has been said of the Lutheran Church in Madagascar that the 1880's were the golden age of literature production. The years prior to 1914 have in many cases been the creative literary period also on the continent of Africa. It is inevitable that translations from that period do not particularly appeal to the African generation of to-day, and this may not be exclusively the fault of this generation.[2]

What happens to the pastor in all this, to the man in charge of a Christian congregation which needs to be nurtured and guided? The question may perhaps appear irrelevant, because in dealing with the medium of teaching, we are concerned only with a methodological problem in the theological colleges, not with the pastors in their various congregations. We beg to differ. The medium of instruction, and the type of book which the young, or not so young, African theologian has to study in his theological school is of great importance for his whole career.

We thought of this when taking part in a small conference in the house of a Swiss missionary in a Mozambique country district in 1953. One of the African pastors who took part in the debate looked around the missionary's room lined with book cases full of books in French and German and Portuguese and English, and

---

[1] *I.M.C. Theol. Report*, II, p. 24.

[2] Cf. our own report on 'The Production of Lutheran Literature and Periodicals' in *Lutheran World Federation Assembly*, Hannover 1952, *Study Document for Section II*, (World Missions), pp. 46–50.

if I remember rightly, also in Greek and Hebrew. 'Look at my European colleague', the African pastor said, 'we are of the same age, and yet I am so much older in spirit than he is. He keeps so much younger than I do, for he has books to read.' He went on to say that there were long periods in the year, particularly during the rainy season between January and March, when the climate made pastoral visitation well-nigh impossible and when he could have plenty of time to read—if only he had books. But there were not many books in his particular language.

The problem of language medium is not concerned solely with the two to four years in the theological college; it affects very vitally the whole life-contribution of the pastor, for he needs to have at his disposal books to renew and refresh his mind and soul. If his theological college has not given him more than a few text books and a set of mimeographed notes, all in a *lingua franca* or some African language—and this *is* the general situation—then he is not happily placed. Mimeographed theological notes, the result of so much hard work, produced at late hours by the flickering light of an unsteady kerosene lamp, are not ever-lasting. The termites, or a house fire, soon play havoc with these papers. A look at the personal libraries of African pastors and catechists is revealing. It is amazing that so much has been achieved by these men in their church work in spite of the limitations represented by an almost non-existent library.[3] I am speaking here of the pastor whose theological education was, according to the programme, given exclusively in an African language and whose literary horizon therefore will necessarily be limited. In a country in 'Latin' Africa one pastor, when asked about his library told us, 'At the theological school I got my own copy of Bunyan, and I have read it, I do not know how many times'. Apart from the Bible— or the New Testament—a hymn-book and a catechism (a book which in this particular context must not be called catechism, for

---

[3] The principal of the theological school in an important Anglo-Catholic diocese in East Africa develops his view on lecture notes: 'The teaching consists largely of dictating notes, partly to ensure that those ordained have a reference library of their notes for use when they get to their parishes. This is by no means a wholly satisfactory method but it has its advantages.' Unfortunately these advantages are not mentioned, and it is difficult to guess where they might lie. From one of the reports to the Inter-territorial Theological Staffs' Conference, Limuru (Kenya), April–May, 1956.

that was resented 'back home'), the Pilgrim's Progress was very
likely his only solid literary possession.

Stubborn 'Africanists' will happily argue that their African pastor has in his vernacular at least one or two 'Introductions', such
as they are, to the Old and New Testaments, and that these will
keep him busy. That may be true, up to a point, but at that point,
which is soon reached, the pastor discovers the intellectual isolation caused by the linguistic policy of his mission, a situation
common not only among the younger generation of pastors, but
also among very many of the older men, who have been trained
in the vernaculars or a *lingua franca*. It is simply not true to say
that they clamour for an exclusive use of their particular vernacular as the medium of teaching in the theological school. The
statement made by the I.M.C. theological commission to 'Latin'
Africa has a very strong body of African opinion behind it:

> A considerable number of the Africans consulted have strongly
> favoured the use of French, Portuguese, or English, where there was
> any question of policy; and many others have assumed from the start
> that only the European language was a workable medium of instruc-
> tion. Where an African language is now employed [as the medium
> of teaching in the Theological College] some Africans felt that the
> church is losing out in society; and almost all of our consultants
> dwelt upon the inadequacy of materials for study in the African
> language.[4]

The debate about the teaching medium has been hampered by
a confusion between two problems: (1.) the language of personal
prayer and congregational worship and (2.) the linguistic tools of
theological study. These two are not necessarily identical. This
was pointed out to us by a Congo pastor, Josef Samba, himself a
theological teacher at Ngouédi. He was deeply concerned over
the need of preserving the African languages. 'A people which
does not struggle to uphold its native language loses its self-respect
and its soul.' 'But', he added, 'precisely in order to prepare our
pastors for this struggle we need French, and good French, as the
teaching medium in the theological school.' It is the man with
the wider outlook, perspective, and culture mediated by the
European language who most strongly experiences the need for

---

[4] *I.M.C. Theol. Report,* II, p. 75.

preserving the African language.[5] We think that his wise and considered statement has wide implications. It is not a question of two antagonistic alternatives but rather of a constructive combination of both. In order to serve as a theological teacher in Africa, the Westerner of course needs a thorough knowledge of the official language(s) of the country and at least one African language which he must be able to use freely. Teacher and students together should aim at discovering the rich treasures of the African languages. The rising generation of theological students will in the new climate of nationalist Africa see to it that the very study undertaken in a Western medium will stimulate their interest in their African language.

The language issue is not confined to the theological college; that particular problem is only one sector of the present argument in Africa as to the choice between African and Western culture media. The question is more subtle than some like to believe. We must take into account an attitude brilliantly represented by the well-known Dahomean writer and politician Hazoumé. He shows no hesitation in choosing, and incidentally reveals an attitude which some well-meaning Westerners may have overlooked.

Westerners who insist on an African language medium believe that Western culture is 'indigestible to the African mind', Hazoumé says.[6] They overlook the bewildering multiplicity of African languages. Enforcing one single African language on the various peoples of a country could possibly foster a dangerous chauvinistic spirit in people whose language was selected for a kind of official recognition. Westerners who advocate the use of African languages hide their real motives, Hazoumé claims. 'They are motives of a sordid egoistic interest, of a prestige to be safeguarded, fear of

---

[5] This can be seen also in the Asian setting. Cf. the important debate in *Universities Quarterly*, May 1957, p. 277, between Robin Mayhead, C. R. Hensman and E. F. C. Ludowyk. Mayhead writes: 'The most heartening evidence [is that] the student interested in Sinhalese literature is often one whose work in English is of a particularly high quality. One student who recently obtained a First Class in English is now researching on Sinhalese folk-poetry. Cf. J. McLeod Campbell, *African History in the Making*, p. 42.

[6] M. Hazoumé's address on 'L'Humanisme occidental et l'humanisme africain' was given at a conference on African culture in Paris and printed in *Présence Africain*, Juin–Sept., 1957, p. 29–45. In October 1953 we had the privilege of discussing these problems personally with M. Hazoumé at Cotonou, Dahomey.

competition from those members of the African élite who have been nourished, up to the present, by the same culture as the Occident—and this is a competition which these foreigners fear although they do not wish to say so.' They seem to fear on the part of the African a kind of profanation and degradation of Western languages. Such Westerners wish the African to be 'permanently established in his traditionalism and in a certain immobility. But it is about time for a sound and peaceful revolution to be produced in that traditionalism.'

Those are bitter words, and there is, perhaps, not a little of the demagogue in them. We are fully aware of the fact that there are at present also other trends among the African élite. An example is the venture of Nkundu-Mongo intellectuals in Coquilhatville, Belgian Congo, who make the defence of their Nkundu-Mongo language a rallying-point for a neo-traditionalist movement—one indication of a wider tendency.[7] We believe however that Hazoumé points to a very important trend, and African nationalism in the next few decades will emphasize the importance of his attitude; the Church cannot afford to give the appearance of holding back future African leaders by ignoring it.

Both the European language *and* the African are needed as tools in the theological school where they have different functions to perform.

1. There are important areas where the European language is the only possible *lingua franca*. Ndoungué in the French Cameroons is a case in point. In a school with twenty-two students speaking seven different Cameroon languages and with a likely supply of students also from Togo and other parts of French-speaking West Africa, it is unthinkable to use any other language than French. Here, to insist on the 'mother tongue' is absurd.

2. The text-book position in the African languages gives decisive support to the claim for the use of a European language in teaching. We repeat here what was said above. It is not merely a question of the three or four years in the theological school; we are concerned with the whole of the active ministerial life of the

---

[7] Cf. G. E. J. B. Brausch, 'The Problem of Elites in the Belgian Congo', *Internat. Soc. Science Bull.*, No. 3, 1956, p. 455.

African pastor. The miserable collection of torn compendia is no enduring help.

3. Above all, the teaching and text-books in English, French or Portuguese open up wider horizons for the pastor and make it possible for him to establish and maintain contacts with a more comprehensive, a more 'Catholic' interpretation of the Christian message.

This does not, in any way, exclude a teaching programme which aims at, and has its very point in, the translation and transformation of ideas into the African languages. We shall readily admit that we feel that too little of this 'translation' has been going on in recent years in the theological schools. Some European teachers have not had sufficient opportunity of learning an African language well, which is regrettable from many points of view. In the next two or three decades it will become increasingly dangerous to ignore this issue, dangerous because in an increasingly race-conscious and nationalist Africa, the omission of interest in the African languages on the part of the missionary will be interpreted as lack of appreciation of African values.

Apart from this general observation, it is obviously necessary to aim at a real 'translation' of the teaching in order to make sure that what is taught has been brought home to the student. We must not take it for granted that this necessarily follows just because the student seems efficient in a particular European language. Some of the best-equipped students report that in the course of teaching they have constantly to carry on a process of silent translation to the vernacular. It is perhaps significant that this has been expressed most forcibly by theological students who have studied in the West. A young Ibo pastor (from Nigeria), studying in Birmingham, and a young Douala pastor (from the Cameroons) studying in Paris, expressed very vividly to me that they had a much more complicated task of assimilation than their European fellow students: 'As I listen to the French in the theological class, I have to translate within myself into Douala, and to give to myself a running commentary in my own language. We have our own concepts and I must transpose the foreign ideas into my own concepts.' We mention this not in order to capitulate to the 'Africanist' argument, which in the Cameroons linguistic situation is an absurdity anyway, but in order to show how exacting is the task of teaching and learning on this frontier of the spirit. And the example set by the Douala pastor is one to be followed on a wide scale; the teaching in the Western language becomes relevant and rewarding only in so far as it aims at this process of transposition into African concepts.

There has been a marked tendency in the direction of the European languages. It is characteristic that in such schools as clung until 1939–1945 to the African medium there was a decisive new orientation after the war. The dramatic change at Ndoungué is typical of what happened in other similar schools at the time. Paris Mission policy between the two world wars was to treat Douala as the potential ecclesiastical language, and teaching at Ndoungué was in this language. Following earlier traditions some of the students were also taught in German, because of the undeniable fact that there exists an excellent theological literature in German. But in the modern city of Douala a pastor trained on these assumptions would have very serious difficulties. At a meeting held in the Cameroons, in 1944, Pastor Boury maintained that teaching in French was the only possible course for the future. This argument carried the day, and instruction at Ndoungué from 1947 onwards, under the remarkable leadership of Jean Nouvellon, was in French. A similar re-orientation in the last decade has taken place at such leading schools as Kimpese, Belgian Congo.

Obviously, the use of French implies important problems as to French theological literature, and the same can be said of Portuguese. We came across a Western missionary in a high-rating theological college who told us with that emphasis which only blissful ignorance can provide: 'I do not believe in French theological books. They are all too simple, on a Sunday-school level, and we cannot use them.' This learned gentleman prepared his own mimeographed notes in his own French. Seriously, there exists an urgent problem in adapting French theological literature to the actual level of the needs in Africa.

> Franco-Swiss Protestant literature is that of some three million persons, all educated with traditions of a highly trained ministry on university levels. The number of simple books is not great, and many works are distinctly technical or professional in their character. Much remains to be done in French with an eye to use in Africa. It is also true, however, that scarcely a missionary, or even a mission in sum, had knowledge of the total literature available in French; and many

fixed their judgments and practices upon slight information, early discouragement, or lack of well-directed effort to discover the resources of France and Switzerland.[8]

Largely through the labours of Professor Michaeli and his consultants, steps forward in this matter have been taken. In *Comme des Flambeaux* (1954), there is a list of French-language books now in print, of interest primarily to training schools for pastors, but also to other schools and to Christian workers generally. The list is classified by subject and by grade of difficulty, and contains brief descriptive notes.

The I.M.C. Commission to Southern Africa (p. 49) reports a concern which is a living issue in the whole of Africa.

> The ideal solution would seem to be to publish text-books growing out of the actual teaching situation. There is undoubtedly good manuscript material in the hands of lecturers, much of it tested and improved by use. Publication would only be possible by co-operation between the colleges, but it is very desirable that some of this material should be examined with this end in view. Despite the service which the International Committee on Christian Literature for Africa tries to render as a clearing-house, we were given the impression that there is very little interchange of information and experience between the colleges regarding such text-books as are being used and their proved value or otherwise. A useful service could be rendered by this interchange.

In the language-medium controversy we thus advocate the use of the official European language—English, French, Portuguese, with Afrikaans or Flemish or Arabic (S. Sudan) as the case may be—keeping in mind all the time that the aim of the teaching in the theological class is creative translation and transposition into African concepts. We have not hidden the difficulties involved in this programme, and do not offer a simple formula. Yet having seen the complexity and difficulty of the situation, the Churches cannot any longer allow themselves further procrastination. We would hope to challenge the Protestant forces in Africa to adopt a determined policy on these issues. The overall situation at present, particularly in 'Latin' Africa, but also in East Africa, is character-

---

[8] *I.M.C. Theol. Report*, II, p. 76.

ized by hesitation and a vacillation which is not conducive to results. This lack of determination is, we suggest, not in the best
interests of the Church of the future.

The situation is of course complicated by the fact that sometimes not one, but two European languages claim the interest.
This is particularly so when, in 'Latin' Africa, some Anglo-Saxon
missions insist on English, for many, though frequently uncon-
vincing reasons. In one important Church in a French-speaking
country we were told that theological education had to be given
partly in English in order to give African pastors an opportunity
of studying the constitution of the particular American home
church with which the African body was connected. The device of
translating that constitution into French and/or an African language seemed far too simple an idea to be acceptable. In another
Church in the same country we were told that the teaching media
were English and one African language because of the limited
knowledge of French among the missionaries! Contact with African
leaders revealed some uneasiness on their part over the tendency to
ignore French. In fact, we gained an impression which makes this
issue into something far more than merely a matter of passing interest. The future of Protestant witness in French-speaking countries
in Africa is linked with the role of the French language among
church leaders to an extent which does not seem to be fully appreciated at present. For this reason it is important that Western
missionaries and African pastors should be fully conversant with
the language.

Great determination is required here. A leading union seminary
in Belgian Congo presented a syllabus including three hours a
week for French and five hours a week for English. But the
principal of the college, after discussion, was prepared to devote
the eight hours available entirely to French. On another level of
academic attainment, the Baptist Bible School at Carnot, Ubangui-Chari, endeavoured to ensure some contact with French text-
books for the pastors of the Church, in a situation where the
educational background and consequent entrance requirements
are low, by stipulating that the teaching medium should be Gbaya
in the first years, but that French theological text-books should
be used from the start, and that French should be substituted for
the vernacular in the concluding period of the course. The advantage of this expedient is obvious; the training has the total

career of the pastor in view, and not only his three years in the theological school. Being used to French text-books, he can orientate himself in a way which could never be assured by a collection of tattered vernacular compendia.

In 'Latin' Africa, French and Portuguese missionaries are convinced that a theological education given in the official language is in the best interests of the Church, but in British East and Central Africa, a characteristic difference in approach can be seen. In some schools run by British missions it is only with reluctance that British missionaries will give up Swahili or Luganda. When forced to accept English as teaching medium, they will, in all sincerity, regard this an 'unfortunate' expedient enforced by the lack of literature in African languages. Yet, as a non-Englishman, I suggest that this reluctance—becoming as it may appear—is nevertheless unnecessary. I should add here that this argument refers to lower levels of theological training. As soon as a higher level has been reached, there has never been any doubt as to the use of English.

The language issue is closely linked with the recruitment problem. Students from secondary schools and teacher training schools used to a wide variety of inspiring text-books on different subjects are simply not going to accept a situation where they will be taught for three to four years from compendia in some vernacular which very probably is not their own. They want a wider view and a larger horizon. The paradox is that in broadening their outlook they also rediscover their own mother tongue. In fact, the language issue reflects the wider problem of the universality and locality of the Church. The Church is a universal society, an *internationale* in the midst of a new Africa, in which nationalism will increasingly make its total demands on the religious expressions of the people. To a considerable extent the Protestant ideal of the autonomous church has already taken, or is now taking, shape and form in tribal settings, which is all well and good provided that it is realized that the Tribe of Christ transcends national limitations. When nationalism brings about a fundamental crisis in the Church, some African leaders will discover, anew or possibly for the first time, the Catholic dimension of the Church. It is good then to have access to the wealth of Christian experience mediated by great international languages. The languages will then appear as bridges, built across the gulf, by the Spirit.

The Wider Perspective

After College.

'We turn the catechism and the Bible over and over without fresh understanding. We need intellectual and spiritual renewal', one well-trained minister declared. African pastors have often stated quite vigorously their individual and collective need of training while in the service of the Church. To meet the problem, missions and churches have sporadically attempted certain make-shifts in the form of short courses, directed reading programmes and correspondence courses, as well as retreats. Some of these are discussed by the I.M.C. theological commission reports.[9]

While their recommendations are no doubt useful and practical, there is obviously some danger of their being overlooked, because there are too many of them. We wish to crystallize the whole problem in two theses which we would like to make as incisive and inescapable as possible.

Thesis I: *Without organizing regularly recurrent Refresher Courses for pastors, the Church in Africa is not doing its job.*

Thesis II: *Pastors should attend a four–six months' theological course every five years after ordination.*[1]

Reasons: 1. In a rapidly changing African society, with its growing industrialization and urbanization against the background of a fast-moving world scene, the Church is exposed to strong forces, both external and internal, which condition her ever-changing position. The ordained leaders of the Church, as far as possible together with responsible lay leaders, need guidance on the relevance of the unchanging Gospel to changing conditions.

2. Our recommendations apply also to the Churches in the West: but in Africa, they point to a condition of crisis. In all too many Churches, pastors are not trained through a European language medium and are therefore reduced to the pitifully meagre theological iron rations provided by a few printed vernacular books and some tattered mimeographed lecture notes. As long as this state of affairs prevails, the Church simply must put its own house in order

---

[9] Cf. particularly *I.M.C. Theol. Report,* II, p. 88–90.

[1] This does, perhaps, not apply in the same compelling measure to churches with an already developed 'in-service training'.

and through recurrent refresher courses keep interest alive. The pastor is often an isolated person in the African society at present; therefore efforts to break through this intellectual and spiritual isolation are needed.

3. The pastor's task of teaching his local leaders by taking Bible Schools and refresher courses for them will, as we have seen already, become more and more an important aspect of his contribution to the life of his church. He cannot perform this without himself receiving fresh inspiration and renewed orientation.

4. As far as possible these courses should be connected with retreats; the unity of theological activity and Christian worship and meditation is thereby stressed.

5. As far as possible the courses should have a central core, common for all, but also an individual aspect, aiming at tutorials with supervised expression work in certain subjects such as exegesis, local church history and music.

6. This move probably implies a re-allocation of missionary personnel. We feel assured that a 'new deal' of this nature on the part of the missions will have a refreshing and lasting effect on the life of the Churches in Africa.

A few Churches and missions have done a good deal in the form of brief refresher courses; a very few have done more than that; and some, in certain areas, very much less than that. The problem is faced realistically by the Methodist Church in West Africa. Since the time of John Wesley, Methodism has had the idea of a 'probationer minister', in which the young minister, fresh from his theological college, is placed in a 'circuit' with two or three other older and more experienced ministers, to learn from their experience, in daily contacts and inspiring co-operation. In West Africa, however, this system clashes with hard and unwieldy facts of sheer geography, and with the insufficient number of ministers, since the majority of circuits have only one minister. In 1954 single-minister circuits in Sierra Leone amounted to 14 out of 17; in French West Africa 3 out of 9; in the Gold Coast 24 out of 36; in Western Nigeria 5 out of 13; and in Eastern Nigeria 10 out of 18.[2] That this meant very great difficulty for the Methodist practical post-collegiate training is obvious.

In a recent report a Lutheran missionary (S. Hagman) from

---

[2] Cf. Stenneth and Beetham, *Report of a Secretarial Visit,* 1953–1954, p. 19.

Southern Rhodesia stresses the African pastor's need of recurrent two-week practical courses in the care of the local congregations. 'Two weeks in the Theological School for worship and study—without those never-ending discussions of grants for motorbikes and school supervision—would soon lead to real results in the life of the Church.'

We do not claim that the suggested recurrent Theological Refresher Course is a novelty. Steps forward have been taken by schools such as Lovedale Bible School, Cape Province. The only thing that is new about our suggestion is our insistence that the situation in the Protestant Churches everywhere in Africa is critical at this particular point and that determined steps must be taken.

A United Effort.

Perspective is important. The problem as to whether theological schools should be united and interdenominational is to some extent a matter of perspective; it concerns the standpoint from which the situation is viewed. There are Western tutors who for a long time have been used to their 'one-man college' idea and who do not seem to discern any resultant ill-effects, and there are 'home' boards who for various reasons strongly support this idea. The African students seem to feel at home in these 'one-man colleges' and they too, if asked, tell their tutor that there should be no change.

There is another perspective, however, that of the Ecumenical Church. An African pastor in Mozambique had caught a glimpse of that as he exclaimed in a discussion on union theological schools: 'We Africans want to see one United Church of Christ, and as a means to that goal we need a united theological school. That alone would make us all into one family. Now we Protestants waste our time in protesting against one another.'[3] As far as we can judge from continent-wide personal interviews with Africans, this Shangaan pastor is representative of an overwhelming majority among his colleagues throughout Africa, though there is also among African pastors a great deal of complacency about the divisions of Protestantism. In the same meeting a colleague of this speaker said with that supposedly endearing, docile smile

---

[3] For a similar view from another part of Africa see Isaac O. Delano, *One Church for Nigeria,* London, 1945.

which has enchanted so many Westerners: 'We Africans are little birds in a nest and we are waiting for food from the Mother. She knows what food is best for us.' As long as this likeable, amiable, hat-in-hand docility persists, there will not be sufficient pressure on the powers-that-be to amend the map of torn and divided Protestant Africa at the point where the most important change of outlook can be made: in theological education.

We mention some of the considerations which seem to work against united theological schools. There are misgivings from a denominational point of view. It is altogether understandable if a Church with a strong emphasis on the role of worship finds it difficult to be enthusiastic over union plans with another Church which has not even considered setting aside a chapel for the envisaged Union Theological School. There are fundamentalist groups who prefer to believe that neighbouring missions are more or less riddled with an out-of-date liberalism.

But apart from considerations of this nature, problems of Faith and Order have so far played an astonishingly limited role on the African scene. Other interests are more important. In the case of two or three Churches with great statistical disparity in Church membership there is a fear on the part of the smaller groups of being 'swamped' by a dominant party—examples from both East and West Africa could be quoted.

In one mandate in Central Africa where Roman Catholicism is very strong, the scattered Protestant forces were sure that 1. they were all conservative Bible believers, 2. they all believed in the importance of 'Christian experience' and that they all could claim what was called 'spiritual infilling subsequent to regeneration'. There was thus no doctrinal barrier between them. But they were kept apart by different attitudes to 'the Revival', and could for this reason not unite in theological education. There had of late come to the area a strong revival movement, beginning in the 1930's in the Anglican Church. The others, themselves products of American and Scandinavian revivals from the 19th and early 20th centuries, were not convinced that the latest revival movement was of the right kind. This had its effect on the organization of Protestant theological education in the area. The various groups preferred to stick to their little one-man-colleges tucked away in the hills.

Some point to 'differences in ethics' as the reason for keeping theological schools apart. They refer to certain differences between European and American *mores* projected on to the African screen; various attitudes to tobacco-smoking provide a case in point. As it happens, the present writer is a convinced non-smoker, but he has observed with some surprise that this matter has been allowed to attain the dignity of a *shibboleth* in discussions about union of theological schools. He has listened to all the arguments, but thinks that there are more important issues to consider. A special case of keeping related schools apart (the adverb is carefully chosen) is the issue formulated in terms of the multi-racial or uni-racial character of the Church. It affects the situation of three small theological schools within the one 'Church of Central Africa, Presbyterian', in Nyasaland. The I.M.C. Commission to Southern Africa has a pithy phrase summing up the situation: 'The C.C.A.P. is one Church, not two', and thinks that this fact should be translated into terms of a united theological school, which would assure a pooling of such resources as staff and library.

In view of the pressure for united schools—from African leaders, and from many Westerners who have an eye to greater efficiency —one wonders how far some of our ecclesiastical arguments are real, and how far they are perhaps rather rationalizations of attitudes formed by old social conventions which are not necessarily relevant in new situations. If 'non-theological factors' condition part of the organization of theological education in Africa, it is important that the issues be faced squarely and that a new advance be made. The I.M.C. Commission to 'Latin' Africa said:

> Where there is a will to join with other Christian bodies in a common task, a way can be found. Some missions, in Africa and elsewhere, have sent a teacher into a school of another body, for a period of mutual acquaintance and trial. Federated schools have been established in various countries, where each of the participants maintains its own life and policy, but with agreed pooling of much teaching and equipment. United schools can and do maintain separate courses in church polity, doctrine, or other subjects, taught for the students of any church body by an instructor of that body. It is, however, the frequent experience of united schools that in all classes such Christian consideration is shown for the various groups of students and their needs, and for the cherished emphases and concerns of the participating denominations, that few distinctive courses are necessary. Each denomination can maintain, if desired, a hostel for its own students, with its particular worship services and other charac-

teristic provisions. Over and above all these options, each mission or church body can arrange a year or other period of instruction or interneship within the area, the language-situation, and the church traditions, of that body. All in all, the stage is now set for efforts to provide one strong interdenominational training school for each territory.

Co-ordination in theological education, unions on a national or regional basis, was one of the main recommendations of the three I.M.C. theological commissions to Africa 1950–1953. Whatever the merits or otherwise of the analyses of the situation presented in the reports of the commissions, they did stress the importance, indeed the necessity, of bolder advance in this field. Together with many important efforts in the same direction on the part of Churches and individual mission or church leaders, the commissions had some catalysing effect in this emphasis on union schools. The 1950's saw a more determined swing in this direction than ever before in Africa.

The following types of united schools exemplify the development.

1. The first we would call the *C.S.I.-type* of union school—after the examples of Church union in South India, i.e. a combination of (a usually Evangelical) Episcopal Church together with Presbyterians, Methodists and others (as it happens Congregationalists are not involved in the particular united schools in Africa to which we refer here). This type is represented by colleges such as Limuru in Kenya and Umuahia in Eastern Nigeria. At least in the case of Eastern Nigeria, the united theological school of Umuahia plays an important role in Church union discussions.[4] In Tanganyika the St. Philip's Theological College, Kongwa belongs to the same pattern. Here Anglicans (C.M.S. Australia) and Moravians (Swiss, Danes, Germans) co-operate. Immanuel College, Ibadan in Western Nigeria, is of the same pattern, as Anglicans (C.M.S.) and Methodists (British) have pooled their resources as from 1958.

We stress the role of the C.M.S. in these union schools in Africa; Anglo-Catholics (S.P.G. and U.M.C.A.) on the other hand have so far not joined in union schools, though they are, as is well-known, represented in the Church of South India. An interesting excep-

---

[4] Cf. H. Sumitra, *Twenty Questions on Church Union*, 1952.

tion in the direction of union was an imaginative attempt of the Bishop of Accra, subsequent to Bishop Neill's visit in 1950 (on behalf of the International Missionary Council). However, opposition from within the ranks of the Anglican Church in that country prevailed against this proposal.

2. The 'free church' type is largely conditioned in theology, worship and ethos by British and American free church traditions. We mention Trinity College, Kumasi, Ghana, where Methodists, Presbyterians and (Swiss) Reformed together have built a strong college; Kimpese, Belgian Congo, with co-operation of Baptists (American and British) and Congregationalists (Swedish); Dondi, Angola, and Ricatla, Mozambique 1958, where Episcopal Methodists collaborate on the one hand with American Congregationalists and the United Church of Canada, on the other with Swiss Reformed; or Modderpoort, Orange Free State, which carries on theological education earlier provided at Adams, Natal.

3. Of a third type (which should be placed only conditionally under the heading 'United Schools') are institutions for students of one denomination, representing different churches and a variety of national backgrounds. The new Epworth Theological College, near Salisbury, is an important example, taking students of British Methodist and American Methodist Episcopal backgrounds. Ecumenical width characterizes the programme, and it is hoped that other churches from Southern and Northern Rhodesia will eventually join the School (cf. p. 269). The Oskarsberg Lutheran Theological College, Natal, and the Makumira Theological Seminary, Tanganyika, take Lutheran students from the various Churches of that one denomination in Southern Africa and Tanganyika.

4. Among United *Bible Schools,* the Sweetwater institution in Natal is of particular significance on the South African scene. Sweetwater has at present some 80 students from eleven different church groups, among whom are some local leaders of Bantu Separatist Churches. That these have been accepted as students is a fact of great promise. Applications from these groups to some other theological institution in South Africa have not met with the same response—have in fact had no response or reply whatever. The Sweetwater experiment in accepting prospective Separatist Church leaders attests to sturdy belief, on the part of the staff and School Board, in the effect of three years' sound Bible teaching.

Two conferences in East Africa took the united college idea one step further, now with post-ordination training in view. Steps in this direction were taken by Lutherans at the All-Africa Conference at Marangu in 1955 and by the Inter-territorial Theological Staffs' Conference at Limuru in 1956. The Limuru scheme was from the beginning related to the planning of the International Missionary Council, and the meeting resolved that the greatest service which the Council and the several missionary societies involved could render to the younger churches would be to sponsor and support financially such a scheme as 'a Pilot scheme for post-ordination Theological training'.[5] The Lutheran post-ordination course at Marangu for pastors from Africa and Madagascar started in 1959.

Theology and the African universities

The 1950's brought a new challenge to ministerial training in Africa through the establishment of university colleges at Makerere (Uganda), Ibadan (Nigeria), Achimota (Ghana), Salisbury (Rhodesia) and, as to South Africa, the decision, in the name of *apartheid,* to reorganise Fort Hare and create 'ethnic' universities. Plans for a French-speaking theological faculty were mooted. We shall not enter into all these problems in detail, but must however briefly indicate these opportunities as a new point of reference for theological education on the rapidly changing African scene in the 1960's.

Three factors are of special importance towards creating the new situation in this field.

1. The rapid rise of the secondary school system in Africa in the 1950's and the parallel and subsequent establishment of university colleges.

2. The role of the universities in bringing out and helping to emphasize needs within the Churches themselves. These were obliged to take cognizance of the fact that they were living in an era in which secondary and university education would increasingly be a dominant influence.

3. The Theological Education Fund, as established by the International Missionary Council in 1958, and as fitting this situation.

---

[5] Minutes and Reports of the Inter-Territorial Theological Staffs' Conference, Limuru, Kenya, 1956, p. 13 (mimeographed). cf. also (F. Birkeli ed.) *Marangu,* 1956, p. 63 f.

This fund, serving the improvement of theological education at strategically selected interdenominational centres, gives preference to supporting ministerial training of high quality and competence. Its work is of special relevance to our study as the attention of the Fund was first drawn to Africa. The visits to Africa in 1958 and 1959 by Dr. C. W. Ranson and Dr. C. W. Forman, Director and Associate Director of the Fund, have been of importance. The Fund has had a catalyzing effect on much of the planning in this field, and its presence has together with other factors accentuated the need for co-operative action in ministerial training. The new planning brought about by the situation in the Churches and by the discussions with representatives of the Fund seems to hold out an important promise. It is an innovation that in a somewhat stagnant situation may well have a long-range cumulative effect on the life of the Churches.

South Africa. At the end of the 1950's, the South African situation with regard to the ministerial training of Africans had become more fluid and uncertain than ever. This was one indication of the tremendous upheaval caused by the enforcement of the Governments *apartheid* policy, the blue-print of which was laid down in enactments such as the Group Areas Act of 1950, and the Bantu Education Act of 1953. Far-reaching changes in the university education of the Bantu were foreseen in the Tribal Universities Plan and the Fort Hare University Bill, 1958. The character of fluidity and uncertainty in the situation is emphasized by the fate of Fort Hare.

Fort Hare, established in 1916 as the 'South African Native College' and 1951—1959 affiliated to Rhodes University, Grahamstown, as a university college, has from the beginning had close connexions with the Churches. The majority of the students are accommodated in three church hostels, Wesley House (Methodist), established in 1921, Iona House (Presbyterian) 1924 and Bede Hall (Anglican) 1934. There is a senior lecturer in theology appointed by the University College, whilst the wardens of the three hostels are ordained men and teach theology. In principle, there is a B.D. course, but so far no students have availed themselves of this. The B.A. course with optional Divinity is a three-year course for students with matriculation. The main bulk of future pastors who have hitherto gone to Fort Hare have studied for a certificate in theology; this two-year course is open to students accepted, not by the University College but by their Churches. For entrance to the course the Junior Certificate is in principle required but even this modest standard has not always been maintained. Apart from these openings, there is also a diploma in theology for both post-graduates and non-graduates.

Fort Hare, as we have known it, is now however something of the past. The *apartheid* policy for South African education aims at the establishment of three 'ethnic' university colleges for Bantu students, one in Transkei, another in Zululand and still another in Northern Transvaal. The University College is placed under the direct control of the Minister of Bantu Education; and the minister shall 'assume control' of the Church hostels attached to the college.

The Federal Missionary Council of the Dutch Reformed Church has adapted itself to this government policy. The best theological institution of the Church, Stofberg near Johannesburg, is like most other centres of ministerial training hit by the Group Areas Act. Instead of one central higher theological institution at Stofberg there will now be four centres placed at or near the proposed ethnic universities. Stofberg will be removed to the projected Northern Bantu University at Pietersburg, and the present D.R.C. theological school at Dingaanstad would probably establish close contacts with the Zulu University College near Empangeni. There will be one joint governing body for all these four theological schools. These plans have quickened the move for joint theological training of Bantu leaders in the three Afrikaans Churches, and steps have been taken to invite other Churches, particularly in Northern Transvaal, to co-operate in this form of theological education, under Bantu Education auspices and in a tribal context.

But the application of the *apartheid* policy has also had an effect in another direction. This was foreshadowed in 1958 by an important debate on ministerial training at the University level.

Professor A. G. Rooks, previously head of the Department of Divinity at Fort Hare, has emphasized the value of theological education at a university:

> The educational minimum level ought to be B.A. with Divinity Majors, such as offered at present at Rhodes University (Grahamstown) and University College of Fort Hare. One or two years of the course should preferably be spent completely integrated into the life of a

university in the company of other undergraduates. Later on, say
during the last two years, the candidates may be housed in special
hostels. It is beneficial to the divinity candidates themselves, because
they are introduced early and very effectively to the type of men and
women who are most likely to lead their respective communities in
future. I prefer infinitely such a university training to the frequently
advocated separate 'Ivory Tower' education of ministers outside the
vital contact with university life, away from real life. I advocate a
training that at least in its essential features is identical with that of
European ministers.[6]

A well-known Methodist minister, Rev. G. M. Setiloane, B.A.,
B.D., himself one of Dr. Rooks' graduates from Fort Hare, replied
that the Church cannot, without selling out on the Gospel, continue to train its ministers, 'when Fort Hare goes', i.e. when it
becomes a 'Xhosa University' according to the programme of
apartheid. He advocated a united church college drawing its staff
and students from what was the Fort Hare Department of Divinity
and from other centres for ministerial training such as Modderpoort, Orange Free State (previously Adams, Natal).

In 1959 the Churches belonging to the Christian Council of
South Africa met to discuss the situation among themselves and
with Dr. Ranson of the Theological Education Fund. They refused to go along with the *apartheid* policy and the majority of
the Churches concerned were prepared to consider a radical real-
ignment of theological institutions which would bring a number
of existing schools into union on a federal basis on a common site.
Out of this situation of great uncertainty which of late has hampered any long-range planning there seems to emerge a united
scheme which could, and should, be of very great importance in
South Africa with its many divisions.

British West and East Africa. During and after the Second World
War, the Asquith Commission and the Elliot Commission had
made far-reaching recommendations for university colleges in
British Africa, and in 1948 Makerere, Ibadan and the University
College of the Gold Coast (Ghana) were established. Some
Churches, both in West and East Africa, followed these plans with
eager expectations. Sierra Leone had of course its own centre,

---

[6] *Christian Recorder* (Standerton), June–July, 1958.

Fourah Bay, established as a theological college in 1827 and affiliated to the University of Durham in 1876.

The principals of Ibadan and the Gold Coast College in 1948 asked Dr. H. C. L. Heywood, Provost of Southwell, to report on the teaching of theology at university level. The Christian Council of Nigeria had urged the setting up of a faculty of theology at the new college at Ibadan, and the Methodists particularly, in both countries, stressed that theological education must aim at a B.D. degree. For Nigeria, Dr. Heywood suggested a General Arts degree, a B.A. with 'Religious Studies' as one of the three parts of the examination. Whether there would be any students available for such studies was very much a matter for conjecture at the time. The African headmaster of one important Grammar School predicted that there would be fifty entrants a year, while more realistic observers estimated a tenth of that figure.[7]

The upshot of the discussions was the formation of a Theological Faculty at the University College of the Gold Coast with a staff of five professors and, at Ibadan, a Department of Theology in the Arts Faculty with one lecturer as from 1949 and a faculty from 1950, which now has three European members of staff. The Ibadan B.A. in 'Religious Studies' is modelled on the London University Theology papers in the B.A. General (for a full B.A. the student has to take two other subjects besides Religious Studies). The numbers of students in this department has risen very satisfactorily: 4 in 1950, 18 in 1951, 32 in 1956 and 50 in 1957. The Ibadan course of Religious studies has many interesting points. One of the European members of the staff is a Roman Catholic priest, who teaches Old Testament and Philosophy. Professor G. Parrinder, the well-known sociologist who taught at Ibadan 1949–1958, worked out a new paper compulsory for all Religious Studies students, on Indigenous Religious Beliefs of West Africa. Several Muslim students have taken courses in the Department, particularly in the 'neutral' subjects offered: History of Islam, Philosophy of Religion and Indigenous Religious Beliefs of West Africa. It should be made clear that this course is not primarily designed for ordinands but is taken mainly with a view to give the students competence in teaching in Secondary Schools. As from 1959

---

[7] It was pointed out that in the period 1913–1948 seven people in British West Africa, five of them Nigerians, had graduated with B. D.

Ibadan gives a B.D. course on a syllabus adapted to local needs and approved by London University.

The Department of Theology in the University College of Ghana started in 1950. A number of students have read Intermediate Arts with Theology as one subject (out of two) or B.A. General with Theology as one subject (out of three). In 1950, two students took this course, in 1952 nine (of whom one was a woman) with rather lower numbers later on. The B.D. graduates were two in 1956 and 1958, while at present eleven are studying for a four-year Bachelor of Divinity course.

The Fourah Bay Theology Faculty has a staff of four Europeans and two Africans. One of the Africans is a part-time lecturer; the other, Rev. Harry Sawyerr, became Senior Lecturer in Theology in 1952 and Head of the Department in the same year. The Religious Knowledge course for B.A. started in 1945 with one student. At the beginning of the 1950's the average studying for this course was five, at the end of the 1950's between 12 and 15. The number of students in the Faculty of Theology has been about ten.

The West African university colleges have been fortunate in their theological staff appointments of scholars who have kept a close contact with the Churches and who at the same time have been engaged in significant research.[8]

At Makerere (where the debate for and against the establishing of a Theology Department was a controversial issue about 1949–1950) the Academic Board now offers a Certificate in Religious Studies to men and women who have attended a voluntary course of two lectures per week during their first two years at Makerere and one in their third year and have successfully written an examination paper.[9] The non-Roman course covers Biblical Theology (especially St. Mark); the History of the Expansion of Chris-

[8] An interesting venture is *The Ghana Bulletin of Theology*, ed. Professor N. Q. King. A. F. Walls, lecturer of theology at Fourah Bay, contributed an Introduction to A. M. Stibbs, *The First Epistle General of Peter*, 1958. The quality of scholarship achieved by some of the theological teachers in Africa is indicated by a reviewer who said of Walls' Introduction that it showed 'complete impartiality, massive erudition, staggering familiarity with the literature of the subject'.

In 1959, Fourah Bay started its own *The Sierra Leone Bulletin of Religion*.

[9] W. D. Lamont, (then Principal, Makerere, opposed a theology department at Makerere), 'The Essentials of University Education in East Africa', *Makerere*, Vol. 3, No. 1; and Rev. F. B. Welbourn (then Chaplain, Makerere) 'The Place of a Department of Theology in an East African University'. *Ibid.*

tianity, with special attention paid to the Acts of the Apostles; and Introduction to Christian Philosophy. On an average six non-Roman students per year have attended this course, which obviously is of great value to future East African Government teachers who wish to deepen their understanding of Christian theology.

There has been an increasing demand for this certificate course, so that recently it was taken by no less than thirty students (both Science and Arts students). Apart from its intrinsic value this achievement is of great importance for a further advance towards providing facilities which would eventually enable students to take Divinity as one part of a General B.A. course. These B.A. courses with Religious Knowledge are not primarily designed, as been emphasized, for the ordained ministry of the Churches. The ministerial training is the task of the denominational and union colleges with which we are particularly concerned here.

A far-sighted suggestion was made early in 1950 by a leading British educationist, E. R. J. Hussey. He proposed that the Christian Councils should established well-equipped and well-staffed theological colleges 'close to Government-supported university colleges which are gradually growing, so that they might share the staff of the theological faculty where such a faculty is established'.[1]

Bishop Neill's I.M.C. report fits into this situation. He suggested 'wise planning and confident action on the strategic scale', in view of the fact that 'the future of tropical Africa will be determined in the next twenty years'. He offers a master-key to the situation, the establishment of central church colleges, one for East Africa, located near to, but independent of, the Makerere College; another at Ibadan, Nigeria, on a site adjacent to that of the University College; and a third in Ghana where, parallel with the already existing theological faculty at the University College, there was to be a church college on a site near the University College (alternatively this united college was to be situated at, or near, Kumasi). For Sierra Leone, there was already a university college. Bishop Neill wished to strengthen its theological staff of three, by a fourth member of staff and a much-needed building programme.

Bishop Neill's church-college idea had strong local support in

[1] E. R. J. Hussey, 'Note on Theological Studies in Africa', 26.1.1950. Edinburgh House.

the important conferences which he arranged in 1950 to discuss theological education in British East and West Africa, though other counsels soon prevailed; it was felt that the idea was out of touch with the actual level of the churches and of the recruitment situation in the secondary schools. Generally speaking, the plan was not seriously followed up until 1958, when Bishop Neill made a new visit to East Africa. He pointed out that the Churches, by concentrating their attention on the supposedly impossible problem of recruiting candidates for higher theological training, are 'in danger of becoming imprisoned in a vicious circle.' 'There is no doubt that a number of students at Makerere and elsewhere have considered the possibility of ordination, but have been deterred by the lack of facilities for training.' If the Churches were to begin by appointing a director of a theological centre affiliated to Makerere—and the great problem is to find the right man for this task—he could, together with the chaplains and certain other members of the staff of the college, initiate a flexible scheme. Even if no students should appear in the first two or three years, making a start would eventually attract the right kind of student and the theological centre would be of fundamental importance both to Makerere and to the churches of East Africa. 'All emergent questions can be tackled as they emerge. The *great thing is to make a beginning,* to leave the future open, and to believe that the guidance of the Holy Spirit will be granted to the churches, as they attempt to meet a great and obvious need.'

Efforts have been made to reshape and locate some of the leading theological union colleges in such a way as to give the ministerial candidates the benefit of contact with university education and university library facilities, along with the ethos of a university. The plan is closely related to the Bishop Neill's church-college idea. In 1959, it was decided to move the Immanuel College (formerly Melville Hall) from its present site near Ibadan to another site in the vicinity of the University College. In the same year Trinity College, Kumasi, prepared to move to Legon, the area of the University College of Ghana. The theological college will be administrated by the Churches as hitherto, but there may emerge a valuable kind of relationship between the theological college and the university college. The scheme was generously supported both by the Churches of Ghana and by the Theological Education Fund.

Similar plans are afoot as far as Makerere is concerned. If implemented, they may affect the ecumenical climate in East Africa to a considerable extent.

In 1955, the new University College of *Central Africa* was founded in Salisbury. Contact was established between the Southern Rhodesia Christian Conference and the College and the possibility of a Divinity course was carefully explored. In the immediate future, however, the number of candidates for a Divinity course would be too small to warrant the organization of such a course. The new Epworth Theological College, which, as we have seen, is interdenominational in principle, is placed in strategic relation to the University College, and this situation may possibly hold great promise for the future. It is significant that the Paris Evangelical Mission has shown interest in the development as far as it may affect the training of Barotse pastors, and other missions and Churches may eventually come to join the theological College, which itself may possibly become affiliated to the University College.[2]

The scene in the Central African Federation changes very rapidly. There is a new awareness on the part of all the Churches of the need of a much more thorough ministerial training than hitherto and of unification of the forces at the strategically important level of theological education. Here again, contacts with the Theological Education Fund have been of importance. In a situation of political crisis and mistrust the new move towards a united theological college on a broad interdenominational basis (we should add that the Anglican bishops, here as elsewhere, have shown great constructive interest in these plans) seems to hold out great promise for the Church in Central Africa.

The Paris Society has been particularly engaged in planning for a theological faculty for *French-speaking Africa*. Here the university situation is very different from that which obtains in British Africa; here, too African church leaders ask for postmatriculation education in theology. Both Africans and Westerners are, however, conscious of the fact that it is not practical politics to base calculations on the possibility of establishing a Theological Faculty, or Department, at a State University. The

---

[2] J. P. Burger, 'La formation des pasteurs au Zambèze', *Journal des Missions Evangéliques*, mars 1958, p. 47.

aim was to build up an independent Faculty of Christian Theology for French-speaking Africa. Dr. Emory Ross was in 1949 already remarking on the problem in very strong terms, 'There is not in the whole of Congo or in any French or Portuguese area in Africa a single Protestant theological seminary of conventional European or North American standard. That may seem incredible, but it is so.'[3]

The approach to this problem in French-speaking Africa has an interesting parallel in Madagascar. The International Missionary Council's theological commission to Madagascar stated, 'We do not think that a Faculty of Theology in Madagascar would necessarily offer all the advantages of a period spent overseas, but it would still provide the means of increasing the number of students capable of proceeding to more advanced studies. It would also, we hope, be a stimulus to theological activity in the Church of Madagascar, in the widest sense of the word.'[4]

To an even greater extent, the Churches in French-speaking West Africa feel that they would be stimulated by the establishment of a Theological Faculty.[5] The I.M.C. Commission to Latin Africa in 1953 suggested that the problem be approached 'with fresh mind and purpose'. The plans were worked out in local conferences in 1956–59, in which latter year the Evangelical Federation of the Cameroons and Equatorial Africa declared itself in favour of the opening of a faculty at Yaounde, the capital of the Cameroons. It was here that the Theological Education Fund made its first significant contribution, towards the building of the new Seminary, including the equipping of the theological library.

An interesting parallel to the Yaounde scheme is to be found in the plans of the Protestant Churches in the Belgian Congo and Ruanda-Urundi to establish a Seminary, or a Theological Faculty, affiliated to the new State University at Elizabethville.

Studies in the West

The idea of sending African students for theological training in the West is not new. The first African who received such training

---

[3] *World Outlook,* (New York), Dec. 1949, p. 603.
[4] *I.M.C. Theol. Report,* IV, p. 49.
[5] Cf. Ch. Bonzon, in *Journal des Missions Evangéliques,* August 1958, p. 143.

at a Western Protestant university was Jacobus Elisa Joannes Capitein (1717–1747), a freed West African slave, who studied at Leiden University from 1737 to 1742. Before he left Holland in 1742, he defended an academic thesis, a Latin dissertation, with the title *De Servitute, libertati Christianae non contraria*.[6] After a decade, another West African, Philip Quaque, was sent to England in 1754, completed his training there and took Anglican orders. In 1765, the S.P.G. appointed him as 'Missionary, School Master and Catechist to the Negroes on the Gold Coast';[7] as such he served for fifty years (d. 1816). Among Africans who studied theology in Britain in the first part of the nineteenth century we should mention at least one name, that of S.A. Crowther.

Efforts at the end of the nineteenth century are noteworthy. From East Africa, the U.M.C.A. directed some Africans for ministerial training to St. Augustine's, Canterbury, among whom Canon Samuel Sehoza is the best known. In West Africa, the Bremen mission decided to educate some of the most promising Ewe preachers in Westheim, Germany. Pastor R. Baëta belongs to this group. He had more than three years in Germany, 1897–1900, and received in German a very thorough grounding in the Western theology of the time.[8]

At present, study opportunities in the West (Europe or the U.S. and Canada) follow as a rule only upon ministerial training already received in Africa. In some Churches with a comparatively limited number of candidates for the ministry, the policy is to send students to the West for the whole of their theological training. An interesting example is the Anglican diocese of Ghana, which now as a rule sends ordinands to English theological colleges, normally Kelham. Anglican priests from the whole of the Anglican communion throughout the world go for post-ordination training to St. Augustine's Theological School, Canterbury. The college caters for men with some years of experience in the ministry, especially those who appear to be potential leaders within their respective Churches.

---

[6] A. Eekhof, *De Negerpredikant J. E. J. Capitein*, Gravenhage, 1917.

[7] C. P. Groves, *The Planting of Christianity in Africa*, I, p. 175 and literature quoted there.

[8] In 1924, Pastor Baëta paid a second visit to Germany. He preached in the Berlin Trinity Church and one of the Berlin newspapers had a sensational headline: 'Der schwarze Prediger auf Schleiermachers Kanzel.' cf. *Pastor Baëta's Besuch im Europa im J. 1924* (Bremen) 1925.

In the U.S.A. the Methodist Church, among others, has arranged for post-ordination theological studies also for Africans. In the period 1945–1958 four Africans seem to have used this opportunity.[9]

Advantages and disadvantages of study in the West are summarized by one of the I.M.C. Commissions.[1]

Advantages:

(1) Students have the choice, much broader in some countries than in others, of seminaries better-staffed and better-equipped, able to provide specialized studies.

(2) Such candidates are able to see and know the life of churches in Europe and America, where they are much larger and stronger than in Africa.

(3) They learn something of general society in the more developed parts of the world. They have the opportunity to understand more clearly that Christianity is not identical with European civilization.

(4) Because of study and experience abroad, they have the prestige to stand up with men of other professions who have had comparable privileges.

The Commission then goes on to speak of the disadvantages and difficulties:

(1) Life abroad is so greatly different that the African striving to adapt himself to it and to make his way within it, may lose contact with his own people, who are very sensitive to the change in him.

(2) Problems of marriage or family are critical.

(3) Expense is a burdensome matter, often utterly unrelated to the man's economic base and future income in Africa. Also, from the point of view of church and mission, the money required to send one man abroad could care for several in Africa.

A significant alternative, perhaps most appropriate for those territories closest to Europe, is found in the experiment of the Methodist Missionary Society (Great Britain), sending pastors from West Africa to England and Europe for a visitation period of six or eight months, which may include a short course of study but is aimed mainly at acquaintance with churches and at a general broadening of outlook. Variations of this principle have been tried by European and American societies also. However, there remains a case for serious theological study, which this useful enterprise does not provide.[2]

---

[9] The Librarian, Bd. of Missions of the Methodist Church, 2.10.1958, to the present writer.

[1] *I.M.C. Theol. Report*, II, p. 90–91.

[2] *I.M.C. Theol. Report*, II, *ibid.*

At the All-Africa Lutheran Conference held at Marangu, 1955, Rev. Simon A. Mbatha said:

'I cannot emphasize strongly enough that future African ministers should be trained on the spot. Americanized and Europeanized African pastors will not do much for Africa. I speak from experience. I know a man who received a scholarship and went abroad for two years. After he came home, he pulled down almost everything. He is not even willing to marry a Zulu girl. We plead that future pastors should be trained on the spot where they will have to fight their battles rather than sending Africans and Malagasy people outside of Africa. We would ask that arrangements be made that we can get American and European professors to come and do something here in Africa to really train the soldiers on the battle front.'

Some African leaders in the Marangu Conference shared this view; others held that, alongside with the best possible training in Africa, there should also be opportunities for study in the West.[3]

In most other cases where African tutors had spent some time in Western theological faculties or seminaries, they felt the time abroad had been far too short. One of the men had this to say 'You are sent to England to study for a year. But it takes you six months there to get your bearings alone. Then they say: "You have had your study; go back!" That is not study—it is only a visit.'

Some pastors who have had a year's post-ordination study and other contacts in the West, have obviously benefited greatly from the experience. To some, the visit appears frustrating, if too brief, and unsettling, if too long. A happy medium here is largely a matter of adaptation on the part of the individual student and wise planning on the part of church and college authorities in the West. In certain countries, particularly in French Africa, the study in Europe and the prospect of an academic diploma from there, is at present a very important issue in the minds of many African pastors, and an object of ambition in the minds of his family.

For African tutors in 'Latin' Africa the studies in the West are something of a problem. Those connected with Anglo-Saxon or Scandinavian missions have in some cases had short spells of study in the home countries of these missions, while some connected with the French Protestant mission in the Cameroons have studied in the Protestant faculties in France. While the one group is

---

[3] *Marangu* (Lutheran World Federation, Geneva), p. 64.

intellectually and spiritually enriched by contacts with both American and—to some extent—Scandinavian theological traditions, their brethren concentrating on French theology seem to score as far as integration of Church and culture is concerned.

The Church of Old — and the Land of the Free

As this book deals with the churches South of the Sahara, we have not included Ethiopia in our survey. Likewise Liberia, a country with ecclesiastical problems of its own, has not received here the keen attention which its problems demand. In the circumstances, we attach to this chapter a few notes on ministerial training in Ethiopia and Liberia.

Ethiopia
The Ethiopian Orthodox Church.

We have asked Dr. K. M. Simon to write a brief statement on the Ethiopian Orthodox Theological School at Addis Ababa. Dr. Simon, a priest of the Syrian Orthodox Church in South India, is the director of the School:

'The Theological School of the Orthodox Church was established by His Imperial Majesty Haile Selassie I in 1944. The primary purpose of starting such an institution was to give the young monks and priests of the Church something of the secular education on modern lines. Practically all these monks and priests would have already gone through the long traditional theological training of the Ethiopian Church before they joined this institution. Actually, until the Emperor came to the throne, education was entirely in the hands of the Church, and this mainly consisted of religious education.

A brief note on the traditional theological learning which the students—the normal Ethiopian monks or priests—have gone through before they come to the School: Every church has a school nearby, generally within the precincts of the church compound. Here the children first master the alphabet in Geez. The second stage is the study of the Apostles, learning by heart the first and second chapters of the First Epistle of St. John in Geez. This is followed by the reading of all the general Epistles. The fourth stage is the reading of the Psalms *(Dawit)*. By this time the boy will be able to write also. Generally the whole book of the Psalms is learnt by heart in Geez. They also learn by heart praises to God and praises to the Mother of God, arranged for each day of the week. To the Ethiopian, *Dawit* normally means the devotional Manual carried by every adult Christian containing besides the Psalms, the prayers of the Prophets, the Songs of Solomon and the Praises of St. Mary and the prayers of Zachariah and Simeon.

After this, those who have the inclination and opportunity for further education will proceed to a monastery and study one of three main branches of learning while sharing the community life. The three branches are: 1. Church music; 2. Philosophy and Composition; 3. Theology and History.

The House of Church Music is called the "Zema School". After the study in the "Zema school" a student may proceed to the "Kene School", which is the school of Philosophy and Religious Verse in Geez. Books containing important extracts from the world philosophers like Socrates, Plato, Aristotle, Diogenes, Cicero, Gregory, David, Solomon, Ahikar and many others are studied.

Then there is *Masahaf Bet*, the School of Interpretation. This is divided into classes for the Old and the New Testaments, and special books on the monastic life. The main theological books to be studied at this school are collections of documents describing the early history of the Universal Church. The Didascalia is a discourse on church life and society. Another book is *Haimanot Abbau* or the Faith of the Fathers. Gradually the students also will be acquainted with the "Synaxer" or the Breviary of the Ethiopian Church, the history of the Martyrs and Saints. Those who are called to become monks will study the rules of the monastic life contained in the three large books—the writings of Mar Issac of Nineveh, and Argawai Manfasawi, the spiritual fathers, and Mar Philexinos. There are many other books in addition to these which could be described under the headings Hagiology, Chronicles and Romance. They contain mainly the lives and miracles of the saints.

In the initial nine years of this school, the students were taught many secular subjects alongside theology and method of teaching, and graduates were sent as Religion teachers to the various government schools.

In 1953 the policy was changed and this was converted into a full-fledged Theological Secondary School. The school has a strength of 300 boys. In addition to the theological subjects, the secondary school curriculum of the Ministry of Education was also accepted and our students sit for both the Ethiopian School Leaving Certificate Examination and the General Certificate Examination of the University of London. This step was taken because of the conviction of the authorities that to be a Minister of the Word of God in the modern world he must have at least the minimum secular education. A separate and parallel course was also started for those who intended to become Religion teachers.

The minimum qualification for admission to the new Theological College is a pass in the Secondary School Leaving Examination, preferably from the Theological Secondary School. But graduates from the other secondary schools are not excluded if they have the necessary church background. This College is to become the Theological Faculty of the University. At the end of a course of study which will last for four and a half years the successful candidates will be awarded the degree of Bachelor of Divinity (B.D.). It is hoped that this institution, when it is completed, will become the main theological centre of the Oriental Apostolic Churches, numbering approximately 20 millions (Ethiopian Orthodox, Coptic Orthodox, Armenian Orthodox, Syrian Orthodox in the Middle East and India). The institution will naturally maintain the recognized theological standards of similar faculties in other parts of the world. Emphasis will be placed on the special doctrines and cultural heritages of the Orthodox world and the Ethiopian Orthodox Church in particular.

Along with the college, plans are also ready for the starting of a missionary centre. The duration of this course will be for three years. Arrangements are also being made for the inclusion of a Youth Workers' Training Centre and another for the training of workers among women and children. Every summer vacation, refresher courses for the clergy and Religion teachers are conducted.

The Theological School is situated in the very heart of Addis Ababa, adjacent to the Cathedral of the Holy Trinity and opposite the University College of Arts and Science. A new hostel building which can accommodate 300 students has been completed and occupied. A few flats for the members of the staff have also been built along with this. The second stage of the building consisting of lecture rooms, auditorium, administration block, library and theological museum was started in 1959.

The management of this institution is vested in the hands of a Board appointed by His Imperial Majesty the Emperor and presided over by His Beatitude Abuna Theophilos. The day-to-day administration is carried on with the co-operation of the Ministry of Education. The Rev. Dr. K. M. Simon is its director.

It is the desire of His Imperial Majesty that when the country is making rapid progress in the material field, her ancient Church which is the very fountain-head of her culture, spirit of independence and unity, should not be left behind. His Majesty's abiding interest in the institution is indeed its main source of inspiration and support. It is legitimately to be expected that this institution will play a vital role not only in the life of the Christian Church in Ethiopia, but also in the whole of Africa.'

The Protestants.

Ethiopia provides an outstanding example of dramatically rapid mass movement to the Protestant groups. This movement has above all taken place in Southern Ethiopia, beginning in the years of the Italian occupation.[4]

The total number of baptized Protestants in 1925 was only a handful of 21 (sixteen belonging to the Swedish Fosterlandsstiftelsen, and five to the Seventh-Day Adventists). Thirty years later, the Protestant community comprised 123,000, of whom the great majority, 100,000, belonged to the Sudan Interior Mission, an organization which in 1938 counted only some 500 followers in the country. Unfortunately, the great numbers were not matched by a corresponding group of well-instructed Ethiopian leaders. A total of 613 pastors and 140 evangelists (and 246 missionaries) was reported by the Sudan Interior Mission. These Ethiopian 'S.I.M.' pastors had only had some three-four years of primary school followed by three years training in a Bible School. Not always were they able to withstand the influence from Seventh-Day Adventists, who have won over a certain number of these pastors. We have the impression that the great numbers gathered by the Sudan

---

[4] A remarkable study of the beginnings of the Ethiopian Protestant revival in D. Wassmann, *Durchbruch des Evangeliums im Gallaland*, 1948.

Interior revivalist groups lack cohesion and have not sufficient Ethiopian leadership.

The German and Swedish Lutherans (with a Christian Community of some 12,500) run a theological school together. After six years primary, there is special training in English (up to Std VIII) and three years theology. Numbers are small. The course which ended in 1958 had seven students. The course of study is an adaptation of the preachers' course at the Theological Seminary, Stockholm, without Greek. Medium of teaching is mostly Amharic, but English is used for certain subjects, and the textbooks are English. The rapidly growing Norwegian Lutheran mission with some 7,000 members has 85 evangelists and no Ethiopian pastors. In Norway the mission concerned is a laymen's movement without ordained leaders, and the rule 'back home' is followed in Africa.[5] There is a Bible school with a two-year course, for church leaders (building on 3–4 years primary school). Plans are afoot for combining the Lutheran institutions into a common seminary, possibly in the early 1960's.

The close connexion between revivalism and pastors' training in some of these missions is apparent from the development within the American United Presbyterian Mission (6,000 members). During the Italian occupation, there was a radical revival in the field, and twelve of the local leaders were trained and set aside as pastors. It seems, however, that these men for various reasons, not excluding financial reasons, opposed the suggestion that their number should be increased by training and ordination of younger men. The first outburst of revival has been followed by a stagnating tendency—and this was closely connected with the particular problems of the first group of twelve pastors. Other groups, such as Baptists and Mennonites, do not seem to have proceeded very far with respect to theological education.

Liberia

Each country has its own peculiarity, and from the point of view of the Church and of theological education Liberia has its own special atmosphere and ethos. Here, also on account of space,

---

[5] This group, Norsk Luthersk Misjonssamband (N.L.M.), must not be confused with Norsk Misjonsselskap (N.M.S.).

we can only hint at the situation. In a population of some 1–2 millions, there has since the 1820's been an influential element of American Negroes. Their Churches, mainly Protestant Episcopal and Methodist Episcopal, have determined the development.

Church statistics in the first half of this century have remained fairly static, with only one or two innovations. The Christian community, which in 1925 was nearly 20,000, had in 1957 risen to 63,000, but in this latter figure are included the new arrivals after 1925: over 25,000 Pentecostals and some belonging to 'Open Bible Standards Inc.'. There were some 100 ordained men in 1925 and 135 pastors in 1957. More than a quarter of the 1957 figure comprised ordained Pentecostals. The African Methodist Episcopal Church and the African Methodist Episcopal Church, Zion, belong to the more prominent groups, besides the Protestant Episcopal and Methodist Episcopal Churches and various Presbyterian, Baptist and Lutheran groups. Among the missions there are also some interdenominational groups, the worship of which provides a bridge of emotionalism over to African syncretism, secret societies and the like.

A leading official of the University, Monrovia, informed the I.M.C. Theological Commission in 1953 that attempts had been made to establish a Theological Faculty in connexion with the University. 'But I thought that would become a racket. I fought against it, and won.' On another level, there are in Monrovia certain Bible Institutes, mostly under the form of sporadic evening classes in religious subjects. The most spectacular project in the 1950's was the building of a School of Religion under the forceful leadership of the A.M.E. Bishop E. C. Hatcher, author of a book with the characteristic title *Sermons I Have Preached* (Nashville, Tenn. 1951). Eight students received three hours' theology a week (1 hour Bible, 1 hour preparation of sermons, 1 hour A.M.E. Church History).

Quite a few of the ordained men in Monrovia are prominent officials in the administration, although in some cases the theological training has been on the short side. 'Private tuition for three weeks' was cited in the case of one very prominent man who admittedly has much else to do besides preaching.

The future for theological education in Liberia lies with Cuttington College, at Suacoco. The result of Episcopal and Methodist Episcopal co-operation, the college takes B.A. students to a B.D.

after three years' theology. In exceptional cases students with lower academic qualifications are accepted, although these are not eligible for a B.D. There were four students of theology in 1959, all college graduates. Cuttington also provides post-ordination refresher courses and takes an active interest in the local catechists' school.

· 6 ·

TOWARDS CHRISTIAN THEOLOGY IN AFRICA

The Bible, or some section of it, has been translated into four hundred African languages—an amazing achievement in circumstances which most often have been far from easy. But when the Holy Scriptures have been made available in a tongue understood by the people, another and no less important work of translation remains to be tackled. Until that second task is taken in hand, the Bible will largely remain an alien book.

Theology is, in the last resort, translation. It is an ever-renewed re-interpretation to new generations and peoples of the given Gospel, a re-presentation of the will and the way of the one Christ in a dialogue with new thought-forms and culture patterns. Translation to Africa, on this level of theological encounter, has hardly begun. If it be true that the Christian Church in Africa has 're-mained an alien institution' (K. Busia), this is to a large extent due to the absence of conscious and creative theological work on the part of both Western and African leaders. Theology, in essence, is to understand the fact of Christ; theology in Africa has to interpret this Christ in terms that are relevant and essential to African existence. Here the background in the myths of African religion is important, for it provides certain broad patterns of which theology in Africa must take account. If in India Jesus Christ, the *Guru,* may appear as the Truth who saves from the unreality of the world of phenomena, so in Africa the same Christ, the King, proves Himself to be the Life and the Fullness with power to liberate from sickness and death and devil.

A theologian who with the Apostle is prepared to become to the Jews as a Jew, to them that are without law, as without law, and *therefore,* unto Africans as an African, must needs start with the fundamental facts of the African interpretation of existence and the universe.

Traditional African thinking was mythical. It was bound up with the Beginning of Things, with Creation and the Primeval Age; the Myths of the Origin of the First Man and of Mankind are fundamental to this conception of life and the world. They constitute an 'original revelation', which is re-enacted in annually recurrent festivals, in a rhythm which forms the cosmic framework of space and time. The myths span the whole of existence, from heaven to the hut and the heart of the individual; in fact, from cosmos to clan. Macrocosm and microcosm are tuned to each other and are included in an all-embracing order.

In the theological encounter in Africa there are certain aspects of the Biblical message which tend to carry a particular emphasis, and which take on overtones that are partially or entirely lacking in other Churches. It is with this emphasis alone that we shall be concerned here, while acknowledging that this account should have its counterbalance in the sum total of the theological tradition of the Church. We concentrate our interest on what appear to be the two foci of the theological encounter in Africa: the Beginnings of Mankind and of the People of God *and* the clan community of the Living and the Dead. After that we shall briefly discuss the African preacher's ideas on the Church and the ministry. The source material for our analysis on this point is scanty, and we have assumed that the most important theological work by Africans at present is to be found in the living voice of African sermons, in the act of preaching itself; it is mainly sermons and hymns by pastors and catechists that provide a basis for our tentative conclusions.

The Links with the Beginning

Listening to a sermon by a catechist in the tropical bush or by certain pastors on the Rand one will inevitably be brought to the Beginning of Things. The European listener says to himself, 'Now he is repeating that old story once again! It is as if he didn't know much more of the Bible!' But the listener may be wrong, and he may come to realize it.

The present writer began to realize it for the first time on a beautiful Easter morning in Natal some years ago. A congregation of five hundred Zulu men and women had come together for four days at the central mission station; together we experienced Holy Communion on Maunday Thursday, and the Passion on Good Friday; together we meditated on our Lord's Descent to

Hell and the Burial on Saturday. At last, the moment of great longing had arrived. Very early on Easter Morning the procession wound its way through the little town towards the cemetery, that is the Native cemetery. As the procession went along, the Paschal hymn was sung:

> *Kusasa lapha laphuma,*
> *uMagdalena wa hamba*
> (At dawn, Magdalene went out).

Standing among the graves, facing a cross with the inscription 'I am the Resurrection and the Life', the congregation sang, and witnessed the coming sunrise.

Then Rev. Michael Mzobe started to preach. He is one of the finest preachers I have ever heard, in any land. The text for his Easter morning message was taken from the Old Testament, the Resurrection chapter in Ezekiel, ch. 37.

Then he began where all Zulu sermons begin, in the Beginning. In the Beginning God created heaven and earth, and the sea, and the animals—and man. That man He created in His own image. But Adam fell, and through the Fall of Adam death and disaster came into the world. But after all, he was Adam, and as he died, he was brought to Paradise. There he was given an honoured place, sitting all by himself on a balcony, and from the balcony in heaven he followed the history of mankind. He saw his eldest son, Cain, murder his brother, Abel. And Adam sitting in that honoured place in the balcony in heaven had to cry out aloud, for sorrow and shame: *Icala lami, icala lami elikhulu,* 'My guilt, my great guilt!' And then the Flood came! People went about, forgetting their God, living in sin; then the Primeval Waters from below began to rise. People tried to flee and hide but were soon overtaken; in another direction he heard children crying and saw men and women caught in terror and despair, to no avail. And Adam—in Paradise!—had to cry, overcome by sorrow: *icala lami, icala lami elikhulu!* Thus the whole of the well-known 'Bible History' passed in review for the Zulu congregation in the Native cemetery; in Dundee, South Africa and before Adam in Paradise was unfolded a history of dramatic events that changed the world. Even David the Anointed King, fell into sin—because of Adam. Generation after generation was born on earth only to sin and die—for the sake of Adam's sin. 'Ye Zulus', cried Michael Mzobe, 'consider that heavy weight of sorrow on the heart of our Great Forefather Adam; suffering and sorrow—and it was all for his sin's sake!

But—Zulus, men and women, *Yekanini lentokozo engakanani!* Consider that incredible joy, that indescribable jubilation which filled Adam's heart on the First Easter Morning, as the Hero of Heaven (*iqhawe la sezulwini*) came in through the Gate of Heaven, with His Crown of Thorns, now a brilliant Crown of Victory, walking the central aisle in the heavenly Temple, straight up to the Throne of the Almighty. There He gave His report that from this day Satan and Sin and Death had been overcome. For now He, the Second Adam, had won the victory.

And the First Adam had peace.

Here is a width of vision that takes in the whole history of Redemption and displays the whole drama of the Bible, from the Beginning to the consummation; this is living African theology, born in the act of preaching. It is significant that it is the great Day of the Church's year, Easter Day, which calls out a message of this magnitude. But Easter is clearly related, as everything must be in the theology of Mzobe, to the *Initium,* the Origin, to that which was in the Beginning. History is, to him, a *remembrance* of that which was in the Beginning. This is why the Old Testament is so central to the whole theological conception of African preachers; their interest in the stories of *Genesis* has often been noticed. It has been referred to in general terms by Bishop Neill and Dr. Welch, the former claiming that 'the African mind is more Hebrew than Greek', the latter asserting 'that African society and values are akin to Hebrew society and values'. We need perhaps to be somewhat more specific than that. If there is a connexion between African and Hebrew concepts, in what does it consist? The parallelism between the great Hebrew stories and African myths can in fact be established in some detail.[1] African myths have close connexions to the Hebrew account of Creation, Cain and Abel and the Flood, while the Crossing of the Red Sea has parallels among the tribes in one uninterrupted series from Ethiopia to the Limpopo. Whether in fact we have to do with

---

[1] We refer particularly to H. von Sicard's important study, *Ngoma Lungundu, Eine afrikanische Bundeslade,* Uppsala 1952. For a comparison of Hebrew and Greek thought, see Th. Boman, *Das hebräische Denken im Vergleich mit dem griechischen,* 2nd ed., Göttingen 1954.

an early Old Testament influence carried over the continent by Islam-influenced Falasha elements (cf. the famous Lemba of S. Rhodesia) or whether, perhaps, at a very early stage both Hebrew and African thought-worlds have been under Babylonian influence, is a matter of conjecture. But the fact of this connexion between African and Hebrew ideas cannot be explained away.

This fact helps to elucidate the significant reaction of African preachers to the Old Testament, a reaction expressed in a representative manner by Rev. Meya, a theological teacher in the French Cameroons, who told us, 'We recognize our own history in the Pentateuch. We feel that we possibly stem from this history of the Hebrews, because our customs and those of the Hebrews are so similar.' In a most dramatic way this attitude was shared by a whole Church as the Fang people (Gabon) in 1950 received the Old Testament. The New Testament was first translated and only after thirty years did they receive the whole Bible in their own tongue. As they were confronted with this new book, the *Old Testament*, it appeared as a tremendous revelation to them. The Old Testament was so much closer to them than the New.

The Old Testament in the African setting is not just a book of reference. It becomes a source of remembrance.[2] The African preacher feels that Genesis belongs to him and his Church, or rather vice versa—that he and his African Church belong to those things which were in the beginning. From this sacred charter in the Book, his own people and Church receive their recognition. They are no longer a dry little branch, 'independent' and cut-off. They belong to the original tree of Life, being grafted into it and receiving its reviving sap.

A word of C. G. Jung on the archetypes comes to mind in this connexion. Using an image that belongs to the African scene, he says, 'Archetypes resemble the beds of rivers: dried up because the water has deserted them, though it may return at any time'.[3] The great primordial images of the Old Testament for a time seemed to be desiccated by Western scepticism and rationalism, but in the African Christian's encounter with the Biblical message, Living Waters begin to flow again over dry river beds.

There is another side to it, which becomes particularly clear in

---

[2] Cf. Ad. Jensen, *Mythos und Kult bei Naturvölkern*, 1951, p. 243-244.

[3] C. G. Jung, *Psychological Reflections*, ed. J. Jacobi 1953, p. 36. Cf. Jung, *Über die Psychologie des Unbewussten* (1943), pp. 161-202.

Bible-interpretation by independent African church leaders, but of at least potential importance to many African preachers within 'orthodox' mission churches. In the great and universal stories of the Patriarchs and the Exodus they discover a charter giving authority to their own race and Church, and the Hebrew myths are re-interpreted in the light of their own fate and aspirations. This re-interpretation serves to link the African Christian group with that which was in the Beginning.

From this point of view I felt that the most 'cocksure' of all Western theological teachers we met in Africa was, perhaps, just a bit off the mark as he confided to the I.M.C. Theological Commission to 'Latin' Africa in 1953: 'I am deathly afraid of Old Testament Christians. I have killed the interest of my students in the Old Testament.'

It is conceivable that in killing that interest he had succeeded in eradicating more than just the *Old* Testament.

To remember (*ukukhumbula* in Zulu) is a fundamental word in this theology. Adam had to remember, against his will, his guilt, and when the African hears of the Christians' God, he 'remembers', at last, what was there, half-forgotten, all the time. Adam and Abraham and Moses and the Exodus from Egypt are archetypes of things that were from the Beginning and which are 'remembered', as the Book is opened. The lively interest shown by African preachers in Abraham and Moses reflects the fact that these Old Testament figures are recognized as archetypes and reproduced, in simple and tangible terms, in the person of the pastor as leader of his flock, bringing them out of bondage into the unknown lands of the future. Thus the stories of Genesis offer more to the African preacher and theologian than to the Westerner. In meeting its message the African leader and his flock 'remember' that they are part of that which was from the beginning. In the same way, possibly, the whole of the Bible tradition as the sacred charter of the Church is 'remembered' in the common African worship with its deep fellowship of preacher and congregation. Particularly is the Holy Communion of significance in this context. The pre-Nicene Church referred to the eucharist as an *anamnesis,* a re-calling or re-presentation of the Body and Blood of Christ.[4] There are remarkable parallels be-

---

[4] Cf. Dom Gregory Dix, *The Shape of the Liturgy,* p. 245.

tween the Early Church and the Young Church in Africa on this fundamental point. Obviously there is a tendency and a propensity to interpret the liturgical drama in a 'realistic' way, different from the rationalistic approach of nineteenth-century Western expressions of the Christian religion.

The Easter sermon we have quoted was preached in an African cemetery; the men and women who listened, and the man who preached, were very familiar with death. Sickness and death were unwelcome but well-known guests, often paying fatal visits to their houses and huts and hovels. In that situation, the message of Easter as expounded by Michael Mzobe became tremendously relevant, and the listerners 'remembered' that which was from the Beginning and which was recreated in their midst. *Uvukile*—He is arisen!—was a great message in the Valley of Death.

We believe that the Church in Africa will discover, and through its preachers and theologians interpret, new riches in the message of Easter, as one of the foremost festivals of the Church's year, making priest and congregation 'remember' the sacred rhythm brought into their lives by the Church. The mythological pattern in traditional African religion had prepared them for a yearly rhythm; but there is a fundamental difference between the ever-returning cycle of mythological existence and the new rhythm of the history of Redemption, expressed in the Bible and in the life of the Church. This new rhythm challenges the former in a fundamental way as it looks to the 'Telos' of all things, in which creation is consummated in the enthronement of the Second Adam.

The Links with the Living and the Dead

The other focus of theological encounter is the corporate life of the clan. However corroding the acids of modern detribalization may appear, the patterns and the attitudes of the clan still play a great role in African life, and we have seen how in the modern city there is a tendency towards an emphasis on tribal values, including those of the clan. The African clan is the link between the generations living on earth and the generations in their existence as ancestors. In the system of the clan, the fundamental facts of life are all represented: the vitality and fertility of the individual and the family, marriage, procreation, birth and death

—all linked up with the continuing existence of the clan; the demands of the clan consequently present the Church with its most persistent challenge. This concerns the life of the extended family on the one hand and death and the ancestors on the other. It is with these two sets of problems that the African preacher, church leader, and theologian has to contend in a very special way.

In the Church there is a fundamental encounter between Bantu fertility cults and the new religion of the White Christ. It is here that the African preacher has to tackle the problem of legalism, since for the most part the Church, in its attempt to conquer human nature to the greater glory of God, has so far appeared as a legalistic body. Ninety per cent of all cases dealt with in Protestant church discipline belong to this category. The Ten Commandments have virtually been reduced to the one Commandment forbidding adultery. In the exercise of church discipline—from the level of the local village church council to the highest courts of the Church—this encounter between Bantu fertility religion and Christianity is made sharp and uncompromising. The African church leader is personally involved in this problem. The encounter as he sees it, between polygamy and the demands of Christian sanctification, is not irrelevant to him personally. I remember Rev. Absalom N., a Zulu, one of the most virile of men and possessing tremendous personality (*isithunzi*, as the Zulus say). On more than one occasion I sensed the personal struggle behind that impressive façade of a great Bantu personality. The son of a chief, he compared his own fate with that of his non-Christian brothers. 'I have only one son and one daughter. Our brothers (*abafo wethu*) have taken wives and have many children. No matter—I have made my choice. I have chosen Christ.' One felt that one witnessed an existential struggle in the life of that Bantu pastor, and that he experienced the problem of fertility and the survival of the clan as a personal problem.

On a somewhat different level, this relationship to his own clan presents the pastor with ever-recurrent problems. He is part of the clan, and has to be loyal to it. The fundamental fact that *the Protestant pastor is a family man,* with some privileges and wide responsibilities to his clan, affects the situation of the African ministry to a greater extent than is commonly realized. So, for instance, recruitment to the ministry is to a certain degree conditioned by these relationships. The pastor's relationship to the clan

7. "Bread of the world, in mercy broken;
Wine of the soul, in mercy shed'.

is ambivalent, for the traditional clan-fellowship is charged with
pagan values; the struggle of sanctification in the pastor—in dream
or personal prayer or public testimony—is, we have suggested,
mainly an encounter with these powers of the clan.

There is a possibility—but of course not more than just a
possibility—that the African Protestant theologian of the future
will build on this fact of the family as one of the main pillars of
his theology, particularly of his ecclesiology. He may come to
regard it as his particular task to see the Church in terms of the
Great Family.

A vitally important section of the new African theology must
concern the dead and the meaning of their after-life, or death. It
is generally recognized that African theologians are sometimes
prone to take over, without much discussion, the teaching from
the Church in the West, but on this aspect of doctrine the Africans
feel that they have something of their own to say and that it must
be said soon. It was well said by Dr. C. G. Baëta, of the University
of Ghana, in 1955:

> For, whatever others may do in their own countries, our people
> *live* with their dead. This is plain for anybody to see who participates
> sympathetically in a ceremony of the pouring of family libations; the
> intimate and affectionate tone of the prayers, the sense of the imme-
> diate presence of the dead, all that can leave no one in any doubt.
> And yet when Church bodies make rulings in the matter of funeral
> observances the reasons given for the repressive measures recommended
> —they are almost that—are not even religious reasons, but merely such
> irrelevancies as expense, inconvenience and waste of time. So the
> decisions get nowhere and the problems persists.
>
> ... There will be an uneasy position for some time followed, as
> soon as concern about the missionary's good opinion is gone, by chaos.
> Exactly as we have chaos now in the matter of libations, because the
> real problem was dodged.
>
> The better way of dealing with such-like intractable remnants of a
> previous or passing culture, now no longer desired, would seem to be
> not to proscribe them out of hand but to prune, purify and guide them,
> making them fit for new and higher service.

Baëta goes on to quote the view of H. St. John T. Evans, Bishop
of St. John's, Ciskei. Writing on the Ashanti, he says:

> The important thing to be noticed about this cult (i.e. ancestor
> worship) is that it in no sense seeks to raise the '*asamanfo*' (practically

ancestors) to the status of gods. Their sphere of influence is not thought to extend beyond the particular family or clan group; nor can the reverence in which they are held be regarded as worship, in the strictly religious sense. It is rather a recognition of the essential unity of all members of the clan, living and departed.

Baëta then concludes:

'Clearly we have to hand here all the material required for a theological battle royal, and the issue is indistinguishable from that of the controversies of the Middle Ages regarding saints, namely the shades of meaning in the words "reverence", "worship" and "service", and who gets what.[5]

The problem concerns not only West Africa. The way in which African local church leaders are groping for an answer here can be seen from the essay of a Zulu theological student. Many theological schools throughout Africa report that their students show an extraordinary interest in the fate of the dead. This Zulu student (Lutheran, 35 years of age) regards it as the central point from which to judge the whole problem of the missionary approach to Africa. We quote from his essay 'Why and how I became a student of theology'.

'The missionaries came with Christianity but missed the open gate for Christianization. The message was not applied to the existing forms of worship. They brought good news for mankind, containing forgiveness of sins by Christ alone, who died for all and *went to the dead to show them who He was,* and *came up from the dead to show himself to the living ones.* As the missionaries preached this Christ, they missed the gate.

How was it missed? The missionaries did not show the Africans that they were a considerable nation by respecting their ways of worship and the belief they had; they did not encourage and tell them that the Bible itself says that the deceased are not dead but are living or resting, and that their spirits were living because they *belonged to God,* from whom they came by the creation of Adam (Gen. 2: 7). Since then, it is a continuous thing—until Christ

---

[5] *Christianity and African Culture* (ed. Chr. Council, Gold Coast), 1955, pp. 51–61.

comes again (Mt. 24: 31). If the missionaries had considered this, they would have won more than they in fact gained.

It was only one foot from the missionaries to the gate. In what way? The missionaries could e.g. have said: You Africans are fortunate that you have such a belief of the deceased living and of *Umvelinqangi,* as the Bible witnesses to this. There is only one thing for you to know. Take a step forward. Your deceased ones can do nothing for you because they are powerless, since they themselves are subjected to and guided by their Owner who had created them, the Most High God, even higher than your *Umvelinqangi* who alone can help the Zulus and all Africans. Your deceased ones can work only for the people of one kraal— if at all, not for the whole nation; and *Umvelinqangi* can only work for the nation, if at all. What about the whole world? This God that we bring to you through the Bible is the owner of all nations of the world. His Son is the one who can save the whole world, being the Son of the Almighty.

Our first missionaries missed the gate. They would have won many people by transforming the old belief into the new and by changing the way of approaching the Almighty. The deceased could have been compared with the angels of God which are never worshipped but just praised as Gods messengers. Something must be done [to establish contact] between the old belief and Christianity. Connect both—there is the key to enter the African door and the African's heart.'

We find particular interest in one aspect brought out by this theological student. The *descent into Sheol*—regarded by the Early Church to be so important that it was given a place in the Creed—does not take a central position in modern Western preaching. African theology no doubt will make a special contribution. Here, the *descent into Sheol* indeed becomes—in the words of this African student—a key to an understanding of the life of the deceased ancestors. The young African pastor stresses that it is the death and *descensio* of Christ which creates the new condition for the dead. He descended to the dead 'to show them who He was'. The full implications of the connexion between His death and the death of all men have, of course, not been brought out by this short statement, and we should add that in the theology of the West at present there are only very few who manage to assimilate in their thinking something of the real meaning of the *descensio*-clause in the Creed. An outstanding recent contribution is Rahner's penetrating study in which he shows to what depths theology needs to go in order to begin to understand Scripture and Creed on this point.[6] It is to be hoped that African priests, pastors and potential theologians will wrestle with the problem; they will have to do this from the point of view of their own recent religious background in an encounter with Christian revelation, and we expect that as this encounter develops, African theologians with their great existential understanding of the Christian sacraments will emphasize new dimensions of depth in both Holy Baptism and Holy Communion.

Obviously the nearest parallel to this relationship between cosmological vision and the depth dimension of *descensio* in African theological encounter, is to be found in the writings of Iraeneus and in the Early Church as a whole. We suggest that there is a difference between them, however. When Iraeneus asks, *Ad quid enim descendebat?*—Why did Christ descend?—he refers to the Incarnation; our African preachers lay their stress on the descent to the Realm of the Dead. But the two concepts have the main interest in common, for both in Iraeneus and in the modern Africans, the meaning of *descensio* is soteriological. It is also mainly from the point of view of Death and *Descensio Christi* that the African pastor verbalizes the sense of the Holy, to an extent which is not always fully understood by Westerners. We ourselves once witnessed a significant occasion which goes to prove this point. In a Zulu congregation, a new mortuary had just been built half-way between the mission hospital and the church. The new building was to be dedicated by the leading Western missionary after the Sunday morning service, and a large crowd had assembled outside the mortuary. One of the Zulu pastors was asked to open the meeting with a free prayer. So he began: 'Oh Lord, our heavenly Father, here we are assembled in this awesome place (*kulendawo esabekayo*) and we pray...' As he had concluded his prayer, the old Western missionary patriarch turned to him, in the presence of that great crowd, saying, 'You, M., this is not an awesome place. This is a place of light and joy and Christian hope, etc.' The social situation being what it was (and

---

[6] Karl Rahner S.J., 'Zur Theologie des Todes', *Zeitschrift für Katholische Theologie*, 1957, p. 1–44.

is), our Zulu pastor bowed his head, apparently in deep gratitude for the higher wisdom thus bestowed upon him and the congregation, but he may possibly have felt at the time that there was somehow a deeper wisdom in his own existential reaction to Death. We suggest that our African colleagues through this reaction have possibilities of reaching new depths of theological understanding.

This endeavour will also have to be directed to the problem of the commemoration of the dead. The Anglican Commission report *'The Commemoration of Saints and Heroes of the Faith in the Anglican Communion'* (1957) was the result of a request from the Church in Africa. The Anglican Diocese of Nyasaland wrote in 1937 to the Archbishop of Canterbury asking for his guidance in this field, and a Commission, the report of which was published twenty years later, was appointed as a result of this initiative. The Report is characterized by sober restraint.[7] It includes a helpful comment from the Bishop of Mombasa (Dr. Leonard Beecher):

> It would be salutary if more were done to make and keep the Church in Africa mindful of that great encircling cloud of witnesses amongst whom there are now so many of their own. I would deprecate anything that departed from a Catholic into a regional or even national tradition of observance. Let Apolo Kivebulaya rank alongside Krapf, and both alongside their Indian, Chinese, and Japanese counterparts. But at the same time, let us not produce a Kalendar so full that it has lost its special significance. I should like an African village congregation to feel from time to time just what their heritage is in respect of this great cloud of witnesses, and feel from it an urge to lay aside encumbering sins and run their race with eyes set on the Lord.

We have tried to indicate one potential trend in the emerging theological encounter in Africa. It is not primarily an intellectual encounter carried out in secluded libraries and academic lecture halls: it is an encounter with the stark realities of Suffering (social and physical), Sickness and Death. 'We Africans live very close

---

[7] *The Commemoration of Saints and Heroes of the Faith in the Anglican Communion* (1957). We realize that some of our readers will think it reckless and irresponsible even to mention the existence of this problem and of the report. We ask such readers to look at the report, an unanimous statement of Anglican leaders, including Dr. M. A. C. Warren of the C.M.S. Cf. Lambeth 1958, Report *1*.48 and 2.94.

to death', an African co-worker of mine, in Western Tanganyika, once told me; he and his wife had had sixteen children, of whom the first twelve had died. The survival of the man and his clan is a matter of primary importance to him and to his people, and the survival of the dead, the after-life, is a matter of existential interest to him and to his Church. The Easter sermon we quoted suggests that the theology which emerges on the African frontier will be 'a theology of the Second Adam, a theology of Resurrection.'

From the Valley of Death, the African Church is looking towards Him who overcame Death. In their own way the Douala Christians, in the French Cameroons, express their conviction in a hymn sung antiphonally by two groups in the Church.

> Christ ascended on to the Cross;
> Christ descended into the Grave;
> Christ overcame the Power of Death.
>> Yes, he overcame him.
>>> Did he overcome him?
>> Yes, he overcame him.
>>> Did he overcome him?
>> Yes, he overcame him.
>>> Did he overcome him?
> Christ overcame the Power of Death.
>> Yes, he overcame him.
>>> Did he overcome him?
>> Yes, he overcame him.
>>> Did he overcome him?
>> Yes, he overcame him.
>>> Did he overcome him?
> Christ overcame the Power of Death.
>> Yes, he overcame him.[8]

The Worshipping Community

'My parish is like all the others. All parishes resemble one another.' Thus the famous country priest of Ambricourt, in the

---

[8] Cf. W. Ringwald, *Die Religion der Akanstämme*, 1952, p. 266.

opening sentence of *Diary of a Country Priest* by Bernanos. He was right, and we are quite sure that he meant all the parishes in Africa to be included in his generous sweeping statement. The task of the Church of Christ is one and the same wherever it is at work. And yet, there *are* differences, brought about by a whole set of old and new factors, for while essentially the Church in Africa is the same as that in Sweden or in New Zealand, it has its own 'peculiar honours' to bring.

In preceding chapters we have tried to analyse in sociological terms the place and function and status of the pastor in African society and in the religious groupings which go to constitute a church. But this approach, while possibly helpful, can only lead us to a certain point, to a line drawn by the fact that the Church of Christ is something *sui generis,* which cannot, in the last resort, be reduced to sociological factors.

The Church has theological dimensions, and it also has a right to claim that it should be understood on its own terms. But here again we have to be careful; theological concepts fashioned in order to measure conditions in the Churches of the West may turn out to be rather blunt tools when we attempt to estimate some of the factors that are determinative for the Church and its ministry in such a culture as that of Africa. The Universal Church, being essentially the same in all climes, expresses itself in particular national and indigenous thought-forms, and with varying accents and emphases. And more important: as the given Gospel is preached in new languages and the Church planted in new soil, there may appear hitherto forgotten or hidden treasures of truth which will enrich the Church as a whole.

In the following few pages we shall make an admittedly daring attempt to understand the Church and the ministry in terms of concepts which at present seem to emerge in the theological encounter in Africa and which are expressed, not in tomes of academic theology, but in tones, and overtones, of preaching and song and movement. In so doing we shall try to do two things: to show in what direction African theological encounter is moving at present and to emphasize some of the great themes on which African theologians will have to carry out particular tasks of re-interpretation in the years to come. If the attempt points in the right direction, it may possibly help to set in motion a much needed theological debate in Africa, by African theologians.

We have suggested that African theological encounter is an ellipse with two foci[9]—the Links with the Beginning and the Links with the Living and the Dead, held together by a particular understanding of the Church, the interpretation of whose nature presents the African theologian with one of his most urgent tasks.

Theological re-orientation by African theologians will necessarily challenge the patterns of church life brought by Protestant missions from Europe and from America. Looking at the canvas of Protestant Africa in broad perspective, it appears that Protestant Christianity was brought to Africa by nineteenth-century Pietism, Puritanism and Evangelicalism and twentieth-century Holiness and Pentecostal groups. While these historical expressions of Christianity made lasting contributions to the evangelization and education of the African masses, their strongest impact probably lay elsewhere than in the ecclesiological field. As Western individualists, the missionaries representing these groups had not always sufficient understanding of the corporate nature of the Church and still less, perhaps, an appreciation of the supra-individual and corporate forces which are at work in African group life.

We have seen how in the modern Christian movement in Africa the school became one dominant interest in the activities of the Church. Historically the school grew out of the catechetical teaching of the Church, and was felt as a necessary part of, and supplement to, the worship of the Church. But often there was a tendency towards an identification of school and church. A common Zulu term for church is characteristically, *'isikole'* (school). The word *umfundisi* (of *ukufundisa*, to teach) was used for both teacher and pastor—with a very slight differentiation in tone.[1] This Zulu term is now employed almost exclusively of the pastor, the term for Christian in Uganda and adjacent countries being *omushomi* (reader, i.e. who can read).

The effect of this identification of school and Church can be studied in the very fixtures of the building. Richard Niebuhr has recently suggested that the interior of a church building, in

---

[9] The use of the term 'focus' in this connexion should be seen as related to the concept 'cultural focus', discussed by M. J. Herskovits, *The Myth of the Negro Past*, Beacon ed. (1958), p. xxvi.

[1] The differentiation in tone: umfundisi, 2.6.6.3.9 (teacher) and 2.6.3.9.9. (pastor). The term nowadays for teacher is the loan-word *utisha*. Dr. D. McK. Malcolm 15.10.1956 to the present writer.

one or other Christian organization, gives an important indication of the particular conception of the Church and its ministry. 'The place in which the minister mainly functions always signalizes the Church's idea of his task.' This conception is symbolized by the dominance of altar (possibly with a confessional) or pulpit in the church.[2] Now, in very many local Protestant church buildings throughout the continent of Africa, besides the pulpit, another fixture has a prominent place, namely the black-board of the school. The church building is given over to the school for five days in the week. A Protestant pastor at Alexandra, Johannesburg, has sensed a problem here.

> A school in the church building consecrated to the service of God alone, is in my mind a mistake. The children are beaten and scolded and very often the language used is as it should not be in a school. All in all, these things are contrary to what it should be, viz. a place where love is preached and God is hallowed. I venture to deduce from this, that the disrespect for the Church and the sacred places allotted to the service of God has its origin all over Transvaal in schools being conducted in church buildings. The children are misled as to what it means: In the presence of God. The purpose of the church is lost. It is considered a place of learning or of where to get worldly knowledge. I mean that the church is a place for the gospel alone and nothing else and should be consecrated to the service of the HOLY GOD.

This reaction is possibly not representative of a very wide opinion among Bantu Christians. It overlooks the fact that, in some places, one building used for all purposes is a practical necessity. Yet this pastor by his approach finds his way towards a theological solution of the concept of the Church. He has to do this in an encounter with the somewhat exclusively intellectualized and catechetical approach which characterized much of nineteenth-century Protestant civilizing and evangelizing efforts.

Many writers noticed that the African Christian apparently has an immediate and existential understanding of the Church as an organic and corporate fellowship. Bruno Gutmann, E. W. Smith and D. W. Shropshire, a Lutheran, a Methodist, and an Anglo-Catholic respectively, have from different viewpoints reminded us of this fact. The great Biblical terms for the Church—the

---

[2] H. Richard Niebuhr, *The Purpose of the Church and its Ministry*, 1956, p. 80.

People of God, the Body of Christ, the Household or Family of God —find a vibrant sounding-board in the structure of African social patterns, particularly of the clan. Our previous remarks on the clan suggest that the *communion of saints* of the Creed may in African worship take on overtones that are not to be found to the same extent in Western congregations, and that the Church will come to life as the new Clan of Christ and the Family of God.

Often, to their surprise, the missions discovered that there emerged in Africa a church structure which was quite different from that known by the missionaries in their home countries. In the African context the *cellular* structure of church organization gave vitality to local village groups and authority to responsible local leaders; the present writer, belonging to the Church of Sweden (Lutheran), discovered when coming as a young missionary to Zululand that there the combined influences of African social patterns and the surrounding, dominant Methodist 'class' organization had formed the Zulu Church into an organic unity of living cells, as part of the Body of Christ in South Africa.

In the worshipping community in Africa, the relationship between the Church and followers often reaches deep into the 'collective personality' of the group. When Rev. B.S.R., on the Rand, preaches a stirring sermon to his Methodist flock (A.M.E.), they cannot simply sit there unmoved and unmovable; both men and women feel the urge to move up to the altar, and there they kneel: members 'of good standing' round the altar; another group of those who have fallen by the wayside and who now wish to revive their faith; and perhaps a third group of new converts—all surrounding the preacher who offers a prayer on their behalf and who himself, in a most tangible way, experiences that he is carried by the prayers of his faithful. Similarly between pastor and those baptized by him exist strong bonds of spiritual fellowship, and between confessor and the penitent—in those few cases where the Church carries out this particular function of pastoral care.

The fully African understanding of the nature of the Church is to be found particularly in an interpretation of the *leitourgia,* the worship of the Church. Here the heartbeat of African church life is felt, and it is at this central point that the encounter between modern Africa and Western Protestantism will take place. An indication of this trend was a statement by a Presbyterian Church leader in Ghana, Rev. E. A. Asamoa. At the I.M.C. meeting at Willingen in 1952, he made an eloquent plea against Western individualism and intellectualism, asking instead for an approach which aimed at the heart of African man. 'The Church', he insisted, 'thinks of itself too much as an institute of social gospel and of preaching. The Church in Africa needs to be shown powers beyond itself. The re-orientation we need implies a more determined emphasis on the sacramental life of the Church.'[3] He and many of his colleagues throughout Africa feel the innate propensity of the African for sacramental life.

Corporate religious life and fellowship express themselves in song and rhythm. The new and radical group expressions found by Separatist churches in the South and in the West are indications of the fact that the really indigenous African Church in the future will orientate itself away from Western intellectualism and show a sense for the rich and generous orchestration of African emotional life. In 1958, living for some time with a small village congregation in one of the Zululand valleys, I compared the worship of the mission flock with that of the adjacent 'Separatist' groups. The obviously foreign tunes made the singing of the former heavy and hesitant, while the 'Separatists' apparently found much joy and satisfaction in their lively worship. The African Church comes to life and realizes its special charisma at the level of music and song and rhythm.

One can see this trend in the surprisingly central place of church choirs in Presbyterian or Baptist congregations at Douala, in the Cameroons, or in the Congregational group at Lobito, Angola, or in Methodist women's weekday prayer-meetings in Sierra Leone. In Mozambique, an African pastor and I were discussing the Christian attitude to the African cultural heritage. My friend said: 'We Africans knew God but not Jesus Christ and the Holy Spirit. Because of this insufficient knowledge, before the arrival of the Gospel, we could not *sing and pray aright.*' A Tonga (Northern Rhodesia) in making known his desire to join the Church says *ndiyanda kurimba,* (I want *to learn to sing*). What strikes them as constitutive for a particular church is the way in which its members sing; churches are different because they sing differently. Similarly, the preaching at its best becomes corporate African worship and the sermon a sacramental act by pastor and congrega-

---

[3] Notes by B. S. from a contribution by E. A. Asamoa to the discussion of Group II at Willingen.

tion, bound together in an electrifying atmosphere of challenge and living response.

The Church as a Family, a corporate fellowship, is expressed also in the cycle of events of the Church's year, with its climax at Easter, sometimes the occasion for a huge church gathering lasting from three to four days (cf. p. 282). Some Protestant churches have shown imagination in creating and adapting regular church gatherings, and thus investing them with deep significance. The Methodists in Northern Rhodesia have revivalist rallies lasting a few days; the Church of the Nazarene in Mozambique gathers once a year to a meeting in the month of August, which lasts for three days and attracts a thousand or more of the faithful: a big tent constitutes the tabernacle of this pilgrim People of God. In this particular group the camp meeting is the occasion when all the catechumens are baptized and when the yearly Communion service is held. In this connexion we should perhaps point to the central place taken by one or two annual festivals, on some sacred mountain, in South African prophet movements, such as the January and July festivals of the Nazarite prophet movement, a bold Bantu re-presentation of the Old Testament Feast of Tabernacles. We ourselves can see no reason why the more 'orthodox' churches in other parts of Africa should not adopt such important group-integrating forms of expression. We venture to suggest that as African pastors more and more come into their own and have a say in the Churches, such forms will be found.

The roots of the matter are reached only as we approach the African minister's interpretation of the sacramental life of the Church. We know, of course, regrettably little about such interpretations, for the difficulty of approach has brought it about that few valid observations have been made—and we are all the poorer for it.

Two examples must suffice in order to show the tendency. The preparation addresses for Holy Communion offer precious material here. We listened to one such address in a Lutheran Church in Zululand, and we quote extracts from the carefully prepared manuscript.

> *Can a women forget her sucking child, that she should not have compassion on the son of her womb? Yea, they may forget, yet will I not forget thee!* Isaiah 49: 15.

Consider the greatness of a woman's love of her child ... The child lives from the mother and receives strength from her day by day. The child eats from the mother, drinks her blood, and yet, the mother never tires of the child. But if the child falls ill and no longer wishes to take his mother's breast, then the mother's hope sinks. Her breasts smart for sorrow, and they remind her of her sick child.

God has born us through Jesus Christ. Jesus is our Mother. He was constrained by his love for us. On the Cross of Golgotha there were opened wounds in his hands and in his feet and in his side, and from these flowed his Blood so that whosoever cometh to him can eat his flesh and drink his Blood.

Jesus is saddened because of the many who no longer want to receive life from his wounds. He died for them. Because of their sins they resemble the sick child that no longer wants to drink from the mother and no longer holds her breast when the mother wants the child to drink.

My friend: Jesus has opened his wounds. Take life from him, and you shall live and grow for Heaven. It spears him that you keep away from him, and his wounds smart.

The other example we take from the Islam-dominated area on the East African Coast. How is the reality of the Christian claim to be demonstrated in this environment? How is Incarnation to be made known, and translated, in this atmosphere?

It is quite possible, of course, to bring all one's more or less intellectual weapons to bear on the argument. In our tour of Africa, we had just come from another part of the same territory, having been invited by a Pentecostal missionary to accompany him to the Moslem village to see how Moslems are approached. This is what actually happened A.D. 1955:

In the village he called some of the hefty, turbanned Africans together and put his first question: *'Nani aliye mkuu, Isa au Muhammed?* — *'Nabii Muhammed.'* — *'Hukufahamu, Nani aliye mkuu?'*[4] So it went on. The visitor was not at all surprised that our Muslim friends seemed to be quite reassured in their position, by *that* meeting.

There is another way; we saw it in action, and experienced how the Presence of the Holy was made vivid in the midst of an African Christian congregation, in a Muslim district in Tanganyika. It

---

[4] 'Who was greater, Jesus or Muhammed?—Prophet Muhammed.'—'You have not understood! Who was greater, Jesus or Muhammed?'

happened in a 'Benediction' service, one Sunday afternoon, at Magila near Tanga (U.M.C.A.).

Canon Sipekho took the service, in Swahili, with the utmost reverence and earnestness. Early that morning the congregation had received the heavenly Food in the Eucharist. At the Benediction service the quietness and expectation in the big crowd was tense. At the appointed moment, the African priest lifted the monstrance and showed it to the congregation. They all prostrated themselves in worship and adoration.

The reading of God's word, the singing of God's praise, the breaking of the Bread and drinking of the Cup—the African sense of table fellowship is very relevant here—all this is expressed in the new rhythm of togetherness made sacred by prayer and song. Here is indicated another vital aspect of the African conception of the Church. We do not, in fact, begin to understand the African Christian's concept of the Church until we have discovered on a sufficiently deep level the connexion between *ecclesia* and *leitourgia*.

Further, the *leitourgia* of the Church is the common worship of the whole *People* of God, of the *laos theou*. By this great term with its deep allusions to the history of salvation both in the Old and the New Testaments, the totality and wholeness of God's people are brought out. In the West, one particular aspect only of this term has been stressed and the term has in this specialized meaning come to indicate the laity as *distinct from* the clergy. This has led to a lamentable impoverishment of our ecclesiology, and the real meaning of the great key term in 1 Peter 2 has been missed. A new and richer understanding of *laos theou* is needed. 'The recovery of this "laos"-consciousness is the heart of church renewal in our times' says Dr. H. R. Weber, Department on the Laity, World Council of Churches. The Church in Africa and its theologians have a special responsibility for that recovery: in their understanding of 'wholeness' and group fellowship they have an important point of departure. But obviously it needs to be placed in dynamic relationship with other fundamental New Testament terms for the Church, particularly the concept of the Church as the Body of Christ. This will give the necessary eschatological counter-point to the understanding of the Church.

It is in this connexion that the unity of the Church becomes a living issue. In private debates or group discussions African Church leaders invariably claim that the concern for organic Church unity will have the priority, 'when the Whites go', or, 'when the missionaries have left us'. Whether this will in fact be so is as yet an open question. But strong pressures from within and from without are at work—and the quality of theological education in the 1960's and 1970's will determine the outcome of the search for Church unity in Africa.

We have suggested certain trends along which the theological encounter in Africa may come to develop in the next few decades. The situation understood in these terms has great risks and very great opportunities. Risks—because an over-emphasis on patterns derived from the 'African heritage' may lead to heresy. or spiritual stagnation, or both. But also very great opportunities —for it may very well be that the Church in Africa is called to help the Universal Church recover indispensable understandings of Biblical faith. Whether or not these opportunities will be translated into life and reality depends to a large extent on the training and the scope for leadership accorded to the African servants of the Church.

The Pastor — the Mid-man

'The Church will be what its ministry makes it. That stands to reason.' In this oft-quoted phrase, P. T. Forsyth, writing from the Free Church camp, indicated one of the cornerstones of the ecumenical 'Great Church' which was his great concern.[5] As the Gospel was translated to Africa, it was represented not so much by a Church and a ministry, but by a number of organizations, referring to themselves as Churches, carrying various names of national and denominational character, and by a number of ministries; episcopal and non-episcopal. We shall not analyse here the ways by which *A*nglicans, *B*aptists, *C*ongregationalists, *D*isciples, *E*piscopalians, *F*ull-*G*ospel, and *H*oliness groups and the whole alphabet of churches brought their various patterns of church order—or lack of order—to the tribes and peoples of Africa.

Here we shall only make one point as we attempt to under-

---

[5] P. T. Forsyth, *The Church and the Sacraments*, p. 130 and p. xv.

stand the kind of ministry that is now emerging in the Churches. It is not so much the professed and verbally expressed theology of the ministry that is shaping the attitude of African office-bearers. It is rather the phenomonology of the ministry: that which was *seen* and observed in the actual practice of the missionary and his first African co-workers conditions their outlook. If the Westerner largely represented the minister to be an efficient administrator, *or* an ordained school inspector, *or* an excellent and painstaking accountant, *or* an interested master-builder and architect, *or* again, an impressive combination of mechanic and preacher, these patterns will influence his younger African colleagues and to some extent determine their conception of the ministry. The different manifestations of ordained men from the West to a certain degree modify the teaching of the various missions as to the nature of the Church's ministry, whether sacramental, kerygmatic, revivalist, teaching, or organizing.

In all this there is, however, emerging something of an African pattern, and it is with this pattern that we must be particularly concerned here. Our quotation from P. T. Forsyth (p. 303) could be altered slightly when applied to Africa: 'The ministry will be what Africa and the African Church makes it. That stands to reason.' A fundamental pattern in traditional African society is the representative character of the chief over against his tribe or people. The representative idea is carried over into the Church and applied to its African office-bearer. The ministry is regarded as a representation *of* the Church and *to* the Church. Whether it is the case of an Episcopal or a Baptist congregation, the pattern of representation imposes itself on the emerging African Church. We have already seen how in even a characteristically Protestant context the minister is sometimes referred to as a 'mid-man' between God and His flock (p. 129). It is felt that he was sent to the flock to represent the Word and Will of God.

We suggest that there is a tension—although seldom explicitly stated—between the official Protestant-'democratic' teaching on the priesthood of all believers, on the one hand, and on the other, the African propensity for representative leadership. We suggest that in the near future, with some measure of *real* leadership accorded to Africans, this tension will be felt even more acutely than hitherto. In that case it illustrates a lesson which Church history has taught before, that forms of group leadership are to a

8. "I, if I be lifted up..."

Mondoro, Southern Rhodesia.

certain extent expressions of particular sociological conditions.
Such forms as have developed in nineteenth-century 'frontier'
situations of the West in America are not necessarily congruent
with conditions in Bantu society. But, on a deeper level than
that, the Church with its African ministry is, even in groups with
the most definite Protestant emphasis on preaching and sermons,
recovering a greater awareness of the place in the life of the
Church of the ministry of the sacraments. Here we are—I believe—
on the threshold of great things for the future of the Church in
Africa.

Because of his position as a 'mid-man', the pastor has special
authority in relation to his team and his flock. Weight of personality and the fact of ordination go together to form that unmistakable authority which the African minister can exercise with regard
to his flock. We shall quote a somewhat drastic example.

Rev. K. L., a young man (32) of a noble family, pastor in a
church in the neighbourhood of Lake Victoria, had to tackle a case
of church discipline. One of the church elders had used the altar
vessels for brewing beer in his hut. His case was brought before the
Church Council, K. L. being present. The pastor told the elders:
'I am one of you. I am listening. You speak to him now.' The
elders tried to show that the man had sinned exceedingly, but he
was adamant and retorted: 'You have no authority over me. I am
just as good as you are.' Their efforts were all in vain. Then pastor
K. L. began to speak, slowly and deliberately: 'Now I am
going to say my words, as a priest and as a man of God. Yes, of
course you were right in doing what you did. Of course you were
right in using the sacred vessels of the church for this unholy
purpose. Of course you were right in carrying on like this. You
will end by harvesting what you have sown, that which must be
the obvious outcome of this, on the last Day before the Throne of
Almighty God. You yourself have chosen. Carry on! Nobody will
hinder you any longer.' Overcome by fright and despair the elder
cast himself to the ground. Reduced to tears, he cried for forgiveness.

In that congregation the pastor had established himself as something more than a mere group leader. Here was a priest of God,
backed by the sanctions of the Holy Church, wielding the sword of
the Spirit.

The fact of ordination, of being set aside for a sacred task, is of particular importance to the pastor or priest himself. To many an African pastor, the link of his Church with the Church of the Apostles will afford the guidance he needs in order to understand his own ministry. A South African theological student—an Anglican—writes in his autobiographical sketch: 'Deep down in me I find myself linked up with the Apostles.' The ministry to which in his studies he is looking forward is anchored in sacred history; to become a member of its to 'remember' that which was in the Church's Beginning. A Lutheran pastor in Western Tanganyika (b. 1907, made deacon 1939, ordained pastor 1947) expressed his view on the nature of ordination in terms which were experiential rather than theological, but which precisely because of this have a realistic tone. 'Through ordination I have given a promise. I can no longer go just in any direction wherever I please. I can do nothing but God's work now. Ordination makes it clear that I am really a priest in the Church of God. Therefore this sacred act is a great help.'[6]

In that same church the African pastors help one another to uphold the sacred character of the ministry as they gather to their own ministers' fraternal. In this exclusive group of African ministers (with neither missionaries nor African laymen present) there is often very outspoken, mutual criticism of colleagues as the ministers handle corporately their own private disciplinary problems. One pastor is warned by the others because as a revivalist enthusiast he has perhaps shown certain sectarian tendencies; another colleague—a young, somewhat headstrong pastor—who does not co-operate with his most effective elder in the local congregation, is censured by the group. In their pastors' meetings, these men are possibly not guided by very much of the premeditated theology of the ministry, and yet by their decisions, taken as nearly as possible in accordance with the precepts of the Book, they evolve in practical encounter with their own personal problems a pastoral ideal and a view of the ministry which is of real relevance to themselves and to their Church.

---

[6] The problem of the nature of the ministry was of course also felt by the missionaries of the period. Perhaps the most remarkable indication, on the African scene, of a world-wide tendency towards 'catholicity' or of a 'return to orthodoxy' is the article by an ex-Methodist missionary in South Africa, now an Anglican priest. Cf. Arthur Matthews, 'Regress from Methodism', *The Church Quarterly Review*, Oct.–Dec. 1957.

The real authority wielded by the individual pastor depends to an immeasurable extent upon the way by which he himself demonstrates his message in his practical life. Bishop Neill expressed this in unforgettable words on the need for the devotional training and the pastoral preparation of the African minister: 'What matters above all else is that he should be a saint. Given that, nothing else matters nearly as much.'[7] We are concerned in this book with theological education and we know, again quoting Bishop Neill, that 'saintliness is not enough'. And yet, renewal has in many cases come to the Church in Africa through the personally experienced rediscovery by the pastor that the Bible's fundamental message about *The New Being* must be lived out by him, the preacher, in ordinary daily life. At this level too, a quite moderately educated pastor can influence the educated groups in his church. A student from West Africa, himself a son of the manse and studying medicine in Britain, stressed this as the fundamental issue for the future of the Christian ministry in Africa: that the pastor himself must be born again.

In certain cases there is a definite tendency to stress 'supernatural' qualities in the ministry. There are African pastors who have a measure of healing power. One highly respected Ghana Methodist pastor is known to have been instrumental in healing folk in his church. In this he is only one among many throughout Africa.

To a greater extent than is generally realized dreams play a role on this level of relationship between minister and followers in the churches. F. Grébert, French missionary in French Equatorial Africa, in his book *Au Gabon* reports a case where some months after the death of a certain catechist his congregation went through a deep spiritual experience. Living near an alcohol factory, the people had eventually become alcoholics and no longer showed any interest in the life of the Church. Suddenly, however, they stopped drinking and began as a group to take a lively part in the church services. One man in the village had in a dream heard the very voice of the deceased catechist calling out, 'Return to God!' On this level of psychic collective experience are formed strong ties of fellowship between pastor and followers in the Church in Africa.

---

[7] S. C. Neill, *I.M.C. Theol. Report,* I, p. 59.

And here, perhaps, we begin to dig down to the real issues involved in the leadership of the Protestant Church in Africa. Generally speaking, few great African leaders have emerged in the mission Churches during the last fifty years. Some of the greatest religious leaders, in South Africa, in Northern Rhodesia and Nyasaland, in Belgian Congo, on the Ivory Coast, have been those who, as prophets or bishops of their particular sects or revival movements, have wielded a remarkable influence over the faithful. They have been men with undoubted 'charismatic' gifts who have been allowed and encouraged to develop those gifts on a grand scale.

In the mission Church, the presence of the Westerners, helpful as it was, sometimes prevented the African leader from developing all his potential gifts. The behaviour patterns and the valuations of the West left too strong an imprint, and also contributed a kind of uncertainty, a split somewhere in the mind, which did not always allow the African pastor to develop a wholly integrated personal authority.

This is the price which the pastor in the mission Churches had to pay, a very heavy price indeed, but one which probably, in the circumstances, could not be avoided. The solution, to my mind, is certainly not be found in a proliferation of Western and African sects, although this for a time will inevitably be one fate of Protestant Africa. Rather it should be found in a deepening concern for the care of souls, excercised by a ministry which has competence, time, opportunity (in terms of sufficiently small congregations) and authority to deal with these things. Some pastors and priests engaged in the various movements of church renewal are examples of what we mean. Some priests in churches with a developed sacramental life are other instances of the same thing.

The priest or pastor thus is regarded as 'mid-man', either because of ordination through the Church or on account of special charismatic gifts. But the pastor is a 'mid-man' also in another sense. He it himself part of the flock and belongs to it. As a family man, he has immediate personal experience of his congregation's most intimate questions. When as a preacher he interprets the message of the Book, he is very well qualified to speak relevantly to a fellowship in which the problems of family and clan and the wider community are ever-present. This 'mid-man' stands in the middle of the African village and in the middle of his flock.

This is only the one side of the picture, however. There is another side. Leadership anywhere has its own problems and in Africa—no less than elsewhere—church leadership has peculiar dangers. In the West there was sometimes a tendency to regard the Church as a *'Pastoren-Kirche'*—as the Germans say. The ministry was identified with the clerical profession as such. There was not always a real understanding of the ministry as a concern of the whole Church, and the vision of the Church as the Body, and the Family and Household of God was to some extent lost. We believe that the Church in Africa has a special task in helping to recover this vision, as we have already pointed out. But this cannot happen unless the Churches in Africa realize that they have to face a similar danger in the form of an unmistakable tendency towards clericalism. This tendency is to be found not only in Churches in which ordinarily the role of the ordained ministry is emphasized. It is to be seen in the most unexpected quarters, in the form of a predilection for power and influence, power over institutions such as schools or interest in holding the purse-strings. The tendency towards clericalism was in some cases a latter-day reflection of a patriarchal and perhaps autocratic attitude on the part of Western missionaries in an earlier or later generation. In one autonomous West African church, ordination to the pastorate tends to be regarded as a reward for old men who during a long life as teachers have served the Church well. In one well-known church in Belgian Congo we are told that ordination tends to be interpreted rather in the nature of a promotion to a position where the pastor as the 'Big Massa' no longer needs to exert himself but rather can direct his subordinates.

Sometimes the vernacular term for 'ordination' was misleading and would cause certain misunderstandings. An example of this could be taken from Eastern Nigeria. A missionary S. H. Childs, who served the Anglican Church in Eastern Nigeria 1926–1946 writes:

'In the Ibo Prayer Book the phrase "The Form and Manner of Ordering of Priests" is translated "Uzo na usoro esi echi Ndi Presbita." "Presbita" is obviously a transliteration of "Presbyter" which is used for "priest". It is the use of *"echi"* or *"chi"* which is open to serious criticism.

In the old customs the people passed through various grades or "titles" which gave them their place in the society. The most important was the last but one, called "*Ozo*". To attain this title a fair amount of money had to be paid in, which was shared by those who held the title and certain sacrifices and religious rites were performed. The holders of the title largely regulated the affairs of the town. In the old system the paying in of the money ensured that the man had experience and a certain amount of ability, and in a simple form of society probably was quite a good method of selecting the "aristocracy". The term for taking the title was "chi *ozo*".

In the period 1926–1946 certain changes took place. First, Christians were not allowed to take a title, because of the sacrifices involved. Secondly, with the contact with Western civilization two opposite things were happening. Some young men who had become rich quickly were able to pay the fees, and the "*ozo*" title was thereby losing its prestige. Further, many of those who had money preferred to invest or save in other ways, which again led to an undue emphasis on the money side. It was generally felt that Ordination was the equivalent to the taking of "*ozo*" and the ordained clergy were given the respect of the "*ozo*" titled men. There was a suggestion that Christians could take the title by paying the money, but would be excused the sacrifices. All this meant that the "*ozo*" titles were changing their character.

It was felt therefore to be unfortunate to use the word "*chi*" for Ordination which inevitably suggested the idea of taking a title, with very little sense of "vocation".'

To a large extent, clericalism is caused by a weakness in the system of church organization at the present time. Many parishes consist of some fifty or more local village congregations, spread out over a wide geographical area. One priest in Kenya remarks that he has under his care a number of local congregations which he can manage to reach only once a year, and that there are some congregations which he has never visited. His case is no exception; in some Churches, this state of affairs is a dominant feature. In these circumstances, the pastor tends to become an itinerating administrator rushing from place to place—'worked to death', as an experienced American Baptist mission leader in Belgian Congo said—only seldom aware of one particular local congregation as being his own special responsibility. The bond of immediacy and fellowship which, ideally, seemed to constitute the very *charisma* of the African ministry is torn asunder in such circumstances. The 'mid-man' becomes a manager separated from his flock. He conceives the task of the ministry of the Church as if it were to administer rather than minister.

How can this be changed? How can the minister become a 'mid-man' again, in the sense of standing as pastor and priest in the midst of his flock as God's servant?

There is something wrong with the system, but the system itself is not peculiar to Africa. It has been well analysed by Bishop L. Newbigin. In South India, he says, the missionaries had made an

> attempt to impose upon a Church largely made up of landless agricultural labourers, and scattered in small groups among hundreds of villages, a pattern of ministry developed over many centuries in much larger, more compact, and wealthier Churches. Instead of asking 'How many people can one pastor effectively care for?' our predecessors had to ask 'How many people will it take to pay for a pastor with these qualifications?' And since in most places it needed 20 or 30 village congregations to support one pastor, most of the responsibility for pastoral care continued to fall on agent, catechist, or grant-aided teacher. It is this agent who in the great majority is in day-to-day pastoral charge of the congregations.

Some of the most constructive ideas towards a solution of this problem are to be found in the discussion on a part-time ministry. In 1930, Roland Allen published his *The Case for Voluntary Clergy*, and the question has recently been raised with new urgency by Bishop Newbigin and others. How far does it afford a 'solution' to the problems of the Church in Africa? The Willingen meeting of the International Missionary Council raised the matter in a way which was relevant also to conditions in the African Churches.

> In many parts of the world there is great concern over the paucity of suitable men hearing and responding to the call to the ministry. Where there are large accessions to the Church through group movements the question is specially urgent. The proposal for a part-time, *ordained* ministry should be considered in this connection. This proposal raises many fundamental issues; in fact, it touches on the basic question of the nature and function of the Christian ministry and the churches' traditional conception of this office. The dangers of a part-time ministry are serious. Nevertheless, the prevailing assumption that a full-time, paid ministry is the norm needs to be reconsidered.

Is it fundamental to the nature of the Christian ministry or is it an uncritical transplantation to another soil of what was appropriate to a different environment? Amongst other gains, the development of a part-time ministry would bring the sacraments within reach of many remote congregations who are at present denied them except on rare occasions. It would also enable a newly-planted church the more effectively to extend its witness.[8]

Our own observations support, and modify, these suggestions. First, the term 'part-time ministry' is not altogether happy with reference to Protestant Africa for the simple reason that most ministers in rural Africa have always been, and still are working on a part-time basis. 'All our pastors are part-time ministers. They only give half of their time to the Church', a leading layman in a Central African church told me. Being a teacher himself he had wished to be ordained and become a minister. As his younger brother was already ordained, he preferred, however, to continue as a teacher on a comparatively good Government salary in order to help his brother's family. In this way the ordained brother would be able to devote himself to his ministerial task. But the great majority of the pastors in his church, and in many others like it, have *de facto* to act as *half-time* pastors, the remaining part of their time being in farming or fishing, or some other specialized job.

This only goes to show how urgent the problem is. It cannot be solved by a simple formula or a single new idea. The Churches must be prepared to experiment in different directions, but before commitment it would be well to heed the warning of Dr. W. O. Chadwick in an article on a part-time ministry. He writes on church conditions in Britain, but his metaphor is taken from a controversy over Africa, in another field: 'Every kind of experiment carries with it dangers: and it would be fatal to embark upon a vast ground-nut scheme without first proceeding to a period of experiment and testing.'[9] He adds a phrase which is vastly relevant to the Church in Africa at present: 'The Church is not in a position where danger lies in one direction and safety in another.

---

[8] See *The Missionary Obligation of the Church* 1952, p. 10, and *Missions under the Cross* (1953), pp. 197–198.

[9] W. O. Chadwick, 'Tent-makers', *Theology*, 54, 1951, p. 51.

There is danger on either hand, in conservatism and in radicalism; and it is our business to determinate which danger must be faced for the sake of the salvation of souls.'

Such experiments have of late been made by various churches. In the diocese of Masasi, Tanganyika (U.M.C.A.), a limited number of teachers and catechists were ordained deacons with the understanding—in the case of five ordained in 1950—that they were to remain as 'permanent deacons'. There was no thought that they were to go on to be priests, because they were all already elderly men, the eldest being about seventy.[1] In this case, the ordination of permanent deacons (carefully selected men who had had three months' special theological training) was a temporary expedient necessitated by the acute shortage of priests in the diocese. So, for instance, at an Easter Communion service, one priest had single-handed to give Holy Communion to more than seven hundred communicants. But there have been warnings against these measures. A missionary with special experience of the training of African clergy (E. A. Maycock) says that 'in practice it has often been found that African deacons who were not later chosen to train for the priesthood have become disgruntled men, their ministry increasingly vitiated'.[2]

In French Equatorial Africa, the Mission Covenant Church and particularly its leader, Rev. M. Lundgren, have suggested that leading *evolués* of good standing in the Church may after a short course in theology wish to exchange their ordinary work for the Christian ministry. Here again, it is recognized that the idea is an expedient and cannot on a wider scale solve the problem of the shortage of ordained men. But Lundgren's suggestion for a non-professional ministry in Central Africa has a stimulating parallel in an important venture in the Anglican Church. We refer to Dr. A. R. Vidler and his famous 'doves'. At Windsor, Dr. Vidler has for periods of five nine-week terms taught theology to classes of six or seven laymen at a time, the average age of each group being about 50. The variety of professions has been considerable: officers, doctors, schoolmasters, civil servants, one bank manager, men engaged in industry, agriculture, commerce and administra-

---

[1] *Central Africa*, 1951, p. 44.
[2] *Central Africa*, 1951, p. 53.

tion. In a decade more than forty priests have been prepared in this way, most of them now incumbents in the Church of England.[3]

In themselves these examples are valuable and imaginative experiments but admittedly makeshifts and far from adequate in the present critical situation. When the ordained minister has to look after fifty or more local congregations, he is to a large extent cut off from effective personal contact with the members of his local groups. As the ordained minister is only very exceptionally able to visit particular local groups, the celebration of the sacrament of Holy Communion tends to become a rare occasion in the village church, and if the African pastor does not have sufficient time for the care of his people and for confessions, neither will he have sufficient opportunity to visit homes, or take burials and other acts of fundamental importance in the life of his parishioners.

In the I.M.C. Commission to 'Latin' Africa, Dr. Baëta of the University of Ghana maintained that the Church should acknowledge two levels, or degrees, of ordained ministers. He did so from his experience in the Ewe Presbyterian Church (Togoland and Ghana) and in the Christian Council of Ghana, but suggested the measure as one which might be applied to the situation in Africa on a wide scale. In the present circumstances, he maintained, only a relatively limited number of pastors will in any case have a secondary school education and theological training on a higher level. Generally speaking, these men will necessarily be selected for urban work and in administrative capacities. The groups of highly trained leaders ought to be supplemented by the ordination of deserving catechists, who will fill vacancies in rural districts.

Together with a number of those who have attempted to analyse the Church situation in Africa we would align ourselves with this proposal. It is a realistic and constructive attempt to remedy a precarious situation. At the same time, we are conscious of the fact that the plan is no solution for the root problem of the Church in Africa, the shortage of well-educated ordained ministers. The obvious argument against this plan is that it tends to accept something other than the highest academic standards for the ministry. But to those who in this world and in the Church prefer reason-

---

[3] A. R. Vidler, 'Doves', *Theology*, Oct. 1956. Here the training and syllabuses of these courses, lasting rather more than a year each, are described.

able and realistic measures to utopian panaceas, however fascinating, it is obvious that here is a plan that ought to be tried out.

We thus advocate for the Churches in Africa, at the present juncture, two degrees of pastors: 1. A regular ministry whose educational background and theological training shall be as advanced as the present situation demands and directed to the needs of the future. 2. Deserving village catechists who, after ordination, shall have regular authority to administer the Sacraments of the Church. Whether this authority should be locally restricted or not is a matter for the particular Church to decide. We notice that a similar plan for the Medak Diocese, Church of South India, provides for the 'Honorary Presbyter' that in the first place his appointment should be 'limited to a particular locality'.[4] Practically, this ought to be intended also for Africa, for the local village church needs its own pastor and priest again to be a 'mid-man' fully equipped with all the authority of the Church, administering the Word and the Sacraments in the midst of the village.

This plan implies an extended theological teaching programme. The Theological School and the Bible School have to be staffed and organized in such a way as to make recurrent intensive refresher courses possible, and higher theological education should include training in the running of courses of this nature. There will most probably be different salary scales for the two degrees of pastors, since the longer period of training and higher academic attainment of one group should be rewarded. On the other hand, the rural pastors will in fact not suffer, for their comparatively low income is compensated by economic opportunities in farming and other activities. But apart from such practical differences, the two groups will have the most important thing in common. For as far as we can see the plan will not work unless there is in the Church a sufficiently high view of the nature of ordination. From the point of view of intellectual training and capacity the plan admits two degrees of pastors. But both groups are effectively united by *the fact of ordination;* both are pastors and priests in the one Church. At this juncture in the development of some of the Churches in Africa this idea may contribute to the effective presence of the ordained servant of the Church, commissioned to administer the word and the sacraments of the Church, placed once more in the midst of the village congregation.

[4] W. Scopes, *Training Voluntary Workers,* N.C.C. India, 1957, p. 144.

LOOKING TOWARDS THE FUTURE

'All that red—that's my dream.' When receiving visitors to his residence, Groote Schuur, Cape Town, Cecil Rhodes used to take them to a wall map of Africa. With an impetuous gesture of his strong hand he drew a broad line from Cape to Cairo indicating the sphere of British interests in the new continent, in an era when the red on the map represented the Empire he loved and served.

That map is being re-drawn to-day. Large-scale pan-Africanism and small-scale tribalism compete in reshaping and modifying frontiers of countries and regions. New ideologies supply modern geo-political dynamics, and even as we write, Africa is changing before our eyes with breath-taking speed. One might speak of a new colour scheme, as it were: the black of African nationalism, the green of conquering Islam, the brown of India and of Gandhi's *satyagraha* ideas; and again, the red, this time indicating a new radical political creed appealing to the emerging industrialized masses of the world.

In this turmoil, the Church is set: 'in the world, but not of the world'. Studying the work of the Church in Africa Bishop Neill in 1950 was burdened with 'a sense of immense opportunity and immense peril'. That is still the formula for 1960. In the last decade, the peril has become no less acute, the danger of remaining foreign and becoming irrelevant to the stark and harsh facts and demands of the new day, the danger of preaching a nineteenth-century Western message to Africa in the second half of the twentieth century; in other words, a possible failure to translate to this day and generation in Africa the life-giving, integrating and saving gospel of Jesus Christ.

And yet, there is opportunity, indeed 'immense opportunity'. A decade ago, Neill affirmed 'with some confidence that there is no area in the world in which the Church is faced with so unexampled an opportunity as in tropical Africa, and none in which the resources of the churches may at this moment be more advantegeously deployed'.[1] Our study in the preceding pages has shown

---

[1] *I.M.C. Theol. Report*, I, p. 59.

that this healthy understanding must include proper recognition of failures and dangers. But we have also attempted to convey an understanding of the role of the African ministry in seizing this opportunity of service and witness in the Church's new day. It is against this background that relevant ministerial training becomes important. For the ideologies of to-day are of course not without influence in the Church (or churches). Pan-Africanism on the one hand and tribalism on the other will in the new and 'free' Africa increasingly make their various impacts on the churches.

In this situation, while the servants of the Church must be awake to the aspirations of the emerging 'African personality' and aware of its needs, their job is also, and above all, to raise the Christian voice in Africa. If there should come a temptation for the Church to be used as a sounding-board for continent-wide or tribal ideologies, it will be effectual contact with ecumenical Christian theology which will give added strength to that Christian voice.

In the last resort therefore it will be on a level of ecumenicity and catholicity that the contribution to ministerial training and theological interpretation in Africa will have to be judged. Here again, the situation points to the tension between peril and opportunity, a tension which ultimately is the 'normal' form of existence of the Church everywhere and at all times.

It is a tension the solution of which is prefigured in the form of the Cross, in the form of the Servant who came not to be ministered unto, but to minister and to give his life a ransom for many. Once again, there is the colour of red, the red of the blood of the sacrifice of Christ. It is *that* red which, in the midst of peril, transforms the task of the Church into a compelling opportunity in the new day.

APPENDIX

APPENDIX I

Field Studies and Material.

Author's field studies for the book

1953, June–November 10: Member of a theological commission to 'Latin' Africa under the auspices of the International Missionary Council. Starting in Ruanda-Urundi, this tour included Mozambique and Angola, Belgian Congo, French Equatorial and French West Africa, Liberia; certain tasks in British West Africa.

1953, November–December: Tanganyika, Uganda and Kenya.

1955, November–December: Tanganyika, Uganda and Kenya.

1957, December–1958, August: After visits to Ghana (I.M.C. Assembly) and Leopoldville, seven months' studies in the Union of South Africa and Swaziland, mainly on the subject of 'Separatist Churches' but with constant contacts with African church leaders in 'orthodox' Churches.

The I.M.C. Commission's journey throughout 'Latin' Africa gave me an opportunity of visiting in June–December 1953 some thirty theological colleges and Bible schools, and in 1955 and 1958 another 15 colleges and Bible schools in East, West and South Africa. Perhaps I should also state that I have myself been engaged in theological teaching in Africa, although admittedly for only very brief spells of time.

As preparatory material for this book I may mention my work in Swedish called *Young Church in Tanganyika*, 1948, a study of the structure and faith of the Protestant Church in the Bukoba district in Tanganyika, including a study of leadership problems. Out of this early book and my work in the Research Secretariat of the International Missionary Council grew a research programme on the Younger Churches under the title *Missionsforskningens arbets-uppgifter* (The Tasks of Missionary Research), published in Swedish in the early part of 1952.

In 1954, I sent out a printed questionnaire to 250 correspondents in all parts of Africa on the following categories of material: (1) autobiographies by pastors and by theological students; (2) detailed diaries of pastors kept for at least a week; (3) sermons by African pastors and catechists; (4) essays by youth in fourteen selected

Teacher Training Schools and Secondary Schools on 'The Pastor in our Local Church' (some three hundred essays). The net was flung widely, to Christian Councils, theological colleges, responsible Church authorities, and other individuals. The catch seemed to me good, and I am grateful to Africans and Westerners, too numerous to mention here, for their co-operativeness. In many cases particular points in autobiographies, essays or other material were followed up by personal correspondence or by personal interviews.

In 1956, I supplemented the diary material by selecting African pastors or priests in different denominations and regions of Africa, who consented to write a detailed diary for two months that year. A few of these have been reproduced under the heading 'Meet Pastor Ulwendo!' (p. 138) and others have been used in other connexions in the book.

The autobiographies of pastors, catechists and theological students collected by me for this study are about 100. Some of them should be published separately and with a commentary, and I hope to do something about this.

A special questionnaire on African lecturers in theological colleges was sent out to 50 correspondents in 1957 and another on the role of women leaders in the Methodist Church in South Africa sent to 300 correspondents in 1958.

The work has entailed a great deal of correspondence and I express my admiration for the tenacity of my African and European correspondents in all parts of Africa who in spite of more pressing duties have taken time to answer my questionnaires and letters and telegraphic reminders of letters. As a rule I have not quoted the name and locality of the correspondent. In some cases it has been important to safeguard his anonymity. I have therefore omitted any detailed apparatus with footnotes containing name and date of letter. On the other hand, I realize that from a historian's point of view it would be valuable, a generation hence, to know about these correspondents. I have prepared three copies of the book, annotated in detail as to names and sealed them for forty years and have had them placed in the Missionary Research Library, N.Y., the Institute of Social Research, University of Natal, Durban, South Africa, and the International Missionary Council, London.

Special studies for this book include a series of twelve essays on the social position of African clergy written by members of Dr. J. E. Goldthorpe's seminar at Makerere and later summarized by him in his book *Outlines of East African Society*, 1958; also a study (1954) by M. Henri Wullschlager, then in Togo, on the Ministry in the Ewe Church in Togo, and by M. Daniel Pfender, then of the Protestant faculty in Paris (both typed).

As far as possible I have tried to make use of available material in books, theological and missionary magazines, etc. 1900–1958. Translations of passages from other European or African languages into English as reproduced in this book are in each case my own.

In chapter V particularly I draw upon the reports of the International Missionary Council Survey of the training of the ministry in Africa 1950–54, abbreviated 'I.M.C. Theological Report', or 'I.M.C. Theol. Report' I, II, III, IV:

Part I, by Stephen C. Neill; theological education in British East and West Africa, 1950.

Part II, by M. Searle Bates, Christian G. Baëta, Frank Michaeli and Bengt G. M. Sundkler; theological education in 'Latin' Africa and Liberia, 1953; report published in 1954.

Part III, by Norman Goodall and Eric W. Nielsen; theological education in Southern Africa, 1953; report published in 1954.

Part IV, by Fridtjov Birkeli, Frank Michaeli and Charles W. Ranson; theological education in Madagascar, 1955.

Theological Schools in Africa, May, 1959

This summary represents an attempt by the Theological Education Fund to compile a list of all non-Roman Catholic schools training candidates for the ordained ministry in the areas with which the Fund is concerned. It draws upon lists prepared by the three International Missionary Council theological commissions 1950–1953 and on the book by Yorke Allen, Jr., *A Seminary Survey,* New York 1959. It offers summary information regarding the entrance standards, length of training, numbers of staff and students and the denominational connections of each institution.

The list, though extensive, is probably incomplete. The detailed *data* may not, in every case, be accurate and up-to-date.

Notes

1. *Entrance requirements:* The symbols used in this column are to be interpreted as follows:

Standards of admission are so varied and flexible, that precise classification is not possible. These categories are offered only as a rough approximation to the three main 'levels' of entrance to theological training.

IA, College or University Graduation; IB, Full Secondary School Course or University matriculation; II, Part Secondary School Course; III, Primary School Course.

Some institutions admit students from two or three 'levels' of formal education.

2. *Staff:* Figures in parenthesis indicate part-time teachers. Some institutions in making returns did not observe a distinction between part-time and full-time teachers.

3. *Students:* Numbers have not, in all cases, been confirmed by the institutions concerned. In some cases, they are probably inflated by the inclusion of persons who are not candidates for ordination.

Summary

Africa	No. of Schools	Staff	Ordinands
North of Sahara-Egypt	1	2 (6)	34
East Africa	10	45 (7)	252
West Africa	10	41 (5)	185
'Latin' Africa	15	47 (32)	214
Southern Africa	23	54 (18)	354
South West Africa	2	4	26
Totals	61	193 (68)	1065

Name and location	Entrance require-ments	Length of course	Staff	Students (ordinands)	Denominational support
RTH OF SAHARA					
pt					
vangelical Theological Seminary, Cairo	IB	3	2 (6)	34	Synod of Nile, Coptic Evangelical Church
Sub-Total			2 (6)	34	
ST AFRICA					
iopia					
oly Trinity Seminary & College, Addis Ababa	II	5	8[1]	53	Ethiopian Orthodox Church
an					
ishop Gwynne College, Mundri, via Juba	II	4	6	20	Anglican and Presbyterian
ya					
t. Paul's United College, Limuru	II	3	2 (1)	20	Anglican, Church of Scot., Meth., U.K.
nganyika					
ll–Africa Theological Seminary, Moshi	III	2	3	17	Lutheran World Federation
utheran Bible School, Moshi	III	2	6 (4)	10	National Lutheran Council
lakumira Lutheran Theological School, Usa River	II	4	3 (1)	50	Lutheran
t. Cyprian's Theological College, Tundru via Lindi	III	2	2	22	Anglican
t. Philip's Theological College, ongwa	III	2	3 (1)	0[2]	Anglican and Moravian
anda					
ishop Tucker Memorial College, Mukono	III	2	8	15	Anglican
uwalasi Diocesan College, Mbale	III	2	4	45	Anglican
Sub-Total			45 (7)	252	

[1] T.E.F. Survey adjusted by B.S.
[2] No students at present.

Name and location	Entrance require-ments	Length of course	Staff	Students (ordinands)	Denominational support
WEST AFRICA					
Ghana					
Trinity College, Kumasi	II	3	4	24	Meth., U.K., Basel Mission
University College of Ghana, Legon	IB	4	5	8	Government
Liberia					
Cuttington College and Divinity School, Monrovia	IA	3	2 (2)	9	Protestant Episcopal Meth.
Nigeria					
Immanuel College, Ibadan	IB	3	6	50	Anglican, Meth.
Nigerian Baptist Theological Seminary, Ogbomosho	IB	4	10	15	Southern Baptist
Theological Training Center, Nyososo	IB	3	2	13	Presbyterian Church Cameroons
Theological College of Northern Nigeria, Barakin Ladi, via Jos	IB	3	2 (1)	22	Union (Ch. of Brethren Dutch Reformed of Africa, Sudan United Mission, etc.)
Trinity College, Umuahia	II	3	3	35	Anglican, Ch. of Scotland Meth., U.K.
University College of Ibadan, Ibadan	IB	4	3	0 [1]	Government
Sierra Leone					
Fourah Bay College, Freetown	IB	♄	4 (2)	9	Government
Sub-Total			41 (5)	185	
'LATIN' AFRICA					
Angola					
Seminário Emanuel Dondi, Bela Vista	II	3	4 (7)	16	Americ. Board; Meth. USA, United Church Canada

[1] B.D. Course from September, 1959.

Name and location	Entrance requirements	Length of course	Staff	Students (ordinands)	Denominational support
gian Congo					
cole des Pasteurs, Kimpese, via Leopoldville	II	4	(7)	18	Baptist, USA, Baptist, U.K. and Swedish Mission
cole des Pasteurs, Bolenge	II	4	8	14	Disciples
cole de Théologie, Kakinda	II	4	2	6	United Presbyterian, USA
cole de Théologie Unie, Mulungwishi, Élizabethville	II	4	(5)	13	Methodist (USA)
nch West Africa, Cameroons					
cole Biblique de l'Église Évangélique, Atakpame, Togo	III	2	3 (1)	0[1]	Swiss Mission
cole de Théologie Ndoungue, N'kongsamba	III	4	2 (1)	29	French Reformed
cole de Théologie Luthérienne, Meiganga	III	4	2	0[1]	Norwegian Missionary Society
ager Biblical Seminary, Bibia, Lolodorf	III	3	6	27	United Presbyterian, USA
éminaire Évangélique, Ngouedi, Loutété	III	4½	9 (2)	12	Swedish Covenant
homey					
rotestant Seminary, Porto Novo	II	4	(3)	6	Methodist (U.K.)
anda-Urundi					
iocesan Training School, Ibuye, Ngozi	II	5	3	10	Anglican
Iweya Bible School, Usumbura	III	3	4	35	Free Methodist, USA, Friends, National Holiness
zambique					
t. Augustine's Theological College, Vila de João Belo, via Lorenço Marques	III	4	1 (2)	12	Anglican

[1] No students at present.

Name and location	Entrance require- ments	Length of course	Staff	Students (ordinands)	Denominational support
Seminário Unido de Ricatla, Ricatla	III	4	3 (4)	16	Methodist Episcopa Ch. & Swiss Missi American Board,
Sub-Total			47 (32)	214	
SOUTHERN AFRICA					
Basutoland					
Morija Theological College, Morija	III	3	2 (4)	15	French Reformed, Sw Mission
Federation of Rhodesia and Nyasaland					
Nyasaland					
St. Andrew's College, Likoma Island	III	3	1	7	Anglican
Theological College, Living- stonia	III	3	4	16	Church of Scotland
Theological College, Mkhoma	III	4	2 (1)	12	D.R.C. Mission
Northern Rhodesia					
Madzimoyo Theological Col- lege, Fort Jameson	III	4	2 (1)	8	D.R.C. Mission
The Seminary of St. John Bap- tist, Lusaka	III	4	2 (2)	17	Anglican
Southern Rhodesia					
African Baptist Seminary, Gwelo	III	3	2 (2)	20	Southern Baptist
Epworth Theological College, Salisbury	III	3	4	19	Methodist, USA a U.K.
Theological College, Morgen- ster	III	4	1 (1)	5	D.R.C. Mission
Union of South Africa					
Adams United Theological School, Modderpoort, Orange Free State	III	3	2	11	American Bd., L.M African Methodist Episcopal Church
College of Resurrection and St. Peter, Rosettenville, Transvaal	III	3	1 (5)	29	Anglican

Name and location	Entrance require-ments	Length of course	Staff	Students (ordinands)	Denominational support
ecoligny Theological School, Umtata, Cape Province	III	4	4 (5)	4	D.R.C., Bantu Ch. of South Africa
ingaanstat Theological School, Dingaanstat, Natal	III	4	3	1	D.R.C., Church of Natal
ereformeerde Kerk Theolog-cal School, Dube, Johannes-urg	III	4	2	24	Gereformeerde Kerk
ermannsburg Seminary Grey-own, Natal	—	—	1	7	Lutheran (German)
larang Lutheran Theological Seminary, Rustenburg, Trans-vaal	III	4	2 (1)	10	Lutheran (German)
foravian Theological College, Port Elizabeth, Cape Province	III	3	2	10	Moravian
scarsberg Lutheran Theolog-cal Seminary, Rorke's Drift, Natal	III	4	3	39	Lutheran
. Bede's Theological School, Umtata, Cape Province	III	3	2	25	Anglican
ofberg Gedenkskool, Viljoena-drift, Orange Free State	III	4	2	34	Dutch Reformed
raining School (coloured), Wellington, Cape Province	III	4	5	12	Dutch Reformed
niversity College of Fort Hare, Alice, Cape Province	IB	3	3	30	Methodist Ch. of S.A. Presbyterian
onnebloom Institute (coloured), Capetown, Cape Province	III	3	2	0 [2]	Anglican
Sub-Total			54 (22)	354	
UTH WEST AFRICA					
innish Mission School, Ona-jena	—	—	2	15	Lutheran (Finnish)
aulinum Theological Semi-nary, Karibib	III	4	2	11	Evangelical Lutheran in S.W. Africa
Sub-Total			4	26	
TOTAL			210 (72)	1065	

[1] Opening 1959.
[2] No students at present.

APPENDIX III

Note on Church Statistics for Africa

As our study deals only with Africa south of the Sahara, these church statistics for 'Africa' have disregarded the numbers for North Africa and Madagascar. We include, however, Ethiopia and Eritrea in the totals.

Obviously the overall statistics for Africa depend on each item of local returns from the churches. A few examples serve to show that the accuracy of these returns is not always what might be expected.

South Africa, with 520 ordained men in 1925, is supposed to have 2420 in 1938. But one church, the Bantu Presbyterian Church, claimed in 1938 to have 1381 ordained, while 11 years later, with a doubled church membership (from 20,000 to 40,000), the number of pastors in this particular group is reported as 32. Clearly the 1938 figures should be disregarded. The total for this Church and the African Methodist Episcopal Church in 1938 represented two-thirds of the total number of African ministers for the whole of South Africa—which is absurd. The number of ordained men in South Africa in the period 1925 to 1938 has in fact risen only from 520 to *890*. But these figures, unfortunately, affect the totals not only for South Africa, but for the whole of Africa. The figures must be adjusted accordingly.

The number of ordained men in Belgian Congo has risen from 5 in 1925 to 336 in 1938. The latter figure should be handled with care. One Swedish mission which claimed to have 100 ordained men in 1938 had reduced that figure to 6 by 1952. A number of Pentecostal and Baptist groups that each claimed to have upwards of 40 ordained in 1938, have none in 1952. For French Equatorial Africa, one Swedish mission claming to have 175 ordained in 1938 (and in that year the total for the whole of the territory was only 180) had in actual fact only 5 ordained at the time.

Pentecostal and similar groups in the Lake Victoria area, Kenya, do not make the task of the missionary statistician any easier. Canadian Pentecostals in this area, with no ordained men in 1938, believed that they had 245 ordained in 1952, but this latter figure was reduced to the round figure of 100 in 1957. American Friends, who in principle do not have an ordained ministry, had none ordained in 1938, one in 1949, 137 in 1952 and 75 in 1957. During this time the strength of this particular group rose from 25,000 to 100,000. A British group, 'The Apostolic Church Missionary Movement', working in Nigeria, had none ordained in 1938, 200 in 1949 (to 16,000 full members) and 118 in 1957. Seventh Day Adventists in the French Cameroons, with a total community of some 16,000, reported 242 ordained in 1957 as compared with none in 1949.

The statistical returns for the 1957 edition of *World Christian Handbook*—valuable and indispensable as the book is—should not always be taken at their face value. The total of ordained nationals for the whole of the Belgian Congo for 1957 must be reduced from 1,969 to approximately 545, as one mission—the African Inland Mission—under 'ordained nationals' has returned a figure of 1,474, including *all* national workers: the actual number of pastors in this particular case could probably by deduced from the 1949 figure, which is 50. In South Africa, the Free Presbyterian Church of Scotland has 1000 ordained for 1957. This should be *one* ordained instead, and he is not in South Africa, but in Southern Rhodesia—according to information supplied by the executive secretary of the mission to the present writer. Two Swedish Free Church groups in South Africa have together claimed a total of 274 ordained men which should read 19 plus 18 instead. Considering these and a few other similar points we have accordingly reduced the ambitious number '*3,186*' ordained for South Africa 1957 to '*1,951*'.

The rise 1949–1957 for ordained missionaries is less dramatic than it appears to be in the first two editions of the *World Christian Handbook* (from 2,810 to 5,508). The 1957 figure should be considerably reduced. The Salvation Army in the Belgian Congo, Northern Rhodesia and South Africa, etc. has placed its 'total number of officers' under the heading 'European ordained' missionaries (about 1,000). There is also an error of 300 in the addition for Kenya. Thus: 5,508 *less* 1,300 is 4,208.

The totals for South Africa have also necessarily had to be adjusted in order to compute the figures for the Bantu Christian community in certain Churches with large European totals. This has been more difficult than one would expect. The total for the

D.R.C. has here been reduced by 1,045 mill. in 1949 and by 1,2 mill., a conservative estimate of the European *plus* Coloured community, obviously included in the 1949 and 1957 figures, but *not* 1938 and prior to 1938. The Mission Secretariat of the D.R.C. has supplied figures showing that at the time of the 1951 census the Bantu Christian community of the D.R.C. was about 300,000.

A missionary serving a North European missionary society which in 1938 had returned rather fanciful figures for the number of ordained men, is quoted as saying in the Congo Missionary Conference: 'Statistical lies are the worst lies, but God's statistics are correct'.[1] That may well be so, but we still need human statistics as accurate as we can get them. These inconsistencies, however, reveal one thing: the general vagueness over the term 'ordained minister' and over the concept of ordination in certain sections of Protestantism. This vagueness is not only a matter of arithmetic. It goes deeper than that. To many groups in Africa ordination was in fact not a matter of theology, but a manner of terminology.

---

[1] Report, *Congo Missionary Conference,* 1924, p. 54.

APPENDIX IV

J. S. Mwale: *Life and Work of the Elder. (Moyo ndi Nchito za Oyang'anira Mpingo)* D.R.C. Mission, Mkhoma, Nyasaland, 1956.

Table of Contents

In respect of which things must he be prudent and guard himself?

a. When speaking to any woman, he should avoid words that are foolish, childish, worthless, or words conveying the sense of cousinship, sistership or playing. With a woman he should use words of spiritual encouragement and advice.

b. When accepting any kind of drink, he must be certain that it is not beer, or sweet beer that has been left over till it has fermented. He must avoid any drink that can cause intoxication.

c. When handling any Church money, he must guard himself, he must be trustworthy. He should fear the eye of God.

d. In speaking to any person, he should speak the word of the Lord. No corrupt word should proceed from his mouth; also any words of argument in a bad sense he should avoid, knowing that this is the source of anger, which produces strife and fighting.

Chap. VI. His Work of Governing the Congregation

1. To speak to every person, Christians (church members), catechumens, by visiting them in their homes; he should appear at every village, every family, every home, to every individual. He should know the name of every member in his area.

2. To encourage and to assist the sick, the bereaved, the orphans, the widows, the lame and aged.

3. To supervise and arrange everything required for meetings of worship.

4. To visit and inspect all Church work in the area, so that everything is done properly: Sunday schools, catechumen's classes, the upkeep of Church buildings and their grounds, youth instruction, women's Christian guilds, prayer circles, Bible-study groups.

5. To visit and speak to heathen and strayed members personally about the salvation in Christ.

6. To feed his flock through the preaching of the Gospel.

7. To arrange and to adjudicate in cases of discipline.

8. To supervise the proceedings at funerals (so as to avoid all heathen and unwonted practices).

9. To supervise at marriage ceremonies and feasts (for same reasons as in para. 8).

Chap. VII. Cooperation between the Elder and other Church workers
Cooperation between Elder and (1) Minister, (2) Evangelist,

APPENDIX V

Women as Local Leaders in the Methodist Church, South Africa.

Cf. p. 176. To the 300 questionnaires on the role of women as local leaders, full replies were received from 60 Methodist ministers in the Union of South Africa and—although on a small scale—from the Protectorates, and one reply from Portuguese East Africa. The questionnaire included a question about the number of "class" leaders, the "class" organization of the local groups being a fundamentally important category in the Methodist Church. These 60 circuits return a total of 6026 class leaders, of whom no less than 3555 are women. In the older Methodist strongholds, such as the Eastern part of Cape Province, the number of men as class leaders is comparatively high. The women play a preponderant role as class leaders in a) the Bantu Areas such as e.g. Zululand and Transkei and b) to a surprisingly high degree also in some of the urban areas. The three Northern circuits of Zululand have together 274 class leaders, of whom 207 are women, while in Ixopo circuit, Southern Natal, 345 of 460 class leaders are women. In some Transkei circuits the trend is the same: Myanjane 50 out of 83, Ngqeleni 100–184, Bizana 172–202, Umtata 80–108. This reflects the general social situation: the men are working in the mines and in the cities, and the local church groups in the Reserves are under the care of the women. On the other hand, there are also on the Rand remarkable examples of a high percentage of women as class leaders. This is sometimes mainly the result of the organizing activity and dedication of the minister's wife. So, for instance, in Benoni 80 out of 168 class leaders are women, and in the Rama Section of the Pretoria circuit 60 out of 90. In Bloemfontein 200 out of 400 class leaders are women; in Newcastle (Natal) 137 out of 186.

The activities of Methodist church women include *manyano* work (p. 173), Sunday school, church choir, youth work, and temperance work. Good Hope (N. Transvaal) reports: "Preaching on Sundays; some societies are entirely in the women's charge." Aliwal North (Cape Province), and Nongoma (Zululand) report deep-seated prejudices against the preaching activities of women.

For special tasks of the minister's wife, see p. 176. The answers to the Methodist questionnaire indicate teaching and nursing as the main avenues of work, besides the regular congregational work, but there are also cases of a Methodist minister's wife as a shop-owner, or a clerk, or two cases of dressmaking: one on the Rand, the other in Zululand. When asked to compare the role of women as local leaders in the Church at present with the situation ten years ago, 4 ministers claim that no difference can be observed, while 56 claim a more or less rapid increase in the role of women. To a certain degree this increase is linked with the rise in educational opportunities.

INDEX